A Sourcebook on Byzantine Law

Medieval Law and Its Practice

VOLUME 34

The titles published in this series are listed at *brill.com/mlip*

A Sourcebook on Byzantine Law

Illustrating Byzantine Law through the Sources

By

Daphne Penna
Roos Meijering

BRILL

LEIDEN | BOSTON

Cover illustration: From the Mausoleum of Galla Placidia mosaics. UNESCO World heritage site. Ravenna, Italy. 5th century AD Photo by Petar Milošević – Own work, CC BY-SA 4.0: https://commons.wikimedia.org/w/index.php?curid=97313612. Last accessed 9th February 2022.

The Library of Congress Cataloging-in-Publication Data is available online at https://catalog.loc.gov
LC record available at https://lccn.loc.gov/2022028518

Typeface for the Latin, Greek, and Cyrillic scripts: "Brill". See and download: brill.com/brill-typeface.

ISSN 1873-8176
ISBN 978-90-04-51470-6 (hardback)
ISBN 978-90-04-52068-4 (e-book)

This book is printed on acid-free paper and produced in a sustainable manner.

IOANNIS HENRICI ANTONII LOKIN ANTECESSORIS
ΜΝΗΜΗΣ ΧΑΡΙΝ

Contents

Preface, or What This Book Is Not

When it comes to Byzantine legal sources, the Greek book by Spyros Troianos, *Οι Πηγές του Βυζαντινού Δικαίου* [= *The Sources of Byzantine Law*], which was revised and edited in Athens in 2011, remains indispensable. It is indeed fortunate that we now possess Italian and German translations of this book. In 2015, Pierangelo Buongiorno translated Troianos' book into Italian (*Le Fonti del diritto Bizantino*, Turin). Two years later, in 2017, Dieter Simon and Silvia Neye translated it into German (*Die Quellen des byzantinischen Rechts*, Berlin/Boston), also bringing its bibliographical references and indices up to date. Moreover, despite its age, the book *Historiae Iuris Graeco-Romani Delineatio. Les Sources du droit byzantine de 300 à 1453* by Nicolaas van der Wal and Jan Lokin, published in Groningen in 1985, still remains useful. In short, a student of Byzantine law has sufficient and excellent material that will help him or her to learn about and investigate the sources of Byzantine law.

What, then, is the point of the present book? To begin with, the book that you have before you derives from the classroom. It was born from our teaching experience. After the abolition of the study of Byzantinology in Groningen, the course on Byzantine law continued to be offered both to Dutch and foreign law students. In 1990, Roos Meijering had taken over teaching it from Jan Lokin. From the academic year 2007/2008, Meijering and I started teaching the course together, and, following the retirement of Meijering in 2017, I have been teaching it on my own, being assisted from time to time by my colleagues Frits Brandsma and Tom van Bochove. The core of the present book is based on the so-called 'Sourcebook' that Meijering and I have used in class for all these years. This 'Sourcebook' consisted of fragments of sources of Byzantine law which Meijering had selected and translated throughout the years, and in a later stage, a few sources were also added by myself. The 'Sourcebook' broadly followed the structure of the *Historiae Iuris Graeco-Romani Delineatio* mentioned above, but the 'Sourcebook' gathered all discussions of canon law into a single chapter (unlike the *Delineatio*, which includes multiple chapters on canon law, one after each of the chronological periods covered in the book). It was partly inspired by a short source reader compiled by Herman Scheltema and entitled *Florilegium jurisprudentiae graeco-romanae*, published in 1950. For many years now I had been thinking of using this 'Sourcebook' as the core of a book. In the year 2020, when the lives of all of us changed because of the pandemic, I decided that it was high time to begin this project, and Roos Meijering once again helped me throughout the process. Using Meijering's selection of Greek sources as a base, I started writing a theoretical text and introduction to accompany these sources, which would provide something like a basic background to help the reader understand the source under discussion and its relationship to other Byzantine sources. In some cases, I expanded the text and made additions to the sources. The result is the book that you have before you.

The present book is not intended to provide a thorough discussion on the sources of Byzantine law, nor is it a textbook about Byzantine law in general. Rather, the purpose of this book is to explain and illustrate Byzantine law through some sources; it provides a selection of sources drawn from across the timeline of Byzantine law. It is by no means exhaustive. In other words, this book is only a tool that can help a student of Byzantine law (or anyone who is interested in Byzantine law) to find out what some of the sources actually look like and provide information about their basic background. As far as the timeline is concerned, the book begins with the sources before the time of Justinian and ends in AD 1453, which marks the end of the Byzantine empire. Byzantine law, of course, continues even after 1453, but in this book we will not address post-1453 Byzantine legal sources. The book is further divided into six chapters, and the reader will notice that some chapters are much lengthier than others. Chapter length depends on the actual material and the importance of each period; for example, the second chapter is lengthy because it deals with the legislation of Justinian, which forms the backbone of most later Byzantine legislation, the new curriculum of legal studies and the teaching of law during this period. The last chapter includes only a brief selection of Byzantine sources of canon law.

As far as the language is concerned, we have opted for simple language. At many points, the reader will also notice some patterns of classroom teaching, a bit of '*antecessorian* teaching' to use a Byzantine term; for example, sometimes we provide some 'theory in advance' or a legal commentary, or we point out the special characteristics of a source that should help the reader better understand the material. In some cases, we also provide tables, schematic approaches to the sources or other features that may help further elucidate the source and understand its nature and relationship to other sources. We have also decided not to include many footnotes in the actual text, but to add relevant select bibliographies after every section. As far as the translations of the sources are concerned, if no translator is specifically named, they have all been done by Roos Meijering. At the final stage of this book, we also had considerable help from Bernard Stolte, whom we would like to thank for his invaluable comments and suggestions on our manuscript. Matthew McHaffie had the courage to read and reread this book, edit the English and help us with the bibliographical references. We thank him not only for his highly professional work, but also for his genuine effort to make this book better in many ways. We owe further thanks to Marios Tantalos for his suggestions on the bibliography and his great patience in reviewing the manuscript and helping with all kinds of corrections. We would also like to thank Marcella Mulder and Kate Hammond from the editing house Brill who have helped us in all practical matters arising from transforming the manuscript into an actual book. The costs for the three beautiful maps made by Peter Palm were covered by the foundation *Het Groningsch Rechtshistorisch Fonds*, which we would also like to thank.

Teaching the Seminar of Byzantine Law all these years together with Roos Meijering has always been a highlight of the academic year, and my favourite course to teach. There is nothing better for a young scholar of Byzantine law, to be thrown into the sources and try to teach this material with the assistance of an experienced and cunningly intelligent scholar. The knowledge that imbues teaching conditions such as these is remarkable, and there is an immense amount of fun to be had in teaching a difficult subject with someone else for the select few. For we knew from the beginning that we were teaching for a select few, and there have been years in which the number of the instructors was actually larger than the number of students. The small number of students, however, created a sphere of intimacy, and there have been students who were extremely motivated and provided excellent pieces of work, something that all teachers dream of. Moreover, our two different characters and approaches to Byzantine law gave some extra colour to the actual teaching, for we were both present at almost all lectures: on the one hand, Meijering insisted on discussing (Byzantine legal sources about) plants, 'coppiced wood' and trees, scaring the students away on the first day with the difficult Greek and emphatically letting them know that they should temper their expectations about the course; I, on the other hand, tried to focus on more legal matters in an attempt to open up the course and make the material easier and more attractive, all the while building my case for the importance of Byzantium. I recall so many funny moments between Meijering and myself, and I hope that the students enjoyed the lessons. I know we did.

Daphne Penna
Groningen, September 2022

Figures and Maps

Figures

Maps

Abbreviations

B.	*Basilicorum libri* LX, ed. H.J. Scheltema, D. Holwerda, and N. van der Wal, Groningen: 1953–1988, available also online at: https://referenceworks.brillonline.com/browse/basilica-online (date of access: 19/03/2022)
BS	B., Series B: Scholia (quoted after page and line)
BT	B., Series A: Textus (quoted after page and line)
Ca	Codex Graecus Coislianus 152
C.	*Codex Justinianus*, ed. P. Krüger, *Corpus Iuris Civilis*, vol. II, 9th edn, Berlin: 1914
cap.	Caput, chapter
CTh.	*Codex Theodosianus*, ed. Th. Mommsen, Berlin: 1905
D.	*Digesta*, ed. Th. Mommsen, *Corpus Iuris Civilis*, vol. I, 12th edn, Berlin: 1911
Frier, *Codex*	*The Codex of Justinian: A New Annotated Translation, with Parallel Latin and Greek Text*, 3 vols., ed. B.W. Frier et al., Cambridge: 2016. This translation is based on an earlier translation by Justice Fred H. Blume.
F	Codex Laurentianus plut. LXXX 11
FM	*Fontes Minores*, vols. I–XIII, Forschungen zur byzantinischen Rechtsgeschichte, Frankfurt am Main/Berlin: 1976–2021
JGR	J. Zepos and P. Zepos, *Jus Graecoromanum*, vols. I–VIII, Athens: 1931 (repr. Aalen: 1962)
JÖB	Jahrbuch der Österreichischen Byzantinistik
Nov.	*Novellae*, ed. R. Schöll, and G. Kroll, *Corpus Iuris Civilis*, vol. III, Berlin: 1895. This is the critical edition of the *Novels*. On the right side of every page directly facing the Greek text the so-called *Authenticum* text is also given.
ODB	*The Oxford Dictionary of Byzantium*, ed. A.P. Kazhdan, 3 vols., New York/Oxford: 1991 (published online in 2005)
Pa	Codex Parisinus Graecus 1348
Pc	Codex Parisinus Graecus 1349
pr.	*principium*, that is the first unnumbered section of a constitution in the *Code*, or of a fragment in the *Digest* or the *Institutes*.
RhP	G.A. Rhalles and M. Potles, *Σύνταγμα τῶν θείων καὶ ἱερῶν κανόνων*, 6 vols., Athens: 1852–1859 (repr. 1966)
RIDA	*Revue internationale des droits de l'antiquité*
sch.	scholion
Scheltema, *Opera Minora*	*H.J. Scheltema, Opera Minora ad iuris historiam pertinentia*, ed. N. van der Wal, J.H.A. Lokin, B.H. Stolte, and R. Meijering, Groningen: 2004
SG	*Subseciva Groningana. Studies in Roman and Byzantine Law*
SZ	*Zeitschrift der Savigny-Stiftung für Rechtsgeschichte: Romanistische Abteilung*
Theoph.	*Theophili antecessoris Paraphrasis Institutionum*, ed. J.H.A. Lokin, R. Meijering, B.H. Stolte, and N. van der Wal; trans. by A.F. Murison, Groningen: 2010

Troianos, *Pèges* = *Quellen*	Sp. Troianos, *Οι πηγές του βυζαντινού δικαίου*, 3rd edn, Athens-Komotini: 2011, which has been translated into Italian: *Le fonti del diritto bizantino*, trans. by Pierangelo Buongiorno, Turin: 2015. This book has also been updated and translated into German: Sp. Troianos, *Die Quellen des byzantinischen Rechts*, trans. D. Simon and S. Neye, Berlin/Boston: 2017.
Van der Wal and Lokin, *Delineatio*	N. van der Wal, and J.H.A. Lokin, *Historiae Iuris Graeco-Romani Delineatio. Les Sources du droit byzantine de 300 à 1453*, Groningen: 1985

General Note on the Bibliography

As mentioned in the preface, at the end of every chapter—and in some cases after a specific section—we provide a select bibliography. The bibliography is divided into: i. primary sources, including editions and translations, and ii. secondary literature. The proposed bibliographies are by no means exhaustive.

For all chapters of the present study, the following two books addressing the sources of Byzantine law are invaluable:

1) Troianos, *Pèges = Quellen*.
2) Van der Wal and Lokin, *Delineatio*.

The following bibliographical resources remain useful despite their age:

- Pieler, P.E. 'Byzantinische Rechtsliteratur', in H. Hunger, *Die hochsprachliche profane Literatur der Byzantiner*, vol. 2. Munich: 1978, pp. 341–480. Pieler's study has been updated and translated into modern Greek by E. Papagianni and Sp. Troianos, which can be found in the Greek edition of Hunger's book, as follows: P.E. Pieler, 'Νομική Φιλολογία', in H. Hunger, Βυζαντινή λογοτεχνία. Ἡ λόγια κοσμική γραμματεία τῶν Βυζαντινῶν, vol. 3 (Athens: 1994), pp. 183–379. Finally, K.E. Zachariä von Lingenthal, *Geschichte des griechisch-römischen Rechts* (Berlin: 1892; repr. Aalen: 1955) remains indispensable.

The following contributions represent general works on Byzantine law:

- Lokin, J.H.A. and Th.E. van Bochove. 'Compilazione—educazione—purificazione. Dalla legislazione di Giustiniano ai Basilica cum scholiis', in J.H.A. Lokin and B.H. Stolte, eds. *Introduzione al diritto bizantino. Da Giustiniano a Basilici*. Pavia: 2011, pp. 99–146.
- Morolli Ceccarelli D. *Il diritto dell'impero romano d'Oriente: Introduzione alle fonti e ai protagonisti*, Rome: 2016.
- Pitsakes, C. 'Byzantine Law: A Constituent of European Legal Tradition', in Sp. Flogaitis and A. Pantelis, eds. *The Eastern Roman Empire and the Birth of the Idea of State of Europe*. London: 2005, pp. 251–289.
- Scheltema, H.J. 'Byzantine Law', in J.M. Hussey, ed. *The Cambridge Medieval History*, vol. 4: *The Byzantine Empire*, part II: *Government, Church and Civilisation*. Cambridge: 1967, pp. 55–77, repr. in Scheltema, *Opera Minora* (see abbreviations), pp. 38–57.
- Simon, D. 'Anfang und Ende der byzantinischen Rechtgeschichte', FM, 8 (2021), pp. 1–23.
- Stolte, B.H. 'Byzantine Law: The Law of the New Rome', in H. Pihlajamäki, M.D. Dubber, and M. Godfrey, eds. *The Oxford Handbook of European Legal History*. Oxford: 2018, pp. 229–248.
- Stolte, B.H. 'Legal Thought', in A. Kaldellis and N. Siniossoglou, eds. *The Cambridge Intellectual History of Byzantium*. Cambridge: 2017, pp. 141–166.

- Stolte, B.H. 'The Law of New Rome: Byzantine Law', in D. Johnston, ed. *The Cambridge Companion to Roman Law*. Cambridge: 2015, pp. 355–373.
- Stolte, B.H. 'Justice: Legal Literature', in E. Jeffreys et al., eds. *The Oxford Handbook of Byzantine Studies*. Oxford: 2008, pp. 691–698.
- Stolte, B.H. 'Is Byzantine Law Roman Law?', *Acta Byzantina Fennica*, n.s., 2 (2005), pp. 111–126.
- Stolte, B.H. 'Balancing Byzantine Law', FM, 11 (2005), pp. 57–75.

Useful too are the contributions of E. Papagianni to J.N. Dillon, ed., and D.A. Smart, trans. *Brill's New Pauly Supplements II—Volume 10: History and Culture of Byzantium*, published online: 2018 (orig. as M. Landfester, J. Rupke and H. Schneider, eds. *Byzanz: Historisch-kulturwissenschaftliches Handbuch*. Der Neue Pauly—Supplemente, 2, ed. F. Daim. Stuttgart: 2016). Papagianni's contributions include the following:

- 4.1. Byzantine law: a new legal system on an ancient foundation
- 4.2. Canon law and its status in the Byzantine legal system
- 4.3. Legislation
- 4.4. Courts and justice

It is also highly recommended that you consult the following bibliography, compiled by Th.E. van Bochove, which is available online and is (ir)regularly updated by its author:

- Van Bochove, Th.E., *A Bibliography of Byzantine Law, A: Books on Byzantine Law, New, Revised and Augmented Edition*, published 5 January 2021 on Academia.edu (https://www.academia.edu/45025705/A_Bibliography_of_Byzantine_Law)
- Van Bochove, Th.E., *Bibliography of Byzantine Law, B: Articles on Roman and Byzantine Law, History and Culture*, new, extended version published 10th June 2021 on Academia.edu (https://www.academia.edu/49198096/Bibliography_of_Byzantine_Law_B_Articles_on_Roman_and_Byzantine_Law_History_and_Culture_New_extended_version)

Both these bibliographies can also be found at the author's personal website: https://www.rug.nl/staff/t.e.van.bochove/research.

Van Bochove has also collected and categorised into sections (and subsections) the bibliography related to the *Basilica*. His *Basilica* bibliography is available online by BRILL at the following link: https://referenceworks.brillonline.com/browse/basilica-online.

Finally, the journal *Subseciva Groningana. Studies in Roman and Byzantine Law* focuses on Byzantine law, and all ten volumes that have been published up to now are available online at the following link: https://ugp.rug.nl/sg.

CHAPTER 1

The Sources of Law before the Time of Justinian

1 Introduction

In the fifth century AD, the Western Roman Empire gradually disintegrated following numerous invasions by Germanic tribes. The king of the Visigoths, Alaric I, sacked Rome in 410, and in 476 the last emperor of the Western Roman Empire, Romulus Augustulus, gave up his throne to the Germanic leader Odoacer. The year 476 traditionally marks the end of the Western Roman Empire. But if the Western Roman Empire collapsed, the Eastern Roman Empire, also known as Byzantine Empire or Byzantium, remained very much alive.[1]

The conventional term 'Byzantium' was first used in a scholarly way in the sixteenth century to describe the Eastern Roman Empire, a medieval state that lasted for more than a thousand years and covered a large part of south-eastern Europe. It is generally accepted that Byzantium or the Byzantine Empire begins with the foundation of the city of Constantinople by Emperor Constantine I in AD 325–330. He chose as the capital of this Empire the city Byzantion, situated on the European side of the Bosporus, a narrow strait dividing Europe and Asia and giving access to the Black Sea. The strait was so narrow that an ox could pass over it. The word Bosporus, deriving from the Greek words 'βοῦς' (= ox/cattle) and 'πόρος' (= passage) literally means a 'cattle-passage'. The city of Byzantion was originally a colony founded in the seventh century BC by the Greek city of Megara, and it was renamed Constantinople after Emperor Constantine, 'City of Constantine', today's Istanbul. The Byzantine Empire collapsed in 1453 when the Ottomans conquered Constantinople, but Byzantium's influence on Eastern Europe in the legal field and in other fields, including art, for example, continued even after 1453. Geographically, the Byzantine Empire was extended over a large part of the Mediterranean Sea, the Black Sea and the Balkans including parts of nowadays Italy, Greece, Turkey and the North of Africa, but the actual Byzantine territories and borders changed often, as is the case with any Empire. Its population consisted mainly of Greeks, Slavs and Armenians; the dominant language was Greek; and the presiding religion was Orthodox Christianity. The Byzantines were and considered themselves Romans. They called themselves 'Rhomaioi' ('Ρωμαῖοι) and their state was called the 'basileia ton Rhomaion' (ἡ βασιλεία τῶν 'Ρωμαίων), meaning the Roman Empire.

In AD 527 an ambitious man ascended the Byzantine imperial throne. His name was Justinian (*c.* 482–565) and he wanted to restore the *imperium Romanum* in all its glory. To do so he used two methods: 'arms and laws'. On the one hand, in the military field he

1 See map no. 1 at the end of the present chapter.

 | DOI:10.1163/9789004520684_002

wanted to reconquer the western part of 'his empire' and he partly succeeded in this plan: during his reign, Italy, part of southern Spain and North Africa were for a short period reconquered.[2] On the other hand, under his reign the codification of Roman law was achieved, which was to become one of the most influential legal works in history. That the emperor used 'arms and laws' (*arma et leges*) to achieve his goals is something that he himself mentions in an introductory law of his.

TEXT 1 ***Constitutio Imperatoriam*** **pr.: aims of Emperor Justinian**[3]

Imperatoriam maiestatem non solum armis decoratam, sed etiam legibus oportet esse armatam, ut utrumque tempus et bellorum et pacis recte possit gubernari [...]	Imperial majesty should not only be graced with arms but also armed with laws, so that good government may prevail in time of war and peace alike [...]

This is a fragment of the so-called *Constitutio Imperatoriam*, a law by Justinian introducing a part of his legislation, the *Institutes* (533). The legislation of Justinian consisted of the following four parts: i. the *Code*, which included the most important imperial laws up to the time of Justinian; ii. the *Digest*, an anthology of the best opinions and commentaries of the Roman jurists, who had mostly lived in the second and third century AD; iii. the *Institutes*, a legal manual addressed to students which also received the status of a law; and finally, iv. the *Novels*, the new imperial laws which were issued after the promulgation of the *Code*.[4] The law in TEXT 1 is referred to as the *Constitutio Imperatoriam* because the first word of the law is the word *'Imperatoriam'*. The majority of Justinian's legislation was issued in Latin, even though Greek was the dominant language in the Byzantine Empire. The fact that Justinian promulgated most of his legislation in Latin comes down to two reasons. First, this was practical because the sources used for his legislation were mostly written in Latin. Secondly, there was an ideological reason behind the use of Latin: Justinian's ambition of restoring the *imperium Romanum*, the Roman Empire. Latin was, after all, the language of the Roman Empire.

When Justinian became emperor in 527 he had many problems that needed solving. In order to understand these problems and before examining Justinian's legislation, it is necessary to provide a short overview of the legal sources from before Justinian's time, namely, the sources of Roman law.

2 See map no. 2 at the end of the present chapter.

3 The Latin text is cited from the edition of P. Krüger (= C.). The English translation is from P. Birks and G. McLeod, Justinian's Institutes (London: 1987; repr. 2001).

4 On Justinian's legislation, see below, pp. 22–32.

2 A Brief Summary of the Sources of Roman Law

The Byzantines who wanted to study law also needed to learn something of Roman legal history. We read this in the following passage, which comes from a handbook addressed to law students of the sixth century. The handbook was written in Greek by a sixth-century law professor named Theophilos.[5]

TEXT 2 Theophilos, *Paraphrasis Institutionum*, 1,2,4: about legislation in ancient Rome

Ἡδέως δὲ ἐμάνθανον πόσοι παρὰ Ῥωμαίοις εἰσὶ νομοθέται καὶ τίνες οὗτοι καὶ πῶς τὰ παρ' ἑκάστου νομοθετούμενα κέκληται. ἓξ παρὰ Ῥωμαίοις εἰσὶν οἱ νομοθέται· δῆμος, χυδαῖος δῆμος, σύγκλητος, βασιλεύς, ἄρχοντες τῆς Ῥώμης, σοφοί.[6]	It would be well to learn how many law-making authorities there are among the Romans, and who these are, and how the laws made by each of them are designated. The law-makers among the Romans are six: the people (*populus*), the common people (*plebs*), the Senate, the Emperor, the magistrates of Rome, and the jurists.

According to this fragment, the people who were responsible for making laws in Roman times were: the people (δῆμος), the *plebs* (χυδαῖος δῆμος), the senate (σύγκλητος), the emperor (βασιλεύς), the magistrates of Rome (ἄρχοντες τῆς Ῥώμης) and the jurists, mentioned in the text as '(*iuris*) *prudentes*', 'the wise' (σοφοί). The Roman citizen body was originally divided into two social groups. On the one hand there were the patricians, a small, privileged group who came from rich Roman families. On the other hand there were the plebeians (*plebs*), who formed the majority and were rather disadvantaged in various ways. If there was doubt about the application of a customary rule to a particular case, a college of priests, the pontiffs (*pontifices*) would decide. This body of pontiffs consisted of patricians. The plebeians became somewhat suspicious of these decisions, and argued that if customary law were written down, then they would at least know what the law was. The first Roman laws committed to text is known as *The Law of the Twelve Tables* (*Lex Duodecim Tabularum*), which was written around 450 BC. Because of its redaction into a text, it became law, *lex*, a noun that derives from the Latin verb *legere*, which means 'to read out'. It was called Twelve Tables because it was written on twelve bronze tablets. Although the bronze tablets themselves have not survived, the contents of the Twelve Tables have been substantially reconstructed from the many quotations draw-

5 On Theophilos, see below, pp. 42–46.
6 The Greek text and the English translation are cited from Theoph.

ing from it that can be found in later writings. The original Twelve Tables were placed at the *Forum Romanum*—the Roman market that was the center of Roman public life—so that every citizen could read them. Even five hundred years after the enactment of this legislation, Romans looked back on the Twelve Tables with immense pride. Cicero (106 BC–43 BC) informs us that in his time schoolboys had to learn its contents by heart; and the historian Livy (59/64 BC–AD 17) calls it 'the source of all public and private life'. The Twelve Tables were the basis of public and private law, but of course Roman law continued to grow and develop. The Romans called their own law the *ius civile* ('the civil law') which meant the state law, namely, the law that was applied only to Roman citizens. The Romans were proud of their law and they would not extend it unconditionally to all foreigners. They distinguished their own *ius civile* from the *ius gentium*, that is, the law for all peoples, a universal law applicable to relations between Romans and non-Romans.

In the same handbook of Theophilos, we also learn about the different types of Roman laws. Note that in his text, Theophilos partly uses the original Latin names in Latin letters.

TEXT 3 Theophilos, *Paraphrasis Institutionum*, 1,2,3: about types of law in ancient Rome

[…] ἔγγραφος δὲ νόμος ἐστίν οἷον ἡ *LEX*, τὰ *PLEBISCITA*, *SENATUS CONSULTA*, διατάξεις βασιλικαί, ἀρχόντων ἤδικτα, τῶν σοφῶν ἀποκρίσεις.[7]	[…] Written law is, for example, *lex*, *plebiscita*, *senatusconsulta*, imperial constitutions, edicts of magistrates and responses of the jurists.

The *lex*, the *plebiscitum* and the *senatusconsultum* were laws made by collective authorities, assemblies: the first by the assembly of the patricians and the plebeians together; the second (*plebiscitum*) by the plebeians only;[8] and the last by the assembly of the patricians only, known as the senate. There were also laws that owe their existence to the *imperium*, the authority of certain persons: the magistrates and the emperor. The *edicta*, the general laws of the Roman magistrates were valid for the duration of any given magistrate's appointment to office. Most of the imperial constitutions were rescripts (*rescripta*), answers given in the emperor's name to questions of law put forward by litigants or public officials.

7 The Greek text and the English translation are cited from Theoph.

8 The *plebiscita*, the resolutions of the assembly of the plebeians, received the force of law by the *lex Hortensia* in c. 287 BC.

The *praetor* was a special magistrate who dealt with the administration of justice. His office was established in its basic shape in 367 BC. Later on, a second *praetor* was introduced for matters arising between foreigners or between a foreigner and a Roman citizen. It is important to note that the Romans thought in actions and not in rights. Hence, in the Roman law of procedure, the crucial question was whether there was an action available for your legal situation. The Roman legal procedure that was applied in the classical period and is known as the formulary system included two stages. The first stage involved the categorization of the issue in legal terms, the drawing up of a *formula*; in the second stage, an actual trial took place before the judge. The *praetor* was concerned with the first stage. For each cause of action there was an appropriate form of action, and each form of action was expressed in a set of words or a *formula*. The *formula* consisted essentially of a direction to the judge (*iudex*) to condemn the defendant if he found the plaintiff's case proved, and to absolve him if he did not. The *praetor* made known the laws according to which he would rule in his edict (*edictum*). Every year the *praetor* would publish his edict where he outlined the legal remedies available and set out the various circumstances in which he would grant a *formula*. In theory, every *praetor* issued a new edict each year, but in practice, *praetor*s tended to follow previous edicts, and simply made additions to them. In the first half of the second century AD (c. 135), the Emperor Hadrian ordered the jurist Salvius Julianus to make a final revision of edictal law. A definitive version of the *praetor*'s edict was thus made and was called the *edictum perpetuum* (= the eternal edict). Only the emperor could henceforth alter or amend the *praetor*'s edict.

Theophilos refers also to the Roman jurists, the *iurisconsulti*, the scholars or wise (οἱ σοφοί), who were important for the interpretation of laws. These *iurisconsulti* were professional jurists who could be consulted for advice on practical cases. Neither the *praetor*, nor the *iudex* (the judge, who was a private person) nor the advocates who represented the parties before them were trained in law, and all of them needed expert help from time to time. The Roman jurists, the *iurisconsulti*, advised all these persons in matters of law. In other words, the Roman jurists did not have an official role to play in the actual administration of trial procedure. Yet, through their advice and their writings, they played a significant role in the development of Roman law. They were also favoured by the emperors, and these experts gradually received a sort of official approval from the emperor which made their advice automatically binding. Emperor Augustus, in the first century AD, had granted certain jurists the right to give opinions with the emperor's authority (*ius publice respondendi*). This is described by Theophilos in the following fragment:

TEXT 4 **Theophilos, *Paraphrasis Institutionum*, 1,2,8: about jurisprudence**

[...] ἐπετέτραπτο δὲ τούτοις δημοσίᾳ νομοθετεῖν ἤτοι τοὺς νόμους ἑρμηνεύειν· οἵτινες καὶ *IURIS CONSULTI* προσηγορεύοντο, τουτέστιν οἱ περὶ τοῦ νόμου ἐπερωτώμενοι· *CONSULERE* γάρ ἐστι τὸ ἐρωτᾶν. ὧν αἱ *SENTENTIAE* καὶ αἱ *OPINIONES* ταύτην ἔχουσι τὴν αὐθεντίαν ὥστε μὴ ἔχειν παρρησίαν δικαστὴν ταῖς αὐτῶν ἀπειθεῖν ἀποκρίσεσιν, ὥσπερ καὶ βασιλέως βοᾷ διάταξις.[9]	[...] The jurists (the wise or scholars, the 'σοφοί') were empowered to make law—that is, to explain the laws—with public authority; and they were also designated *iurisconsulti*, that is, persons consulted on the law, for *consulere* means 'to consult'. And their *sententiae* and *opiniones* are of such authority that a judge is not at liberty to disregard their answers; as is indeed laid down by an imperial constitution.

Roman jurists not only wrote on request; they also wrote commentaries on the laws and on the edict of the *praetor* as well as commentaries on the writings of other Roman jurists. In short, the Roman jurists were very productive. We also know that there were two important law schools in Rome: the Sabinians and the Proculians. There is much debate over what distinguished these two schools. The *iurisconsulti* did not explain legal issues in an abstract way, but instead used real or hypothetical cases to explain the law. In other words, the Roman jurists explained their concepts not by defining them but by testing them against particular cases. To a great extent, their typical form of their writings was casuistic, collections of opinions or problems in which the jurist argued his way to a particular solution. These answers, views and opinions were published, and they were still available by the time of Justinian. After the end of the third century AD, the only source of new law was the emperor himself, but the immense textual output of previous centuries remained.

Already by the fourth century, jurists must have found it difficult to identify the most recent rules valid for particular cases. On the one hand, jurists needed to trawl through the constitutions; on the other, they had to look at the opinions of the legal experts. The quantity of all these writings is clearly reflected in later legal sources. Another problem was whether or not the text of the law in a specific manuscript was reliable; many mistakes were made when copying the manuscripts, and falsifications remained a possibility. Even before the time of Justinian's compilation, it was necessary to arrange the existing legal chaos into some kind of order. In the end of the third century, two private collections were compiled: the *Codex Gregorianus* and the *Codex Hermogenianus*. These were not official codifications because they were made by private persons on their own initiative, rather than on the order of an authority. These collections were certainly useful, but

9 The Greek text and the English translation are cited from Theoph.

since they lacked official status, any constitutions that were not found in these collections retained the force of law.

The next step was taken in 426 when Emperor Theodosius II issued an important constitution. In fact it was issued by Theodosius and his co-emperor in the western part of the Roman Empire, Valentinian III. This constitution took the form of a letter, addressed to the senate. It dealt with various subjects, and TEXTS 5 and 6 are quotations from it. It was a very long constitution, but later emperors broke it into pieces, which are found in different parts of their own codifications. TEXT 5 is found both in the *Codex Theodosianus* and in the *Codex Justinianus*.[10]

TEXT 5 ***Codex Theodosianus* 1,4,3 / *Codex Justinianus* 1,14,3: about general and special *leges* or constitutions**

Idem AA. [*sc. Theodosius et Valentinianus*] *ad senatum.*	The same Augusti [who also issued the previous law in this Code title, namely in this case Theodosius II and Valentinian III] to the Senate.
pr. Leges ut generales ab omnibus aequabiliter in posterum observentur, quae vel missa ad venerabilem coetum oratione conduntur vel inserto edicti vocabulo nuncupantur, sive eas nobis spontaneus motus ingesserit sive precatio vel relatio vel lis mota legis occasionem postulaverit. [...]	pr. From now on, the following laws must be observed by everybody alike as being general laws: [1] those which are established by an oration addressed to this venerable assembly (the Senate); [2] those which are explicitly labelled 'edict'. It makes no difference whether they were made on our own spontaneous initiative, or were occasioned by a request, a consultation, or by a case brought before us. [...]
1. Sed et si generalis lex vocata est vel ad omnes iussa est pertinere, vim obtineat edicti; interlocutionibus, quas in uno negotio iudicantes protulimus vel postea proferemus, non in commune praeiudicantibus, nec his, quae specialiter quibusdam concessa sunt civitatibus vel provinciis vel corporibus, ad generalitatis observantiam pertinentibus.[11]	1. But also when a law is called 'general', or when it is said to be valid for everybody, it is accorded the force of an edict. Special arrangements, however, which we have put forward as a judicial sentence in one specific case, or which we shall put forward as such in the future, do not possess this common validity for subsequent cases. Nor are the special privileges granted to specific cities, provinces, or corporations generally valid.

10 For more on the *Codex Justinianus* and all parts of Justinian's legislation, see below, pp. 22–32.
11 The Latin text cited comes from P. Krüger's edition (= C.).

This passage deals with the constitutions or *leges*. It distinguishes between general and special laws. This distinction is the first step towards the *Codex Theodosianus*, which was published in 438 and contained all imperial laws issued dating from AD 312 to 438. Although this *Code*, was issued in the East, it was sent to the West where it was approved and held to be valid there. In contrast with the *Codices Gregorianus* and *Hermogenianus*, the *Codex Theodosianus* has survived to this day.

With so many writings by Roman jurists, it was difficult to find out what the applicable law actually was. The same Emperors Theodosius II and Valentian III also tried to create some order out of this legal chaos by promulgating the law of citations (*lex citandi*). According to this law, issued in AD 426, the courts could henceforth take into account only the writings of the five following jurists: Papinian, Paul, Ulpian, Modestinus and Gaius. If there were conflicting opinions over a legal issue, the majority view should be followed. If there was an equal number, then the opinion of Papinian prevailed; but if Papinian had not written about that issue, the judge could, in that case, choose whose opinion (from the equal number) to follow. Other jurists were acceptable provided that they were considered sufficiently competent to have been cited by the five main jurists and if more than one manuscript was submitted to the judge to make sure that they were not falsified. Here is a fragment of the *lex citandi*, the law of citations, which is included in the *Theodosian Code*, but not in Justinian's *Code*.

TEXT 6 *Codex Theodosianus* 1,4,3: the *lex citandi*, the law of citations, AD 426[12]

Impp. Theod. et Valent. aa. ad senatum urbis Romae. post alia:	Emperors Theodosius and Valentinian Auguses to the Senate of the City of Rome (After other matters):
Papiniani, Pauli, Gai, Ulpiani atque Modestini scripta universa firmamus ita, ut Gaium quae Paulum, Ulpianum et ceteros comitetur auctoritas lectionesque ex omni eius corpore recitentur. Eorum quoque scientiam, quorum tractatus atque sententias praedicti omnes suis operibus miscuerunt, ratam esse censemus, ut	We confirm all the writings of Papinian, Paulus, Gaius, Ulpian and Modestinus, so that the same authority shall attend Gaius as Paulus, Ulpian and the others, and passages from the whole body of his writings may be cited. We also decree to be valid the learning of those persons whose treatises and opinions all the aforesaid jurisconsults have incorporated in their own work, such as Scaevola,

12 The English translation of this fragment of the *Theodosian Code* is by C. Pharr, *The Theodosian Code and Novels and the Sirmondian Constitutions: A Translation with Commentary, Glossary, and Bibliography* (Princeton: 1952). The Latin is cited from the edition by Th. Mommsen (= CTh.).

TEXT 6 (*cont.*)

Scaevolae, Sabini, Iuliani atque Marcelli omniumque, quos illi celebrarunt, si tamen eorum libri propter antiquitatis incertum codicum collatione firmentur. Ubi autem diversae sententiae proferuntur, potior numerus vincat auctorum, vel, si numerus aequalis sit, eius partis praecedat auctoritas, in qua excellentis ingenii vir Papinianus emineat, qui ut singulos vincit, ita cedit duobus. [...] *Ubi autem eorum pares sententiae recitantur, quorum par censetur auctoritas, quos sequi debeat, eligat moderatio iudicantis.* [...]	Sabinus, Julianus, and Marcellus, and all others whom they cite, provided that, on account of the uncertainty of antiquity, their books shall be confirmed by a collation of the manuscripts.[13] Moreover, when conflicting opinions are cited, the greater number of the authors shall prevail, or, if the numbers should be equal, the authority of that group shall take precedence in which the man of superior genius, Papinian, shall tower above the rest, and as he defeats a single opponent, so he yields to two. [...] Furthermore, when their opinions as cited are equally divided and their authority is rated as equal, the regulation of the judge shall choose whose opinion he shall follow [...]

3 Teaching Law before the Time of Justinian

In the early Byzantine period, one could study law in several places: in Alexandria, Caesarea; or, better yet, in Rome and Constantinople; or, best of all, in Beirut. Legal studies were part of a general curriculum of liberal studies including philosophy, rhetoric, Greek and Latin. A constitution by Theodosius II, dated from 425 (TEXT 7), survives and gives us information about Constantinople's school of higher education. We know that there were freelance teachers who taught at home, but in the following example, we read about real *magistri* who were members of a civil service; there were also teachers of Latin and Greek, and other subjects such as philosophy and law.

13 Pharr renders this as 'a collation of the codices'.

TEXT 7	*Codex Theodosianus* 14,9,3,1 (by Theodosius II and Valentinian III, AD 425): about state schools
[...] *Et quoniam non his artibus tantum adulescentiam gloriosam optamus institui, profundioris quoque scientiae adque doctrinae memoratis magistris sociamus auctores. Unum igitur adiungi ceteris volumus, qui philosofiae arcana rimetur, duo quoque, qui iuris ac legum formulas pandant.* [...][14]	[...] Since it is Our desire that Our glorious youth should be instructed not only in such arts [Latin and Greek], We associate authorities of more profound knowledge and learning with the aforesaid professors. Therefore, it is Our will that to the other professors, one teacher shall be associated who shall investigate the hidden secrets of philosophy, two teachers also who shall expound the formulas of the law and statutes. [...]

In AD 425, there must have been two law professors in Constantinople, and an unknown number in the schools of Beirut and elsewhere. We know some of their names, and we can get an impression of their qualities and competence from the fact that these were the people who taught the professionals who would work on Justinian's codification. We even know the curriculum followed in the study of law because Justinian provided a description of it when he reformed it, as we will see in Chapter 2. The fact that Latin was the standard language for law created a problem for the Greek-speaking majority of the Eastern Roman Empire. However, the study of law itself was immensely popular precisely because of its focus on Latin, and that needs some explanation. As Latin was the language of Roman law, legal studies necessarily comprised a certain amount of Latin schooling. This was useful enough for many purposes if you wanted to start any career, even outside the field of law. Moreover, contrary to the situation in old Rome, legal schooling had become imperative for a career as a lawyer. In the old Rome, barristers used to be orators, schooled in rhetoric rather than in law; legal specialists simply provided the technical arguments, whereas the orators were trained to make the most of them in court. But that had changed. Constantine the Great, in particular, had organized the courts: supreme courts were established in Constantinople (and in Rome, at first); in addition, every provincial capital had a law court. Each law court had a fixed, limited number of barristers. If you applied to such a post, you had to prove your legal schooling. This is confirmed by a constitution promulgated in 460 by Emperor Leo I (TEXT 8). It states that persons who want to practice law have to prove their legal schooling by providing a document in which their law teachers promised that the applicants

14 The Latin comes from the edition by Th. Mommsen (= CTh.). The English translation of this text is by C. Pharr, The Theodosian Code (see n. 12, above).

are qualified as jurists. Here is the relevant fragment of this law by Leo I, preserved in Justinian's *Code*:

TEXT 8 C. 2,7,11,2 (by emperor Leo I, AD 460): certificate required

Iuris peritos etiam doctores eorum iubemus iuratos sub gestorum testifactione depromere, esse eum, qui posthac subrogari voluerit, peritia iuris instructum. [...][15]	We order that from now on lawyers also present a certificate, in which their teachers swear that the person applying for an office has received instruction in jurisprudence. [...]

As far as the law schools were concerned, we know from the sources that Beirut was already an important centre of legal learning from the third century, up until the year AD 551, when a catastrophic earthquake destroyed the whole city. Several testimonies confirm the prominent role that Beirut played in legal studies. Authors of the fourth and fifth centuries characterise Beirut, which was originally a Roman colony, as 'the mother of laws', 'the most Roman city' and 'the seat of Roman laws'. The prominent role of the city of Beirut in legal studies is confirmed by Justinian himself. In an introductory law to the *Digest* and the *Institutes*, the emperor refers to Beirut as 'the most excellent *civitas* of Beirut, which might well be called the nurse of the law'.[16] The fact that Justinian had invited law professors from the law school of Beirut to take part in the committees of his legal reforms offers further proof of this law school's fame.[17]

The earliest likely reference to Beirut as a centre of legal training is the testimony of Gregory the Thaumaturgus[18] from the beginning of the third century AD. Gregory writes that he and his brother Athenodoros had intended to study law in Beirut. However, after attending the lectures of the Christian philosopher Origen in Caesarea, the two brothers were so inspired by him that they changed their minds; they gave up law studies in Beirut and became Origen's pupils instead. The importance of Beirut as a popular centre of legal studies by the fourth century is also confirmed by Libanius, a fourth-century Greek teacher of rhetoric. He complained in his letters about young students—especially the wealthy ones—who abandoned the study of rhetoric to flock to the law school of Beirut. We also have some testimonies of students who attended classes at the law school of Beirut. For example, Severus of Antioch,[19] after having studied rhetoric and philoso-

15 The Latin text cited comes from P. Krüger's edition (= C.).
16 *Constitutio Omnem*, 7: '... in Berytiensium pulcherrima civitate, quam et legum nutricem bene quis appellet ...'.
17 See below, pp. 24–27.
18 Gregory Thaumaturgos (*c.* 213–270), 'the Wonderworker', became bishop of Neocaesarea.
19 Severus of Antioch (*c.* 465–538) was a Monophysite theologian who became bishop of Antioch.

phy in both Greek and Latin in Alexandria, travelled in 486 to Beirut and studied law and philosophy at the law school. One year later, Severus was followed by his friend and fellow student Zacharias of Mytilene,[20] who had also studied rhetoric and philosophy in Alexandria. Zacharias wrote a biography of Severus which gives us a glimpse of student life in Beirut.

The last fragment of sources of the pre-Justinianic period (TEXT 9.2) is a part of the so-called *Fragmenta Sinaitica*, which were papyrus fragments once found in the library of the monastery of St Catherine at Mount Sinai, but which now seem to be lost. These papyrus fragments contain notes by an unknown author on the work of the Roman jurist Ulpian entitled *Libri ad Sabinum*: a commentary on the work of the first-century Roman jurist Sabinus. This work of Ulpian is now lost, but fragments of it have been preserved, mainly because they were included in Justinian's *Digest*.[21] The chosen example (TEXT 9.2) comments on a passage of Ulpian that we still find in the *Digest*.[22] In fact, the commentary is not on the *Digest* passage itself, but on the separate, original commentary of Ulpian. TEXT 9.1 is the beginning of what has become *Digest* title 25,1 and contains fragments from Ulpian's book 36 *ad Sabinum* alternating with Paul's book 7 *ad Sabinum*.[23] This *Digest* title deals with expenses made by a husband for the benefit of his wife's dowry. The dowry was a separate part of his property, which a husband had to return when the marriage was dissolved, but he could deduct all so-called 'necessary expenses'. Therefore, it was clearly important to define 'necessary expenses' in this context, and that is what Ulpian is doing here, after giving several examples (*generaliter definiemus*). Ulpian explains that only long term investments are counted as 'necessary expenses' and can thus be deducted from the dowry.

TEXT 9.1 From *Digest* 25,1: about expenses made for things that belong to a dowry

Liber vicesimus quintus *I DE IMPENSIS IN RES DOTALES FACTIS* *1 Ulpianus libro trigesimo sexto ad Sabinum.* *pr. Impensarum quaedam sunt necessariae, quaedam utiles, quaedam vero voluptariae.*	Book twenty five I EXPENSES INCURRED IN CONNECTION WITH DOTAL PROPERTY 1 Ulpian, on Sabinus, book 36: pr. Some expenses are necessary, some are useful, but some are incurred for pleasure. 1. Expenses are said to be necessary where they arise out of necessity. But where there

20 Zacharias of Mytilene, also called Zacharias the Rhetor or Scholastikos (*c.* 465/6–after 536), was a churchman and ecclesiastical historian and became bishop of Mytilene.

21 On Justinian's legislation, see below, pp. 22–32.

22 The fragments of Ulpian and his fellow *iurisconsulti* have been edited by O. Lenel, *Palingenesia* (see bibliography at the end of this chapter): this particular fragment is no. 2805.

23 There is also one fragment from Paul's commentary on the *Edict*.

TEXT 9.1 *(cont.)*

	is no necessity for them, other rules apply to them.
1. Necessariae hae dicuntur, quae habent in se necessitatem impendendi: ceterum si nulla fuit necessitas, alio iure habentur.	
2. In necessariis impensis hoc sciendum est eas demum impensas dotem minuere, quae in dotem factae sunt: [...]	2. As far as necessary expenses are concerned, note that they only reduce the dowry when they are incurred in connection with it. [...]
3. Inter necessarias impensas esse Labeo ait moles in mare vel flumen proiectas. [...]	3. According to Labeo, dikes built in the sea or a river count as necessary expenses. [...][25]
2 Paulus libro septimo ad Sabinum. *vel* [...]	2. Paul, on Sabinus, book 7: or [...]
3 Ulpianus libro trigesimo sexto ad Sabinum. *pr. vel* [...]	3 Ulpian, on Sabinus, book 36: or [...]
1. ***Nos generaliter definiemus*** *multum interesse, ad perpetuam utilitatem agri vel ad eam quae non ad praesentis temporis pertineat, an vero ad praesentis anni fructum: si in praesentis, cum fructibus hoc* ***compensandum****: si vero non fuit ad praesens tantum apta erogatio,* ***necessariis impensis computandum****.*	1. Let us lay down as a general rule that it makes much difference whether expenses have a lasting effect on the field's value, not just for the current period, or merely contribute to the proceeds ('fruits') of this particular year. In the latter case, the expenses must be compensated with the fruits. But if they were long-term investments, they must be counted as necessary expenses.
4 Paulus libro trigesimo sexto ad edictum. [...]	4 Paul, Edict, book 36: [...]
5 Ulpianus libro trigesimo sexto ad Sabinum. [...]	5 Ulpian, on Sabinus, book 36: [...]
6 Paulus libro septimo ad Sabinum. *veluti.* [...][24]	6 Paul, on Sabinus, book 7: for example [...]

24 The Latin text is cited from the standard edition of Th. Mommsen (= D.).

25 The English translation up to this *Digest* fragment is from A. Watson, ed. and trans., *The Digest of Justinian*, 4 vols., Philadelphia: 1985 (rev. edn, Philadelphia: 1998), here vol. 2, p. 273, reprinted with permission of the University of Pennsylvania Press.

TEXT 9.2 ***Fragmenta Sinaïtica*** **VIII (18): anonymous Greek notes to the same fragment before it was inserted in the *Digest***

Nos generaliter: ὁρᾷς, πῶς καὶ ***Ulpianos*** κανονίζει ἡμῖν, ὅσα δαπανήματα πεποίηκεν ὁ ἀνὴρ πρόσκαιρα τῶν καρπῶν ἕνεκεν, ταῦτα τοῖς καρποῖς ***compensateuεται***, οὐ μὴν ποιεῖ τὴν ***retentiona***. ὅσα δὲ διηνεκῆ ᾖ καὶ ἐπὶ πολὺν χρόνον παρέχει τὴν χρείαν, οἷον μῶλος ἢ ἀρτοκοπεῖον ἢ τὸ φυτεῦσαι, ταῦτα ***necessaria*** ἐστι καὶ μειοῖ τὴν προῖκα. τοῦτό φησι καὶ ὁ ***Paulos*** βιβλίῳ ζʹ τῶν ***ad Sabinum*** αὐτοῦ τίτλῳ λεʹ.[26]	You see how Ulpian too gives us the general rule: the husband is compensated for all short-term expenses which he has made to improve the proceeds (fruits) with those fruits. So he cannot deduct them [from the dowry]. All lasting expenses, however, which have a long-term effect, such as for a dam, a mill or a plantation, are necessary and can be deducted from the dowry. This is also said by Paul, in book seven of his *libri ad Sabinum*, title thirty-five.

We observe, first of all, that in this fragment (TEXT 9.2) the anonymous commentator uses Latin words in the Greek text.

- '**Nos generaliter**' is the lemma: it only serves to mark the text of Ulpian which is under discussion; it means: the following paragraph deals with the passage that starts with *nos generaliter*.
- '**Ulpianos, Paulos**': Latin names have the Greek ending *-os*.
- '**compensateuεται**': this word is a combination of the technical Latin term *compensare* (= to compensate) and the Greek verb ending (-τευεται).[27] This is a well-known phenomenon that we also still find in modern languages, namely, when a word combines elements from a language that is broadly used, mainly English, with another, native language.
- '**retentiona**': this word is also a combination of a Latin noun (*retentio*, which means 'to keep back', here 'to deduct') and the Greek accusative ending *-ona*.

There are two important differences between the Latin fragment by Ulpian (TEXT 9.1) and the Greek commentary (TEXT 9.2). First, the Greek adds some examples of 'long term investments' (dam, mill, and plantation). Secondly, in the Greek text there is a reference to a work by another Roman jurist, Paul's book *ad Sabinum*. This is precisely the book which was later combined with Ulpian in the *Digest* (see TEXT 9.1). One might compare this reference to a present-day footnote when writing a paper: 'see also …'. This Greek fragment is one of the few traces of law teaching that survives before the time of Justinian.

26 P. Krüger et al., *Collectio librorum iuris anteiustiniani*, vol. III (Berlin, 1890), p. 274.

27 On technical legal terms and linguistic problems, see below, pp. 41–42.

4 Select Bibliography

General Literature on Byzantium

An important and useful work for Byzantine literature is A.P. Kazhdan, ed., *Oxford Dictionary of Byzantium*, 3 vols. (New York/Oxford: 1991; online edn.: 2005). This work contains numerous entries, each including a basic bibliography on various Byzantine subjects. Since there is an abundant scholarly literature on Byzantium and different Byzantine topics, the references below provide only a selection of general Byzantine literature.

Angold, M. *Byzantium: The Bridge from Antiquity to the Middle Ages*. London: 2001.
Browning, R. *The Byzantine Empire*, rev. edn. Washington, D.C.: 1992.
Cameron, A. *The Byzantines*. New York: 2009.
Gregory, T. *A History of Byzantium*. Oxford: 2005.
Herrin, J. *Byzantium: The Surprising Life of a Medieval Empire*. London: 2007.
James E., ed. *A Companion to Byzantium*. Chichester: 2010.
Jeffreys, E., J.F. Haldon, and R. Cormack, eds. *The Oxford Handbook of Byzantine Studies*. Oxford/New York: 2008.
Mango, C., ed. *The Oxford History of Byzantium*. Oxford: 2002.
Mango, C. *Byzantium: The Empire of New Rome*. London: 1980.
Sarris, P. *Byzantium: A Very Short Introduction*. Oxford: 2015.
Shepard, J., ed. *The Cambridge History of the Byzantine Empire, c. 500–1492*, rev. edn. Cambridge: 2019.
Stathakopoulos, D. *A Short History of the Byzantine Empire*. London/New York: 2014.
Stephenson, P., ed. *The Byzantine World*. London: 2010.

For general works about Byzantine law, see the section *General note on the bibliography* at the beginning of the book.

Other Literature for This Chapter

Primary Sources[28]

Krüger, P et al., ed. *Collectio librorum iuris anteiustiniani in usum scholarum*, vol. III. Berlin: 1890.
Krüger, P. 'Die Sinai-Scholien zu Ulpians ad Sabinum', SZ, 4 (1883), pp. 1–32 (with apograph).
Lenel, O. *Palingenesia juris civilis; juris consultorum reliquiae quae Justiniani Digestis continentur ceteraque juris prudentiae civilis fragmenta minora secundum auctores et libros*. Leipzig: 1889 (with reprints).
Pharr, C. *The Theodosian Code and Novels and the Sirmondian Constitutions: A Translation with Commentary, Glossary, and Bibliography*. Princeton: 1952.

28 See also the abbreviations of the sources cited in this chapter.

Secondary Literature

Atzeri, L. *Gesta senatus Romani de Theodosiano publicando. Il Codice Theodosiano e la sua diffusione ufficiale in Occidente*. Berlin: 2008.

Collinet, P. *Histoire de l'école de droit de Beyrouth*. Paris: 1925.

Corcoran, S. 'Roman Law and the Two Languages in Justinian's Empire', *Bulletin of the Institute of Classical Studies*, 60/1 (2017), pp. 96–116.

Dimopoulou-Piliouni, A. 'Les corporations d'avocats au début de l'ère Byzantine', in Ch. Papastathis, ed. *Byzantine Law, Proceedings of the international symposium of jurists, Thessaloniki 10–13 December 1998*. Thessaloniki: 2001, pp. 307–316.

Goria, F. 'Il giurista nell'impero romano d'Oriente (da Giustiniano agli inizi del secolo XI)', FM, 11 (2005), pp. 147–211.

Hall Jones, L. *Roman Berytus, Beirut in Late Antiquity*. London: 2004, esp. pp. 195–220.

Harries, J. and I. Wood, eds. *The Theodosian Code: Studies in the Imperial Law of Late Antiquity*, 2nd edn, London: 2010.

Liebs, D. 'Rechtsschulen und Rechtsunterricht im Prinzipat', in H. Temporini, ed. *Recht (Methoden, Schulen, Einzelne Juristen)*, Aufstieg und Niedergang der römischen Welt II/15. Berlin/New York: 1976, pp. 197–286.

Markopoulos, A. 'Education', in R. Cormack, J.F. Haldon, and E. Jeffreys, eds. *The Oxford Handbook of Byzantine Studies*. Oxford: 2008, pp. 785–795.

McNamee, K. 'Another Chapter in the History of Scholia', *The Classical Quarterly*, 48/1 (1998), pp. 269–288.

Nicholas, B. *An Introduction to Roman Law*, rev. edn. Oxford: 2008.

Salway, B. 'The Publication and Application of the Theodosian Code. NTh 1, the *Gesta senatus*, and the *constitutionarii*', *Mélanges de l'École française de Rome: Antiquité*, 125/2 (2013), pp. 327–354.

Sirks, A.J.B. *The Theodosian Code: A Study*. Friedrichsdorf: 2007.

Thüngen, L. 'Anmerkungen zu den Scholia Sinaitica', RIDA, 64 (2017), pp. 313–366.

Watson, A., ed. and trans., *The Digest of Justinian*, 4 vols., Philadelphia: 1985 (rev. edn, Philadelphia: 1998).

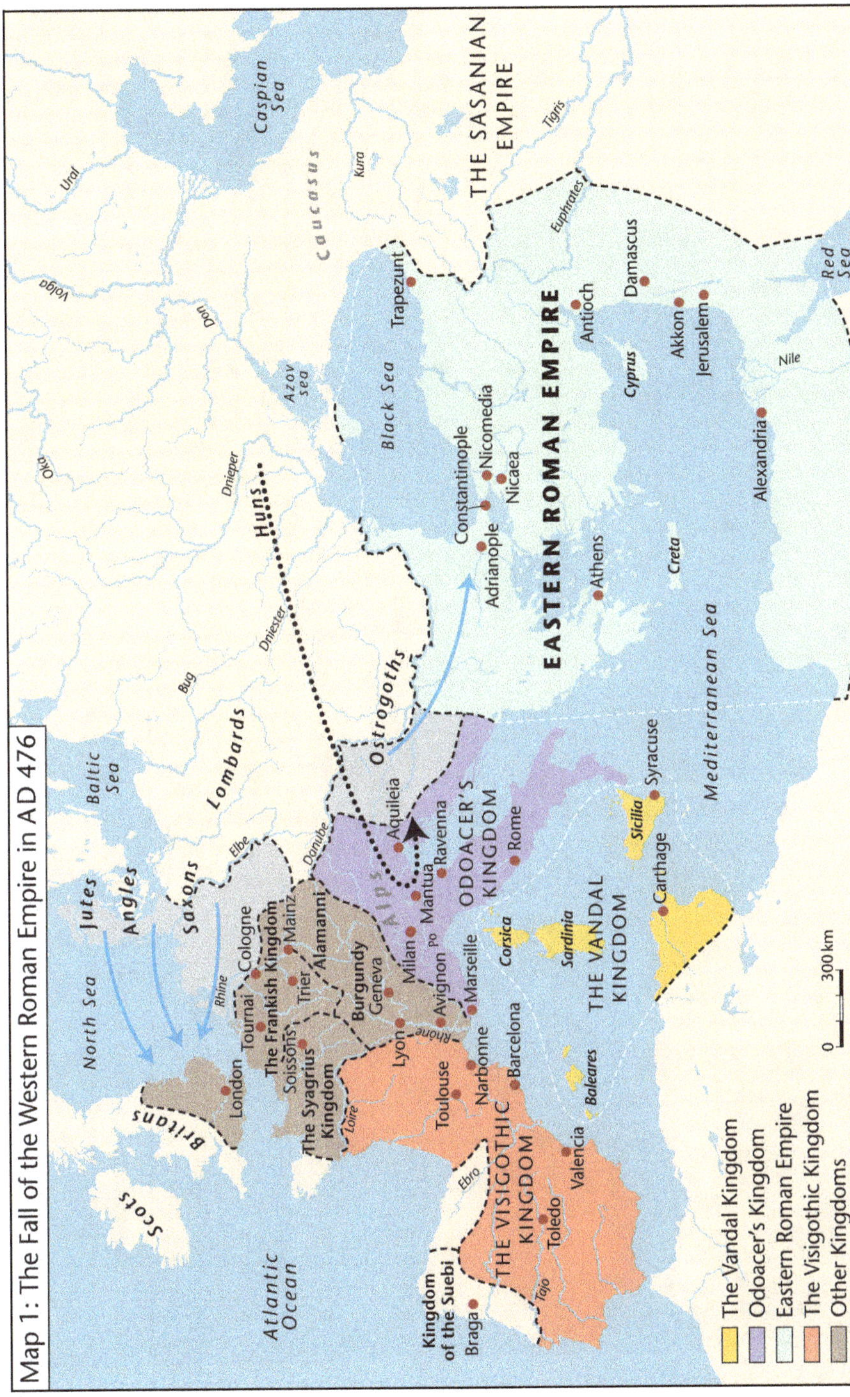

MAP 1 The Fall of the Western Empire in AD 476

DRAWING: PETER PALM

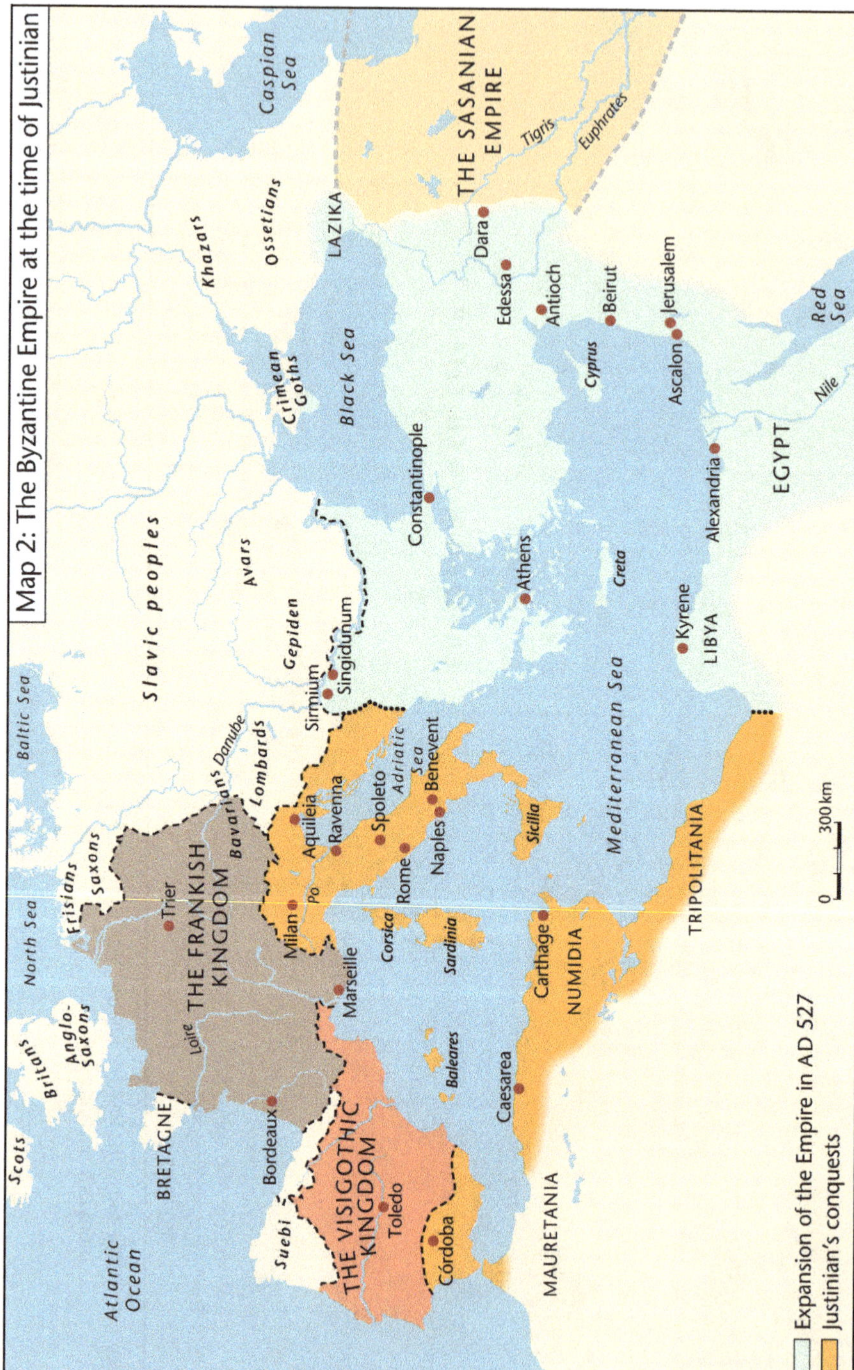

MAP 2 The Byzantine Empire at the time of Justinian
DRAWING: PETER PALM

FIGURE 1 Mosaic from the church of Hagia Sophia of Constantinople (Istanbul, Turkey), depicting on the right Emperor Constantine I offering a model of the city to the Virgin Mother. On the left, Emperor Justinian offers to the Virgin Mother a model of the Hagia Sophia.
PHOTO: MYRABELLA, HTTPS://COMMONS.WIKIMEDIA.ORG/WIKI/FILE:HAGIA_SOPHIA_SOUTHWESTERN_ENTRANCE_MOSAICS_2.JPG. LAST ACCESSED MARCH 14, 2022

FIGURE 2 Detail of the mosaic in Ravenna, in the church of San Vitale, depicting Emperor Justinian. PHOTO: PETAR MILOŠEVIĆ, CC BY-SA, HTTPS://COMMONS.WIKIMEDIA.ORG/W/INDEX .PHP?CURID=40035957. LAST ACCESSED MARCH 14, 2022

FIGURE 3 Mosaic in the church of San Vitale, in Ravenna, depicting Emperor Justinian (middle) and bishop Maximian (right), surrounded by officers and guards.
PHOTO: ROGER CULOS: HTTPS://COMMONS.WIKIMEDIA.ORG/WIKI/FILE:SANVITALE03.JPG. LAST ACCESSED MARCH 14, 2022

CHAPTER 2

The Time of Justinian

This chapter is dedicated to the Justinianic period and is divided into three parts. The first part focuses on Justinian's legislation, the second part deals with the teaching of law during the time of Justinian and the third part is dedicated to some contemporary works written for more practical purposes in this period.

1 Justinian's Legislation

The *Code*

The word *codex* derives from the Latin word *caudex*, which means a tree trunk or a piece of wood. A *codex* consists of sheets of paper, papyrus or other material, that has been put together into one book. Thus, the original meaning of the word *codex* was any bound book, in order to distinguish it from a papyrus scroll. In a more technical, legal sense, the Latin word *Codex* and the English Code gradually acquired the meaning of a codification, that is, a legal book in which the law has been codified. The *Codex Justinianus* (hereafter the *Code*) consists of so-called constitutions, namely the imperial laws up to and including part of the reign of Justinian. In compiling Justinian's *Code*, the *Theodosian Code* was used as a source, as were several other private collections, such as the *Codices Gregorianus* and *Hermogenianus*. The first edition of Justinian's *Code* was issued in 529, but it was updated some years later. It was written in Latin. The following fragment is from the *Constitutio Haec*, which was formally a letter addressed to the senate by which Justinian announced the appointment of a committee whose task was to draft up the first *Code*:

TEXT 1.1 ***Constitutio Haec* § 3: commissioning the first *Code* (AD 528)**

[...] *studentes certas et indubitatas et in unum codicem collectas esse de cetero constitutiones, ut ex eo tantummodo nostro felici nomine nuncupando codice recitatio constitutionum in omnibus ad citiores litium decisiones fiat iudiciis.*[1]	[...] what we wish to effect is, that from now on all constitutions can be found, in a distinct and reliable form, in one single book [a 'codex'], so that constitutions shall be cited **only from this codex**, which is to be called by our own blessed name [i.e. *Codex Justinianus*]. This will result in faster decisions in each lawsuit.

1 The Latin text is cited from the edition of P. Krüger (= C.).

 | DOI:10.1163/9789004520684_003

The committee had to collect all imperial constitutions and compile them into one code which would be named after the emperor. Justinian made his *Code* the exclusive source of law by stating that 'constitutions shall be cited only from this *codex*'. This implied that all other constitutions which were not included in his *Code* would no longer be valid. It also implied that other collections of constitutions were considered superfluous, and were therefore not to be consulted. Further instructions for the committee were included in the *Constitutio Haec*. The idea was to arrange all of the constitutions into books according to their contents and then to subdivide the books into titles, placing the laws within each title in their chronological order. If, for example, one book was about the law of obligations, it included titles about purchase and sale, titles about lease, titles about partnership, and so on; furthermore, the title about purchase would have included all imperial laws concerning purchase in their chronological order. If Justinian, for instance, had issued a law about purchase, his constitution would be placed at the end of the title because it was the most recently promulgated one. In fact, it was not so much the full texts of the laws that were inserted in the *Code*, but parts of them. In other words, the imperial laws were to be cut into bits and pieces, and were to be inserted into the appropriate thematic and chronological order of the *Code* itself. The committee was allowed to introduce changes to the laws if necessary. They could omit material deemed irrelevant, like prefaces to laws, or they could excise invalid laws or contradictions. They could also, for example, include the so-called *rescripta*. A rescript is a reply to a request or a question brought before an emperor. The name of the emperor is given in the beginning of every fragment in the *Code*, as is the name of the person who has posed the question or filed the request. At the end of every constitution in the *Code* we also find the date of its promulgation.

The *Constitutio Haec* provides information about the members of the committee. It consisted of ten men, including Theophilos, a law professor in Constantinople, and Tribonian. Tribonian was later appointed as *quaestor of the sacred palace*, an office that can be compared to the minister of justice of nowadays. He supervised the drafting of all parts of Justinian's legislation. A year later, the emperor announced that his *Code* was completed and that it would henceforth be enforced. The first edition of the *Code* of 529 was revised some years later by a smaller committee, which resulted in an updating of the *Code* in 534 (the *Codex Justinianus repetitae praelectionis*): this is the version that is preserved today. Justinian's *Code* is divided into twelve books in tribute to the earlier Roman *Law of the Twelve Tables*. After the promulgation of the first *Code*, Justinian also published the so-called 'Fifty Decisions' (*Quinquaginta Decisiones*) which were discussions of disputed points resolved by Justinian. This work has not been preserved as such, but many of the individual decisions contained within it have presumably survived as rescripts included in the second *Code*. It has been suggested that this work was related to the celebration of the fiftieth birthday of the emperor.

The *Digest* or *Pandects*

In his second legislative project, Justinian focused on the 'body of writings of authoritative Roman jurists'. This was something that Theodosius II had originally also planned to do. After the completion of his *Code*, Theodosius had planned to make a collection of writings of the Roman jurists, but he did not continue with this plan. Justinian, however, did succeed in this plan, and the result was the *Digest* or *Pandects*. The *Digest* was an anthology of extracts from the writings of the great Roman jurists who had lived mostly in the second and third century AD. The word 'digest' derives from the Latin verb *digerere*, which indicates 'to distribute and arrange in an order'. The Greek name of the *Digest* was the *Pandects* (Πανδέκτης), a term which signifies the comprehensiveness of this work, as it derives from the words 'πᾶν', which means 'everything' and the verb 'δέχομαι', which means 'to receive'; hence, the *Pandects* literally means 'containing everything'.

Making the *Digest* was an enormous effort. Thanks to the introductory constitutions we know what Justinian's intentions were and how he proceeded. The emperor described the works that had to be read as 'an ocean of learning' and mentioned that the compilers were required to read more than three million lines of text. The committee which undertook this project was supervised by Tribonian, and consisted of two imperial officers, four law professors (Theophilos and Cratinos from Constantinople and Dorotheos and Anatolios from Beirut) and eleven professional lawyers. The *Digest* was produced in three years. It consists of fifty books, divided into titles, and most of it was written in Latin. Fragments of texts were taken from writings of thirty-nine authors, but the fragments that made their way into the *Digest* also sometimes cite the names and works of other authors as well. Writings of Paul and Ulpian occupy a substantial part of the *Digest*. It has always been a mystery how the committee managed to complete such a massive work in such a short period of time. In 1818, the German scholar F. Bluhme developed a theory about the compilation of the *Digest* known as the 'Massentheorie'. He showed that the *Digest* fragments can be divided into three main groups, or three 'masses', and concluded that the compilers had been divided into three committees, each committee being responsible for one group or one mass of fragments. According to Bluhme, in the final stage, the full committee brought together the three groups and unified the whole text.

In the following fragment the emperor acknowledges the improvements that were made to the texts by the *Digest* compilers. The fragment is taken from the introductory law to the *Digest*, the so-called *Constitutio Tanta/Dedōken* (*Δέδωκεν*) which was a bilingual constitution, promulgated in both Latin and Greek.[2]

2 We will provide only the Latin text for the passages that we cite from this constitution; the Latin text is cited from the standard edition of Th. Mommsen (= D.).

TEXT 1.2 *Constitutio Tanta*, pr.: improvements

nostra quoque maiestas semper investigando et perscrutando ea quae ab his componebantur, quidquid dubium et incertum inveniebatur, hoc numine caelesti erecta emendabat et in competentem formam redigebat.	Also, our majesty, by a consistent investigation and thorough examination of those texts that were arranged by them, has amended with the support of heavenly divinity anything that was found to be dubious or uncertain and has turned this into a suitable form.

The instructions of the emperor were to select what was useful, to omit what was superfluous, to avoid contradictions and to make any necessary changes (see TEXT 1.3). The compilers were also authorised to make alterations to the texts in order to ensure that the result would reflect the law of sixth-century Byzantium. From the time of the humanists and up to the twentieth century, establishing the extent of the changes made by the *Digest* compilers has remained significant issue in the study of the *Digest*. These modifications or amendments to the texts have been known as interpolations (*interpolationes*) or *emblemata Triboniani*.

The opinions of the Roman jurists were valid only if they had been included in the *Digest*. Furthermore, the opinions that were included in the *Digest* were only valid not because they were from Ulpian or Papinian, but because they came from the emperor who spoke with the words of the jurists. This is very well illustrated in the following fragment from the *Constitutio Tanta/Dedōken* (*Δέδωκεν*).

TEXT 1.3 *Constitutio Tanta* § 10: instructions to the committee about opinions of Roman jurists in the *Digest* (AD 533)

Tanta autem nobis antiquitati habita est reverentia, ut nomina prudentium taciturnitati tradere nullo patiamur modo: sed unusquisque eorum, qui auctor legis fuit, nostris digestis inscriptus est: hoc tantummodo a nobis effecto, ut, si quid in legibus eorum vel supervacuum vel imperfectum vel minus idoneum visum est, vel adiectionem vel deminutionem necessariam accipiat et rectissimis tradatur regulis. et in multis similibus vel contraris quod rectius habere appare-	However, we have such reverence for antiquity that we absolutely do not allow the names of those learned in law to be surrendered to oblivion: no, each of the original authors of the laws is specified in our *Digest*. All we have done is the following: wherever anything in their legal writings was regarded as superfluous or incomplete or less suitable, it has been either expanded or diminished to the necessary extent, and adjusted to the most correct form. And in many places where texts were similar or incompatible, that which appeared to be more correct has been set down instead

TEXT 1.3 (*cont.*)

bat, hoc pro aliis omnibus positum est unaque omnibus auctoritate indulta, ut quidquid ibi scriptum est, hoc nostrum appareat et ex nostra voluntate compositum.	of the others, and one single authority has been accorded to all, so that everything that has been written there is shown to be ours and to have been composed by our will.

The names of the Roman jurists, as well as the original titles of their works and the numeration of the books from which passages of their writings were taken, are indeed mentioned in the *Digest*. For example, we already saw in Chapter 1, TEXT 9.1 an extract of the *Digest* from title 25,1 'about expenses made for things that belong to a dowry', in which fragments of Ulpian and Paul are used. Each fragment is preceded by the name of the Roman jurist and the specific work and number of the book from which the fragment derives. This is called the inscription. For instance, the first fragment is from Ulpian, from his work on Sabinus, book 36; the second fragment is from Paul, on his work on Sabinus, book 7, and so on. The names of the Roman jurists and their works are mentioned in the *Digest* out of respect for them. The *Digest* owes its force of law solely to Justinian's own authority, as the emperor clearly mentions in TEXT 1.3. Indeed, the *Digest* had the force of a single constitution, which means it was one law enacted in 533 and it is presumably the lengthiest law ever written. Justinian clearly announces the exclusive character of the *Digest* in the following fragment from the same *Constitutio Tanta/Dedōken* (*Δέδωκεν*):

TEXT 1.4 ***Constitutio Tanta* § 19: exclusivity of the *Digest***

Hasce itaque leges et adorate et observate omnibus antiquioribus quiescentibus: nemoque vestrum audeat vel comparare eas prioribus vel, si quid dissonans in utroque est, requirere, quia omne quod hic positum est hoc unicum et solum observari censemus.	So these are the laws that you must revere and observe whereas all the old ones are laid to rest; and none of you must dare either to compare them with earlier ones or, if there is some disharmony between them, to investigate this, because we determine that only and solely all that has been set down here is to be observed.

The emperor further proudly and in a rather threatening tone announced that no contradictions could be found in the *Digest*:

TEXT 1.5 ***Constitutio Tanta* §15: no contradictions in the *Digest***

Contrarium autem aliquid in hoc codice positum nullum sibi locum vindicabit nec invenitur, si quis suptili animo diversitatis rationes excutiet. [...]	However, there is nothing in this book that one can claim or find to be contradictory, provided that one carefully executes the methods of differentiation. [...]

According to this fragment, the emperor makes clear that if someone tries to find a contradiction in the *Digest*, such an effort would be in vain, for even if someone thinks that he has found a contradiction, he should better read the text more carefully and he will come logically to the conclusion that there is no contradiction whatsoever.

The *Digest* has been preserved in one sixth-century manuscript, the so-called *Littera Florentina* or *Codex Florentinus*, which is kept in the Laurentian library in Florence and has a complicated history of transmission. We know that the manuscript was kept in Pisa in the middle of the twelfth century, and in 1406 it made its way to Florence as war booty. However, we do not know how and when exactly the *Digest* manuscript reached Italy in the first place. According to some studies, for example, the *Codex Florentinus* was first kept in Amalfi and then it was taken by the Pisans. Regardless, there is strong evidence that the *Digest* manuscript that did eventually reach Italy was first written in Constantinople.

The *Institutes* or *Elements*

The *Institutes* or *Elements* was a manual for first year law students and it was addressed, as the emperor mentions in its title, to 'young enthusiasts of the laws' (*cupidae legum iuventuti*). The word *Institutes* derives from the verb *instituere*, which means 'to teach'. Apart from being a law manual for students, the *Institutes* also had the force of a law and enjoyed equal status with the *Digest* and the *Code*.[3] It too was written in Latin. The committee that drafted the *Institutes* consisted of Tribonian and two law professors: Theophilos from the law school of Constantinople and Dorotheos from the law school of Beirut.

TEXT 1.6 ***Constitutio Tanta* § 11: commissioning the *Institutes***

Et ideo Triboniano viro excelso, qui ad totius operis gubernationem electus est, nec non Theophilo et Dorotheo viris illustribus et facundissimis antecessoribus	We have therefore invited the eminent man Tribonian, who is chosen as the supervisor of the whole project, and also the illustrious and most competent profes-

3 The *Digest* and the *Institutes* became law on 30 December, in the year AD 533.

TEXT 1.6 *(cont.)*

accersitis mandavimus, quatenus libris, quos veteres composuerunt, qui prima legum argumenta continebant et institutiones vocabantur, separatim collectis, quidquid ex his utile [...] *invenitur, hoc et capere studeant et quattuor libris reponere* [...]	sors of law Theophilos and Dorotheos, and ordered them to make a separate collection of the books that have been composed by the old jurists, which comprised the first principles of law and were called *Institutes*, and to endeavour to select from them whatever is found useful [...] and to lay it down into four books [...]

The *Institutes* comprises four books. They are based on previous *Institutes* of Roman jurists, in particular that of Gaius, who had lived in the second century AD. Gaius' *Institutes* is the only complete work we possess from the Roman jurists. Gaius' *Institutes* was accidently discovered in a library in Verona in 1816 by the German scholar B.G. Niebuhr. While he was reading a manuscript containing some of the works of St Jerome, Niebuhr realised that the manuscript was a so-called palimpsest. The word 'palimpsest' derives from the Greek word 'παλίμψηστος'/palímpsēstos, which literally means 'scraped again', and it indicates a manuscript whose surface has been scraped off in order to prepare it for reuse. Thus, a palimpsest is a manuscript that contains two or even more layers of writing. In the palimpsest that Niebuhr was studying, the lower layer contained the lost work of Gaius.

Justinian's *Institutes*—just as the *Institutes* of Gaius—employs the Roman threefold division of law into persons, things and actions. In the following example, we will briefly compare a fragment of Justinian's *Institutes* to the corresponding part of Gaius's *Institutes*. Both fragments deal with obligations and their classification.

TEXT 1.7 Justinian's *Institutes* 3,13: obligations and beginning of 3,14: obligations contracted by conduct[4]

3.13. *De obligationibus.* *Nunc transeamus ad obligationes. obligatio est iuris vinculum, quo necessitate adstringimur alicuius solvendae rei secundum nostrae civitatis iura.*	3.13. Obligations. We turn to obligations. An obligation is a legal tie which binds us to the necessity of making some performance in accordance with the laws of our state.

4 Latin text and translation from P. Birks and G. McLeod, *Justinian's Institutes with the Latin text of Paul Krueger* (London: 2001; orig. 1987).

TEXT 1.7 *(cont.)*

1. *Omnium autem obligationum summa divisio in duo genera diducitur: namque aut civiles sunt aut praetoriae. civiles sunt, quae aut legibus constitutae aut certe iure civili comprobatae sunt. praetoriae sunt, quas praetor ex sua iurisdictione constituit, quae etiam honorariae vocantur.*	1. They divide first into two: legal and praetorian. Legal obligations are those recognized by statute or, of course, by the state law. Praetorian obligations are those which the *praetor* recognized in the exercise of his own jurisdiction. These are also called honorarian.
2. *Sequens divisio in quattuor species diducitur: aut enim ex contractu sunt aut quasi ex contractu aut ex maleficio aut quasi ex maleficio. prius est, ut de his quae ex contractu sunt dispiciamus. harum aeque quattor species sunt: aut enim re contrahuntur aut verbis aut litteris aut consensu. de quibus singulis dispiciamus.*	2. The next classification is into four: obligations arise from a contract, as though from a contract, from a wrong, or as though from a wrong. Those from contract are our first concern. They also fall into four classes: they are contracted by conduct, by words, by writing, or by agreement. We will take these in turn.
3.14. *Quibus modis re contrahitur obligatio.* *Re contrahitur obligatio veluti mutui datione.* [...]	3.14 Obligations contracted by conduct. One case where an obligation is contracted by conduct is when a loan is made, of the kind called '*mutuum*' [...]

TEXT 1.8 **Gaius's *Institutes* 3,88–90: classification of obligations**[5]

88. *Nunc transeamus ad obligationes, quarum summa divisio in duas species diducitur: omnis enim obligatio vel ex contractu nascitur vel ex delicto.*	88. We turn to obligations. They divide first into two: all obligations arise from a contract or from a delict.
89. *Et prius videamus de his, quae ex contractu nascuntur. harum autem quattuor genera sunt : aut enim re contrahitur obligatio aut verbis aut litteris aut consensu.*	89. Those from contract are our first concern. Now, they fall into four classes: they are contracted by conduct, by words, by writing, or by agreement.
90. *Re contrahitur obligatio velut mutui datione;* [...]	90. One case where an obligation is contracted by conduct is when a loan is made, of the kind called in Latin 'mutuum'. [...]

5 Translation from W.M. Gordon and O.F. Robinson, *The Institutes of Gaius with the Latin text of Seckel and Kuebler* (London: 2001; orig. 1988).

There is a similar didactic style in both fragments since both books were, in principle at least, legal textbooks for students. The fragment from Justinian's *Institutes* is more extensive than that of Gaius. It includes a definition of an obligation and it also explains the distinction between legal and praetorian obligations, something that is not explained in the fragment from Gaius' *Institutes*. For the rest, both fragments are rather similar and, in fact, the subsequent fragments in Justinian's *Institutes* 3.14 pr and 3.14.1 (Obligations contracted by conduct) are almost identical to the corresponding fragments in Gaius's *Institutes* 3.90–3.91.

The *Novels*

The word 'novel' derives from the Latin word *novella*, which means 'new'. In this case, a *novella* (*novella lex/constitutio*) or in Greek a νεαρά/*neará* (νεαρὰ διάταξις) is a 'new law', a 'new constitution'. Even after the promulgation of Justinian's *Code* it was necessary to make new laws, or as Justinian himself admits in the following fragment, legislation never ends. This fragment is taken from the *Constitutio Cordi*, which was the introductory law of the second version of Justinian's *Code* promulgated in 534.

TEXT 1.9 ***Constitutio Cordi* § 4: future *Novels***

[...] *hoc etenim nemini dubium est, quod, si quid in posterum melius inveniatur et ad constitutionem necessario sit redigendum, hoc a nobis et constituatur et in aliam congregationem referatur, quae novellarum nomine constitutionum significetur.*[6]	[...] Everybody can be assured that if in the future any improvement should be discovered, which would absolutely deserve a place in the legislation, we will certainly make a law about it. We will adopt such laws in a separate collection, which will be referred to as 'novel constitutions'.

Hence, the *Novels* were the new laws, the imperial laws that were issued after 534, after the promulgation of the second, updated *Code*; their full name was *Novellae post Codicem constitutiones*, meaning the imperial laws after the *Code*. The majority of the *Novels* were written in Greek. Prefaces of laws, the so-called *prooimia*, reflect in many cases imperial ideology. It is also typical to point out in prefaces of Byzantine laws the close relation between God and the emperor, as well the legislative role of the emperor. It is often emphasised that the emperor has been placed in that position by God and that he is a responsible ruler who takes care of legal affairs in the best way.[7] Rhetoric plays an important role in the justification of a law. We quote in the following example a characteristic fragment from the preface of *Novel* 69, which deals with issues of court competency and

6 The Latin text is cited from the edition by P. Krüger (= C.).

7 See the examples presented in Troianos, *Pèges*, pp. 60–64 = *Quellen*, pp. 28–31.

attempts to encourage that trials be held in the provinces, thereby limiting the number of cases heard in Constantinople.

TEXT 1.10 *Novel* 69, preface[8]

Μίαν εἶναι πασῶν τελεωτάτην ἀρετὴν ὑποληπτέον ἐν ἀνθρώποις τὴν τὰ δίκαια πᾶσι βραβεύουσαν, φαμὲν δὲ τὴν τοῦ πράγματος ἐπώνυμον δικαιοσύνην. καὶ γὰρ ἑκάστῃ τῶν ἄλλων ἀρετῶν εἰ μὴ παρακολουθοίη τὰ ταύτης ἀγαθά, γένοιτο ἂν οὐδὲν τῶν προσηκόντων. τοιγαροῦν οὐδὲ ἀνδρείαν τὴν μὴ μετὰ δικαιοσύνης ἐπαινέσομεν, καίτοιγε ἡ πάτριος φωνὴ τὴν ἐν ὅπλοις ἰσχὺν ἀρετὴν ὀνομάζει μόνην· εἰ δέ τις αὐτῆς τὸ δίκαιον ἀφέλοιτο, πλημμελημάτων ἀφορμὴ μόνων, οὐ μήν τινος γένοιτο ἂν τῶν βελτιόνων. ταύτην ἐν ταῖς ἡμετέραις ἐπαρχίαις ὁρῶντες παρεωραμένην, νόμῳ θεραπεύοντι θεὸν ἀναρρῶσαι καὶ πρὸς ἰσχὺν πρέπουσαν ἀγαγεῖν ᾠήθημεν χρῆναι.	Of all human virtues, there is one that must be held the most perfect, because it awards to all their just deserts; we mean justice, named from that fact: unaccompanied by its benefits, none of the other virtues would have its proper character. For that reason, even courage, if not associated with justice, is not something that we shall praise, despite the fact that the ancestral language uses 'virtue', on its own, to mean prowess in arms;[9] should one remove the element of justice from that, it would become merely a means for crime, not for anything better. As we observe that justice has been disregarded in our provinces, we have thought it necessary to reinforce it by means of a law in the service of God, and to bring it up to its proper strength.

In this fragment, Justinian uses a rather rhetorical tone to emphasise the importance of justice, assuring readers that he will take care of legal affairs in the provinces and will hereby promulgate a law that settles these matters in accordance with God's will.

Despite his original intention (see TEXT 1.9), Justinian did not succeed in publishing a collection of the *Novels*. There was no official collection of the *Novels*, but most of them were later on assembled—together with a few laws of Justinian's immediate successors—in a private collection, the so-called 'Collection of the 168 Novellae', which we still possess today. There also was a Latin summary of a number of the *Novels*, composed by Julian, a law professor in Constantinople; this summary is known as the *Epitome Juliani*.[10] Another

8 The Greek text is from the standard edition by R. Schöll and G. Kroll (= Nov.) and the English translation is from D.J.D. Miller and P. Sarris, *The "Novels" of Justinian: A Complete Annotated English Translation*, 2 vols. (Cambridge: 2018).

9 The editors of the English translation include the following note here: '"Virtue" (Greek ἀρετή) referring to the Latin *virtus*, in a military context "courage". Note the description of Latin as the "ancestral tongue"'.

10 For examples from the *Epitome Juliani*, see below, pp. 60–63.

Latin translation of the *Novels* was known as the *Authenticum*, a word that can be misleading. As is well known, Roman law (the *Digest*, in particular) was 'rediscovered' roughly at the end of the eleventh century in Italy, in Bologna. During the period of 'the rediscovery or revival of Roman law' in the Middle Ages, people started to study and use Roman law as it was codified in Justinian's legislation. The fact that most of Justinian's legislation had been promulgated in Latin made it possible for the people in the medieval West to read it and use it, since Latin was the common language in the western parts of Europe during the Middle Ages. If the medieval jurists wanted to consult the *Novels*, they relied on the Latin version of that text by Julian (the *Epitome Juliani*); but they also discovered another Latin text of the *Novels*, which was a word-for-word translation of the Greek text into Latin. Presumably because of the peculiar Latin of this text, the medieval jurists thought that it must have been an official, original text and therefore named it the *Authenticum*, which means the authentic, original text—in this case, that of the *Novels*. We know, however, that the *Novels* were in their majority originally promulgated in Greek. Finally, for the whole of the legislative collection of Justinian, the term *Corpus Iuris Civilis* is used, which literally means 'the body of civil law'.

Table of Justinian's Constitutions about the Commission and Promulgation of His Legislation

Constitutio Haec (13 February, 528)	Commissioning the first *Code*
Constitutio Summa (7 April, 529)	Publishing the first *Code*
Constitutio Cordi (16 November, 534)	Publishing the second *Code*
Constitutio Deo auctore (16 December, 530)	Commissioning the *Digest*
Constitutio Omnem (16 December, 533)	Establishing the new curriculum of legal studies[11]
Constitutio Tanta/Dedoken **(Δέδωκεν)** (16 December, 533)	Bilingual constitution in Latin and Greek, by which the *Digest* was published and by which the *Digest* and the *Institutes* were entered into force.
Constitutio Imperatoriam (21 November, 533)	Offering the *Institutes* to law students

11 We will refer to this *constitutio* later in this chapter, at pp. 34–40.

Select Bibliography

There is a vast amount of literature on the different parts of Justinian's legislation, and especially on the *Digest*. See, for example, the relevant bibliography cited in Troianos, *Pèges* = *Quellen*. The following list of books represents only a small selection.

Primary Sources

On the editions and translations of the four parts of Justinian's legislation, see also the abbreviations provided at the beginning of the present volume.

Birks, P. and G. McLeod. *Justinian's Institutes with the Latin text of Paul Krueger*. London: 2001.

Gordon, W.M. and O.F. Robinson. *The Institutes of Gaius with the Latin text of Seckel and Kuebler*. London: 2001.

Kaiser, W. *Die Epitome Iuliani: Beiträge zum römischen Recht im frühen Mittelalter und zum byzantinischen Rechtsunterricht*. Frankfurt am Main: 2004.

Miller, D.J.D. and P. Sarris. *The Novels of Justinian: A Complete Annotated English Translation*, 2 vols. Cambridge: 2018.

Secondary Literature

Baldi, D. 'Il Codex Florentinus del Digesto e il 'Fondo Pandette' della Biblioteca Laurenziana (con un' Appendice di documenti inediti), Segno e Testo', *International Journal of Manuscripts and Text Transmission*, 8 (2010), pp. 99–186.

Bluhme, F. 'Die Ordnung der Fragmente in den Pandectentiteln', *Zeitschrift für geschichtliche Rechtswissenschaft*, 4 (1820), pp. 257–472 (repr. *Labeo* 6, 1960, pp. 50–96, pp. 235–277, pp. 368–404).

Corcoran, S. 'The Codex of Justinian: the Life of a Text through 1,500 Years', in B. Frier, ed. *The Codex of Justinian: A New Annotated Translation, with Parallel Latin and Greek Text*, vol. 1. Cambridge: 2016, pp. xcvii–clxxxi.

Hallebeek, J. 'Structure of Medieval Roman Law: Institutions, Sources, and Methods', in H. Pihlajamäki, M.D. Dubber, and M. Godfrey, eds. *The Oxford Handbook of European Legal History*. Oxford: 2018, pp. 286–308.

Honoré, T. *Tribonian*. London: 1978.

Humfress, C. 'Law and Legal Practice in the Age of Justinian', in M. Maas, ed. *The Cambridge Companion to the Age of Justinian*. Cambridge: 2005, pp. 161–184.

Kaiser, W. 'Justinian and the Corpus Iuris Civilis', in D. Johnston, ed. *The Cambridge Companion to Roman Law*. Cambridge: 2015, pp. 119–148.

Kaiser, W. 'Schreiber und Korrektoren des Codex Florentinus', SZ, 118 (2001), pp. 133–219.

Kaiser, W. 'Zur Herkunft des Codex Florentinus. Zugleich zur Florentiner Digestenhandschrift als Erkenntnisquelle für die Redaktion der Digesten', in A. Schmidt-Recla, E. Schumann, and F. Theisen, eds. *Sachsen im Spiegel des Rechts*. Cologne/Weimar: 2001, pp. 37–55.

Lokin, J.H.A. 'The End of an Epoch: Epilegomena to a Century of Interpolation Criticism', in R. Feenstra et al., eds. *Collatio iuris romani. Études dédiées à Hans Ankum à l'occasion de son 65e anniversaire*. Amsterdam: 1995, pp. 261–273 (repr. in Th. van Bochove, ed. *J.H.A. Lokin, Analecta Groningana ad ius graeco-romanum pertinentia*. Groningen: 2010, pp. 17–31).

Mantovani, D. *Digesto e masse bluhmiane*. Milan: 1987.
Osler, D.J. 'The Compilation of Justinian's Digest', SZ, 102 (1985), pp. 129–184.
Radding, C.M. and A. Ciaralli. *The Corpus Iuris Civilis in the Middle Ages: Manuscripts and Transmission from the Sixth Century to the Juristic Revival*. Leiden/Boston: 2007.
Stolte, B.H. 'The Partes of the Digest in the Codex Florentinus', SG, 1 (1984), pp. 69–91.
Wallinga, T. *Tanta/Δέδωκεν: Two Introductory Constitutions to Justinian's Digest*. Groningen: 1989.
Wilson, N.G. 'A Greek Palaeographer Looks at the Florentine Pandects', SG, 5 (1992), pp. 1–6.

2 Teaching Law in the Time of Justinian

Justinian's New Curriculum of Legal Studies[12]

With the promulgation of the *Digest* and the *Institutes* under his belt, Justinian proceeded to a thorough revision of the curriculum of legal studies. The *Constitutio Omnem*, promulgated in 533, was one of the introductory laws to the *Digest* and was addressed to the law professors at that time, the so-called *antecessores* (ἀντικήνσορες). The Latin word *antecessor* was a military term. It literally meant 'the man leading the way', and was used to describe the officer who walked in front of the army in order to investigate whether the ground was safe to proceed. The law professor had a similar task too because he 'walked in front' and opened up the path of knowledge to his students. In the following example, we quote the heading of the *Constitutio Omnem* and its first line:

TEXT 2.1 *Constitutio Omnem*, heading and *praefatio*[13]

IMPERATOR CAESAR FLAVIUS IUSTINIANUS ALAMANNICUS GOTTHICUS FRANCICUS GERMANICUS ANTICUS ALANICUS VANDALICUS AFRICANUS PIUS FELIX INCLUTUS VICTOR AC TRIUMPHATOR SEMPER AUGUSTUS THEOPHILO, DOROTHEO, THEODORO, ISIDORO ET ANATOLIO ET THALELAEO ET CRATINO VIRIS ILLUSTRIBUS ANTE-	THE EMPEROR CAESAR FLAVIUS JUSTINIANUS, ALAMANNICUS GOTTHICUS FRANCICUS GERMANICUS ANTICUS ALANICUS VANDALICUS AFRICANUS, PIOUS, FORTUNATE, RENOWNED CONQUEROR AND TRIUMPHER FOR EVER AUGUSTUS, GREETS THEOPHILOS, DOROTHEOS, THEODOROS, ISIDOROS AND ANATOLIOS AND THALELAIOS AND

12 Please note that this section and the following are partly based on a contribution by D. Penna for a chapter in a book currently under preparation in the series Brill's Companions to the Byzantine World (ed. W. Brandes). The book's title is *Byzantine law from the foundation of Constantinople (330) until the end of the Macedonian dynasty (1056)*, and the volume editors are E. Papagianni and D. Penna.

13 All Latin fragments that follow from the *Constitutio Omnem* are cited from the edition by Mommsen (= D.).

TEXT 2.1 (*cont.*)

CESSORIBUS ET SALAMINIO VIRO DISERTISSIMO ANTECESSORI SALUTEM *Omnem rei publicae nostrae sanctionem iam esse purgatam et compositam tam in quattuor libris institutionum seu elementorum quam in quinquaginta digestorum seu pandectarum nec non in duodecim imperialium constitutionum quis amplius quam vos cognoscit?*	CRATINOS, ILLUSTRIOUS PROFESSORS OF LAW, AND SALAMINIOS, MOST ELOQUENT PROFESSOR OF LAW The whole legislation has now been purified and arranged into four books of the *Institutes* or *Elements*, into the fifty books of the *Digest* or *Pandects* and into the twelve books of the imperial constitutions: who is better aware of this than you?

Eight *antecessores* are mentioned in this passage: Theophilos, Dorotheos, Theodoros, Isidoros, Anatolios, Thalelaios, Cratinos and Salaminios. In the time of Justinian, there were two law schools, one in Constantinople and one in Beirut, and eight law professors, with four teaching in each school. Both schools were supervised by the state. In the *Constitutio Omnem*, the emperor gives a detailed account of the new curriculum of legal studies based on his brand new legislation. To study law in the days of Justinian took five years. Roughly speaking, the teaching material was divided as follows: in the first year, students were taught the *Institutes* and a small part of the *Digest*; in the following three years, they received instruction in the additional parts of the *Digest*; and in the final year, they learned the *Code*. It was, moreover, common for the mainly Greek-speaking pupils to attend courses in rhetoric in order to familiarise themselves with Latin. In the following example, we will take a closer look at the description of the material studied each year and the information that Justinian provides about the curriculum.

***First year:** students are to be taught the *Institutes* (see TEXT 2.2) and a small part of the *Digest* (see TEXT 2.3)

TEXT 2.2 ***Constitutio Omnem praefatio* and § 2: in the first year the *Institutes***

[…] *itaque dubio procul quidem est necesse esse institutiones in omnibus studiis primum sibi vindicare locum, utpote prima vestigia cuiusque scientiae mediocriter tradentes.* […]	[…] for that reason there is no doubt that the *Institutes* should necessarily claim the first place in all studies, in view of the fact that they impart the first steps of every science in a moderate form […]

TEXT 2.2 (*cont.*)

et primo quidem anno nostras hauriant ***institutiones*** *ex omni paene veterum institutionum corpore elimatas et ab omnibus turbidis fontibus in unum liquidum stagnum conrivatas tam per Tribonianum virum magnificum magistrum et ex quaestore sacri palatii nostri et ex consule quam duos e vobis, id est Theophilum et Dorotheum facundissimos antecessores.*	Accordingly, in the first year they must take in our *Institutes*, derived as these are from almost the whole body of the old institutional works and conducted into one clear reservoir out of all their muddy sources through the agency of Tribonian, glorious man, magister and *ex-quaestor* of our sacred palace and ex-consul, as well as two of you, that is the most eloquent *antecessores*, Theophilos and Dorotheos.

TEXT 2.3 ***Constitutio Omnem*** **§ 2: the first part of the** ***Digest***

[...] *in reliquam vero anni partem secundum optimam consequentiam* ***primam legum partem*** *eis tradi sancimus, quae Graeco vocabulo πρῶτα nuncupatur, qua nihil est anterius, quia quod primum est aliud ante se habere non potest.*	[...] For the rest of the year we order, in accordance with a very good principle of arrangement, that there should be given to them the first part of the law, which is called by the Greek name πρῶτα (Prota), since there is nothing before it, because, in fact, whatever is first cannot have anything else preceding it.

In the first year, students were taught the *Institutes* and the 'first part', the *prima pars* of the *Digest* or the so-called *prota* (πρῶτα), which consists of the first four *Digest* books. Although the term *partes* had been used in the law schools of the empire in earlier periods, the term has come to be associated with the *antecessorian* way of referring to parts of the *Digest*. Further information about the division of the *Digest* books into different *partes* is found in the bilingual *Constitutio Tanta/Dedōken*.[14] According to this *constitutio*, there were seven *partes* in total. In the *Constitutio Omnem*, the emperor mentioned that first-year students will henceforth be called 'new Justinians' (*Iustiniani novi*).

14 *Constitutio Tanta/Dedōken*, § 2–8.

TEXT 2.4 *Constitutio Omnem* § 2: nickname of first-year students

[...] *cuius auditores non volumus vetere tam frivolo quam ridiculo cognomine dupondios appellari, sed Iustinianos novos nuncupari, et hoc in omne futurum aevum optinere censemus* [...]	[...] and we do not want those who participate in it [= in the first year course] to be called by the silly and ridiculous old name of two-pounders; they are to be styled new Justinians, which appellation, so we decree, is to be used for all time to come [...]

***Second year:** students were taught either the second *pars* of the *Digest*, namely the law of procedure (*de iudiciis*), or the third *pars* which was about the law of things (*de rebus*) and, in addition, four *Digest* books which dealt with specific subjects (see TEXT 2.5). The emperor added that second-year students were allowed to keep their existing nickname, which was *edictales*:

TEXT 2.5 *Constitutio Omnem* § 3: in the second year another part of the *Digest* + four *Digest* books which deal with specific subjects

In secundo autem anno, per quem ex edicto eis nomen antea positum et a nobis probatur, vel de iudiciis libros septem vel de rebus octo accipere eos sancimus, secundum quod temporis vicissitudo indulserit [...] [...] *adiungi in secundi anni audientiam volumus quattuor libros singulares, quos ex omni compositione quattuordecim librorum excerpsimus: ex collectione quidem tripertiti voluminis, quod pro dotibus composuimus, uno libro excerpto: ex duobus autem de tutelis et curationibus uno: et ex gemino volumine de testamentis uno: et ex septem libris de legatis et fideicommissis et quae circa ea sunt simili modo uno tantum libro.*	In the second year, for which a name derived from 'edictum' has already been given to them before, a name of which we also approve [second year students were and will continue to be called 'edictales'], we ordain that they should take either the seven books on legal proceedings [Dig. 5–11] or the eight on things [Dig. 12–19], according to what the flow of time allows [...]. Further, we desire that the second year's course should be supplemented with four works in one book each, which we have selected out of the whole composition of fourteen books: one is taken from the collection in three books compiled by us on the subject of dowries [Dig. 23], one from the two books on tutelage and cares [Dig. 26], one from the work in two books on last wills [Dig. 28], and again, in the same way, one only from the seven books on legacies, fideicommissa [testamentary trusts] and related subjects [Dig. 30] (...)

***Third year:** students were taught another part of the *Digest*, either the law of procedure or the law of things, depending on which of the two they had been taught in the second year, and three more *Digest* books on specific subjects:

TEXT 2.6 *Constitutio Omnem* § 4: in the third year another part of the *Digest* + three more *Digest* books on specific subjects

Tertii insuper anni doctrina talem ordinem sortiatur, ut, sive libros de iudiciis sive de rebus secundum vices legere eis sors tulerit, concurrat eis tripertita legum singularium dispositio [...]	Furthermore, the teaching of the third year is to conform to the following course. In addition to the books on either legal proceedings or on things, depending on which of these happens to be scheduled, the students must also take an arrangement of three additional books of law, each dealing with a single subject [Dig. 20, 21, 22].

The emperor added that the *Digest* compilers deliberately included a significant amount of Papinian's writings in one of these books so that the third-year students could keep their existing nickname of the Papinianists (see TEXT 2.7). Part of the rationale for this, the emperor explained, was so students could continue to celebrate a feast dedicated to the famous jurist Papinian:

TEXT 2.7 *Constitutio Omnem* § 4: nickname third-year students Papinianists

[...] *ne autem tertii anni auditores, quos Papinianistas vocant, nomen et festivitatem eius amittere videantur, ipse iterum in tertium annum per bellissimam machinationem introductus est: librum enim hypothecariae ex primordiis plenum eiusdem maximi Papiniani fecimus lectione, ut et nomen ex eo habeant et Papinianistae vocentur et eius reminiscentes et laetificentur et festum diem, quem, cum primum leges eius accipiebant, celebrare solebant, peragant* [...]	[...] lest the third-year students, the Papinianists as they are called, seem to lose the nickname and festal day attached to their patron, he (Papinianus) has again been introduced for the third year by a most exquisite trick, since the book about hypothecs [Dig. 22] is one which we had filled throughout with passages from the same excellent Papinianus, so that they (the students) can have their name from him and be called Papinianists and they can rejoice by commemorating him and continue to observe the festal day which they used to celebrate when they first became acquainted with his legal works [...]

*__Fourth year:__ students no longer took course centred on lectures, but instead had to study on their own ten *Digest* books devoted to specific subjects. They could keep their existing nickname of *lytai* (λύται), a nickname that was presumably given to them because at this stage they could solve difficult legal questions: *lytai* derives from the Greek word lyō (λύω), meaning 'to solve'.

TEXT 2.8 ***Constitutio Omnem* § 5: in the fourth year ten *Digest* books on specific subjects**

Sed quia solitum est anni quarti studiosos Graeco et consueto quodam vocabulo λύτας appellari, habeant quidem, si maluerint, hoc cognomen: pro responsis autem prudentissimi Pauli [...] *decem libros singulares, qui ex quattuordecim quos antea enumeravimus supersunt, studeant lectitare* [...]	But because it is customary that the students of the fourth year will be called by the traditional Greek name, 'λύτας', let them keep this nickname if they like; however, instead of the replies of the most learned Paul [...] they must devote themselves to studying the ten separate books which are left from the fourteen books that we have mentioned above [...]

*__Fifth year:__ students were taught the material of the *Code* and the constitutions, and during this final year of study, they were called *prolytai.*

TEXT 2.9 ***Constitutio Omnem* § 5: in the fifth year the *Codex Justinianus***

[...] *quibus si bene sese imbuerint et in quinti anni, quo prolytae nuncupantur, metas constitutionum codicem tam legere quam suptiliter intellegere studeant, nihil eis legitimae scientiae deerit* [...]	[...] if they have assiduously familiarised themselves with these and dedicated themselves to reading them and thorough comprehension of the *Code* of constitutions in their fifth year, in which they are to be called 'prolytae', nothing will be missing in their legal knowledge [...]

According to this legal curriculum, a significant part of the *Digest* was left out completely, namely books 37–50. According to the emperor, the thirty-six *Digest* books that were part of the curriculum would provide sufficient teaching material. The books taught by the *antecessores* were called 'βιβλία πραττόμενα', meaning literally 'books that are done'; these were books 1–23, 26, 28 and 30 of the *Digest*. All the other books, the ones that students had to study on their own in their fourth year and the untreated ones (books 37–50), were called 'βιβλία ἐξτραόρδινα', extraordinary, i.e. falling outside of the ordinary school curriculum. The emperor trusted students to study these books later on, whereby they would be able to display their knowledge of them in court (see TEXT 2.10):

TEXT 2.10 ***Constitutio Omnem* § 5: the remaining 14 *Digest* books not till after law school**

[...] *duabus aliis partibus, id est sexta et septima nostrorum digestorum, quae in quattuordecim libros compositae sunt, eis depositis, ut possint postea eos et legere et in iudiciis ostendere.*	[...] two other parts of our *Digest*, the sixth and seventh, which are arranged in fourteen books [Dig. 37–50], must be laid to one side, so that students can read them at a later time and display their knowledge of them in court.

Finally, the emperor made it clear that the teaching of law was limited to the two schools of Constantinople and Beirut. He announced that anyone who dared to teach unauthorised courses of law outside the aforementioned two cities had to pay a severe fine and would be banished from the city in which he had taught.

The Teaching Method of the *Antecessores*

In this section, we will first give a general overview of the *antecessorian* teaching method, and in the following sections, we will give specific examples of this method demonstrated through the teaching material itself: namely, the *Institutes*, the *Digest*, the *Code* and the *Novels*. Language was the main problem that the *antecessores* had to tackle. The teaching material—that is, Justinian's legislation—was mostly promulgated in Latin. The majority of law students, however, spoke Greek, and needed additional help with the Latin. As H.J. Scheltema has shown, the *antecessores* developed a two-phase teaching method to help their students.[15] In the first phase, they provided a translation of the original Latin text that they had to teach. This translation was called an *index* (ἴνδιξ), from the Latin verb *indicare*, which means 'to show'. The *index* served as a helpful tool for students, and 'introduced' them to the teaching material. As with all translations, the *index* varied depending on the personal preferences of the given *antecessor*. Some professors gave a translation that was as close as possible to the text, others gave a looser translation, others still simply summarised the original text, and yet others even considered it necessary to add extra details to their translations, such as providing a glossary of difficult words in Latin.

Sometimes, the *antecessores* incorporated into the *index* a 'protheory' (προθεωρία), a piece of theory given in advance that would help the student to better comprehend the material. These *protheories* can be easily recognised because of their context and their

15 Scheltema has examined in detail the *antecessorian* method of teaching, on which see his monograph, H.J. Scheltema, *L'enseignement de droit des antécesseurs* (Leiden: 1970) = *Opera Minora*, A3, pp. 58–110.

standard formulas; for example, they begin with the words 'keep the following in mind in advance' (ἔχε ταῦτα ὡς ἐν προθεωρίᾳ or προθεώρησον) and end with the words 'now that we have considered this beforehand, look at the present text' (ἐπειδή σοι ταῦτα προτεθεώρηται, ὅρα λοιπὸν τὸ προκείμενον or ἐλθὲ ἐπὶ τὸ προκείμενον), or similar such expressions. The *index* was made in order to help the students understand the original text, not as a substitute for it.

In the second stage, the *antecessores* would return to the original Latin text, the so-called *rheton* (ῥητόν), and would provide comments, mostly of a legal nature but also in some cases of a linguistic nature. These Greek comments on various legal aspects were called *paragraphai* (παραγραφαί), meaning 'side writings', because students probably wrote them down in the margins of their copies of the Latin *rheton*. The *paragraphai* referred to the Latin original text even if they were written separately or had been detached from the *rheton*. If the comments had a more general scope, they were called *hypomnèmata* (ὑπομνήματα).

There were additional elements found in the writings of the *antecessores* that contribute to what we describe as the *antecessorian* style of teaching. One example is the *thematismos* (θεματισμός), which was an imaginary case used as an example to explain a legal rule. The student was asked to 'imagine' or 'suppose' (θεμάτισον) certain circumstances in order to understand the legal rule. A *thematismos* was also used to better understand the content of a constitution. In many cases, constitutions resulted from replies to particular requests brought by litigants, who appealed either to a professional jurist asking for advice, or to the emperor himself, presenting their case and asking for his decision. As the original request has, in most cases, not been preserved, a *thematismos* was used to reconstruct the case that had led to the constitution.

Another typical element of the *antecessorian* teaching method was the so-called *erotapokriseis* (ἐρωταποκρίσεις), the question-and-answer type of writing. A student asked a question, which was not so much of an informative character but rather an objection in the form of a question, and the law professor gave the solution, the *lysis* (λύσις). A typical form of an *erotapokrisis* was, for example, when a student was puzzled by the material under discussion because he believed to have come across an inconsistency. The critical student therefore posed his question and the teacher replied: he gave the 'solution' (λύσις), sorting out the material and showing the student how he was mistaken. Throughout the *antecessorian* texts we find several expressions indicating that the text derived from the oral teaching in the classroom, such as the use of expressions like 'I have told you' (εἶπον δέ σοι), 'you have learned' (μεμάθηκας) or similar.

Regarding the language used, the *antecessores* taught in Greek, but many technical terms remained in Latin for reasons of legal clarity and certainty. Sometimes, these terms were written in Greek characters: examples include μόρα for the Latin *mora*, meaning delay; ἐξστιπουλάτου for *ex stipulatu*, meaning from a stipulation;[16] στρίκτης for *stricta*,

16 The stipulation (*stipulatio*) was the most important verbal contract in classical Roman law. It consisted

meaning strict;[17] οὐτιλία for *utilis*, meaning emergency (action), etc. Some legal terms were also written as a combination of Latin and Greek. This was done by adding a Greek ending to the Latin root of a word, making the untranslated Latin word fit within a Greek grammatical sentence, such as the following: COMPENSATEUEIN (*compensa* ⟨*re*⟩ + teuein = τεύειν), which means 'to compensate'; PACTEUEIN (pact ⟨um⟩ + teuein = τεύειν), which means 'to make an agreement'; USUCAPITEUEIN (usucapi ⟨o⟩ + teuein = τεύειν), which means 'being in a status of acquisitive prescription'. Sometimes the continued use of Latin was not limited to legal terms, but was also used for the names of Roman jurists or for Latin names more generally.

Teaching the *Institutes:* Examples from Theophilos

The *Institutes* were the first part of Justinian's legislation that was taught at the law schools in Constantinople and Beirut. There is one important work that has fortunately survived and illustrates how the *Institutes* was taught by the *antecessores*: this is the *Paraphrasis Institutionum* of Theophilos. As its title, probably not authentic, implies, it is a paraphrase: a rather free Greek version of Justinian's Latin *Institutes*. Theophilos' text has all sorts of additions, as we will see below. Theophilos taught at the law school of Constantinople, and was one of the *antecessores* who had taken part in the drafting of the *Code* (its first version), the *Digest* and the *Institutes*. This must have made him a real expert in law at that time, since he was one of the jurists behind the drafting of Justinian's legislation, and students in Constantinople would have been very lucky indeed to have him as a teacher.

As far as the authorship of the *Paraphrasis* is concerned, some have questioned whether it was compiled by Theophilos himself, or by one of his students. According to the most recent editors of the *Paraphrasis*, the text is the work of the *antecessor* Theophilos. H.J. Scheltema had suggested that the *Paraphrasis* is a combination of the *index* and the *paragraphai* redacted by a student, a copyist or by the teacher himself. In other words, the author of the *Paraphrasis* used as a base the *index* and the *paragraphai* of Theophilos' lectures, but also did some editing himself. G. Falcone, on the other hand, believes that the *Paraphrasis* does not combine two separate components, the *index* and the *paragraphai*, but was instead a text produced by teaching the *Institutes* as a single course, and thus represented 'an original antecessorial version' of Justinian's *Institutes*. Whatever the case, the *Paraphrasis Institutionum* certainly reflects the classroom teaching of the

---

of a promise in a form of a question by the creditor and an affirmative answer by the debtor. There were strict formalities that had to be exercised for this verbal contract to be legally valid. Gradually, the classical stipulation degenerated, oral formality became unnecessary and the stipulation was ultimately converted into a written contract. On the classical stipulation and its development, see R. Zimmermann, *The Law of Obligations. Roman Foundations of the Civilian Tradition* (Oxford/New York: 1996), pp. 68–94.

17 In Roman law, contracts were distinguished between those made *bona fide* (in good faith) and *stricti iuris* (of strict law). The difference between them lies in the actions that were available on the basis of each contract. See B. Nicholas, *An Introduction to Roman Law* (rev. edn. Oxford: 2008), pp. 163–164.

sixth-century *antecessores*. It is interesting to add that there are also scholia preserved on Theophilos' *Paraphrasis*.

We will cite in the following an example from the Theophilos' teaching of the *Institutes*. The text of *Institutes* 4,1 is about theft (*furtum*), and § 8 deals with a special case of theft. As a preliminary remark, we should note that theft in Roman law was broader than its modern definition. In Roman law, theft also occurred if people interfered with the property of someone else without the owner's consent. An example of this latter is if someone used a borrowed thing for a purpose other than that for which it was lent; but this only counted as theft if the following two conditions were met: (1) the individual believed that the owner would not consent to this use if he knew about it, and (2) the owner did indeed disagree. This definition had led to a juridical dispute in the time before Justinian but, as we can see from the following fragment of the *Institutes*, the emperor had solved the problem:

TEXT 2.11 Teaching the *Institutes*: Justinian's *Institutes* 4,1,8, (AD 533) and corresponding passage from Theophilos' *Paraphrasis Institutionum*, 4,1,8 (AD 534)[18]

Rheton	***Index* with additional explanations and *protheoria***		
Sed et si credat aliquis invito domino se rem commodatam sibi contrectare, domino autem volente id fiat, dicitur furtum non fieri.	Εἰ δὲ καὶ ἄκοντος τοῦ δεσπότου ταῦτα ποιεῖν ἑαυτοὺς ὑπώπτευον, μαθὼν δὲ ὁ δεσπότης οὐκ ἠγανάκτησεν ἐπὶ τῷ γεγονότι, οὐδὲ οὕτω χώρα γενήσεται τῷ τῆς κλοπῆς λόγῳ.	Moreover, if they supposed they are doing the act against the will of the owner, but the owner, on hearing, was not displeased at what had been done, there will not in these circumstances be room for the doctrine of theft.	*index* (translation)
unde illud quaesitum est,	ὥστε οὖν ἵνα ⟨ᾗ⟩ *FURTI* ἁρμόσῃ δεῖ τὰ δύο συνδραμεῖν, κἀμὲ παρὰ γνώμην κεχρῆσθαι δεσπότου εἰδότα ὡς ἀγανακτήσει ἐπὶ τῷ πραττομένῳ ὁ τοῦ πράγματος κύριος, κἀκεῖνον ὀργισθῆναι μαθόντα·	Accordingly, in order that the *actio furti*[19] may lie, two things must concur: I must use the thing against the will of the owner, knowing that the owner of the thing	addition (summary)

18 The Latin text of Justinian's *Institutes* is cited from the edition of P. Krüger (= Inst.). The Greek text and the English translation are cited from Theoph.

19 In Roman law, the *actio furti* was a penal action that was brought against the thief.

TEXT 2.11 (*cont.*)

	ἓν δὲ τούτων ἐλλεῖψαν οὐκ ἐᾷ τεχθῆναι τὴν *FURTI*.	will be displeased at what is done, and he, on knowing, must be displeased; and the absence of one of those things prevents the *actio furti* from arising.	***index***
	ἀμέλει ἐντεῦθεν τοιοῦτό τι ἐζητήθη.	Hereupon, then, arose this question.	
	ἔχε δὲ ταῦτα ὡς ἐν προθεωρίᾳ. ἐάν τις τὸν ἐμὸν ὑπονοθεύσῃ δοῦλον καὶ χείρονας αὐτοῦ τοὺς τρόπους ἀποτελέσῃ, κατέχεταί μοι ἀγωγῇ τῇ λεγομένῃ *SERUI CORRUPTI*, ἥτις εἰς τὸ διπλάσιον τῆς ἐπὶ τῇ ἐλαττώσει τοῦ οἰκέτου διατιμήσεως ἁρμόζει ἤ, ἡνίκα ἀπώλετο, ἐπὶ τῷ διπλῷ τοῦ τιμήματος.	**But take this by way of preliminary consideration.** If a man corrupts my slave and renders his character worse, he is liable to me on the so-called *actio servi corrupti*,[20] which lies for double the diminution of the value of the slave, or, if he died, for double his value.	addition: ***protheoria***
cum Titius servum Maevii sollicitaverit, ut quasdam res domino subriperet et ad eum perferret, et servus id ad Maevium pertulerit, Maevius, dum vult Titium in ipso delicto deprehendere, permisit servo quasdam res ad eum perferre,	**ἐπειδή σοι ταῦτα προτεθεώρηται, ὅρα λοιπὸν τὸ προκείμενον.**	**With this preliminary remark, go on to consider the case in hand.**	
utrum furti an servi corrupti iudicio teneatur Titius, an neutro?	Τίτιος διελέχθη τῷ ἐμῷ οἰκέτῃ τοῦτον ὑπονοθεύων καὶ φυγὴν ὑποτιθέμενος αὐτῷ, προστιθεὶς ἅμα καὶ τοῦτο ὥστε αὐτὸν ὑφελέσθαι τι τῶν ἐμῶν πραγμάτων. ὁ οἰκέτης γνώριμόν μοι τοῦτο κατέστησεν· οὐ πεισθεὶς ἐγὼ τούτῳ τῷ οἰκέτῃ, βουλόμενος δὲ τὸν Τίτιον ἐν αὐτῷ καταλαβεῖν τῷ ἁμαρτήματι, ἐπέτρεπον τῷ οἰκέτῃ ταῦτα πράττειν. ὁ δὲ λαβών τι τῶν παρ' ἐμοὶ ὄντων σκευῶν ἀπῄει πρὸς Τίτιον. εἰπόμην ἐγὼ λάθρα γνῶναι βουλόμενος εἰ ἀληθῆ	Titius held conference with a slave of mine [of Maevius], trying to seduce him and to persuade him to run away, at the same time adding this, that he should purloin some of my property. The slave discovered this to me. I, not giving credit to the slave, but wishing to catch Titius in the very act of wrong-doing, gave the slave leave to do so.	***index***

20 In Roman law, the *actio servi corrupti* was an action brought by the master of a slave against the person who corrupted the master's slave.

TEXT 2.11 *(cont.)*

	τὰ παρὰ τοῦ οἰκέτου	And he, taking one of the	elabora-
	λεχθέντα. γενόμενος ὁ οἰκέτης	vessels that were in my	tion of
	κατὰ τὸν συντεθέντα τόπον	house, went off to Titius; I	the story
	παρ' αὐτοῦ καὶ Τιτίου ἐπιδέ-	followed secretly, desiring	
	δωκε Τιτίῳ τὸ σκεῦος. εὗρον	to know whether the story	
	διὰ τῶν γενομένων τὸν οἰκέ-	told me by the slave was	
	την οὐ ψευδόμενον.	true; the slave, on reach-	
	ζήτησίς ἐστι ποία μοι κατὰ	ing the place appointed	
	Τιτίου δίδοται προφάσει τῶν	by himself and Titius, gave	
	γενομένων ἀγωγή.	Titius the vessel; and from	
	καὶ τέως οὐ δυνατὸν εἰπεῖν	what took place I found	
	ἁρμόζειν τὴν FURTI· εἰ καὶ τὰ	that the slave was not lying.	
	μάλιστα γὰρ κακῇ διαθέσει	The question is, what sort	***index***
	λαβὼν ἐψηλάφα τὸ σκεῦος ὁ	of action is open to me	
	Τίτιος, ἀλλ' οὐ παρὰ γνώμην	against Titius on the facts	
et cum nobis	δεσπότου συνέβαινε τοῦτο.	stated?	
super hac	ἀλλ' ἡ SERUI CORRUPTI;	First, then, it cannot be said	
dubitatione	ἀλλ' οὐδὲ ταύτην ἐγχωρεῖ	that the *actio furti* lies; for,	
suggestum est	παρέχεσθαι· ὁ γὰρ οἰκέτης	although Titius with wrong-	elabo-
et antiquorum	οὐ χείρων τοὺς τρόπους,	ful intent took and dealt	ration
prudentium	μᾶλλον δὲ καὶ πάλαι διαλαν-	with the vessel, yet it was	of the
super hoc	θάνων εὐνοῶν τῷ δεσπότῃ νῦν	not against the will of the	***index***
altercationes	γέγονε φανερός.	owner that he did so.	
perspeximus,	καὶ συμβαίνει κατὰ ταὐτὸν	The *actio servi corrupti*,	
quibusdam	πολλὰ τὸν Τίτιον πταίσαντα	then? No, neither is it	
neque furti	μηδεμιᾷ κατέχεσθαι ἀγωγῇ.	allowed to give this action;	
neque servi	τινὲς δὲ τῶν νομικῶν ἐδίδοσαν	for the slave's morals were	
corrupti	ἐντεῦθεν τὴν FURTI.	not vitiated: on the con-	
actionem	ἀλλ' ἐπειδὴ ζητήσεις ὑπῆρχον	trary, while his goodwill to	
praestantibus,	τῶν νομικῶν, τῶν μὲν πᾶσαν	his master had not previ-	
quibusdam	ἀρνουμένων ἀγωγήν, τῶν δὲ	ously been demonstrated,	
furti tantum-	παρεχόντων τὴν FURTI, ἐπὶ	now it has become mani-	
modo:	τὸν ἡμέτερον ταῦτα ἀνηνέ-	fest.	
nos huius-	χθη βασιλέα, καὶ γέγονε παρ'	So the result is that, while	
modi calliditati	αὐτοῦ διάταξις ἥτις ἕνεκα τῆς	Titius has been guilty of	
obviam euntes	τοσαύτης κακουργίας τιμω-	many things together, he	
per nostram	ρουμένη τὸν Τίτιον οὐ μόνον	is not liable to any action.	
decisionem	τῇ FURTI ἀλλὰ καὶ τῇ SERUI	Some of the jurists, how-	

TEXT 2.11 (*cont.*)

sanximus non solum furti actionem, sed etiam servi corrupti contra eum dari [...]	CORRUPTI ἔνοχον αὐτὸν ἐκέλευσεν εἶναι [...]	ever, on these facts gave the *actio furti*. But as the jurists continued to dispute the point, some denying all and every action, others giving the *actio furti*, the case was laid before our Emperor, who made a constitution which punishes Titius for his extraordinary wickedness, ordering that he is liable not only to the *actio furti* but also to the *actio servi corrupti*. [...]	***index***

As already mentioned, Justinian's *Institutes* were promulgated in Latin. Latin-speaking students therefore did not face a language problem with this part of Justinian's legislation, but they did need help with understanding the legal contents of the text. And there was indeed a collection of writings that could help them. It was the so-called 'Glossa Taurinensis', which was a collection of Latin *paragraphai*, namely legal comments on Justinian's *Institutes*. It has this name because it comprises a set of notes written in the margin of a manuscript in the Turin library. The style of the author of this collection displays elements of the *antecessorian* teaching method.

Teaching the *Digest:* Examples from Stephanos

As far as the *Digest* is concerned, there are fragments of commentaries from the following *antecessores*: by Theophilos from his *index*, by Stephanos from his *index* and *paragraphai*, by Isidoros from his *index* and *paragraphai* and finally fragments by Kobidas.[21] A significant part of Stephanos' commentary on the *Digest* has been preserved, and that is why we will use some examples from his teaching materials. Fragments of his *index* and *paragraphai* on the *Digest* have been preserved separately.

21 On Kobidas, see Scheltema, 'Subseciva XV. Kobidas', RIDA, 13 (1966), pp. 341–343 = *Opera Minora*, A3, pp. 148–150. An anonymous scholiast of the *Paraphrasis* of Theophilus makes a reference to the 'Kobidianoi and Thylakianoi' (Κωβιδιανοὶ καὶ Θυλακιανοί), which recalls, as Scheltema notes, the schools of the Proculians and Sabinians in Roman times. Thylakas (Θυλακᾶς) must have been the name of an *antecessor*: see Scheltema, 'Kobidas', p. 341 = *Opera Minora*, A3, p. 148.

Stephanos taught at the law school of Beirut after 533. He had not participated in the codification committees. Characteristic of his style is the elaborated analysis of the provisions he comments upon and the rich examples that he uses. His texts are lengthy. Stephanos' commentary on the *Digest* was very influential, and later Byzantine jurists consulted it as well. There are many fragments of his commentary which are preserved mostly as *Basilica* scholia.[22] Because of the 'volume' of Stephanos' works on the *Digest*, later Byzantine jurists also referred to it as the *platos* (τὸ πλάτος), that is 'the breadth' or 'extensive version'.[23] Scheltema's reconstruction of the *antecessorian* teaching method of the two stages, discussed above[24] was mainly based on Stephanos' fragments.

We will cite in the following texts two examples from Stephanos' teaching of the *Digest*.

TEXT 2.12 Teaching the *Digest*: Stephanos, first example D. 22,1,32,5 and corresponding *index* by Stephanos

D. 22,1,32,5 *Marcianus libro* [...] *Item si fideiussor solus moram fecerit,*	Στεφάνου.	Of Stephanos	⟨..⟩ = not in manuscripts
	Ἐὰν ὁ ἐγγυητὴς ⟨μόνος⟩ *μόραν* ποιήσῃ, τόκους ἀπὸ τῆς ἰδίας *μόρας* οὐκ ἀπαιτεῖται διὰ *τῆς ἐξτιπουλάτου, στρίκτης* δηλαδὴ τυγχανούσης καὶ μὴ δυναμένης τόκους ἀπὸ *μόρας* ἀπαιτεῖν.	If it is only the surety who is in default, he is not, on account of being in default, required to pay interest because of the action from a stipulation (*actio ex stipulatu*), as this is, of course, a strict action (*stricti iuris*), which cannot demand interest on account of default.	
	Καλῶς εἶπον τὸ 'μόνος'· ἀπὸ γὰρ τῆς τοῦ *ρέου μόρας* κατέχεται καὶ ὁ ἐγγυητής, ὡς εἶπόν σοι ἐν τῷ κδ'. διγ.	It was with good reason that I said 'only': for if it is the principal debtor who is in default, the surety is certainly liable, as I told you in discussing fragment 24 [D. 22,1,24§1].	'I' = Steph διγ(έστῳ) = *Digest*

22 On the *Basilica* text and scholia, see below pp. 123–129, 137–142 and 152–164.

23 The term *platos*, however, is associated with more texts of Byzantine law. See, for example, how the term *platos* is used below, pp. 54 and 133–134.

24 See The Teaching Method of the *Antecessores*.

TEXT 2.12 (*cont.*)

non tenetur,	Οὐ κατέχεται τοίνυν ὁ ἐγγυητὴς ἀπὸ *μόρας* ἰδίας,	**So *he* is not liable,** (the surety), **if *he* is in default,**	**he/he?**
sicuti si Stichum promissum occiderit:	ὥσπερ οὖν οὐδὲ εἰ τὸν οἰκέτην, ὃν ὁ πρωτότυπος ἐπηρωτήθη παρέχειν, ἀνεῖλεν ὁ ἐγγυητής,	**as when the slave, whom the principal debtor had promised by stipulation to give, was killed by the surety.**	**who killed?**
	ἐπειδὴ ἀναιρεθέντος τοῦ οἰκέτου ἐλευθεροῦται ὁ πρωτότυπος. Εὑρίσκεται ἐκ περιστάσεως ὁ ἐγγυητὴς ἐλευθερούμενος, καὶ οὐ κατέχεται κατὰ ἀκρίβειαν,	For the fact that the slave is dead frees the principal debtor from his debt. In this way the surety turns out to be freed by force majeure, so that he cannot be liable in the strict sense	
sed utilis actio in hunc dabitur.	δίδοται δὲ ἡ *οὐτιλία* κατ' αὐτοῦ.[25]	Instead, the emergency action [*utilis*] is given against him.	

Digest book 22, which Stephanos is teaching here, was taught to third-year-students, as we know from Justinian's description of the curriculum of legal studies. This *Digest* fragment is taken from a work by Marcianus, who was a third-century lawyer. The English text in the third column is the translation of the Greek, and we have highlighted with dark green colour in that text everything which is not found in the Latin of Marcianus. In other words, the passages that are highlighted with dark green colour represent the contribution of Stephanos. One can see how long the Greek version is in comparison with the Latin, and that is why later Byzantine jurists would call it the '*platos*', as mentioned above.

The Latin text deals with a situation involving three different people (not counting the slave): A, B, C. This causes trouble, because the Latin does not express the grammatical subject in every sentence: 'if C fails to do what he promised he would do, then '**he**' is not

25 BS 1678/1–9 (sch. Pa 25 ad B. 23,3,32 = D. 22,1,32).

liable, as when **'he'** killed Stichus, who had been promised.' But who is meant by 'he'? If we look at the context of this *Digest* fragment, then it makes sense to think that the jurist Marcianus meant that B is not liable if C failed to perform the obligation. B had promised, through a formal stipulation, that he would give A the slave named Stichus. C had guaranteed that he would deliver the slave to A, if B should fail to do so. Here follows a scheme of this case:

Creditor A

Principal debtor B promises to give a slave to A

Surety C guarantees that he will deliver the slave to A if B fails to do so

Then the same C kills this particular slave: there is a problem for B, who obviously can no longer provide the slave Stichus, as he had promised. Even so, B is not liable. That would make sense. But Stephanos gives a different interpretation: according to Stephanos, if C kills the slave, C himself is not liable, because as soon as the slave is killed the debt ceases to exist, therefore C is freed as well. In his view, the 'he' refers to the surety. Note that the Latin technical terms are written in Greek characters this time: μόρα (*mora*), which means 'delay', ἐξστιπουλάτου (*ex stipulatu*), which means 'from a stipulation', στρίκτης (*strictis*), which refers to *stricti iuris* contracts, ῥέου (*reou*), which means 'debtor', and οὐτιλία (*utilia*) which refers to 'the special emergency action'. It seems that the students of Stephanos were not quite convinced of their teacher's interpretation, for one of them raised a critical question, as we read in the following fragment:

TEXT 2.13 ***Paragraphè* (of the *erotapokrisis* type) by Stephanos discussing the legal implications of D. 22,1,32,5**

Ἠρωτήθη. Καίτοι ἐν τῷ *δεδόλω* τῶν **Πρώτων** διγ. ιθ'. ὁ Παππιανὸς *δεδόλω* δέδωκε κατὰ τοῦ ἐγγυητοῦ τὸν οἰκέτην ἀνελόντος, ὃν ὁ πρωτότυπος ἐπηρωτήθη.	The question was asked: but in the title *de dolo* of the *Prota*, fragment 19 [D. 4,3,19], Papinianus did grant the action for *dolus* (malice) against the surety who kills the slave promised by the principal debtor!	contradiction?
Λύσις. Ἀλλ' ἐκεῖ θεμάτισον, ὅτι κατὰ δόλον αὐτὸν ἀνεῖλεν ὁ ἐγγυητής· ἐνταῦθα δὲ μὴ κατὰ δόλον. Καὶ ἔχε ταύτην τὴν διαφοράν.[26]	Solution: true, but in that case you have to imagine that the surety killed him in malice, in contrast with the present text, where it was without malice. Please keep this difference in mind!	*thematismos*

26 BS 1678/10–13 (sch. Pa 26 ad B. 22,3,32 = D. 22,1,32).

This fragment is a *paragraphè* of the *erotapokrisis* type, namely, in the form of a question-and-answer (ἐρωταπόκρισις). The question usually raises an objection to an aspect of the taught material, and the teacher gives the 'solution' (λύσις). Stephanos clarifies to his student that in this case the surety has killed the slave without malice, and that is why he is not liable, whereas in the other part of the *Digest*, i.e. the text to which the student refers, the surety acted out of malice and thus was liable.

In this passage we encounter another important term. The critical student is asked to 'suppose' certain circumstances: θεμάτισον in Greek is an imperative form of the verb θεματίζειν, which means 'to suppose', 'to hypothesize'. The *thematismos*, as mentioned above[27], attempts to reconstruct the initial situation to which the solution of a case refers. Further, we may comment on the way Stephanos solves the student's problem. What the student says, in fact, is: in *Prota*, in such-and-such a place, we read this, whereas in *Digest* 22, we read something else; in other words, there is a contradiction here. That may be due to the fact that one fragment was taken from Marcianus and the other from Papinian, but since they are both in the *Digest*, Justinian is responsible for both. Justinian had proudly declared that there were no contradictions to be found in his *Digest*.[28] If you believed that you had found one, just as the student had done at this point, you should look again more closely and you would discover that the laws cover different situations and that therefore there is no contradiction whatsoever. There must be a difference (διαφορά). Difference, distinction, is a key term in Byzantine law: you must distinguish cases that at first sight seem identical, and then your problem is quite beautifully solved.

We quote in the following another example from Stephanos' teaching on the *Digest*, which consists of his *index* and a relevant *erotapokrisis*.

TEXT 2.14 Teaching the *Digest*: Stephanos, second example D. 22,1,45 and *index* by Stephanos

D. 22,1,45 *Pomponius libro* […] *vicesimo* *secundo ad …* *Mucium.*	Στεφάνου. Εἰ καὶ ἄχρηστός ἐστιν ἡ μεταξὺ τοῦ ἀνδρὸς καὶ τῆς γυναικὸς ἐν συνεστῶτι τῷ γάμῳ γενομένη δωρεά,	Of Stephanos. Although gifts between husband and wife dur- ing their marriage are invalid, yet the fruits gathered from gifts to	
Fructus percipiendo *uxor vel vir ex re* *donata suos facit,*	πλὴν ἀλλ' οἱ καρ- ποὶ οἱ ληφθέντες ἐκ τῶν δωρηθέντων	the husband by the wife or to the wife by the husband do become the	

27 See above, The Teaching Method of the *Antecessores*, p. 41.
28 See above, p. 27.

TEXT 2.14 (*cont.*)

*illos tamen, quos suis operis adquisierit, **veluti serendo:***	πραγμάτων τῷ ἀνδρὶ ἐκ τῆς γυναικὸς ἢ τῇ γυναικὶ ἐκ τοῦ ἀνδρὸς εἰς κέρδος προχωροῦσι τοῦ δεξαμένου τὴν δωρεάν· καρποὺς δὲ λέγω ἐκείνους, οὓς ὁ τὴν δωρεὰν λαβὼν ἀπὸ καμάτων οἰκείων ἐκτήσατο.	property of him or her who received the gift. I am talking now about those fruits which the receiver of the gift has acquired by his own efforts [for instance by sowing].	Stephanos omits ***veluti serendo***: for instance by sowing
nam si pomum decerpserit vel ex silva caedit, non fit eius,	Εἰ γὰρ ὀπώρα ἐστί, τοῦτο εἰς κέρδος τοῦ λαμβάνοντος οὐ προχωρεῖ.	For if it was just a matter of harvesting, then the fruits do not become his property.	
sicuti nec cuiuslibet bonae fidei possessoris, quia non ex facto eius is fructus nascitur.	Ταῦτα νόησον καὶ περὶ *βοναφίδε* νομέων.[29]	The same rule applies to possessors in good faith [since these are not fruits of their efforts].	**Stephanos omits** *quia ... nascitur*: since these are not fruits of their efforts.

Erotapokrisis on the same text D. 22,1,45

Ἠρωτήθη. Τί οὖν; Ἐναντιοῦται τὸ κε' διγ.· ἐκεῖ γὰρ καὶ τοὺς μὴ *φάκτῳ* αὐτοῦ, ἀλλ' ἑτέρου *σπαρέντας* εἶπεν εἶναι τοῦ *βοναφίδε* νομέως. **Λύσις.** Ἀλλά φαμεν, ὅτι ἐκεῖ περὶ **σπειρομένων** εἶπεν ὁ νομικός· ἐν αὐτῷ τῷ κε' διγ. ὁ Ἰουλιανὸς τῷ 'σάτι' ἐχρήσατο ῥήματι. Καὶ ἔστι μὲν αὕτη πιθανὴ ἡ ἀπολογία. Ἐναντιοῦται δὲ ἡμῖν τὸ ἐνταῦθα κείμενον ῥητὸν	The question was asked: what is this? This is in contradiction with fragment 25 (D. 22,1,25 § 1), which says that the possessor in good faith also acquires the fruits if they are not due to his own action but were sown by someone else. Solution: certainly, but in that text the jurist is talking about sown fruits, for in fragment 25 Julianus literally uses the word *sati* [sown].[30]

29 BS 1688/4–10 (sch. Pa 1 ad B. 23,3,45 = D. 22,1,45).

30 See the relevant fragment by the Roman jurist Julian, quoted below.

TEXT 2.14 (*cont.*)

ἔχον καὶ αὐτὸ 'ἐρENDO' καὶ διὰ τοῦτο ἐναντιώτατόν ἐστι τὸ θέμα. Σημείωσαι αὐτὸ διὰ τὸ κείμενον ἐν τῷ γ' τῶν δεϊουδικίης βιβ. τιτ. δ' διγ. ιγ' Παύλου ῥητῷ.[31]	This apology may sound plausible enough, but it is contradicted by the fact that the present text (D. 22,1,45) also contains the word *serendo* [by sowing] so the matter is hopelessly contradictory. Take notice of this, because of what is said in the text of Paulus in book 3 of *de iudiciis* title 4 fragment 13.

D. 22,1,25: the text of the Roman jurist Julian that is referred to in the ***erotapokrisis*** above

Iulianus libro septimo digestorum	Julian, *Digest*, book seven:
1. *In alieno fundo, quem Titius bona fide mercatus fuerat, frumentum* ***sevi:*** *an Titius bonae fidei emptor perceptos fructus suos faciat? respondi, quod fructus qui ex fundo percipiuntur intellegi debet propius ea accedere, quae servi operis suis adquirunt, quoniam in percipiendis fructibus magis corporis ius ex quo percipiuntur quam seminis, ex quo oriuntur aspicitur: et ideo nemo umquam dubitavit, quin, si in meo fundo frumentum tuum* ***severim,*** *segetes et quod ex messibus collectum fuerit meum fieret. porro bonae fidei possessor in percipiendis fructibus id iuris habet, quod dominis praediorum tributum est. praeterea cum ad fructuarium pertineant fructus a quolibet* ***sati,*** *quanto magis hoc in bonae fidei possessoribus recipiendum est, qui plus iuris in percipiendis fructibus habent? cum fructuarii quidem non fiant, antequam ab eo percipiantur, ad bonae fidei*	1. I sowed corn on land of another which Titius had bought in good faith. Does Titius as purchaser in good faith acquire the fruits gathered? I replied that fruits gathered from land are like acquisitions which slaves make by their labour, since in taking fruits one looks more to rights over the thing from which they are taken than over the seed. No one ever doubted that if you sow corn on my land, the crops and harvest products are mine. Further, a possessor in good faith has the same right in gathering fruits as the landowner. Besides, since a fructuary takes fruits by whomever sown, how much more so a possessor in good faith, who has greater rights? For a fructuary only acquires the fruits when gathered by himself, but a possessor in good faith acquires them however separated from the soil, like the holder of a long lease of public land.

31 BS 1688/16–22 (sch. Pa 4 ad B. 23,3,45 = D. 22,1,45).

TEXT 2.14 *(cont.)*

autem possessorem pertineant, quoquo modo a solo separati fuerint, sicut eius qui vectigalem fundum habet fructus fiunt, simul atque solo separati sunt.[32]	

This second passage drawn from the teaching of Stephanos is also an example of a critical question by a student and the answer that follows by the *antecessor*. By comparing the *index* of Stephanos and the *Digest* fragment of a text deriving from Pomponius, we observe that the *antecessor* sometimes adds extra information in his *index*, and in some cases he omits a few things from the *rheton*. In particular, Stephanos ignores the words *veluti serendo*, which means 'for instance by sowing': he does not translate them. Perhaps Stephanos considers it superfluous to translate this because it is just an example. However, his *index* led to a critical question by a student as we read in the *erotapokrisis*. The student actually believes that he has discovered a contradiction with another law. He points out that D. 22,1,25 discusses the same situation, but with a different outcome. This would mean that there is a significant contradiction within the *Digest*. Stephanos claims to solve the problem once again by pointing out an essential difference between the two texts. He alleges that D. 22,1,25, a fragment by the Roman jurist Julian, specifically deals with the produce of something 'sown', as can be seen from the Latin word *sati*, which does mean 'sown', whereas the Pomponius fragment under discussion, D. 22,1,45, does not. In fact, however, this is a fake solution, for we saw that Pomponius also spoke of sowing (*veluti serendo*), even if Stephanos did not translate this. We might almost accuse Stephanos of deliberately cheating here. Another possibility would be that Stephanos's manuscript of the *Digest* was corrupt at this point, or simply that he was not quite smart enough on this point. Or, perhaps he did not realise that *serendo* and *sati* (as well as *sevi* and *severim* in D. 22,1,25) are forms of the same irregular Latin verb. The second part of the *erotapokrisis* does point this out: it says that the *lysis* or 'apology' provided by Stephanos does not work, and that there really is a contradiction. Who had the courage to say this so bluntly? It seems unlikely that it was Stephanos, criticising his own 'solution' and accusing his emperor of contradicting himself. Could it be the same clever student who raised the question in the first place? In any event, it was someone who was still able to read the Latin text, the *rheton*. He even refers to a third fragment, originally a text by the Roman jurist Paul (D. 7,4,13), which deals with the same matter.

32 The Latin text is cited from the edition by Th. Mommsen (= D.). The English translation is from A. Watson, ed. and trans., *The Digest of Justinian*, 4 vols., Philadelphia: 1985 (rev. edn, Philadelphia: 1998), here vol. 2, p. 181, reprinted with permission of the University of Pennsylvania Press.

Teaching the *Code:* Examples from Thalelaios and Isidoros

Regarding the teaching of the *Code*, fragments from the following *antecessores* have survived: the *index* and the *paragraphai* of Thalelaios, the *index* of Isidoros, the *index* of Anatolios and a couple of fragments from Stephanos. Thalelaios, Isidoros and most likely Anatolios as well taught at the law school in Beirut. Most of the *antecessorian* material concerning the *Code* derives from Thalelaios. Later Byzantine jurists describe his work with the term *platos* (τὸ πλάτος), which can be translated as 'the extensive form', 'breadth'. As has been said above, the word *platos* can refer in Byzantine law to various other works too. For example, it is also used to refer to the work of Stephanos on the *Digest* or to the work that was done for the *Basilica*.[33]

Thalelaios is also related to the so-called *kata podas* translation (ἡ κατὰ πόδας ἑρμηνεία), meaning a word-for-word translation. As already mentioned, the *Code* comprised imperial constitutions. It was a demanding text for students because of the difficult Latin, not least because the emperors often used a rhetorical style when issuing legislation. It seems that even an *index* was not sufficient for students when being taught the *Code*. This explains why Thalelaios in his courses also provided a *kata podas* to accompany the Latin text, the *rheton* (see TEXT 2.16). Certain characteristics indicate that such Greek translations were written above the Latin lines in manuscripts of the *Code*. Each Latin word had its exact Greek translation placed above it; in other words, it was something like an automatic or mechanical translation. Hence, Thalelaios often used the *kata podas* in his lectures and quoted from it. It could be that he was the one who composed it, but we are not sure about this.

Thalelaios also often made use of a *thematismos*, which can be explained by the material that he had to teach, namely the *Code*. As already mentioned, many of the imperial constitutions had been issued as replies to specific questions about cases, but we do not know exactly what the actual cases were. In other words, we have the replies of the emperor which subsequently acquired the status of a law, but often we do not know the actual facts which led to this decision. Most of the time one had to suppose (θεματίζειν) the actual facts of the case in order to reconstruct it and make sense of it. In the following, we will give two examples from the teaching of the *Code* by Thalelaios which contain various elements of the *antecessorian* teaching method.

TEXT 2.15 Teaching the *Code*: Thalelaios, first example

C. 2,4,38 *Idem* AA. *et* CC. *Theodotiano.* *Transactio nullo dato vel retento seu promisso minime procedit.*	The same Augusti and Caesars to Theodotianus. A settlement has no validity at all when nothing has been given, kept back, or promised (by both parties).[34]

33 On the *Basilica* and the *platos*, see below pp. 133–134.

34 The Latin text is cited from the edition of P. Krüger (= C.) and the English translation from Frier, *Codex*.

TEXT 2.15 *(cont.)*

Index of C. 2,4,38 by Thalelaios

protheoria	Οἶδας τὴν κυριότητα τοῦ συμφώνου καὶ τῆς διαλύσεως, ὅτι σύμφωνον μέν ἐστιν ὡμολογημένου χρέους συγχώρησις, διάλυσις δὲ ἀμφιβαλλομένου χρέους συμβιβασμός· **τούτων οὖν μεμνημένος ἐλθὲ ἐπὶ τὸ προκείμενον.**	You know the definitions of a legally valid agreement [*pactum*] and compromise [*transactio*]: an agreement is to acknowledge an undisputed debt, whereas a compromise is to agree with a disputed debt. **Keep this in mind while you consider the present case.**
example ***thematismos***	Πολλάκις φιλονεικίαν ἔχων πρός τινα καὶ μὴ δυνάμενος αὐτὸν συμπεῖσαι εἰπεῖν μοι τὸ ἀληθὲς ἢ ἀπραγμόνως ἀπαλλαγῆναί μου ἦλθον ἐξ ἀπορίας εἰς τὸ εἰπεῖν αὐτῷ 'ἄπελθε ἑταῖρε, οὐ δύναμαί σοι, διαλέλυμαι πρὸς σέ',	I am permanently having conflicts with someone and I cannot persuade him either to tell me what is the matter, or to leave me in peace. At last my exasperation makes me say to him: 'Please leave me alone, I don't know what to do with you; all right then: I agree with you'.
other example	ἢ καὶ φίλοι μου πολλάκις παρεκάλεσάν με διαλύσασθαι πρὸς τὸν ἐμὸν διάδικον καὶ εἶπον, ὅτι διαλύομαι. Ἆρα τοῦτο διάλυσίς ἐστι;	Or: my friends have often advised me to settle my conflict with my opponent, until I finally say: 'All right then, I do'. Is this a compromise?
paraphrase of the constitution that solves it	Λέγει τοίνυν ἡ διάταξις, ὅτι πᾶσα διάλυσις ἢ δοθῆναι τίποτε ζητεῖ τῷ διαλυσαμένῳ ἢ παρακατασχεθῆναι τίποτε παρ' αὐτοῦ ἢ ἐπαγγελθῆναι αὐτῷ τίποτε, καὶ εἰ μηδὲν τούτων γένηται, οὐκ ἔστι διάλυσις·	Well, the constitution says that every compromise presupposes that something is given to the opponent, or that something is retained by him, or that he is promised something, and that it is not a compromise if none of these three possibilities is realised, for:
kata podas translation	διάλυσις γὰρ οὐδενὸς δοθέντος ἢ παρακατασχεθέντος ἢ ὁμολογηθέντος ἤτοι ἐπαγγελθέντος οὐδαμῶς προβαίνει.[35]	'A compromise, if nothing is given or retained or agreed upon, i.e. promised, no way exists'.

35 BT 672/13–24 (B. 11,2,55 = C. 2,4,38).

This constitution is about a compromise (a settlement) and is very brief. Thalelaios begins his *index* by making a link to what the students have already learned. He gives in advance information about the difference between an agreement and a compromise; this is something that the students know already and he considers this difference important for understanding the examined constitution. The students have already been taught the theory of agreements and compromises, which is covered in first part of the *Digest* (the *prota*), taught during their first year.[36] In the next passage, Thalelaios gives an example illustrating the problem in the form of a *thematismos*, and after that, he gives another brief example. His intention is to define the essence of a compromise. When do we speak of a compromise? In order to answer this question, he examines the actual content of the constitution (C. 2,4,38) but he paraphrases it and elaborates it so that it makes better sense. He concludes his *index* by a literal, *kata podas* translation of the constitution.

TEXT 2.16 Teaching the *Code*: Thalelaios, second example

C. 7,16,4 with the corresponding ***kata podas***

kata podas rheton	*Idem A. [= Alexander] Iucundo.*	The same Augustus [= Alexander] to Iucundus
	Ἐὰν οὗτος, ὅντινα εἰς δουλείαν ᾔτεις, ἐλεύθερος *Si is, quem in servitutem petebas, liber*	If the person whom you (Iucundus) claimed in slavery has been pronounced free,
	κἂν τὰ μάλιστα ἀπόντος σου τῆς αἰτίας διαγνωσθείσης ***quamvis absente te*** *causa cognita*	even if you were absent when the case was decided,
	ἀποφανθεὶς ἐστι, δευτέρα εἰς δουλείαν αἴτησις *pronuntiatus est, secunda in servitutem petitio*	you should not be granted a second possibility to claim him as your slave.
	δοθῆναί σοι οὐκ ὀφείλει. Ἐὰν μεθὸ ἔγνως *eius dari tibi non debet. sed si,* ***posteaquam cognovisti***	But if, after you were informed
	περὶ τῆς ἀποφάσεως τοῦ δικαστοῦ, ἔκκλητον ἐπιδέδωκας, *de sententia iudicis, appellasti,*	of the judge's pronouncement, you entered an appeal,

36 D. 2,14 is about agreements (*De pactis*) and D. 2.15 is about compromises (*De transactionibus*). The *prota* consisted of the first four *Digest* books, as we have already mentioned above, p. 36.

TEXT 2.16 (*cont.*)

	εἰ ἄρα κατὰ νόμον ἐξηνέχθη, ἐν τῷ ἀκροατηρίῳ *an iure **lata** sit, in auditorio*	whether it was pronounced in accordance with the law: in a court session
	ζητηθήσεται. *quaeretur.*[37]	it will be investigated.

TEXT 2.17 Thalelaios' *index* of the same constitution

Ἐὰν κινηθῇ τὸ περὶ τύχης δικαστήριον καὶ ἀποφανθῇ τις ἐλεύθερος, κἂν τὰ μάλιστα ἄπεστιν ὁ δουλαγωγῶν αὐτόν, ὅμως οὐκ ἀνατρέπεται ἡ ἀπόφασις· ἐὰν δὲ ἔκκλητος παρακολουθήσῃ, ζητεῖται ἐν τῷ δικαστηρίῳ τῆς ἐκκλήτου, εἰ καλῶς γέγονεν ἡ πρώτη ἀπόφασις.[38]	If an action is brought for examining someone's status and this person is pronounced to be free, even if the person who claims him as his slave is absent, nevertheless the pronouncement is not reversed. But if it is followed by an appeal, then, in the session where the appeal is dealt with, they investigate the correctness of the first pronouncement.

TEXT 2.18 Three *paragraphai* by Thalelaios at the same constitution

at *quamvis absente te*: Θαλελαίου. Ἔγνως ἤδη καὶ ἐν τῷ α′ βιβ. τῶν *deiudiciis*, ὅτι κἂν ἀπολιμπάνηταί τις τὸ πρᾶγμα, ἐκ μιᾶς μοίρας ὀφείλει τὴν τοῦ πράγματος διάγνωσιν ὁ δικαστὴς ἀναδέξασθαι καὶ οὕτως ἀποφήνασθαι.	Of Thalelaios. You already learned in the first book of *de iudiciis* that, even if someone lets his case run, the judge must accept the view of one [i.e. the other] party and pronounce his verdict on the basis of that.
at *posteaquam cognovisti*: Θαλελαίου. Βλέπε οὖν, ὅτι οὐκ ἔστιν ὁ χρόνος τῆς ἐκκλήτου συναπτός, ἀλλὰ περιμένει τὴν εἴδησιν τοῦ ὀφείλοντος ἐκκαλέσασθαι.	Of Thalelaios. Notice that the term for entering an appeal does not begin immediately after the pronouncement itself,

37 BS 2989/15–20 (sch. Pc 1 ad B. 48,20,4 = C. 7,16,4): 'Τὸ κατὰ πόδας'. The Latin text is cited from the standard edition by ed. P. Krüger (= C.).

38 BT 2251/16–19 (B. 48,20,4 = C. 7,16,4).

TEXT 2.18 (*cont.*)

	but awaits the moment that the person who should enter appeal is informed.
at *lata*: Θαλελαίου. Πρὸς τὸ *sententia* εἶπε τὸ *lata*· 'εἰ κατὰ νόμον ἐξηνέχθη ἡ ἀπόφασις'.[39]	Of Thalelaios. *lata* [grammatically] belongs to *sententia*: 'If the judgment was made in accordance with the law'.

This second example from the teaching of Thalelaios deals with an issue of the law of procedure concerning an allegation about the slave-status of a person. As we can see, Thalelaios provides a *kata podas* translation, an *index*-translation and three *paragraphai* for the same *Code* fragment. Note also the different types of content that a *paragraphè* can have: it can be a grammatical explanation, it can link the material to other examined material, or it can clarify a particular legal issue. One may conclude that the students of Thalelaios must have been lucky to have him as their teacher for the *Code* since all of this material must have been extremely helpful for them.

We will quote one more example concerning the teaching of the *Code*, though this one derives from the work of another *antecessor*, Isidoros. In his treatment of the *Code*, Isidoros had established a different way to help his students. He often added a small list or glossary of difficult Latin words with their Greek translations to his *index* on a *Code* constitution. We cite in the following an example from Isidoros' *index* and an example of the sort vocabulary guide he provided.

TEXT 2.19 **Teaching the *Code*: Isidoros**

the ***rheton***: C. 8,53,17	the ***index*** by Isidoros
Idem AA. *et* CC. *Hermiae.* *pr. Sive* ***emancipatis*** *filiis res donasti sive in potestate constitutis et sui iuris effectis ac tenentibus non ademisti,* ***blandiri tibi***[40] *non debes, velut res donatas ex paenitentia liceat auferre.*	Ἰσιδώρου. Τὰ τοῖς **ἐμαγκιπάτοις** δωρηθέντα οὐκέτι δύναται ὁ πατὴρ ἐφ' ἕτερον μεταφέρειν· καὶ ὅ τι ἐὰν τῷ ὑπεξουσίῳ δωρησάμενος ὁ πατὴρ μετὰ ταῦτα ποιῶν αὐτὸν **ἐμαγκιπάτον** μὴ **ἀdempteus**ῃ, ταῦτα οὐδὲν ἧττον μένει

39 BS 2989/21–27 (sch. Pc 2, 3, 4 ad B. 48,20,4 = C. 7,16,4).
40 See below, on the vocabulary of Isidoros.

TEXT 2.19 (*cont.*)

1. *Sane si ea, quae in tua positis potestate donaveras, post* ***emancipationem*** *contra tuam tenuerunt voluntatem, horum penes te dominium remansit, si quidem nec tempore quo voluisti propter vinculum potestatis sibi quicquam quaerere, nec post invito te de rebus tuis potuerunt.*[41]	ἀναφαίρετα παρὰ τῷ παιδὶ γινομένῳ αὐτεξουσίῳ. Εἰ δὲ **ademptευsei,** μένει παρ' αὐτῷ ἡ δεσποτεία· οὔτε γὰρ ἐξ ἀρχῆς δοὺς ἐν ὑπεξουσιότητι ἐποίησεν αὐτὸν δεσπότην οὔτε μετὰ ταῦτα εἴασεν αὐτὸν γνώμῃ οἰκείᾳ ἔχειν.[42]
Translation of the ***rheton***:	Translation of the ***index***:
The same Augusti and Caesars to Hermias.	of Isidoros.
pr. As for things which **you [Hermias]** have given to emancipated sons, and also things which they held because you did not take them back when you emancipated them, **you should not flatter yourself with the illusion** that you may claim those things back now that you regret it.	**A father** cannot transfer to a different person what he has first given to his emancipated sons. In the same way, what a father has given to his son while he was still under his authority and did not claim back when emancipating him, **that remains** no less the child's property and **cannot be taken away from him.**
1. If, however, it was against your wish that after their emancipation they kept the things you gave them while they were still under your authority, the ownership of those things remained with you, in consideration of the fact that neither at the time you would have wished it they were in a position to acquire ownership, because they were chained to your authority, and later they could not control your property against your wish.	But if he did claim them back, the ownership remains his: for neither did he make him the owner when he first gave it, because he was still under his authority, nor did he later by his own wish suffer him to keep it.

Vocabulary of Isidoros, explaining difficult words of the *rheton*
ulandiritiu· ἀπατᾶν ἑαυτόν[43] (= to deceive yourself)

41 The Latin text is cited from the standard edition by ed. P. Krüger (= C.).

42 BS 2772/4–9 (sch. Pc 1 ad B. 47,1,50 = C. 8,53,17).

43 BS 2772/10 (sch. Pc 2 ad B. 47,1,50 = C. 8,53,17).

The text is about non-emancipated sons. In Roman law, a non-emancipated son, who was still under the authority of his father, could not own property. By comparing the *rheton* with the *index* of Isidoros we observe, first of all, that some legal words have been left untranslated in the *index*: 'ἐμαγκιπάτος' for the emancipated son and 'ἀδεμπτεύειν', which means to 'to take away' (< *adimere*). Further, Isidoros' *index* omits historical details because they are no longer relevant. Thus, the names of the emperors are not mentioned. The constitution was in a form of a rescript, i.e. an answer to a question from an official. The name of the official was Hermias, as we read in the *rheton*, and the emperors address him in the second person singular form. In the *index* of Isidoros, the second person singular 'you' has become 'a father'. As far as the style is concerned, Isidoros is simpler and more sober: 'you should not flatter yourself with the illusion that you may claim back' becomes 'it remains his and cannot be taken back'. In his vocabulary guide, Isidoros provides an explanation for the Latin words *blandiri tibi*, which mean 'to deceive yourself'. It is, however, difficult to recognise the Latin words based on what has survived in the glossary as we now have it: in a manuscript written five hundred years after the time of Isidoros, for example, we find *blandiri tibi* rendered as *ulandiritiu*. This corruption is due to the way the Byzantines pronounced Latin, in particular the Latin letter 'b'.

Teaching the *Novels:* Examples from Julian

Unlike the rest of Justinian's legislation, the majority of the *Novels* were promulgated in Greek. Most students were Greek speaking and only faced a problem with Latin legislation. There were, however, a few Latin-speaking students and they faced difficulties when reading the Greek laws. That is why the *antecessor* Julian, who very likely taught in Constantinople, compiled the so-called *Epitome Novellarum*, also known as the *Epitome Juliani*, which was a Latin 'short version' of the *Novels*. It was based on the *index* of his courses. There was another Latin text of the *Novels*, a Latin word-for-word translation known as the *Authenticum*, but this name is misleading, as we have explained in an earlier section.[44] The following text is an example of a Latin protheory by Julian, directly related to the Greek protheories we saw being used by Theophilos (TEXT 2.11) and Thalelaios (TEXT 2.15); this protheory is followed by Julian's summary of the *Novel*, which we will not cite here:

TEXT 2.20 Formula of a *protheoria* in Julian's *Epitome*, cap. 1 (= Nov. 1,1)[45]

Et in Digestis, et in Constitutionibus didicimus [...] *His itaque eo modo*	We have already learned, in the *Digest* as well as in the *Code* that [...]. So, having

44 See above p. 32.

45 The Latin text of the fragments of Julian's *Epitome* are cited from G. Hänel, *Iuliani epitome latina Novellarum* (Leipzig: 1873; repr. Osnabrück: 1965; repr. with additional tables and glossary in P. Fiorelli and

TEXT 2.20 (*cont.*)

discretis, videamus caput constitutionis propositum. Eius autem vis ac potestas talis est: Si quis [...]	made this distinction let us look at the present chapter of the constitution. Its sense and meaning is as follows: if somebody [...]

The following text illustrates the drastic way in which Julian summarises *Novels* in his *Epitome Novellarum*:

TEXT 2.21 Teaching the *Novels*: Julian Nov. 5,1 (About monasteries, and monks and abbots, AD 535) and Julian's Latin *index* / Epitome of this *Novel*

Nov. 5,1	Julian's Latin *index* *Epitome* cap. 12 (const. 4)
'Εκεῖνο τοίνυν πρὸ τῶν ἄλλων ῥητέον, ὥστε κατὰ πάντα χρόνον καὶ ἐν ἁπάσῃ τῇ γῇ τῆς ἡμετέρας βασιλείας, εἴ **ποτέ τις οἰκοδομεῖν** εὐαγὲς **μοναστήριον βούλοιτο**, μὴ πρότερον ἄδειαν εἶναι τοῦτο πράττειν, πρὶν ἂν	
τὸν θεοφιλέστατον τῶν τόπων **ἐπίσκοπον προσκαλέσαιτο**, ὁ δὲ χεῖράς τε ἀνατείνειεν εἰς οὐρανόν, καὶ διὰ τῆς εὐχῆς τὸν τόπον ἀνιερώσειε θεῷ,	*Qui vult aedificare monasterium,* *prius episcopum vocet,* *et illum exoret,*
πηξάμενος ἐν αὐτῷ τὸ τῆς ἡμετέρας σύμβολον σωτηρίας (φαμὲν δὲ τὸν προσκυνητὸν καὶ **τίμιον** ὄντως **σταυρόν**), **οὕτω τε ἄρξηται τῆς οἰκοδομίας**, καλόν δή τινα τοῦτον καὶ πρέποντα θεμέλιον ἀποθέμενος. Αὕτη μὲν οὖν ἀρχὴ τῆς εὐσεβοῦς τῶν εὐαγῶν μοναστηρίων ποιήσεως ἔστω.	*ut sanctam crucem imponat,* *et postea imponatur aedificium.*
First of all we must lay down the rule, which will hold for all time and for all parts of the world belonging to our empire, that, if someone should want to build a	The person who wants to build a

A.M. Bartoletti Colombo, eds., *Secondo l'edizione di G. Hänel e col glossario d'Antonio Agustìn. Testo, indici, concordanze*, Florence: 1996). The Greek text of all the fragments of the *Novels* are cited from the edition of R. Schöll and G. Kroll (= Nov.).

TEXT 2.21 (*cont.*)

holy monastery, he is not allowed to do so before having invited the most god-loved bishop of the area, and before this bishop has raised his hands to heaven and consecrated the place by his prayer, fastening onto it the symbol of our Salvation (we refer to the revered and truly venerable cross): it is not until after this that he may start building, because in this way he will have laid a fine and fitting foundation. So this must be the first step in establishing holy monasteries in accordance with the rules of piety.	monastery, must first invite the bishop and beg him to place the holy cross into the ground, and after that he may go on to add the building.

Finally, we cite Julian's summary of one paragraph of another *Novel* and his *paragraphè* on it:

TEXT 2.22 Julian and Nov. 12, 1: about illicit marriages (Περὶ ἀθεμιτογαμιῶν)

Nov. 12,1 (also TEXT 2.23)	Julianus *Epitome* cap.110/Const. 32
Θεσπίζομεν τοίνυν, τοῦ λοιποῦ, εἴ τις ἀθέμιτον καὶ ἐναντίον τῇ φύσει (ὃν ὁ νόμος ***incest*όν** τε καὶ **nefariov** καὶ **damnatov** καλεῖ) συναλλάξειε γάμον, [...]	*Si quis nefarium et incestum atque damnatum matrimonium contraxerit,* [...]
ἔστω γε αὐτῷ ποινὴ μὴ δήμευσις μόνον, ἀλλὰ καὶ ζώνης ἀφαίρεσις καὶ ἐξορία, καὶ εἴ γε εὐτελὴς εἴη, καὶ τοῦ σώματος αἰκισμός, ὅπως ἂν μάθοι σωφρονεῖν καὶ εἴσω τῆς φύσεως μένειν, ἀλλὰ μὴ τρυφᾶν τε καὶ ἐρᾶν ὑπερόρια, καὶ τῶν παραδεδομένων ἡμῖν ἐκ τῆς φύσεως καταυθαδιάζεσθαι νόμων.	*Post publicationem autem et cinguli sui patiatur amissionem, et exsilio puniatur. Quod si vilior sit, et corporales coercitiones subsistat.*
καὶ τῆς γυναικός, **εἰ τὸν νόμον ἐπισταμένη** τούτου μὲν ἀμελήσειεν, ἀθεμίτοις δὲ ἑαυτὴν ἐπιδοίη γάμοις, ὑπὸ τὴν αὐτὴν γινομένης ποινήν.	*et uxor eius contra leges nupta easdem poenas patiatur, scilicet* ***si nulla iusta*** *excusetur* ***ignorantia.***

TEXT 2.22 (*cont.*)

Therefore we ordain that in the future, if anyone should contract an unlawful and unnatural marriage, which the law calls incestuous and impious and criminal [...] his punishment must be not only confiscation of property, but also loss of office and exile, and, if he is of a lower status, also physical torture, so that he may learn to have self-control and to remain within the boundaries of nature, rather than to be licentious and love what goes too far and defy the laws that have been given us by nature. And the woman too, if she, knowing the law, chooses to ignore it and lends herself to an unlawful marriage, will fall under the same punishment.	If anyone should contract an unlawful and incestuous and criminal marriage [...] in addition, however, to confiscation of his property and loss of office he must be punished by exile too; but if he is of a lower status, [he must] also undergo physical torture. And his wife, married in opposition to the laws, will suffer the same punishment, unless, of course, legitimate ignorance is put forward as an excuse.

Paragraphè of Julian at Nov. 12,1: scholion 35 to his cap. 110[46]
If women excuse their unlawful marriage by saying that they did not know the law, this excuse needs to be justifiable

Bene dixit; nam si forte mater filio nupsit, non poterit iuris ignorantiam praetendere, quia iure naturali sive gentium talis copulatio prohibita est. [...] *Quaesitum est, quid si minor viginti quinque annis sit? et dictum est: minoribus non permittitur ius ignorare in delictis scilicet.*	This is a sensible addition; for if, for instance, a mother would marry her own son, she could not pretend not to know the law, because such a relationship is prohibited by natural law, i.e. the law of all peoples [...] The question was asked: what if she is under twenty-five years of age? And the answer was: Minors are not allowed not to know the law, at least not in delicts.

The brevity and down-to-earth nature of Julian's summary contrasts with how we find the same section of *Novel* 12 represented in the *Authenticum*:

46 This scholion is cited from the original edition of Hänel in the Appendices A., p. 183 (see the select bibliography at the end of this section).

TEXT 2.23 Nov. 12,1 and its *Authenticum*[47]

Θεσπίζομεν τοίνυν, τοῦ λοιποῦ, εἴ τις ἀθέμιτον καὶ ἐναντίον τῇ φύσει (ὃν ὁ νόμος incestόν τε καὶ nefariov καὶ damnatov καλεῖ) συναλλάξεις γάμον, εἴπερ οὐκ ἔχοι παῖδας ἐκ προτέρων γνησίων τε καὶ ἀμέμπτων αὐτῷ γενομένους γάμων, εὐθὺς μὲν αὐτῷ τὴν τῶν οἰκείων πραγμάτων ἔκπτωσιν ἐπικεῖσθαι, ἅμα δὲ καὶ τῶν ὀνόματι προικὸς ἐπιδεδομένων αὐτῷ μηδενὸς ἀπολαύειν, ἀλλὰ πάντα τῷ ταμείῳ προσκυροῦσθαι. ἀνθ' ὅτου γὰρ ἐξὸν γαμεῖν νενομισμένα παρανόμων ἐρᾷ, καὶ συγχεῖ μὲν γονάς, ἀδικεῖ δὲ τὰ γένη, πράττει δὲ ἀσεβῆ τε καὶ ἀνόσια, καὶ τοιαῦτα γε ἐπιθυμεῖ ὁποία πολλὰ καὶ τῶν ἀλόγων ἀποσείεται ζῴων, ἔστω γε αὐτῷ ποινὴ μὴ δήμευσις μόνον, ἀλλὰ καὶ ζώνης ἀφαίρεσις καὶ ἐξορία, καὶ εἴ γε εὐτελὴς εἴη
[…]
καὶ τοῦ σώματος αἰκισμός, ὅπως ἂν μάθοι σωφρονεῖν καὶ εἴσω τῆς φύσεως μένειν, ἀλλὰ μὴ τρυφᾶν τε καὶ ἐρᾶν ὑπερόρια, καὶ τῶν παραδεδομένων ἡμῖν ἐκ τῆς φύσεως καταυθαδιάζεσθαι νόμων. καὶ τῆς γυναικός, εἰ τὸν νόμων ἐπισταμένη τούτου μὲν ἀμελήσειεν, ἀθέμιτοις δὲ ἑαυτὴν ἐπιδοίη γάμοις, ὑπὸ τὴν αὐτὴν γινομένης ποινὴν […]

Sancimus igitur, de cetero, si quis illicitas et contrarias naturae, quas lex incestas et nefandas et damnatas vocat, contraxerit nuptias, si quidem non habuerit filios ex prioribus legitimis et inculpabilibus sibi contractis nuptiis, mox ei suarum rerum casum imminere, simul autem et ea, quae nomine dotis data sunt ei, in nullo potiri, sed omnia aerario assignari, eo quod, dum licuerit nuptias facere legitimas, contra leges amaverit, et confuderit quidem sobolem, nocuerit autem et generi, egerit vero quae impia sunt et scelesta, et talia concupierit qualia plurima etiam irrationabilia amovent animalia: sitque ei poena non confiscatio solum, sed etiam cinguli privatio et exilium, et si vilis fuerit
[…]
corporis verberatio, quatenus discat caste vivere et intra naturam se continere, non autem delectari et amare ultra terminum et traditis nobis a natura etiam his legibus repugnare. Muliere quoque, si legem sciens hanc quidem neglexerit, incestis autem semetipsam tradiderit nuptiis, sub eadem constituenda poena. […]

As explained above, the *Authenticum* is a literal, word-for-word Latin translation of the Greek original text.[48] Because the translation is so literal, it does not always make sense. For instance the author of the *Authenticum* does not always translate the smaller, easy words, like 'and', 'to', or 'is'. Presumably, the author of the *Authenticum* considers these small words not important enough to translate, since every reader could have easily understood them, provided that he had the original Greek text as well. In other words, these small words are too easy to translate. However, such omissions can have an effect

47 The Greek text and the Latin Authenticum cited from the edition of R. Schöll and G. Kroll (= Nov.).
48 See also above, p. 32.

on the actual meaning of the text. In some cases, the author gives two alternative translations for a single word, without consideration of the context. In the following fragment (TEXT 2.24), we can see some mistakes in the translation of the *Authenticum* which help us understand its nature. For example, in this last fragment (TEXT 2.24) the οὗ (= whose) has been interpreted as οὐ ('not': *neque*) and the word 'περιεργίας' (= curiosity) was not understood at all, but merely transliterated (nepi).

TEXT 2.24 Mistakes in *Authenticum* 126 (Nov. 159, 2), which help to understand its nature

Auth.: Nov.:	... *in proastio vero* **neque** *si dominum codicilli Hierium ostendant* ... ἐπὶ δέ γε τῷ προαστείῳ, οὗ δὴ κύριον ὁ κωδίκιλλος Ἱέριον δείκνυσι ... as for the country house, whose owner the codicil clearly says is *gloriosae memoriae multae nobis visum est plenum esse* τὸν ἔνδοξον τῇ μνήμῃ, πολλῆς ἡμῖν ἔδοξεν ἀνάμεστον εἶναι the late Hierius, it seems to us excessively ⟨***nepi********⟩ *quattuor postea generationes huiusmodi in medium deduci quaestionem* περιεργίας τέτρασιν ὕστερον γενεαῖς τὴν τοιαύτην εἰς μέσον ἄγεσθαι ζήτησιν. exaggerated after four generations to bring such a matter forward in court.

Justinian's (So-Called?) Prohibition against Writing Commentaries

The Greek commentaries which appeared directly after the promulgation of Justinian's legislation seem to contradict the so-called 'ban on commentaries' that Justinian ordered in two of his introductory laws. What we read in these laws is that Justinian prohibited commentaries on his legislation, but with some exceptions. We cite in the following the prohibition of Justinian as found in the *Constitutio Deo Auctore* and the *Constitutio Tanta/Dedōken*.

TEXT 2.25 *Constitutio Deo Auctore* § 12 (AD 530): Justinian's (so-called?) prohibition against writing commentaries

Nostram autem consummationem, quae a vobis deo adnuente componetur, digestorum vel pandectarum nomen habere sancimus, nullis iuris peritis in posterum	We command that our complete work, which is to be composed by you [Tribonian and the members of the drafting committee] with God's approval, is to bear the name of *Digest* or *Pandects*.	

TEXT 2.25 (*cont.*)

audentibus ***commentarios illi applicare*** *et verbositate sua supra dicti codicis compendium confundere:*	And no persons learned in the law are to presume in the future to supply any commentaries thereon, and to confuse with their own verbosity the brevity of the aforesaid work,	ban
quemadmodum et in antiquioribus temporibus factum est, cum per contrarias interpretantium sententias totum ius paene conturbatum est:	as was done in former times, when the whole of the law was virtually thrown into confusion by the conflicting opinions of those interpreting it.	reason antiquity
sed sufficiat per ***indices*** *tantummodo et titulorum suptilitatem quae παράτιτλα nuncupantur quaedam admonitoria eius facere, nullo ex interpretatione eorum vitio oriundo.*[49]	Let it suffice merely to make some reminders by indexes, and minute titles, which are called *paratitla*, in such a way that no offense arises through their interpretation.	exceptions

TEXT 2.26 ***Constitutio Tanta/Dedōken*** **§ 21 (AD 533): Justinian's (so-called?) prohibition against writing commentaries**[50]

Hoc autem, quod et ab initio nobis visum est, cum hoc opus fieri deo adnuente mandabamus, tempestivum nobis videtur et in praesenti sancire,	Ἐκεῖνό γε μὴν εὐθύς τε τὴν νομοθεσίαν ἀθροισθῆναι ταύτην ἐνκελευόμενοι νῦν τε αὖθις αὐτὴν βεβαιοῦντες ἅπασιν ὁμοίως ἀπαγορεύομεν,	Now there is one thing which we decided from the outset, when with divine approval we commissioned the execution of this work, and it seems opportune to us to ordain it now also:	
ut nemo neque eorum, qui in praesenti iuris peritiam habent, nec qui postea fuerint audeat ***commentarios isdem***	τὸ μηδένα θαρρῆσαι μήτε τῶν νῦν ὄντων μήτε τῶν ὕστερον ἐσομένων τούτων δὴ	that no one, of those who are skilled in the law at the present day or shall be hereafter, may dare to append any commentary to these laws,	ban

49 The Latin text is cited from the standard edition of Th. Mommsen (= D.).

50 The Latin and Greek text of this constitution is cited from the standard edition of Th. Mommsen (= D.). The English translation is based on the Latin text and is from A. Watson, ed. and trans., *The Digest of Justinian*, 4 vols., Philadelphia: 1985 (rev. edn, Philadelphia: 1998), here vol. 1, from the Confirmation of the *Digest* § 21 in the beginning (no pagination), reprinted with permission of the University of Pennsylvania Press.

TEXT 2.26 (*cont.*)

legibus adnectere: *nisi tantum si velit eas in Graecam vocem transformare sub eodem ordine eaque consequentia, sub qua et voces Romanae positae sunt (hoc quod Graeci* **κατὰ πόδα** *dicunt), et si qui forsitan per titulorum suptilitatem adnotare maluerint et ea quae* **παράτιτλα** *nuncupantur componere.*	**τῶν νόμων ὑπομνήματα γράφειν**, πλὴν εἰ μὴ βουληθεῖεν εἰς μὲν τὴν Ἑλλήνων γλῶτταν αὐτὰ μεταβαλεῖν, μόνῃ δὲ τῇ **κατὰ πόδα** καλουμένῃ χρήσασθαι τῶν νόμων ἑρμηνείᾳ, καὶ εἴ τι κατὰ τὴν τῶν ὀνομαζομένων **παρατίτλων** ὡς εἰκὸς προσγράψαι βουληθεῖεν χρείαν·	save only insofar as he may wish to translate them into the Greek language in the same order and sequence as those in which the Roman words are written (*kata poda*, as the Greeks call it); and if perhaps he prefers to make notes on difficulties in certain passages, he may also compose what are called *paratitla*.	exceptions
alias autem legum interpretationes, immo magis perversiones eos iactare non concedimus, ne verbositas eorum aliquid legibus nostris adferat ex confusione dedecus.	ἕτερον δὲ παντάπασιν μηδ᾽ ὁτιοῦν περὶ αὐτὰ πράττειν μηδὲ αὖθις δοῦναι στάσεώς τε καὶ ἀμφισβητήσεως καὶ πλήθους τοῖς νόμοις ἀφορμήν·	But we do not permit them to put forward other interpretations—or rather, perversions—of the laws, for fear lest their verbosity may cause such confusion in our legislation as to bring some discredit upon it.	reason
quod et in antiquis edicti perpetui commentatoribus factum est, qui opus moderate confectum huc atque illuc in diversas sententias producentes in infinitum detraxerunt, ut paene omnem Romanam sanctionem esse confusam.	τοῦτο ὅπερ καὶ πρόσθεν ἐπὶ τῆς τοῦ ἠδίκτου γέγονεν νομοθεσίας, ὥστε καίτοι γε οὕτω βραχύτατον αὐτὸ καθεστός, ἐκ τῆς τῶν ποικίλων ὑπομνημάτων διαφορᾶς εἰς ἀναρίθμητον ἐκταθῆναι πλῆθος.	This happened also in the case of the commentators on the Perpetual Edict, who, although the compass of that work was moderate, extended it this way and that to diverse conclusions and drew it out to an inordinate length, in such a way as to bring almost the whole Roman legal system in confusion.	antiquity
quos si passi non sumus, quemadmodum poster-		If we have not put up with them, how far can vain	

TEXT 2.26 (*cont.*)

itatis admittatur vana discordia? […] *si quid vero, ut supra dictum est, ambiguum fuerit visum, hoc ad imperiale culmen per iudices referatur et ex auctoritate Augusta manifestetur, cui soli concessum est leges et condere et interpretari.* […]	εἰ γάρ τι φανείη τυχὸν ἀμφισβητούμενον ἢ τοῖς τῶν δικῶν ἀγωνισταῖς ἢ τοῖς τοῦ κρίνειν προκαθημένοις, τοῦτο βασιλεὺς ἑρμηνεύσει καλῶς, ὅπερ αὐτῷ μόνῳ παρὰ τῶν νόμων ἐφεῖται. […]	disputes be allowed in the future? […] But if, as was said before, anything should appear doubtful, this is to be referred by judges to the very summit of the empire and made clear by the imperial authority, to which alone it is granted both to create laws and to interpret them. […]	emperor

Scholars have put forward several different hypotheses to explain this so-called 'ban on commentaries' and the exceptions that Justinian refers to. It has been suggested, for example, that the prohibition on commentaries was never put to force and was very soon abrogated by another *Novel*, although one that has not been preserved. According to H.J. Scheltema, Justinian's prohibition was not an absolute ban on commentaries on the *Digest*. What the emperor actually forbade was the writing of commentaries in the margins of the *Digest*, i.e. additions to the text (a ban which extended, according to Scheltema, to all manuscripts containing his legislation). The emperor was afraid that the official text would become corrupt by the addition of these comments in the manuscripts themselves. People, and in particular copyists, might consider these comments as parts of the official text, the *rheton*, and this could lead to its alteration. The emperor, however, allowed individuals to publish commentaries separately, according to Scheltema. Moreover, Justinian added that there were three exceptions to his prohibition against adding commentaries within the manuscripts. The exceptions were: the *indices*, the *paratitla* and the *kata podas*. An *index* could reproduce the contents of a law or it could be considered a paraphrase of the law text; the *indices* could be extensive but they could also take the form of a short summary. According to Scheltema, the so-called *paratitla* were brief legal passages in the margins of the manuscripts that had to be written in smaller letters than the main text so that everyone could distinguish the two. The *kata podas* were word-for-word translations. Other scholars have suggested that Justinian's prohibition did not apply at all to the texts written by the contemporary *antecessores*. It was allowed therefore to write texts for didactical purposes, such as *indices*, *paratitla* and the *kata podas*.

A subject that is related to the ban on commentaries by Justinian is his prohibition against using *sigla*, i.e. abbreviations and numerals, while copying the *Digest*. It was not allowed for copyists to abbreviate, for example, the names of the Roman jurists or the titles of their works, including the numbering of books and titles. This could cause confusion and corruption in the manuscripts. Justinian wanted to protect the original text of his precious *Digest*. People who dared to use abbreviations despite the emperor's prohibition were considered as having committed forgery (*falsum*) and were punished as such. We quote the relevant fragment from the *Constitutio Tanta/Dedōken*:

TEXT 2.27 ***Constitutio Tanta/Dedōken*** **§ 22 (AD 533): Justinian's prohibition of abbreviations in the *Digest*[51]**

Eandem autem poenam falsitatis constituimus et adversus eos, qui in posterum leges nostras per siglorum obscuritates aussi fuerint conscribere. omnia enim, id est et nomina prudentium et titulos et librorum numeros, per consequentias litterarum volumus, non per sigla manifestari, ita ut, qui talem librum sibi paraverit, in quo sigla posita sunt in qualemcumque locum libri vel voluminis, sciat inutilis se esse codicis dominum: neque enim licentiam aperimus ex tali codice in iudicium aliquid recitare, qui in quamcumque sua parte siglorum habet malitias. [...]	We also prescribe the same penalty on the ground of fraud for those who in the future may dare to write down our laws by means of obscure signs in code.[52] We wish that everything—that is to say, the names of the legal experts and the titles and numbers of the books—be made manifest through a succession of letters and not in a code, so that anyone who procures for himself one of these books in which coded signs are used in any passage whatsoever of the book or the volume must realize that he is the owner of a useless work; for we do not give to anyone who has objectionable coded signs in any part of such a work the right to cite anything from it in legal proceedings. [...]

The prohibition against using abbreviations (*sigla*) is also included in other constitutions, including the *Constitutio Cordi*, which pronounced the second *Code* of Justinian. In fact, in that *constitutio*, it is clearly stated—as is shown from the following fragment—that the prohibition against using abbreviations applies not only to the *Code* and the *Digest*, but also to the *Institutes*:

51 The Latin text of this constitution is cited from the standard edition of Th. Mommsen (= D.). The English translation is from A. Watson, ed. and trans., *The Digest of Justinian*, 4 vols., Philadelphia: 1985 (rev. edn, Philadelphia: 1998), here vol. 1, the Confirmation of the Digest § 21 in the beginning (no pagination), reprinted with permission of the University of Pennsylvania Press.

52 By 'obscure signs', they mean 'abbreviations'.

TEXT 2.28 ***Constitutio Cordi* § 5 (AD 534)**[53]

[...] *cuius scripturam ad similitudinem nostrarum institutionum et digestorum sine ulla signorum dubietate conscribi iussimus, ut omne, quod a nobis compositum est, hoc et in scriptura et in ipsa sanctione purum atque dilucidum clareat, licet ex hac causa in ampliorem numerum summa huius codicis redacta est.*	[...] We have ordered that, as in the case of Our *Institutes* and *Digest*, the text shall be free of all ambiguous symbols (i.e. abbreviations), so that everything composed by Us may be pure and plain in the writing just as in the enactment itself, even though the size of this *Code* has thereby been increased greatly.

Select Bibliography

Th.E. van Bochove provides a comprehensive bibliography on different items related to *antecessorian* teaching in his bibliography for the *Basilica* Online Brill: see https://referenceworks.brillonline.com/browse/basilica-online (especially the section: VII. Legal education and *antecessores*).

The following provides a selected list of further reading for this section.

Primary Sources

Hänel, G. *Iuliani epitome latina Novellarum*. Leipzig: 1873; repr. Osnabrück 1965; repr. with additional tables and glossary. Florence: 1996, as P. Fiorelli, and A.M. Bartoletti Colombo, eds. *Secondo l'edizione di G. Hänel e col glossario d'Antonio Agustìn. Testo, indici, concordanze.*

Kaiser, W. *Die Epitome Iuliani. Beiträge zum römischen Recht im frühen Mittelalter und zum byzantinischen Rechtsunterricht*. Frankfurt am Main: 2004.

Lokin, J.H.A. and R. Meijering. *Anatolius and the Excerpta Vaticana et Laurentiana. Edition and Commentary*. Groningen: 1999.

Lokin J.H.A., R. Meijering, B.H. Stolte, and N. van der Wal, eds. *Theophili Antecessoris Paraphrasis Insitutionum*, with a translation by A.F. Murison. Groningen: 2010.

Secondary Literature

Brandsma, F. *Dorotheus and his Digest Translation*. Groningen: 1996.

De Jong, H. *Stephanus en zijn Digestenonderwijs* (PhD Diss., University of Groningen). The Hague: 2008.

Falcone, G. 'The Prohibition of Commentaries to the Digest and the Antecessorial Literature', SG, 9 (2014), pp. 1–36.

Falcone, G. 'Premessa per uno studio sulla produzione didattica degli antecessores', in J.H.A. Lokin

53 The Latin text of this constitution is cited from P. Krüger (= C.). The English translation is from Frier, *Codex*.

and B.H. Stolte, eds. *Introduzione al diritto bizantino. Da Giustiniano a Basilici*. Pavia: 2011, pp. 147–157.
Falcone, G. '"Theophilus noster". Zur Benutzung der Theophilos Paraphrasis seitens der humanistischen Jurisprudenz', *Iuris Antiqui Historia. An International Journal on Ancient Law*, 2 (2010), pp. 15–21.
Falcone, G. 'La formazione del testo della Parafrasi di Teofilo', *Tijdschrift voor Rechtsgeschiedenis*, 68 (2000), pp. 417–431.
Kaiser, W. 'Wandlungen im Verständnis der Epitome Iuliani von der Spätantike bis zur Gegenwart', in M. Avenarius, ed. *Hermeneutik der Quellentexte des Römischen Rechts*. Baden-Baden: 2008, pp. 300–353.
Scheltema, H.J. 'Das Kommentarverbot Justinians', *Tijdschrift voor Rechtsgeschiedenis*, 45 (1977), pp. 307–331 = *Opera Minora*, pp. 403–428.
Scheltema, H.J. *L'enseignement de droit des antécesseurs*. Leiden: 1970 = *Opera Minora*, A3, pp. 58–110.
Scheltema, H.J. 'Subseciva XV. Kobidas', RIDA, 13 (1966), pp. 341–343 = *Opera Minora*, A3, pp. 148–150.
Simon, D. 'Aus dem Kodexunterricht des Thalelaios', SZ, 86 (1969), pp. 334–383 and 87 (1970), pp. 315–394 and in RIDA, 16 (1969), pp. 283–308 and 17 (1970), pp. 273–311.
Thüngen, L. 'Digestenunterricht des Antezessors Isidor in den *Baroccianus*-Fragmenten', published online 20.05.2021 on Academia.edu (https://www.academia.edu/48996670/Digestenunterricht_des_Antezessors_Isidor_in_den_Baroccianus_Fragmenten; date of access 11.02.2022)
Van Bochove, Th.E. 'Justinianus Latinograecus. Language and Law during the Reign of Justinian', in A. Garcea, M. Rosellini, and L. Silvano, eds. *Latin in Byzantium I: Late Antiquity and Beyond*. Turnhout: 2019, pp. 199–243.
Wallinga, T. *Tanta/Δέδωκεν: Two Introductory Constitutions to Justinian's Digest*. Groningen: 1989.
Watson, A., ed. and trans., *The Digest of Justinian*, 4 vols., Philadelphia: 1985 (rev. edn, Philadelphia: 1998).

3 Contemporary Writings for More Practical Purposes

The *Digest* Translation by Dorotheos

As already mentioned, a substantial part of the *Digest* was left out of the curriculum of law studies. Students were supposed to study this part on their own and to be able to consult it if needed after they had finished their studies. Fortunately, there was a Greek translation of the *Digest* available. The *antecessor* Dorotheos had translated into Greek all books of the *Digest*, including those that were not part of the formal law curriculum. Dorotheos was a real expert in law since he had been a member of the committees that had drafted the *Digest*, the *Code* (second version) and the *Institutes*. He taught at the law school in Beirut. It is believed that Dorotheos wrote his translation between 536 and 539. The fact that Dorotheos translated the whole text of the *Digest* into Greek, and not only the *Digest* parts of the law curriculum, is an indication that his translation was also aimed at helping practising lawyers. Fragments of his translation have mainly survived in the *Basilica* scholia.[54] In the following, we quote a fragment from Dorotheos' *Digest* translation:

TEXT 3.1 D. 24,3,7,12 and the translation by Dorotheos

Digest text (from Ulpian)	Dorotheos' translation
Si fundum viro uxor in dotem dederit isque inde arbores deciderit, si hae fructus intelleguntur,	Δωρόθεος. Ἐὰν γυνὴ ἀγρὸν δέδωκεν ἐν προικὶ τῷ ἀνδρί, ὁ δὲ ἔτεμεν ἐκ τοῦ ἀγροῦ δένδρα, εἰ μὲν εἰς καρπὸν ψηφίζονται τὰ τμηθέντα (ἦν γὰρ ἐν προσόδῳ τὸ τέμνειν τὴν ὕλην),
pro portione anni debent restitui	κατὰ τὴν ἀναλογίαν τοῦ ἐνιαυτοῦ ὀφείλει ἀποδιδόναι μέρος αὐτῶν ὁ ἀνήρ·
(*puto autem, si arbores caeduae fuerunt*	ἐγὼ δὲ νομίζω, ἐὰν τῶν ἐξ ἔθους τεμνομένων ἦν τὰ δένδρα (ἦν γὰρ τυχὸν ἄκαρπα καὶ σύνηθες ἦν κόπτεσθαι αὐτά)
vel gremiales,	καὶ ἦν τὰ τμηθέντα ὅσα ἐν ταῖς ἀγκάλαις συλλέγομεν,
dici oportet in fructu cedere), *si minus, quasi deteriorem fundum fecerit, maritus tenebitur.* [...][55]	ταῦτα εἰς καρποὺς λογίζεσθαι τῷ ἀνδρί. Ἐὰν δὲ μὴ τοιαῦτα ἦν τὰ τμηθέντα, τότε ὡς βλάψας τὸν ἀγρὸν ὁ ἀνὴρ καὶ χείρονα ποιήσας αὐτὸν ἐνάγεται παρὰ τῆς γαμετῆς αὐτοῦ. [...][56]
If a woman has given her husband land as her dowry and he has felled trees from there, then, if these are considered as fruits,	Dorotheos. If a woman has given her husband land as her dowry and he has felled trees from that land, then, if the felled wood is considered as fruits (because felling the wood counted as revenue),
they must be restored in proportion to the time of the year	the husband must restore part of it, in proportion to the time of the year
and in my opinion, they are to be counted as fruits if it was coppice wood	and in my opinion, if they are such trees as are normally chopped (for perhaps they were of a kind that does not bear fruit, and they were always felled),
or pollard trees.	

54 On the *Basilica* scholia, see below pp. 137–143 and pp. 152–164.
55 The Latin text is cited from the edition by Th. Mommsen (= D.).
56 BS 1890/10–17 (sch. F Pa 11 ad B. 48,8,7 = D. 24,3,7).

TEXT 3.1 *(cont.)*

If they were not, the husband will be held responsible for making the land less valuable.	and if it was such an amount as can be carried in the arms, then they must be reckoned as fruits picked by the husband. If, on the other hand, the felled wood was not like that, then the husband is accountable by the wife for damaging the land and for making it less valuable.

The *Digest* fragment which Dorotheos translates here deals with the general rule that the husband must return the dowry to his wife when their marriage is dissolved, plus part of the fruits of that year. It was therefore important to define what could be considered as 'fruits'. In particular, this text deals with trees: some sorts of trees count as fruits and the husband is allowed to fell them, but then he must restitute it as part of the dowry; other kinds do not count as fruits, and if he has felled such trees, he has made the dowry less valuable. As we can see, the translation by Dorotheos is slightly more elaborate than the *Digest* fragment. He provides a few examples in his translation to clarify the meaning in some sentences and help the reader.

The *summae*

Another of the practice-orientated types of work produced in this period were the *summae*, the Greek summaries, of the *Digest* or the *Code*, for example. Practising lawyers preferred these Greek summaries to the original texts because they were easy to consult. A *summa* would omit the disputed opinions of different Roman jurists and would focus only on the valid rule as settled by Justinian. It was therefore easier and faster for the lawyers to use *summae*, rather than the original texts, although the latter formally remained valid law. The difference between a *summa* and an *index* was that in a *summa* a significant amount of less relevant information was omitted, whereas in the *index* (and the translation of Dorotheos, as we saw), information was added to help the reader and to clarify the material under discussion. In the following, we cite from two *summae* on the *Digest*, which summarise the same fragment that was at the heart of Dorotheos' translation cited above, that is D. 24,3,7 § 12 (see TEXT 3.1). The first *summa* is by an author whose name we do not know and which we call the *summa* of 'the Anonymos'; the second is by Cyrillos.

TEXT 3.2 Corresponding *summae* of 'the Anonymos' and Cyrillos

3.2.1 'The Anonymos'	3.2.2 Cyrillos
Ἐὰν ὁ ἀνὴρ ἐκ τοῦ προικιμαίου ἀγροῦ δένδρα κόψῃ, εἰ μὲν ἐξ ὕλης τεμνομένης ἢ τὰ ἐν ἀγκάλαις φερόμενα, καρπός ἐστι καὶ ἀναλόγως μερίζεται· εἰ δὲ μὴ τοιαῦτα ἦσαν, ἐνέχεται ὁ ἀνὴρ ὡς βλάψας τὸν ἀγρόν.[57]	Κυρίλλου. Εἰ δὲ δένδρα κόψῃ ἐκ τοῦ ἀγροῦ ὁ ἀνήρ, εἰ μὲν τῶν κοπτομένων ἦσαν, ἐν τοῖς καρποῖς ταῦτα λογίζεται, εἰ δὲ μή, ὡς χείρονα τὸν ἀγρὸν ποιήσας κατέχεται [...][58]
If the husband fells trees from land belonging to the dowry, then, if it was from coppice wood or if it was what is carried in the arms, it is fruit and is divided accordingly; if it was not like that, the husband is accountable for damaging the land.	Of Cyrillos. And if the husband fells trees from the land, then, if it was coppice wood, they are counted among the fruits; if not, he is accountable for making the land less valuable [...]

We can now compare the three versions of the same *Digest* fragment: i. the translation of Dorotheos (TEXT 3.1), ii. the *summa* by 'the Anonymos' (TEXT 3.2.1) and iii. the *summa* by Cyrillos (TEXT 3.2.2). As mentioned above, if we compare the Latin text and the translation by Dorotheos, we can see that Dorotheos is slightly more explicit and helpful in some places. The two *summae* of the same passage show how easily the text can be shortened. They closely resemble each other, though the *summa* of Anonymos is slightly more elaborate. The *summa* of Cyrillos has been preserved in the *Basilica* scholia, and the *summa* by 'the Anonymos' has become the *Basilica* text itself.[59] Note that this Anonymos is also known in Byzantine legal scholarship as 'the Anonymos Senior'. He lived in the sixth century and we distinguish him from 'the Anonymos Junior', who lived in the early seventh century.[60]

We will quote another example of a *Digest* fragment and the three Greek versions of it that have survived (TEXT 3.3): i. that of Dorotheos in his translation, ii. that of 'the Anonymos Senior' from his *summa* and iii. that of Cyrillos, also from his *summa*.

The *Digest* fragment (which Dorotheos translates and 'the Anonymos Senior' and Cyrillos summarise) refers to the *pactum de non petendo* (agreement not to sue). This was an informal agreement between the creditor and the debtor by which the first agreed not to bring an action against the latter for his debt. The obligation remained valid, but if the

57 BT 1374/16–19 (B. 28,8,7,12 = D. 24,3,7).
58 BS 1891/1–3 (sch. F Pa 13 ad B. 28,8,7 = D. 24,3,7).
59 See the discussion below, pp. 123–129 and pp. 137–143 on the *Basilica* and their 'old' scholia.
60 More on 'the Anonymos Junior' can be found below, pp. 91–96.

TEXT 3.3 D. 2,14,40pr., the translation by Dorotheos and the *summae* by 'the Anonymos Senior' and Cyrillos

D. 2,14,40 pr.		**Dorotheos' translation**		***Summa* of 'the Anonymos Senior'**		***Summa* of Cyrillos**	
Idem libro primo respon-sorum	The Same (= Papinian) in Book 1 of Replies	**Greek translation by Dorotheos** (scholion at *Basilica* 11,1,40)[61]		**Greek *summa* by 'the Anonymos Senior'** (*Basilica* 11,1,40)[62]		**Greek *summa* by Cyrillos** (scholion at *Basilica* 11,1,40)[63]	
Tale pactum 'profiteor te non teneri' non in personam dirigitur, sed cum generale sit, locum inter	An agreement stated as follows: 'I acknowledge that you are not bound', is not limited to the person, but, since it is general, it will	Δωροθέου. Διαλεγόμενός τις πρὸς τὸν χρεώστην αὐτοῦ οὕτως εἶπεν· ἐπαγγέλλομαι μὴ κατέχεσθαί σε τῷ χρέει. Οὐκ ἔστι τοῦτο τὸ πάκτον	Dorotheos Speaking to his debtor somebody said: 'I acknowledge that you are not bound by your debt'. This agreement is	Idem. Τὸ εἰπεῖν 'ὁμολογῶ σε μὴ ἐνέχεσθαι' καὶ εἰς κληρονόμους διαβαίνει.	The same. The saying 'I acknowledge that you are not bound' is also passed on to the heirs.	Κυρίλλου. Τῷ εἰπεῖν, ὁμολογῶ σε μὴ κατέχεσθαι, ἰν ῥέμ ἐστι τὸ πάκτον καὶ κληρονόμῳ δίδοται.	Cyrillos. By saying 'I acknowledge that you are not bound' the agreement is real (*in rem*) and

61 BS 285/29–31 (sch. Ca 1 ad B. 11,1,40 = D. 2,14,40).
62 BT 636/1–2 (B. 11,1,40 = D. 2,14,40).
63 BS 285/32–33 (sch. Ca 2 ad B. 11,1,40 = D. 2,14,40).

TEXT 3.3 (*cont.*)

D. 2,14,40 pr.		**Dorotheos' translation**		***Summa* of 'the Anonymos Senior'**		***Summa* of Cyrillos**	
heredes quoque litigantes habebit.[64]	also apply to heirs when they are litigants.	περσονάλιον, ὅθεν καὶ εἰς τοὺς κληρονόμους τοῦ δεβίτορος διαβαίνει.	not personal, so that it is also passed on to the heirs of the debtor.				also passed on to the heir.

64 The Latin text is from the standard edition by Th. Mommsen (= D.).

creditor tried to enforce the debt despite this agreement, then the debtor had an exception, a defence at his disposal that he could use against the creditor. What is explained here is that if such an 'agreement not to sue' has been made it would not be fair, if the debtor dies, for the creditor to bring the action against the heirs of the debtor.

As far as the *summae* are concerned, we should also mention another name: the *antecessor* Anatolios and his *summa* of the *Code*. Anatolios taught in Beirut. Anatolios' *summa* on the *Code* was probably intended for primarily practical purposes, and this is because it does not show the characteristics of the *antecessorian* teaching method. It is believed that Anatolios used the *index* of his colleague Isidoros, whom we mentioned above,[65] because there are similarities between their texts. Anatolios, however, is briefer and more straightforward in his style. The following fragments give a good impression of how the *Code* text has been shortened by Isidoros and by Anatolios:

TEXT 3.4 C. 8,2,1 with its *summa* by Anatolios and its *index* by Isidoros

C. 8,2,1 *Impp. Severus et Antoninus AA Iusto*	*Summa* by Anatolios	*Index* by Isidoros
Hereditatem eius, quem patrem tuum fuisse dicis, petiturus iudicibus qui super ea re cognituri erunt de fide intentionis adlega. quamvis enim bonorum possessionem ut	Ὁ παῖς ἐαθεὶς ἀμνημόνευτος παρὰ τοῦ πατρὸς καὶ αἰτῶν τὴν κατὰ τῆς διαθήκης διακατοχὴν	Ἰσιδώρου. Ὁ παῖς ἐαθεὶς πραετέριτος παρὰ τοῦ οἰκείου πατρὸς καὶ αἰτήσας τὴν κοντραταβούλλας διακατοχὴν
praeteritus agnovisti, tamen interdicto quorum bonorum non aliter possessor constitui	οὐκ ἄλλως ἐπιτεύξεται αὐτῆς,	οὐκ ἄλλως δύναται τῷ ἰντερδίκτῳ χρήσασθαι,
poteris, quam si te defuncti filium esse et ad hereditatem vel bonorum possessionem admissum probaveris.[66]	εἰ μὴ δείξει ἑαυτὸν εἶναι παῖδα τοῦ τελευτήσαντος.[67]	εἰ μὴ καὶ παῖδα ἑαυτὸν ἀποδείξει τοῦ τελευτήσαντος καὶ κατὰ τὸ ἔδικτον ᾐτηκέναι τὴν διακατοχήν.[68]
Emperors Severus and Antoninus Augusti to Iustus.	The son who is	Isidoros. The son who is

65 See above, pp. 58–60.
66 The Latin text is cited from the standard edition by P. Krüger (= C.).
67 BT 1815/12–14 (B. 40,9,3 = C. 8,2,1).
68 BS 2399/16–19 (sch. Pb 2 ad B. 40,9,3 = C. 8,2,1).

TEXT 3.4 (*cont.*)

If you [Iustus] intend to claim the inheritance of him whose son you say you are, you will have to provide the judges who will deal with your case with proofs of the rightness of this claim. For even though you claim possession of the goods as being left unrecorded [in the will: neither as heir nor as disinherited], even so the interdict *quorum bonorum* will make it impossible for you to be made possessor unless you have given proof that you really are the deceased's son and [therefore] entitled to the inheritance or the possession of the goods.	left unrecorded by his father and claiming possession because this made the will invalid, shall not receive it unless he proves [himself] to be the deceased's son.	left unrecorded by his father and claiming possession because this made the will invalid, shall not be allowed to use the interdict unless he gives proof that he is the deceased's son and that he claims the possession in accordance with the edict.

In Roman law, the interdict *quorum bonorum* was an interdict for acquiring possession granted by the *praetor* to the so-called praetorian successor or *bonorum possessor*. The latter could use this interdict against anyone who held things belonging to the plaintiff's inheritance. Note that the Greek versions (*summa* and *index*) are more abstract and impersonal than the original Latin text of the *Code*. For example, the second singular form in the *Code* fragment ('you') has become in the Greek text a third person singular ('the son who is …').

Julian of Ascalon

There is one more author to mention before we finish with the Justinianic period. This is Julian of Ascalon, who lived in the sixth century in the town of Ascalon in Palestine. We refer to him as 'Julian of Ascalon' to distinguish him from other Julians, like the *antecessor* Julian who wrote a Latin *Epitome* of the *Novels*, as we saw earlier, or the Roman jurist Julian. The work of Julian of Ascalon is very different from what we have examined until now, primarily because it is not primarily based on Justinian's legislation. Julian of Ascalon was an architect and wrote a treatise on building regulations in his region. He probably wrote the treatise between 531 and 533.

Julian's treatise was incorporated into a late Byzantine compilation, the *Hexabiblos* (which dates from the fourteenth century),[69] but extracts of his work are also preserved in a separate manuscript. They are referred to as 'Extracts from the laws or customs in Palestine by Julian of Ascalon, the architect' ('Εκ τῶν τοῦ Ἀσκαλωνίτου Ἰουλιανοῦ τοῦ ἀρχιτέκτονος ἐκ τῶν νόμων ἤτοι ἐθῶν τῶν ἐν Παλαιστίνῃ). The contents concern rules about building and construction: i.e. distances between buildings, about obstructing someone's view, etc. Some of the rules are indeed by Justinian, others are not, and in some cases, the rules found in Julian of Ascalon's work are even in conflict with Justinian's laws. Presumably, the non-Justinianic rules are Palestinian customs, but there is only one phrase which says so in so many words: 'in Caesarea the custom is ... in Ascalon the custom is ... and the most logical compromise between them is the following: ...'. Thus, Julian of Ascalon describes the existing customs and then provides his opinion, which is a compromise. In the introduction to his writing, Julian attempts to structure his work by referring to the four elements of fire, air, water and earth:

TEXT 3.5 Julian of Ascalon, architect, 'The Laws or Customs in Palestine'[70]

1. Τεσσάρων ὄντων τῶν στοιχείων, πυρός, ἀέρος, ὕδατος, γῆς, ἀπὸ δὴ τούτων ἀμφισβητήσεις τοῖς ἀνθρώποις ἐγγίνονται· ὅθεν ἀναγκαῖον ἡγησάμεθα τὰ κατὰ μέρος ἐκ τούτων καὶ ταχυμερέστερον συμβαίνοντα εὖ τάξαι, εὖ θέντες καὶ τὰς αἰτίας καὶ τὰς δικαίας διαλύσεις ἢ βλάβας. Καὶ ἔστι πρῶτον περὶ πυρός.	1. There are four elements: fire, air, water and earth. These are the sources of all conflicts among people. Therefore we thought it necessary to deal with the difficulties that may arise from them successively, laying down their causes as well as the right ways to solve them or to repair the damages. The first section will deal with fire.
2. Τὸ πῦρ καὶ ὁ καπνὸς καὶ ἡ ἀτμὶς πρὸς τὰς τῶν καύσεων δυνάμεις ἢ καὶ τὰ πλήθη τὴν διαφορὰν τῶν βλαβῶν καὶ τῶν διαστημάτων ἔχουσιν· ὅθεν ταῦτα ἀφορίσαντες, οὕτω καὶ τὰ διαστήματα ἐροῦμεν ἐν πείρᾳ τούτων γενόμενοι.	2. Fire, smoke and steam cause varying degrees of inconvenience and require various distances, depending on the amount of heat involved and on their frequency. Therefore we distinguish them in prescribing the minimum distances, according to our own experience of the matter.
3.1. Χρὴ τοίνυν τὸν ἐπιχειροῦντα ἰδιωτικὸν κτίζειν βαλανεῖον ἀφιστᾶν τοῦ γείτονος τὰς	3.1. If someone wants to build a bathhouse, its hot-water room must keep the follow-

69 More on the *Hexabiblos* can be found below, pp. 182–185.

70 The Greek text is cited from the edition by C. Saliou, *Le traité d'urbanisme de Julien d'Ascalon: droit et architecture en Palestine au VIe siècle* (Paris: 1996).

TEXT 3.5 (*cont.*)

καμίνους· εἰ μὲν νοτιώτερον εἴη τὸ κτιζόμενον βαλανεῖον ἢ δυτικώτερον τοῦ γείτονος, ἔχοντος δευτέραν ἢ τρίτην θέσιν καὶ θυρίδας ἀποβλεπούσας εἰς αὐτὸ τὸ βαλανεῖον, πήχεις εἴκοσι. Χειμερινῶν γὰρ ὄντων τῶν ἀνέμων, οὐ συνεχῶς μὲν αἱ τοῦ γείτονος ἀνοιγήσονται θυρίδες, διασκορπισθήσεται δὲ καὶ ἀναλωθήσεται ὑπὸ τοῦ ὑγροῦ ἀνέμου ἡ τοῦ πυρὸς ἀκμή.

ing distances from his neighbour's house: twenty yards if the building is on the neighbour's south or west side, if this has a second or even a third story, with windows that look at the bathhouse. For these winds blow primarily in winter, when the windows will not continually be open anyway, and the heat and steam will easily be dispersed by the damp winds.

3.2 Εἰ δὲ βορειότερον ἢ ἀνατολικώτερον εἴη τοῦ γείτονος τὸ πριβάτον, δευτέρας ἢ τρίτης θέσεως οὔσης τοῦ γειτνιῶντος καὶ θυρίδων ὑπανεῳγμένων ἐπὶ τὸ αὐτὸ πριβάτον, τηνικαῦτα ἀφιστᾶν τὸν κτίζοντα τὸ εἰρημένον πριβάτον πήχεις οὐκ ἐλάττους τῶν τριάκοντα. Θερινῶν γὰρ ὄντων τῶν ἀνέμων, καὶ τῶν θυρίδων συνεχῶς ἀνοιγομένων, βλάβη τις προσγενήσεται τῷ τὴν οἰκίαν ἔχοντι.

3.2 If, however, the bath faces the north or east side of the neighbour's house, if that has two or three stories and windows at the side of the bathhouse, then the person who builds this bathhouse must keep a distance of at least thirty yards, as these are winds that blow in summer, when the windows are open, so that some damage will arise for the proprietor of the house.

(4. ἀρτοκοπεῖον 5. φοῦρνος κεραμικός....)

(4. Bakery 5. Kiln etc.)

49.1. Ἡ τῶν φυτῶν καταφύτευσις μὴ ἀναλόγως τοῖς μεγέθεσι τὴν ἀπόστασιν ἀπὸ τῶν οἰκιῶν ἔχουσα, οὐ τὰς τυχούσας ταῖς οἰκίαις ἐπιφέρει βλάβας· ῥιζοβολοῦντα γὰρ τὰ φυτὰ ἢ καὶ πρὸς τὸ μεγεθυνθῆναι ἀρδευόμενα καὶ ἐγγίζοντα τοῖς τοίχοις ἢ ταῖς οἰκίαις ἢ ταῖς θυρίσι καὶ μάλιστα ταῖς ληνοῖς ἢ τοῖς τῶν κήπων εὐρίποις, βλάπτει τὰ μέγιστα· ἐκ θεμελίων μὲν γὰρ ὠθεῖ τοὺς τοίχους, κλοπῆς δὲ αἰτία γίνεται διὰ τῶν θυρίδων, ἐπισκιάζει δὲ τοῖς ἐπορρύττειν ἑτέρας βουλομένοις θέσεις, ῥήξεις δὲ καὶ ἐμπτώσεις ἐργάζεται ταῖς ληνοῖς καὶ τοῖς τῶν κήπων εὐρίποις·

49.1. [in the section about 'earth'] Plants within a certain distance from buildings, a distance that should be in proportion to their heights, cause considerable damage to these houses. Indeed, as they develop roots, or are watered for better growing, standing near walls, houses, windows, and especially water reservoirs or garden ditches, they cause enormous damage: they push walls off their foundations, they give rise to theft through the windows, they make shadow where neighbours may wish to make windows, they make the water reservoirs and garden ditches collapse.

TEXT 3.5 (*cont.*)

49.2 ὅθεν χρὴ τὸν θέλοντα καταφυτεύειν φυτὰ ἀφεστάναι τῆς τοῦ γείτονος οἰκίας μέτρα ταῦτα·	49.2 Hence a person who wishes to grow plants must keep the following distances from his neighbour's house:
50.1 Εἰ μὲν ἄμπελον φυτεῦσαι βουληθείη μὴ πρὶν ἔχων, ἀφίστασθαι πήχεις ἓξ καὶ δίμοιρον. 50.2 Μηλέαν δὲ καὶ ῥοιὰν καὶ τὰ τούτοις ἰσομεγέθη πήχεις δέκα. 50.3 Συκομοραίαν δὲ ἢ πλάτανον ἢ αἴγειρον ἢ τὰ τούτοις ἰσομεγέθη πήχεις εἴκοσι.	50.1 If he wants to grow a vine that was not there before: 6 and 2/3 yards. 50.2 Apple, pomegranate and other trees of that size: ten yards. 50.3 Sycamore, plane-tree, poplar or other trees of that size: 20 yards.

In general, the goal of Julian of Ascalon is to compromise on the different interests of parties and to distribute rights and responsibilities in a fair way amongst the parties when changes occur in the built environment. For instance, Julian describes in his treatise the rules and regulations for constructing private baths, ovens, bakeries as well as the regulations on building a tavern. In the last case, for example, the owner of the tavern was not allowed to place benches outside the tavern for the clients because this might cause trouble. For the same reason, drinking was allowed only within the building of the tavern. Julian also included rules about the protection of various kinds of views, such as the protection of the view to the sea:

TEXT 3.6 Julian of Ascalon, architect, 'The Laws or Customs in Palestine'[71]

52. 1. Ἡ ὁρατικὴ δύναμις, πασῶν τῶν αἰσθήσεων ὀξυτάτη οὖσα, ἀπὸ πλείστου διαστήματος τὴν ἐνέργειαν ἔχει, ὅθεν οὐ χρὴ ἁπλῶς οὐδὲ ὡς ἔτυχε περὶ ταύτης ἀποφαίνεσθαι, ἀλλ' ἐνθέντας μέτρα τούτοις στοιχεῖν. Φασὶ μὲν γὰρ νόμους τρεῖς εἶναι ἀπόψεων· θαλάσσης, κήπων, γραφῆς δημοσίας. Ταύτας δὲ ἀορίστως τιθέντες τοῖς κτίσουσιν ἀμφιβολίας τίκτουσιν· ὁρᾶται μὲν καὶ γὰρ ἡ θάλασσα ἀπὸ μιλίων πολλάκις	52. 1. The sense of sight, being the sharpest of all senses, is activated from a very long distance. For this, one should not take decisions about it at random or haphazardly, but specify measurements and stick to them. It is said that there are three laws about views: regarding [the view of the] sea, gardens and public displays. But dealing with all of these indiscriminately, they create an almost hopeless situation for those who want to build anything; for the sea is often visible from a

71 The Greek text is cited from Saliou, *Le traité* (see n. 70).

TEXT 3.6 (*cont.*)

τεσσαράκοντα, καὶ περαιτέρω· ὁρᾶται δὲ καὶ κῆπος καὶ φυτὰ καὶ ἄλση ἀπὸ μιλίων εἴκοσιν· ὁρᾶται δὲ καὶ δημοσία γραφὴ ἀπὸ πηχέων οὐχ ἧττον διακοσίων, καὶ εἰ ταύταις ἐστοιχοῦμεν ταῖς ἀπόψεσιν, οὐκ ἂν οἰκία ἢ κώμη ἢ πόλις ἐκτίζετο. Εἰσὶ δὲ καὶ ἄλλαι ἀπόψεις οὐ κατ' εὐθεῖαν ὁρῶσαι, ἀλλὰ πλάγιαι καὶ βεβιασμέναι καὶ ταύτας ἀπόψεις οὐ φημί.	distance of more than forty miles; yet a garden and plants and parks [are visible] from twenty miles; and a public depiction is visible from at least two hundred cubits, and if we respected these views, no house or village or city would be built. There are also other views which are not seen directly but from sideways or in a constrained manner; but I will not talk about these views.
52.2 Χρὴ οὖν τὸν θαλάσσης ἀπόψει ἐν τῷ οἰκοδομεῖν ἐπιπροσθοῦντα, κατ' εὐθεῖαν οὔσῃ καὶ μὴ πλαγίαν ἐχούσῃ τὴν θέσιν, ἀφεστᾶναι τοῦ τὴν ἄποψιν κατ' εὐθεῖαν ἔχοντος καὶ μὴ πλαγίαν καὶ βεβιασμένην.	52.2 So it is necessary that he who blocks the view of the sea by erecting a building, if it is a direct and not a side view, will keep a certain distance from the person who has the view that is direct and not oblique or constrained.
52.3 Εἰ μὲν ὁρᾷ λιμένα ἢ αἰγιαλόν, κἂν ἁπλῶς τῇ πόλει ἢ τῇ κώμῃ ἢ στάσεις πλοίων τέλειον μὴ ἐχούσῃ λιμένα, τὸ παράπαν μὴ κωλύειν μήτε ἀφαιρεῖν τὴν τοιαύτην ἄποψιν· ἱκανὴ γὰρ ἡ ἀπὸ τούτων ψυχαγωγία τοῖς ὁρῶσιν.	52.3 If he has a view to a harbour and a beach or even simply the village or a city or anchorage grounds, if there is not a complete harbour, then he may absolutely not hinder or block such a view; because a great pleasure derives from them for the spectators.
52.4 Εἰ δὲ ἀπωτέρω καὶ πελάγη ὁρᾷ, ταύτην οὐδεμίαν λογιζόμεθα ἄποψιν· καθὼς γὰρ εἴρηται, καὶ ἀπὸ τεσσαράκοντα μιλίων τὸ τῆς θαλάσσης ὁρᾶται μέγεθος, καὶ οὐ δίκαιον ἀπὸ τοσούτου ἐμποδίζεσθαι τοὺς οἰκοδομεῖν ἐθέλοντας διαστήματος.	52.4 If, however, he sees the pelagic sea in the far distance, we do not consider this as any view; because, as stated, the greatness of the sea is seen even from forty miles and it would not be right to prevent those who want to build from such a great distance.

Similar rules about the protection of views overlooking gardens and trees, or views of public painting, were also included in Julian's treatise. Other rules refer to houses and apartment buildings. Most interesting here is where Julian speaks about the issues that concerned owners of apartment buildings in a multistorey building. Julian discusses, for example, the distribution of construction costs of a new building and the distribution of costs of repairs among the owners.

Select Bibliography

Primary Sources

Lokin, J.H.A. and R. Meijering. *Anatolius and the Excerpta Vaticana et Laurentiana. Edition and Commentary*. Groningen: 1999.

Saliou, C. *Le traité d'urbanisme de Julien d'Ascalon: droit et architecture en Palestine au* VIe *siècle*. Paris: 1996.

Secondary Literature

Brandsma, F. *Dorotheus and his Digest Translation*. Groningen: 1996.

Hakim, B.S. 'Julian of Ascalon's Treatise of Construction and Design Rules from Sixth-Century Palestine', *Journal of the Society of Architectural Historians*, 60 (2001), pp. 4–25.

Scheltema, H.J. 'The Nomoi of Iulianus of Ascalon', in M. David, B.A. van Groningen, and E.M. Meijers, eds. *Symbolae ad jus et historiam antiquitatis pertinentes Julio Christiano van Oven dedicatae* (*symbolae van Oven*). Leiden: 1946, pp. 349–360 = *Opera Minora*, B 6, pp. 247–256.

Saliou, C. 'Le traité de droit urbain de Julien d'Ascalon. Coutumier et Codification', in E. Lévy, ed. *La Codification de lois dans l'antiquité*, Actes du colloque de Strasbourg 27–29 novembre 1997. Paris: 2000, pp. 293–313.

CHAPTER 3

From the End of the Sixth Century up to and including the Iconoclastic Period

1 End of the Sixth Century: The *Scholastikoi*

The two law schools of Justinian's day did not last for very long. The school of Beirut was destroyed in 551 by an earthquake which also practically demolished the whole city of Beirut; and the law school in Constantinople presumably ended about the time of Justinian's death in 565. Justinian's curriculum of legal studies proved in practice to be too expensive and time-consuming. The closing down of these two law schools was thus the end of state education. Law was henceforth taught by professional lawyers, the so-called *scholastikoi*. Their name derives from the way they were organised, i.e. an organisation based on a particular kind of school or college (*scholae*/σχολαί).[1] The term *scholastikos* (plural: *scholastikoi*) had already been in use long before the time of Justinian. It was used during the period of the Roman republic (509 BC–27 BC) to refer to people who were educated in rhetoric, and from the fourth century, it became a title. The term applied to any educated man and was broadly used by lawyers and rhetors, although it was not used as a technical term for describing people who appeared in courts.[2]

We have seen that in their teaching methods, the *antecessores* devoted a considerable amount of time to dealing with the texts themselves and trying to tackle the linguistic problems. The *scholastikoi*, in comparison, had a very different way of teaching. Being legal practitioners, the *scholastikoi* were not so much interested in the linguistic and historical subtleties of the original, official law text; they were basically satisfied if the legal implications of the original text were clear. Hence, there were two main differences between the *scholastikoi* and the *antecessores*. First, the *scholastikoi* taught law in private to pupils and so their teaching was not supervised by the state. Secondly, the teaching of the *scholastikoi* was practice oriented. They focused on the *Novels* and the *Code*, although there are also traces of a contemporaneous version of the *Institutes* which they taught as well. The *scholastikoi* did not really consult the original legislation of Justinian, but instead made broad use of existing Greek *summae*. For example, if they did use the *Digest*, they consulted the *summae* made by 'the Anonymos Senior' and Cyrillos, rather than the *Digest* itself. Their aim was to find the valid rule of Justinian's text as quickly as possible, and they were not interested, for example, in the disputed opinions of Roman jurists

1 See the examples cited in The Online Liddell-Scott-Jones Greek-English Lexicon (retrieved from Thesaurus Linguae Graecae), II, 2: 'σχολή, a group to whom lectures were given; σχολὴν ἔχειν to keep a school; σχολῆς ἡγεῖσθαι to be master of it'; the Lexicon cites all relevant references to such terms.

2 For this description of the *scholastikos*, see ODB, vol. 3, p. 1852.

 | DOI:10.1163/9789004520684_004

which had led to this rule. We will examine in the following sections some fragments of the works of two *scholastikoi*, Athanasios of Emesa and Theodoros of Hermoupolis.

2 Athanasios of Emesa

Athanasios worked as a lawyer at the court of the capital of Syria, Emesa (present day Homs), and he wrote a sort of summary of the *Novels*—or more accurately, a tool that helps the reader consult the *Novels*. He must have written this work after 572 because he includes a *Novel* dated to that year. In Byzantine legal literature, this work is known as *The Syntagma of Athanasios*. It is divided into twenty-three titles which discuss the following subjects:

Titles 1–3	Church and religion
Titles 4–8	Justice, organisation of the administrative authorities and law of procedure
Titles 9–13	Family and succession law
Titles 14–17	Law of obligations and notaries
Titles 18–22	Law of persons and of certain professions (slaves, farmers, soldiers)
Title 23	Miscellaneous

The aim of Athanasios was to provide an easy tool whereby people could consult and read the *Novels*. At first, he tried to present the *Novels* in a logical order according to their subject matter, somewhat like the arrangement of the *Digest* and the *Code*. It was, however, difficult to classify complete *Novels* under just one heading. Although each *Novel* has a title which roughly indicates what it is about, in reality, any given *Novel* often deals with a variety of subjects. Moreover, any particular subject can be viewed from different perspectives. For instance, in the example given below (TEXT 1), a law saying that a legacy made to one's slave implies the master's intention to release him from slavery can be viewed as relevant to the general subject of slavery and emancipation (law of persons), or to that of legacies (law of succession). Athanasios proved to be both practical and creative in his classification. He defined one item as the main subject (in this example emancipation: TEXT 2), but provided an elaborate system of further references as well.

In short, the structure of Athanasios' *Syntagma* can be explained as follows. His work consists of twenty-three titles and each title is subdivided into 'constitutions' (*diataxeis*), which are summaries of more or less related *Novels*, each supplied with notes. Following each title, there are series of 'side-titles' (*paratitla*), which are summaries of related fragments of other *Novels* which were classed under other titles elsewhere in the *Syntagma*. For a few titles there are no 'side-titles' (*paratitla*). Finally, the twenty-third title consists of miscellaneous subjects which the reader might not sufficiently notice otherwise. In a way, this last, twenty-third title acted as a safety net for those subjects that Athanasios might have missed in his classification.

We will give in the following text an example of Athanasios' work. This example shows how a fragment of a *Novel* has been placed by Athanasios into three different parts of his *Syntagma*. We will first quote the *Novel* fragment which Athanasios wants to categorise in his work, which is a fragment from *Novel* 78, and we have highlighted in bold letters the specific part that Athanasios intends to include in his *Syntagma*:

TEXT 1 **Nov. 78,4, preface: a legacy to one's slave implies the intention to release him from slavery**[3]

Καὶ οὕτω τῶν πραγμάτων καὶ τῆς ἀληθείας ὅλοι γινόμεθα, ὥστε εἴ τινι καὶ δουλευούσης τῆς γυναικὸς ἐξ αὐτῆς γένοιντο παῖδες, βουληθείη δὲ ἐκεῖνος ὕστερον τὴν γαμετὴν ἐλευθερῶσαι καὶ προικῷα συντάξαι συμβόλαια, ἅμα τῇ τῶν προικῴων γραφῇ καὶ τοῖς παισὶν ἁρμόσει τό τε τῆς ἐλευθερίας ὁμοῦ καὶ τὸ τῆς γνησιότητος δίκαιον· οὐκ ἐπιζητούντων ἡμῶν ἰδιάζουσαν ἐλευθερίαν ἐπὶ τοῖς παισὶ γενέσθαι, ὥστε ἢ συνελευθερωθῆναι τῇ μητρὶ ἢ καὶ μετ' αὐτὴν ἢ καὶ πρὸ αὐτῆς ἴσως τὴν ἐλευθερίαν λαβεῖν, ἀλλ' ἅμα τῇ γραφῇ τῶν γαμικῶν συμβολαίων εὐθὺς αὐτοῖς καὶ τὴν ἐλευθερίαν χαριζόμεθα. τί γὰρ ἂν μεῖζον δείξειεν ὁ πατὴρ ἐλευθερίας τῶν παίδων σημεῖον ἢ τὸ τὴν γαμετὴν ἀποφῆναι καὶ ἐλευθέραν ὁμοῦ καὶ γνησίαν τῇ τῶν γαμικῶν συμβολαίων γραφῇ; **εἰ γὰρ στρατιώτης καταλιπὼν πρεσβεῖον τῶν οἰκείων τινὶ θεραπόντων αὐτῇ τῇ δόσει τοῦ πρεσβείου καὶ τὴν ἐλευθερίαν διδόναι δοκεῖ**, πῶς οὐκ ἂν πολλῷ μᾶλλον ὁ πατήρ, εἰ γράψειε

So wholly and genuinely are we intent on this matter that, should anyone have had children even while his wife was still a slave, and subsequently decide to manumit her and draw up marriage contracts, he will, simultaneously with the executing of the settlement, be combining with it the children's right to both freedom and legitimacy, together. We are making no separate manumission-requirement for the children, either by having them manumitted simultaneously with their mother, or after her, or even possibly before her; instead, we are also granting them their immediate freedom, simultaneously with the execution of the marriage contracts.[4] After all, what greater indication could the father have evinced of his manumission of the children, than by rendering his wife both free and lawful, by the execution of the marriage contract? **A soldier, by leaving a legacy to one of his own slaves, is regarded as also giving him freedom by means of the gift of the legacy, in itself;** if that is so, how could it not be all the more so that any father

3 The Greek text is from the standard edition by R. Schöll and G. Kroll (= Nov.) and the English translation is from D.J.D. Miller and P. Sarris, *The Novels of Justinian: A Complete Annotated English Translation*, 2 vols. (Cambridge: 2018).

4 We prefer to translate 'γαμικὰ συμβόλαια' as 'marriage contracts', and not as 'matrimonial settlements' which is used in the translation of Miller and Sarris.

TEXT 1 (*cont.*)

συμβόλαιον γαμικόν, ἕξει τοὺς ἑαυτοῦ παῖδας ἐξ αὐτοῦ δὴ τούτου καὶ μόνου καὶ ἐλευθέρους καὶ γνησίους διαδόχους; [...]	who executes a marriage contract will have children who, in mere virtue of that sole act, are free, and his legitimate successors? [...]

Novel 78,4,pr. is found at three different places in *The Syntagma of Athanasios*, as follows:

i. as a 'constitution' in the eighteenth title (18.2.3, TEXT 2), a title that thematically belongs to the law of persons,
ii. as a *paratitlon* in the ninth title (9.P.19, TEXT 3), a title that deals with succession law issues and finally,
iii. as part of the twenty-third title (23.18, TEXT 3), a title which deals with miscellaneous subjects of law.

TEXT 2 **Athanasios' *Syntagma*, title 18 heading and contents**[5]

τίτλος ιη' Περὶ ἐλευθερίας ὑπεξουσίων καὶ δούλων καὶ γεωργῶν καὶ γάμων αὐτῶν καὶ ἐπιμερισμοῦ γονῆς καὶ περὶ χαμευρετῶν βρεφῶν καὶ τῶν εὐνουχιζόντων	**Title 18:** About freeing children from paternal authority, slaves, and serfs; their marriages; dividing their children; abandoned children; those who castrate.

This title consists of eight 'constitutions', *diataxeis* (*Novels*), as follows:

'Constitutions' (*diataxeis*)

18.1 / Nov. 54

18.1.1/Nov. 54.1: children of a serf and a free person

18.1.2/Nov. 54.2: Constantinopolitan churches which wish to exchange immovables [...]

18.2 / Nov. 78

18.2.1 freed persons automatically become Roman citizens

18.2.2 ungrateful freedmen are made slaves again

18.2.3 a legacy to one's own slave automatically frees him

18.2.4 marriage between a freed slave and her/his former owner

18.2.5 a dowry to one's own slave frees her

18.3 [...] **18.4** [...] etc.

5 The Greek fragments from Athanasios' *Syntagma* are cited from D. Simon and Sp. Troianos, *Das Novellensyntagma des Athanasios von Emesa* (Frankfurt am Main: 1989).

TEXT 2 (*cont.*)

In addition this title of the Syntagma (Title 18.) has seven *paratitla*, as follows:

Paratitla ('see also title …'):
 18.**P.**1 = Ath. 1.2 / Nov. 123 legal status of senators and bishops
 18.**P.**2 = Ath. 1.13 / Nov. 5 slaves who apply as monks
 18.**P.**3 […] 18.**P.**4 […] etc.

From the references in the *paratitla* we can see that Nov. 123 and Nov. 5 are found as additional 'side-titles' to the eighteenth title (18.P.1 and 18.P.2). Their real place, however, is in the first title of the *Syntagma*, which is about 'bishops, clerics, monks and monasteries' (Περὶ ἐπισκόπων καὶ κληρικῶν καὶ μοναχῶν καὶ μοναστηρίων). The system also works the other way around: the text of title 18.2.3 is also found as a *paratitlon* (= P.) to the ninth title, which basically deals with the law of succession, and even in the twenty-third title (miscellaneous):

TEXT 3 **Athanasios' *Syntagma* 18.2.3 = 9.P. 19 = 23.18 (deriving from Nov. 78,4pr.)**

Athanasios' *Syntagma* 18.2.3 Ὁ στρατιώτης LEGATEUSAS τι τῷ ἰδίῳ δούλῳ ἐλεύθερον αὐτὸν ποιεῖ.	A soldier who leaves a legacy to his own slave makes him free.
Athanasios' *Syntagma* 9.P.19 Ὁ στρατιώτης LEGATEUSAS τι τῷ ἰδίῳ δούλῳ ἐλεύθερον αὐτὸν ἀποτελεῖ.	A soldier who leaves a legacy to his own slave makes him free.
Athanasios' *Syntagma* 23.18 Ὁ στρατιώτης LEGATEUSAS τι τῷ ἰδίῳ δούλῳ ἐλευθερίαν αὐτῷ χαρίζεται.	A soldier who leaves a legacy to his own slave grants him freedom.

So, when Athanasios considers that a *Novel* is relevant for two titles he places it in both. In one title, it appears as a regular *diataxis*, and in the other one, as a secondary side-title, a *paratitlon*. Moreover, he sometimes also places a *Novel* in the final twenty-third title with other 'miscellaneous subjects', just to be absolutely sure that the reader will be able to find it. This classification undoubtedly meant a lot of work for the author, but it is very practical for the reader, especially for someone who is interested in legal practice. Moreover, Athanasios also allows one to find and consult the whole text of the *Novel* itself. He does this by quoting the details of the authentic text of the *Novels* themselves: the opening words, the name of the emperor who promulgated the *Novel*, the original addressee and the date. Occasionally, he also adds some clarifications to the *Novel*, and sometimes he even provides references to the *Code* and the *Digest*. He also points out whether a *Novel* derogates an older one. All this made *the Syntagma of Athanasios* a perfect tool for a lawyer.

3 Theodoros of Hermoupolis

Theodoros of Hermoupolis (Egypt) made summaries of the *Code* and of the *Novels*. His summaries of the *Novels* are similar to those of Athanasios, but Theodoros used a different system which is not so elaborate as the one used by Athanasios. Theodoros simply offered summaries of the *Novels* in the order in which he found them, and he added simple cross references to relevant sections elsewhere in his text as well. However, his references—in contrast with those of Athanasios—are not fully written-out summaries. A reader of Theodoros' work on the *Novels* would have to check these references himself in the books. The long lists of references are called *parapompai* (παραπομπαί). They are typical of Theodoros and often make it possible to identify certain summaries as his. Fragments of his *summa* of the *Code* have been mostly preserved as *Basilica* scholia.[6] His summaries of the *Novels* are found there too, but they also survive as a separate work.

For a comparison between the work of Theodoros on the *Novels* and *The Syntagma of Athanasios*, we quote the following fragment from Theodoros' work, which summarises the same chapter of *Novel* 78 (78,4), as Athanasios had done in the example provided above:

TEXT 4 Theodoros' *summa* with *parapompai* (references) of the same part of Nov. 78,4 pr.[7]

Ἐὰν στρατιώτης ἐάσῃ λεγάτον τῷ ἰδίῳ δούλῳ ἐλεύθερον αὐτὸν ποιεῖ. καὶ σημείωσαι θαυμαστὸν παρὰ τὰ πανταχοῦ εἰρημένα· ἀνάγνωθι γὰρ βι. ς' τοῦ κώδ. τι. κζ' διάτ. ε' καὶ τί. λζ' διάτ. δ' καὶ τί. μβ' διάτ. κη'· καὶ δέξαι τοῦτο ἰδικὸν ἐπὶ στρατιώτου.	If a soldier leaves a legacy to his own slave, he makes him free. Notice this strange rule, which is contrary to what is said everywhere else, if you read C. 6, 27, 5 and 37, 4 and 42, 28. Hence you should accept this rule as specifically applying to soldiers.

6 On the *Basilica*, see below, pp. 123–129.

7 The Greek text is cited from C.E. Zachariae, ed., *Ἀνέκδοτα. Theodori scholastici breviarium Novellarum,*

TEXT 5 **The relevant parts of the *Code* constitutions referred to by Theodoros in this *summa* of Nov. 78,4 pr.: C. 6,27,5, C. 6,37,4 and C. 6,42,28.**[8]

C. 6,27,5,2 2. *Illo videlicet observando, ut,* ***si legatum vel fideicommissum eis sine libertate relinquatur, maneant in servitute.*** *2a. Non tamen ita impii heredes existant, ut liberalitatem testatoris servilis laboris debita remuneratione defraudare conentur et non derelictum, licet adhuc servis constitutis, donent.* [...]	C. 6,27,5,2 2. Clearly this rule must (also) be observed: if a legacy or trust is left to them without freedom, they remain in servitude. 2a. Still, heirs should not be so wicked as to try to defraud the testator's generosity of the repayment owed for servile labor, and not give what is left (to them) although they are still in the position of slaves. [...]
C. 6,37,4 *Servis testamento dominorum non data libertate legatum seu fideicommissum relictum non valet nec convalescere potest, licet post mortem testatoris libertatem aliqua ratione consecuti sunt.* [...]	C. 6,37,4 A legacy or a trust left to slaves in the will of their master without a grant of freedom is invalid. Nor can they become valid even if after the death of the testator they have acquired freedom in some other way. [...]
C. 6,42,28 *Ex fideicommisso sub condicione sine libertate servis propriis inutiliter dato libertas peti non potest.* [...]	C. 6,42,28 Manumission cannot be claimed pursuant to a trust ineffectually given to one's own slaves upon the condition 'without manumission' [...]

collectio regularum iuris ex Institutionibus, fragmenta breviarii Codicis a Stephano antecessore compositi, appendix Eclogae, fragmenta epitomae Novellarum graecae ab Anonymo sive Iuliano confectae, fragmenta Novellarum ex variorum commentariis, edicta praefectorum praetorio (Lipsiae: 1843; repr. Aalen: 1969).

8 We quote only the Latin text and the English translation of the passages relevant for our present purposes; the texts and translations are taken from the edition of Frier, *Codex*.

4 'The Seventh Century': 'The Anonymos Junior'

Under the term 'the seventh century', we refer to the period roughly between 600 and 717.[9] During this period, the Byzantine empire faced many political and military troubles. This period is not as important so far as the legal field is concerned. Emperor Heraclius (r. 610–641) issued some *Novels* which dealt with ecclesiastical matters. Another name worth remembering from this period—or better, another author with no name—is the so-called 'Anonymos Junior'. In an earlier section we referred to 'the Anonymos Senior', who was the author of the *Digest summa*. The importance of this *summa* is its relationship to the *Basilica*. In a later chapter, we will discuss the *Basilica* in detail.[10] At this point, it is enough to know that the *Basilica* was a massive legal compilation issued around 900 which rendered Justinianic law in Greek. Later on, the *Basilica* text was supplemented with explanatory marginal notes, the so-called scholia. The *Basilica* compilers used the Greek versions of Justinianic legislation which they had at their disposal. For example, for the *Digest*, they used the Greek *summa* by 'the Anonymos Senior'. There were also marginal notes in this *Digest summa*, but these notes (scholia) had been written by another author whose name we do not know, although we do know that he lived in the early seventh century. We refer to this latter, younger author as 'the Anonymos Junior' to distinguish him from 'the Anonymos Senior' of the sixth century. Byzantine jurists of the tenth and eleventh century did not, however, distinguish these anonymous authors. Apparently, these later jurists believed that the person who wrote the *Digest summa* and the scholia on that *summa* was one and the same person. As a consequence, they simply spoke of 'the Anonymos'.

This misunderstanding on the part of the later Byzantine jurists can be explained if one takes into account the manuscripts. Later Byzantine jurists saw manuscripts of the Greek *Digest summa* already filled in with marginal notes, and thus had good reason to believe that both the *summa* and these notes, the scholia, had been written by the same author. There are, however, arguments that prove that these scholia were written by someone else, not the Anonymos of the sixth century but someone who came after him in the following generation, 'the Anonymos Junior'. To start, as the first of the following fragments shows (TEXT 6.1), an unknown author identified as Anonymos (that is, as we now know, 'the Anonymos Junior') who wrote the *paragraphai* (παρέγραψα = I wrote a *paragraphè*) to the *summa* was also the author of a book on legacies and gifts *mortis causa* (Μονόβιβλος περὶ ληγάτων καὶ μόρτις καῦσα δωρεῶν).[11] These *paragraphai* are now *Basilica* scholia. In the second fragment (TEXT 6.2), we read that the person who was called 'Enantiophanes' by the compilers of the *Basilica* scholia, who wrote *paragraphai* to the *summa*, was the author of a book on legacies and gifts *mortis causa*. It follows that this Anonymos ('the Anonymos Junior') must be identified with Enantiophanes.

9 Around 717, the so-called iconoclastic period begins in Byzantium, on which see below, pp. 99–100.

10 On the *Basilica* text and scholia, see below, pp. 123–129, 137–143 and 152–164.

11 A gift *mortis causa* was a gift that was given in the expectation that the person making the gift would soon die.

TEXT 6.1 BS 2806/16–26 (scholion Pc 7 ad B. 47,3,42 = D. 39,6,42) ≈

TEXT 6.2 BS 2796/15–21 (scholion Pc 1 ad B. 47,3,25 = D. 39,6,25)
Identity and date of 'the Anonymos Junior' and 'Enantiophanes'

TEXT 6.1	TEXT 6.2
Τοῦ Ἀνωνύμου. [...]	Τοῦ Ἐναντιοφανοῦς
Εἰσὶ δὲ καὶ ἄλλαι πολλαὶ διαφοραί, ἃς ἀνήγαγον ἐν τῷ γραφέντι μοι **μονοβιβ. περὶ ληγάτων καὶ μορτισκαῦσα δωρεῶν**, ἐγγεγραμμέναι διγ. α' τοῦ λ' βιβ.	Διαφορὰ δέ, ὅτι ..., καθὰ ἐν τῷ θ'. διγ. τούτου τοῦ τιτ. παρέγραψα. [...] Εἰσὶ δὲ καὶ ἄλλαι πολλαὶ διαφοραὶ ληγάτου καὶ μορτισκαῦσα δωρεᾶς, ἃς ἀνήγαγον ἐν τῷ γραφέντι μοι **μονοβιβ. περὶ ληγάτων καὶ μορτισκαῦσα δωρεῶν.**
Of 'the Anonymos'. [...] And there are also many other differences, which I have put forward **in my monograph about legacies and gifts *mortis causa***, and which are found in Dig. 30, 1.	Of Enantiophanes. The difference is [...], as I have pointed out in a marginal note [a 'paragraphè': παρέγραψα = have written in the margin] to fragment 9 of this title [= D. 39,6,9]. [...] And there are also many other differences, which I have put forward **in my monograph about legacies and gifts *mortis causa*.**

There is some additional proof in the following fragments. As we can see from the following two fragments (TEXT 7.1 and TEXT 7.2), the same text is preserved in two different *Basilica* scholia, one of which is credited to Anonymos, the other of which is attributed to Enantiophanes.

TEXT 7.1 BS 2739/13–17 (scholion Pc 2 ad B. 46,2,4 = D. 4,5,5) ≈

TEXT 7.2 BS 2739/26–31 (scholion Pc 5 ad B. 46,2,4 = D. 4,5,5)
Identity and date of 'the Anonymos Junior' and 'Enantiophanes'

TEXT 7.1	TEXT 7.2
Ὁ Ἀνώνυμος 'ὡς ἐν τῇ ἀπαγορεύσει τοῦ πυρὸς καὶ τοῦ ὕδατος' ἔχει, πρὸς ὅ φησιν· ἐν τῷ ις'. τιτ. τῆς α'. ἰνστιτ. τῆς μέσης φησὶν καπίτις δεμινουτίονος τὴν	Τοῦ Ἐναντιοφανοῦς. Ἀνάγνωθι καὶ βιβ. μη.' τιτ. ιγ'. διγ. γ'. καὶ τιτ. ιθ'. διγ. β'.Ἐν μὲν τῷ ις'. τιτ. τῆς α'. ἰνστιτ. τῆς μέσης φησὶν ἐναλλαγῆς καταστάσεως τὴν τοιαύτην τιμωρίαν καὶ μόνην τὴν

TEXT 7.1 & 7.2 (*cont.*)

<table>
<tr><td>τοιαύτην τιμωρίαν καὶ μόνως τὴν πολιτείαν, οὐ μὴν τὴν ἐλευθερίαν φθείρειν· ἐν δὲ τῷ ε'. διγ. τοῦ ιγ'. τιτ. τοῦ ν'. βιβ. καὶ τῆς μεγάλης αὐτὴν λέγει καὶ φθείρει⟨ν⟩ τὴν ἐλευθερίαν.</td><td>πολιτείαν, οὐ μὴν τὴν ἐλευθερίαν φθείρει⟨ν⟩· ἐν δὲ τῷ γ'. (5)[13] διγ. τοῦ ιγ' τιτ. τοῦ ν' βιβ. καὶ τῆς μεγάλης αὐτὴν ⟨λέγει καὶ⟩ φθείρειν τὴν ἐλευθερίαν.'Εκ τῆς κβ'. νεαρᾶς αὕτη ἡ ποινὴ εἰς περιορισμὸν μετέπεσεν.</td></tr>
<tr><td>The Anonymos has 'as in the interdiction from fire and water'. And he adds to this:
In Inst. 1,16 he says that such a penalty is an instance of medium-grade capitis deminutio[12] and that it merely entails the loss of citizenship, not of freedom.
In Dig. 50,13,5, however, he says that it is large-grade and that it does entail the loss of freedom.</td><td>Of Enantiophanes. Read also D. 48,13,3 and 48,19,2.
In Inst. 1,16 he says that such a penalty is an instance of medium-grade degradation of legal status, and that it merely entails the loss of citizenship, not of freedom. In D. 50,13,3 (in fact D. 50,13,5)[14] however, he says that it is large-grade and that it does entail the loss of freedom.
According to Novel 22 this penalty was changed into banishment.</td></tr>
</table>

Note that in the introduction of the left-hand scholion (TEXT 7.1) we read: 'The Anonymos has (the translation) … to which he adds (as a *paragraphè*): …'. We can see from this line that later Byzantine jurists considered the author who wrote the *summa* (whom we call 'the Anonymos Senior') and the one who wrote the scholia (= the *paragraphai*) on the *summa* (whom we call 'the Anonymos Junior') to be the same person.

The next step is to identify this so-called Enantiophanes. The following fragment (TEXT 8) helps us learn more about him. This fragment is taken from the *Nomocanon of Fourteen Titles*, a work to be discussed later when we look at canon law.[15]

12 In Roman law, *capitis deminutio* referred to the deterioration of status and it had different grades; *capitis deminutio media* was the loss of citizenship and family rights, mostly by way of punishment.

13 The number (5) is an addition by the editors of the *Basilica* Groningen edition (BT 2739/29). In other words, the correct number should have been 5 and not 3, and therefore the correct citation should have been D. 50,13,5.

14 See the observation in the preceding note.

15 See below, pp. 195–198.

TEXT 8 ***Nomocanon of Fourteen Titles*, 4,1**

κεφ. ι'. Περὶ ἐγκύου βαπτιζομένης. Συνόδου Νεοκαισαρείας κανὼν ϛ'.	Chapter 10. About baptizing pregnant women: Synod of Neocaesarea canon 6.
Καί τοι ἐν τῇ α.' διατ. τοῦ δ.' τιτ. τοῦ κε.' βιβλίου τῶν διατάξεων φησι, τὸ κυοφορούμενον εἶναι μέρος τῆς ἐγκύου·ἐν δὲ τῇ ι.' διατ. τοῦ γ.' τίτ. τοῦ μα.' βιβλίου, καὶ βιβλίου ν.' τίτ. ιϛ.' διατ. κϛ.', ὅτι τὸ κυοφορούμενον οὐκ ἔστι μέρος τῆς μητρός· καὶ ἄλλα δὲ διάφορα νόμιμα περὶ τούτου συνήγαγον **ἐν τῇ γραφείσῃ μοι περὶ ἐναντιοφανειῶν μόνῃ βίβλῳ**.[16]	In D. 25,4,1[17] he says that the unborn child is a part of the pregnant woman, although in D. 41,10,3 and 50,16,26 he says that the unborn child is not a part of the mother. And there are many other legal differences about this matter, which I have collected **in my monograph 'About seeming contradictions'** (περὶ ἐναντιοφανειῶν).

TEXT 9 **D. 25,4,1 (referred to in the *Nomocanon of the Fourteen Titles*, 4,1)[18]**

De inspiciendo ventre custodiendoque partu.[19]	Concerning the examination of pregnant women, and the precautions to be taken with reference to their delivery.
Ulpianus libro vicesimo quarto ad edictum pr. *Temporibus divorum fratrum cum hoc incidisset, ut maritus quidem praegnatem mulierem diceret, uxor negaret, consulti Valerio Prisciano praetori urbano rescripserunt in haec verba: 'Novam rem desiderare Rutilius Severus videtur, ut uxori, quae ab eo diverterat et se non esse praegnatem profiteatur, custodem apponat, et ideo nemo mirabitur, si nos quoque novum consilium et remedium*	Ulpian, *Edict*, book 24: pr. In the time of the deified brothers, a husband said his wife was pregnant, but the wife denied it. On being consulted about this, they addressed a rescript to Valerius Priscianus, the urban praetor, which stated: 'Rutilius Severus seems to be asking for something new in applying for a person to observe his wife, whom he has divorced and who asserts that she is not pregnant. So no one will be surprised

16 The Greek text is cited from RhP, vol. 1, p. 124.

17 It is strange that the edition of RhP mentions 'διατάξεων' instead of 'διγέστων', as one would expect.

18 The Latin of the following *Digest* fragments are cited from the edition by Th. Mommsen (= D.) and the English translations are from A. Watson, ed. and trans., *The Digest of Justinian*, 4 vols., Philadelphia: 1985 (rev. edn, Philadelphia: 1998), here vol. 2, p. 282 and vol. 4, p. 449, reprinted with permission of the University of Pennsylvania Press.

19 In Watson, *Digest*, the translation of this title reads: 'The examination of pregnant women and the observation of delivery'.

TEXT 9 (*cont.*)

suggeramus. igitur si perstat in eadem postulatione, commodissimum est eligi honestissimae feminae domum, in qua domitia veniat, et ibi tres obstetrices probatae et artis et fidei, quae a te adsumptae fuerint, eam inspiciant. et si quidem vel omnes vel duae renuntiaverint praegnatem videri, tunc persuadendum mulieri erit, ut perinde custodem admittat atque si ipsa hoc desiderasset: quod si enixa non fuerit, sciat maritus ad invidiam existimationemque suam pertinere, ut non immerito possit videri captasse hoc ad aliquam mulieris iniuriam. si autem vel omnes vel plures non esse gravidam renuntiaverint, nulla causa custodiendi erit.'

if we suggest a new plan and remedy. If the husband persists in this demand, it will be best for the house of an extremely respectable woman to be chosen into which Domitia will go, and that three skilled and trustworthy midwives selected by you examine her. If all of them or two of them announce that she appears to be pregnant, the woman must be asked to allow a guard[20] in just as if she wanted this herself. If she does not give birth, the husband should be aware that his reputation and honor are involved, and he will quite rightly be held to have devised this to injure his wife. If, however, all of the women or the majority of them declare that she is not carrying a child, there will be no reason to keep her under guard.'[21]

1. *Ex hoc rescripto evidentissime apparet senatus consulta de liberis agnoscendis locum non habuisse, si mulier dissimularet se praegnatem vel etiam negaret, nec immerito: partus enim antequam edatur, mulieris portio est vel viscerum. post editum plane partum a muliere iam potest maritus iure suo filium per interdictum desiderare aut exhiberi sibi aut ducere permitti. extra ordinem igitur princeps in causa necessaria subvenit.* [...]

1. It is quite clear from this rescript that the *senatus consulta* on the recognition of children will not apply if the woman pretended she was pregnant or even denied it. This is not unreasonable, since the child is part of the woman or her insides before it is born. After the child is born, the husband can legally demand the boy from the woman by using an interdict, or have the child shown to him or be allowed to remove him. Thus, the emperor provides a procedure *extra ordinem* here where necessary. [...]

20 We prefer the word 'guard' to the word 'observer' used in Watson's translation.

21 In Watson, *Digest*, the translation reads: '... will be no reason for an observation'.

TEXT 10 **D. 50,16,26 (also referred to in the *Nomocanon of the Fourteen Titles*, 4,1)**

Ulpianus libro sexto decimo ad edictum. pr. *Partum non esse partem rei furtivae Scaevola libro undecimo quaestionum scribit.*	Ulpian, *Edict, book* 16 pr. Scaevola writes in the eleventh book of his *Questions* that offspring are not part of something stolen.

It is stated that the author of the *Nomocanon of the Fourteen Titles* also wrote a monograph about 'seeming' or 'apparent' contradictions (*peri enantiophaneion*, περὶ ἐναντιοφανειῶν, see TEXT 8). We can therefore identify the author of the *Nomocanon of the Fourteen Titles* as Enantiophanes, the author of the legal treatise 'On seeming contradictions'. We know that this *Nomocanon* dates from the first quarter of the seventh century and this information helps us date 'the Anonymos Junior'. In other words, 'the Anonymos Junior' who wrote notes to the *Digest summa* was a highly critical person; he drew attention to contradictions in the *Digest* and actually wrote a book on the subject. However, he obviously did not dare to call them contradictions—not least because Justinian had proudly declared that there are no contradictions to be found in the *Digest*—so he called them 'seeming, apparent contradictions'. In fact, it is fair to say that we cannot be entirely sure how seriously he took Justinian's claims of consistency, perhaps he was not so much afraid as he was being ironic.

5 Early Legal Treatises: *De Actionibus* and *Rhopai*

We have already mentioned two legal treatises from this period, both written by 'the Anonymos Junior': one was about the apparent contradictions in the *Digest* and the other was about the difference between a legacy and a gift *mortis causa*, i.e. a gift made in contemplation of approaching death. Only fragments have been preserved from these two legal treatises. There are, however, two other texts that deal with special subjects and can roughly be dated to the seventh century. Unfortunately, we know nothing about their authors. Both deal with the law of procedure. The first treatise is about actions and is a rather simple text; it gives information on the different actions and when to use them. It looks a bit like an aid for learning the Latin names of these actions: the format of the text is, 'if situation X, then use the action called Y', without any further explanation or detail:

TEXT 11 ***De actionibus*** **(περὶ ἀγωγῶν) 7–10**[22]

7. Ἐπὶ δὲ τῶν περσοναλίων· εἰ χρέος ἀπαιτούμεθα, τὸν δανειακὸν ὁρισόμεθα *condicticium*. 8. Ἐπὶ δὲ τοῖς τόκοις τὴν *ex stipulatu*, ἤτοι ἀγωγὴν μὴ συγχωροῦσαν ζημιωθῆναί με τόκοις ἀλλὰ ἀπαιτοῦσαν αὐτούς. 9. Εἰ δὲ ὁ πράτης ἐνάγει τῷ ἀγοραστῇ, τὴν *ex empto* [...] εἰ δὲ ὁ ἀγοραστὴς τῷ πράτῃ, τὴν *ex vendito*[...] 10. Εἰ δε ὁ μισθώσας ἐνάγει τῷ μισθωσαμένῳ, τὴν *locati* [...] εἰ δὲ ὁ μισθωσάμενος τῷ μισθώσαντι, τὴν conducti [...]	7. In cases of personal obligations: if we claim a loan, we shall define the *condictio* of loan. 8. In cases of interest, the action *ex stipulatu*, i.e. the action that does not let me suffer damage by losing interest but that claims it. 9. If the buyer takes action against the seller, it is the *actio ex empto* [...] if the seller against the buyer, then the *actio ex vendito* [...] 10. If the lessor takes action against the lessee, it is with the *actio locati* [...] if the lessor against the lessee, then with the *actio conducti* [...].

The second monograph is called *Rhopai* (ῥοπαί), which means 'moments', 'terms', or 'time limits', and this is rather a strange work. It presents legal texts according to the periods of time for which a specific text remains legally relevant. The author also specifies his sources. The text starts with the shortest possible period, namely just one 'moment' = *rhopè* (ῥοπή):

TEXT 12 ***Rhopai*****: 'about deadlines, from one moment to a century' (περὶ χρόνων προθεσμίας ἀπὸ ῥοπῆς ἕως ἑκατὸν ἐνιαυτῶν)**[23]

I Περὶ ῥοπῆς 1. Arescusa, ἐὰν γ' παῖδας τέκῃ, ἐλευθέρα ἐν διαθήκῃ ἐγγραφεῖσα, ἐν πρώτῳ τοκετῷ ἕνα ἔτεκεν, ἐν δευτέρῳ τρεῖς ἔτεκε παῖδας. ἐζητήθη ποῖος ἐξ αὐτῶν ἐλευθερίᾳ ἐτέχθη καὶ λέγει ὁ Τρύφων ὅτι ὁ ἔσχατος ἐξ ἐλευθέρας γαστρὸς ἐτέχθη. ἐπειδὴ γὰρ ἡ αἵρεσις ἡ τῇ ἐλευθερίᾳ ἐπιτεθεῖσα τῷ	I 'The single moment' 1. Arescusa, who is said in a will to be free as soon as she has given birth to three children, bears one at the first delivery and three children in the second. The question is which of them was born from a free woman. Tryphon says that the last one was delivered from a free womb. For since the condition attached

22 The Greek text is cited from the edition of Fr. Sitzia, *De actionibus* (Milan: 1973).

23 The Greek text is cited from the edition of Fr. Sitzia, *Le Rhopai* (Naples: 1984).

TEXT 12 (*cont.*)

τοκετῷ τοῦ τρίτου ἐπληρώθη, καὶ συνωμολόγηται ἡ φύσις οὐκ ἐπιτρέπειν δύο ἐν μίᾳ καὶ τῇ αὐτῇ ὁρμῇ τίκτεσθαι, ἀλλὰ κατὰ τάξιν ἕκαστον καὶ ῥοπὴν μεῖναι ἐν τῷ μεταξὺ τοῦ τοκετοῦ τοῦ κατὰ πρώτην καὶ δευτέραν τάξιν τεχθέντος, διὰ τοῦτο καὶ ῥοπήν φαμεν τῷ τοιούτῳ χαρίζεσθαι τὴν ἐλευθερίαν. ὡς βι. α' τῶν διγ. τίτλος ε' διγ. ιε'. (D. 1,5,15)	to the slave's freedom was fulfilled by the birth of the third, and since we all agree that nature does not permit that two are born on one and the same effort but that they come out in succession, so that there is a moment between the births of the first and the second, for that reason we say that there also exists a moment when freedom is granted him. Thus book 1 of the *Digest* title 5 fragment 15.
2. Ulp. ταὐτόν ἐστι κἂν ἐξ ἀρχῆς δύο καὶ μετὰ ταῦτα δύο ἔτεκεν. (D. 1,5,16)	2. Ulp(ianus). The same is also true when there were two children to begin with and she gave birth to twins afterwards.

TEXT 13 **Source behind *Rhopai* 1: D. 1,5,15–16**[24]

D. 1,5,15 *Tryphoninus libro decimo disputationum.* *Arescusa, si tres pepererit libera esse testamento iussa, primo partu unum, secundo tres peperit: quaesitum est, an et quis eorum liber esset. haec condicio libertati adposita iam implenda mulieri est. sed non dubitari debet, quin ultimus liber nascatur: nec enim natura permisit simul uno impetu duos infantes de utero matris excedere, ut ordine incerto nascentium non appareat, uter in servitute libertateve nascatur. incipiente igitur partu existens condicio efficit,*	D. 1,5,15 Tryphoninus, *Disputations*, book 10: There was a testamentary instruction that if Arescusa should bear three children she should be free. She bore one child at the first birth, but triplets at the second. The question is whether any and if so which of the triplets is free. The condition set upon her freedom must be fulfilled by the woman. There should, however, be no doubt but that the last triplet is born free. Nor indeed has nature allowed that two babies can get out of their mother's womb at the same time with one push, so that from the uncertain order of their being born, there is no way

24 The Latin text of the *Digest* passages are cited from the edition by Th. Mommsen (= D.) and the English translations are from A. Watson, ed. and trans., *The Digest of Justinian*, 4 vols., Philadelphia: 1985 (rev. edn, Philadelphia: 1998), here vol. 1, p. 16, reprinted with permission of the University of Pennsylvania Press.

TEXT 13 (*cont.*)

ut ex libera edatur quod postea nascitur, veluti si quaelibet alia condicio libertati mulieris adposita parturiente ea existat. vel manumissa sub hac condicione, si decem milia heredi Titiove dederit, eo momento quo parit per alium impleverit condicionem: iam libera peperisse credenda est. D. 1,5,16 *Ulpianus libro sexto disputationum. Idem erit, si eadem Arescusa primo duo pepererat, postea geminos ediderat: dicendum est enim non posse dici utrumque ingenuum nasci, sed eum qui posterior nascitur. quaestio ergo facti potius est, non iuris.*	of telling which is born in slavery and which in freedom. Therefore, from the onset of labor, the postulated condition has the effect that the one born last comes forth out of a free woman, just as if any other condition whatever had been set for her freedom and had come to pass while she was giving birth. For example, she is manumitted subject to this condition, that she give ten thousand to the heir or to Titius, and at the very moment of her labour, she fulfils the condition by the hand of another. In that case, it must be supposed that she gave birth as a free woman. D. 1,5,16 Ulpian, *Disputations*, book 6: The answer would be the same, if Arescusa first bore two children and then had twins. For the point is that it cannot be said that both twins are born as free born; only the second born is. So the question is one of fact rather than of law.

6 The *Ecloga*

The period from approximately 717 (or 726) up to 842 encapsulates the so-called iconoclastic period in Byzantine history. The word 'iconoclast' literally means 'icon-smasher', 'image-destroyer'. The followers of the iconoclastic movement were opposed to icon veneration. Throughout this period—with a short interruption between 787 and 813—the display of all figurative art, including icons in the church or anywhere else, was forbidden throughout the Byzantine empire. This is not the place to discuss the reasons and theories behind this movement. In short, some scholars suggest that the iconoclastic emperors wanted to refine religious practice because they believed that God was punishing them because of their idolatry: for example, attacks made against the Byzantine empire by the Arabs during this period, or various natural disasters such as the eruption of the volcano on the island of Thera in 727, could have been viewed as divine punishment. Others scholars suggest that there were economic reasons behind the iconoclastic movement: for example, the emperors confiscated monastic and ecclesiastical property by using the iconoclastic movement as an excuse and justification for so doing.

After AD 842, icons were once again allowed. The Byzantine emperors who ruled after the iconoclastic period considered that their own beliefs were the only correct ones, constituting the right doctrine, the Orthodoxia.[25] In other words, they regarded the iconoclastic emperors as heretics. As far as the legal field is concerned, this meant that hardly any laws from the Iconoclastic period survive. There is one important exception. This is the *Ecloga*, a law book published during the iconoclastic period by Emperor Leo III and his son Constantine V. These two emperors belonged to the Isaurian dynasty, a family that ruled Byzantium from 717 to 802. The *Ecloga* most probably dates to 741. The word *Ecloga* literally means 'selection' (of laws). In its heading we read that it is an abridged selection of laws from the *Institutes*, *Digest*, *Code* and the *Novels* of Justinian, and that this law, i.e. the *Ecloga*, is meant to be more humane, milder or 'more philanthropic': ''Εκλογὴ τῶν νόμων ἐν συντόμῳ γενομένη παρὰ Λέοντος καὶ Κωνσταντίνου, τῶν σοφῶν καὶ φιλευσεβῶν βασιλέων, ἀπὸ τῶν ἰνστιτούτων, τῶν διγέστων, τοῦ κώδικος, τῶν νεαρῶν τοῦ μεγάλου Ἰουστινιανοῦ διατάξεων καὶ ἐπιδιόρθωσις εἰς τὸ φιλανθρωπότερον ...' ('An abridged selection of the *Institutes*, the *Digest* the *Code*, the *Novels* of the great Justinian and corrected to be more humane under Leo and Constantine, wise and piety-loving emperors ...').

The concept of 'φιλανθρωπία' (*philanthropia* = mildness) played an important role in Byzantium. A good emperor must first of all be 'φιλάνθρωπος', that is, he had to show mildness and mercy, and this Byzantine virtue is reflected in many sources. The idea of being mild and merciful fits the idea of a virtuous emperor who—just like a father to his children—cares about his subjects and is willing to show mildness. Yet, the concept of *philanthropia* has another, higher-level resonance in the Byzantine world. It is directly linked to the relationship between the emperor and God. According to the Byzantines, the emperor was thought to be the mirror of Christ, the mirror of God and, just as God was merciful, so too should a good emperor follow His example. Thus, being mild and merciful were qualities necessary for a good emperor. Mildness and mercy are also related to Byzantine justice more generally. As mentioned in several Byzantine sources, a good judge had to be wise and fair, but he also had to display mildness in his decisions.

The relationship between the Byzantine emperor and God is also something that the prefaces to legal texts often stress. Emperors emphasise in prefaces that they are responsible for justice because God has placed them in their position and that good emperors should diligently manage legal affairs. Biblical references are common in context of legal prefaces. TEXT 14, containing a fragment of the emperors' preface to the *Ecloga*, is a characteristic example:

---

25 The word 'Orthodoxia' derives from the Greek words 'ὀρθός', which means 'correct, right' and 'δόξα', which means 'opinion'.

TEXT 14 From the *Ecloga*, preface, lines 32–51[26]

Ὅθεν ταῖς τοιαύταις μερίμναις ἐνασχολούμενοι καὶ πρὸς τὴν τῶν ἀρεσκόντων Θεῷ καὶ τῷ κοινῷ συμφερόντων εὕρεσιν ἀκοίμητον τὸν νοῦν καταστήσαντες τήν τε δικαιοσύνην πάντων τῶν ἐπιγείων προτιμήσαντες ὡς πρόξενον τῶν οὐρανίων ὑπάρχουσαν καὶ τομωτέραν ξίφους παντὸς τῇ τοῦ ἐπ' αὐτῇ θεραπευομένου δυνάμει κατὰ τῶν πολεμίων τυγχάνουσαν ἐν πολλαῖς τε βίβλοις τὰ ὑπὸ τῶν προβεβασιλευκότων νενομοθετημένα γεγράφθαι γινώσκοντες καὶ τοῖς μὲν δυσδιάγνωστον τὸν ἐν αὐτοῖς περιεχόμενον νοῦν, τοῖς δὲ καὶ παντελῶς ἀδιάγνωστον, καὶ μάλιστα τοῖς ἔξω τῆς θεοφυλάκτου ταύτης καὶ βασιλίδος ἡμῶν πόλεως εἰδότες τυγχάνοντα, μετακαλεσάμενοι τούς τε ἐνδοξοτάτους ἡμῶν πατρικίους τόν τε ἐνδοξότατον κυέστορα καὶ τοὺς ἐνδοξοτάτους ὑπάτους καὶ ἀντιγραφεῖς καὶ λοιποὺς τὸν τοῦ Θεοῦ φόβον ἔχοντας πάσας τὰς αὐτὰς βίβλους συναθροισθῆναι παρ' ἡμῖν ἐκελεύσαμεν καὶ πάσας μετ' ἐπιμελοῦς ἐπισκέψεως ἀνακρίναντες διά τε τῶν ἐν αὐταῖς βίβλοις εὐθέτως ἐμφερομένων διά τε τῶν παρ' ἡμῶν νεαρῶς θεσπισθέντων τῶν ἐπισυχναζόντων πραγμάτων καὶ συναλλαγμάτων τὰς κρίσεις καὶ τὰς καταλλήλους τῶν ἐγκλημάτων ποινὰς ἐν τῇδε τῇ βίβλῳ φανερωτέρως τε καὶ λεπτοτέρως

Whence, busied with such cares and watching with a sleepless mind the discovery of those things which please God and are conducive to the public interest, preferring Justice to all things terrestrial as the promise of things celestial, and as being, by the power of Him who is worshipped in her, sharper than any sword against foes; knowing moreover that the laws enacted by previous Emperors have been written in many books and being aware that the sense thereof is to some difficult to understand, to others absolutely unintelligible, and especially to those who do not reside in this our imperial God-protected city, we have called the most illustrious Patricians, our most illustrious *quaestor*,[27] and our most illustrious consuls and *antigrapheis*,[28] and others who have the fear of God, and we have ordered that all these books should be collected in our Palace; and having examined all with careful attention, going through both the contents of those books and our own enactments, we considered it right that the decisions in frequently occurring cases and the laws of contract and the penalties of crimes should be

26 The Greek text is from the edition by L. Burgmann, *Ecloga. Das Gesetzbuch Leons III. und Konstantinos' V* (Frankfurt am Main: 1983).

27 The *quaestor of the sacred palace* was a high-ranking official in the late Roman Empire and early Byzantine period who was responsible for drafting laws. By the eighth and ninth centuries, the *quaestor* had lost some of the office's earlier duties. He acted as a judge and, in the ninth century—marking a departure from earlier practices—he had his own staff. For all this, see ODB, vol. 3, pp. 1765–1766.

28 The *antigrapheis* (= copyists) were subordinate officials to the *quaestor*. They were successors of the late Roman *magistri scriniorum* and acted as secretaries, but it is not clear what their actual functions were when they were moved to the department of the *quaestor*. For all this, see ODB, vol. 1, p. 112.

TEXT 14 (*cont.*)

ἀναληφθῆναι ἁρμόδιον ἡγησάμεθα πρὸς εὐσύνοπτον τῆς τῶν τοιούτων εὐσεβῶν νόμων δυνάμεως εἴδησιν καὶ τὴν ἐν εὐκρινείᾳ τῶν πραγμάτων εὐλύτωσιν καὶ τὴν δικαίαν τῶν πλημμελούντων ἐπεξέλευσιν καὶ τὴν τῶν ἐπιρρεπῶς πρὸς τὸ πλημμελεῖν διακειμένων ἀναστολὴν καὶ διόρθωσιν.	repeated more lucidly and minutely, to ensure a synoptic [good, overall] knowledge of the force of such pious laws, and to facilitate the decision of such causes clearly, and to ensure a just prosecution of the guilty and to restrain and correct those who have a natural propensity for evil-doing.

This single long sentence from the preface to the *Ecloga* expresses the intentions of the emperors. Leo III and Constantine V present themselves as good and responsible emperors because they issue good legislation. They have assembled a committee of competent lawyers and nobles who have studied the law books and have, accordingly, produced a new law book which, according to the emperors, is synoptic and superior to the ones that existed before. The description of the work involved in the process reminds us of Justinian and his legislative activities, but there is a significant difference in the scale of work behind Justinian's *Corpus* compared to the *Ecloga*. As we have seen in an earlier chapter, Justinian produced a monumental codification, whereas the *Ecloga* remains a more modest text. In any case, based on this part of the *Ecloga*'s preface, we can presume that Leo III and his son had intended to emulate Justinian's activities and follow his example; perhaps they had even intended to supersede Justinian and 'steal' some of his glory as well.

The *Ecloga* is divided into eighteen titles, as follows:

Titles 1–8	Mainly the law of persons
Titles 9–13	Mainly the law of obligations
Titles 14–15	Law of procedure
Titles 16–18	Some particular subjects (for example, the distribution of war booty)
Title 17	Criminal law

The seventeenth title, which deals with criminal law, is a very long title and comprises approximately one third of the *Ecloga*.

As already mentioned, the aim of the *Ecloga* was to improve existing legislation so that it would have a milder character: to make it more humane. How was this 'more philanthropic character' reflected in this law book? The most convincing traces of a milder approach are found in the field of criminal law. Indeed, the *Ecloga* abolished various cruel methods of death penalties such as crucifixion and execution by drowning. Capital punishment by cruel execution was restricted to two crimes: i. when someone committed arson in an inhabited area he was put to death by burning and, ii. when a robbery had been committed with murder, the wrongdoer was executed by 'furca'.[29] In the *Ecloga* we find many mutilation penalties, such as the amputation of noses or hands. In some cases, the mutilations also served as a measure to prevent the wrongdoer from committing the same crime again. For example, in the crime of adultery, the punishment was to have one's nose cut off, which made the convicted person less attractive and thus limited the chances for him to commit sexual crimes again. Some of the corporal punishments in the *Ecloga* can be considered as 'mirror punishments', an application of the *lex talionis* ('an eye for an eye'). Examples include cutting off the tongue of someone who has sworn a false oath and has committed perjury, or cutting off the hand of someone who has counterfeited money (see TEXT 15). We quote in the following text some characteristic examples of the *Ecloga*'s title addressing criminal law.

TEXT 15 From the seventeenth title of the *Ecloga*: penalties for criminal cases (Ποινάλιος τῶν ἐγκληματικῶν κεφαλαίων)[30]

17.2 Ὁ ἐκ δικαστικῆς ψήφου ἢ καὶ ἐπὶ μαρτυρίᾳ παραγόμενος ἢ ἐξ ἐπαγωγῆς ἀντιδίκου ἐφαπτόμενος τῶν ἁγίων τοῦ Θεοῦ εὐαγγελίων καὶ ἐφομνύμενος, ἐπίορκος δὲ μετὰ ταῦτα ἀποδεικνύμενος, γλωσσοκοπείσθω.	17.2 Anyone who holds the holy gospels of God and swears on them during a judicial inquiry, either while bearing witness or bringing a dispute, and afterward is shown to have committed perjury, shall have their tongue cut out.
17.18 Οἱ παραχαρακταὶ μονήτας χειροκοπείσθωσαν.	17.18 Forgers of money shall have their hand cut off.
17.26 Εἴ τις εἰς ὕπανδρον σύντεκνον αὐτοῦ τι τοιοῦτον εὑρεθῇ ποιῶν, καὶ αὐτὸν καὶ ταύτην πρὸς τῇ ἐκτομῇ τῆς ῥινὸς καὶ σφοδρῶς τύπτεσθαι.	17.26 If anyone should be found in such a way to have married their godparent, both shall be severely beaten besides having their noses cut off.
17.27 Ὁ εἰς γυναῖκα ὕπανδρον μοιχεύων ῥινοκοπείσθω καὶ αὐτὸς καὶ ἡ μοιχαλίς, ὡς ἐντεῦθεν χωρισμοῦ γινομένου καὶ	17.27 Any man who commits adultery with a married woman shall have his nose cut off; and likewise the adulteress, who henceforth

29 Execution by *furca* or gallows was a brutal capital punishment whereby the individual sentenced to death was hanged from a large, fork-shaped stake.

30 The Greek text is from the edition by L. Burgmann, *Ecloga. Das Gesetzbuch Leons III. und Konstantinos' V* (Frankfurt am Main: 1983). The English translation is from M. Humphreys, *The Law of the Isaurian Era: The Ecloga and its Appendices* (Liverpool: 2017).

TEXT 15 (*cont.*)

ἀπωλείας τέκνων προερχομένης καὶ τοῦ κυριακοῦ λόγου μὴ φυλαττομένου τοῦ διδασκόντος, ὅτι ὁ Θεὸς *εἰς σάρκα μίαν* τούτους συνήνωσεν. μετὰ δὲ τὸ ῥινοκοπηθῆναι τὴν μοιχαλίδα λαμβάνειν αὐτὴν τὰ ἴδια αὐτῆς πράγματα, ἅπερ εἰσήγαγε τῷ ἀνδρὶ αὐτῆς, καὶ μηδὲν ἕτερον, τὸν δὲ μοιχὸν ἐκ τῆς ἰδίας γυναικὸς μὴ χωρίζεσθαι, εἰ καὶ ἐρινοκοπήθη. [...]	is divorced and lost to her children, since she has not kept the words of our Lord, who teaches that God had joined them together as 'one flesh'. And after their noses have been cut off, the adulteress shall receive her own property, which she had brought to her husband, and nothing else. But the adulterer shall not be separated from his wife, even though his nose is cut. [...]

Another attempt to increase mildness in the *Ecloga* can be seen in efforts to achieve some measure of social parity in the punishments meted out for certain offences, regardless of whether the offender was noble or poor. For example, the penalty for some crimes was twelve whips of the lash for anyone found guilty of that crime, irrespective of their social status, whether they were noble or poor. In other cases, however, criminals who had a noble background received preferential treatments. We can therefore definitely not speak of consistency in practice when it comes to closing the gaps in the execution of punishment based on social differences.

The *Ecloga* was an important work in the field of criminal law, and later generations of emperors, even if they despised the work of the iconoclast Isaurian emperors, ended up adopting many of the criminal provisions as articulated and included in the *Ecloga*. The fact that this law text was popular is also apparent in its rich manuscript tradition. Nearly one hundred manuscripts of the *Ecloga* have survived. Furthermore, the work has been translated into several Slavic languages, along with Armenian and Arabic.

The *Ecloga* is the most important contribution from the iconoclastic period to the legal field, but there are also three other legal works that we will discuss in this chapter. These works were not promulgated by an emperor and we do not know the identities of their authors. In fact, we are not even that sure about their dating, but it has been suggested that they date from the eight century and they must be related to the *Ecloga*, at least based on the manuscript tradition, because we find them as an appendix to the *Ecloga*. These three legal works are known as the *leges speciales*, laws about special subjects: one for farmers, one for soldiers, one for sailors. A common characteristic of these three works is that they are more simple and down-to-earth texts than the average imperial law. Much has been written on them concerning their origin, nature and application. In the following, we will only briefly refer to the laws for farmers and soldiers and present a few characteristic fragments of these sources. More attention will be dedicated to the law for sailors, because it is also directly related to the *Basilica*, as we will see.

7 The *Farmer's Law* and the *Military Law*

The *Farmer's Law* (Γεωργικὸς Νόμος, Georgikos Nomos) regulates issues concerning agriculture, peasantry and livestock. We quote in the following examples two fragments from this collection. The first deals with problems that might arise between farmers, such as the theft of a farmer's tool. The second is about cowherds and mostly deals with the duties that cowherds owe towards the owners of the cattle. Note in both texts how practical the problems and solutions are, and how simple the language is, especially when compared to the bombastic style of the preface to the *Ecloga*:

TEXT 16 The *Farmer's Law*, chapters 12, 22–25, 30 and 59[31]

12. Ἐὰν γεωργὸς λάβῃ παρά τινος γεωργοῦ ἀπορήσαντος τὴν ἡμισείαν ἄμπελον πρὸς ἐργασίαν καὶ οὐ κλαδεύσῃ αὐτὴν ὡς τὸ πρέπον σκάψῃ τε καὶ χαρακώσας διασκαφίσῃ, μηδὲν ἐκ τῆς ἐπικαρπίας λαμβανέτω.	12. If a farmer gets from another, disabled farmer half the latter's vineyard for cultivation, but fails to prune at the right moment and to work it with a hack and to bind the shoots onto sticks, then he will receive nothing from the harvest.
22. Ἐὰν γεωργὸς κλέψῃ ἐν σκάφῳ λίσγον ἢ δίκελλαν καὶ μετὰ χρόνον διαγνωσθῇ, παρεχέτω τὸ ἡμερήσιον αὐτοῦ φόλλεις δώδεκα· ὁμοίως καὶ ὁ κλέπτων ἐν καιρῷ κλαδείας κλαδευτήριον ἢ ἐν καιρῷ θερισμοῦ δρέπανον ἢ ἐν καιρῷ ὑλοκοπίας πέλεκυν.	22. If a farmer while digging the ground steals a spade or a hack, and if this theft is later discovered, then he must pay one day's wages: twelve *folles*.[32] This also applies to someone who steals the hook in the pruning season, or the sickle in harvest time, or the axe when it is time for wood-chopping.
23–30 Περὶ ἀγελαρίων 23. Ἐὰν ἀγελάριος βοῶν ἕωθεν παραλαβὼν παρὰ γεωργοῦ βοῦν συγκαταμίξῃ αὐτὸν μετὰ τῆς ἀγέλης καὶ συμβῇ τὸν βοῦν λυκωθῆναι, δειξάτω τὸ πτῶμα τῷ κυρίῳ καὶ ἀζήμιος αὐτὸς ἔσται.	23–30: About cowherds 23. If a cowherd gets a cow from a farmer in the morning and includes it in the herd, and if the cow is then caught by a wolf, then he must show the corpse to the owner and will not be liable for the damage.

31 The Greek fragments are from the critical edition by W. Ashburner, 'The Farmer's Law', *The Journal of Hellenic Studies*, 30 (1910), pp. 85–108 (repr. in JGR, II, pp. 65–71). There is a more recent critical edition by I. Medvedev et al., *Vizantijskij zemledel' českij zakon* (Leningrad: 1984), but we have used the one by Ashburner because it is easier to consult.

32 A *follis* was a type of bronze coin in Byzantium.

TEXT 16 (*cont.*)

24. Ἐὰν ἀγελάριος βοῦν παραλαβὼν ἀπολέσῃ καὶ τῇ αὐτῇ ἡμέρᾳ ἐν ᾗ ὁ βοῦς ἀπώλετο οὐ καταμηνύσῃ τῷ κυρίῳ τοῦ βοὸς ὅτι 'τὸν βοῦν ἕως ὧδε καὶ ὧδε ἑώρακα, τί δὲ γέγονεν οὐκ οἶδα', μὴ ἔστω ἀζήμιος, εἰ δὲ κατεμήνυσεν, ἔστω ἀζήμιος.	24. If a cowherd loses a cow which was under his care and fails to report to this cow's owner on the very day that it was lost: 'Until there-and-there I saw it and what happened next, I do not know', then he will not come away without paying; but if he does report, then he does not have to pay.
25. Ἐὰν ἀγελάριος βοῦν παραλαβὼν ἀπὸ γεωργοῦ ἕωθεν ἀπέλθῃ, καὶ χωρισθεὶς ὁ βοῦς ἐκ τοῦ πλήθους τῶν βοῶν ἀπελθὼν εἰσέλθῃ ἐν χωραφίοις ἢ ἀμπέλοις καὶ πραῖδαν ποιήσῃ, τοῦ μισθοῦ αὐτοῦ μὴ στερείσθω, τὴν δὲ πραῖδαν διδότω.	25. If a cowherd starts out with a farmer's cow in his care in the morning, but if then the cow strays off from the herd and enters into a little farm—or vineyards—and causes devastation there, then, although the cowherd is not to miss his wages, he is liable for the damages.
30. Ἐάν τις κόψῃ κώδωνα ἐκ βοὸς ἢ ἐκ προβάτου καὶ διαγνωσθῇ ὡς κλέπτης, μαστιγωθήτω· εἰ δὲ ἀφανὲς γένηται τὸ ζῷον, διδότω αὐτὸ ὁ τὴν κλοπὴν ποιήσας τοῦ κώδωνος.	30. If someone cuts the bell from a cow's or sheep's neck and is exposed as a thief, he will be flogged. And if the animal is not found, then the person who stole the bell must compensate for the animal as well.
59. Ὁ κόπτων ἀμπέλους ἀλλοτρίας ἐγκάρπους ἢ ἀνασπῶν χειροκοπείσθω ζημιούμενος.	59. The person who cuts or pulls out vines with fruits of someone else shall have his hand cut off and is fined.

In the last provision cited from this fragment (59) of the *Farmer's Law*, we see a remarkably severe punishment imposed on those who destroy vines. There is a distinction here between the civil aspect of the act (payment of damages) and the criminal one (mutilation). It seems that trees with fruits—and vines especially—were particularly protected (and had already been so at least from Roman times), presumably because they were valuable owing to their fruit. Another reason can be that vineyards take on average about five years to established as well—in contrast to agricultural crops—so part of the severity may be linked to the temporal investment required to (re)grow vineyards.

The *Military Law* (Ὁ Στρατιωτικὸς Νόμος, Stratiotikos nomos) is a collection of military criminal provisions, which address on the one hand issues that arise within the army, such as when somebody refuses to obey orders or deserts the army, and, on the other, which deal with issues that more generally concern military justice and the law of war, such as looting, etc. We quote in the following a fragment from the *Military Law*:

TEXT 17 The *Military Law*, chapters 15, 18, 19, 21[33]

15. Ὁ πρὸς τοὺς πολεμίους ἀποφυγὼν καὶ ὑποστρέψας βασανίζεται καὶ ἢ θηρίοις παραδίδοται ἢ εἰς φοῦρκαν καταδικάζεται.	15. Someone who defects to the enemy and comes back will be tortured and either fed to the animals or put on the 'fork'.[34]
18. Ὁ στρατιώτης κλέπτων ὅπλα ἀλλότρια τοῦ βαθμοῦ τῆς στρατείας ἐξωθεῖται.	18. The soldier who steals someone else's weapons will be deprived of his military rank.
19. Ἐάν τις ἀταξίαν τραχεῖαν στρατιωτῶν ὑφάψῃ ἢ διεγείρῃ, εἰς κεφαλὴν κολάζεται· εἰ δὲ ἄχρι φωνῆς μόνης τὴν στρατιωτικὴν ἀταξίαν παρεσκεύασεν γενέσθαι μέχρι ψιλῆς κατά τινων μέμψεως ἢ ἀταξία διανέστη, τότε τοῦ βαθμοῦ τῆς στρατείας ἀποβάλλεται· καὶ ὅτε δὲ πολλοὶ ἅμα στρατιῶται συμπνεύσωσιν εἰς ἄτοπόν τι ἢ λεγεὼν αὐτῶν ἀτονήσει, ἀποστρατεύεσθαι εἰώθασιν. [...]	19. If somebody kindles or stirs up mutiny in the army, he will get a capital punishment. And if he causes such mutiny solely by his words, not proceeding beyond abusing certain people, and if then mutiny breaks out, he will be deprived of his military rank. And if a great number of soldiers conspire to some wicked plan, or if an entire legion deserts, then they are usually kicked out of the army. [...]
21. Οἱ ἐπὶ μοιχείᾳ ἢ ἐν ἄλλῳ ἐγκλήματι πουβλίκῳ κατακριθέντες, οὐκ εἰσὶ δεκτοὶ βουλόμενοι στρατευθῆναι.	21. People convicted for adultery or another crime are not admitted into the army.

8 The *Rhodian Sea Law*

The *Rhodian Sea Law* is a collection of maritime legal provisions which were probably compiled in the seventh or eighth century. It deals with the dangers that one would encounter during maritime travels (e.g., piracy, shipwreck, fire), with issues that pertain to the crew, the captain and passengers (e.g., responsibilities, theft, payments); and with matters concerning the transportation of goods, maritime contracts, general average (see below), jettison and contributions to compensation, etc. The *Rhodian Sea Law* has a complicated history of manuscript transmission. To begin with, as the title *Rhodian Sea Law* implies, this collection presumably derived from or was related somehow to an ancient text originating from the Greek island Rhodes. Rhodes had in antiquity been a major sea

33 The Greek comes from the critical edition by W. Ashburner, 'The Byzantine Mutiny Act', *The Journal of Hellenic Studies*, 46 (1926), pp. 80–109 (repr. in JGR, II, pp. 75–79).

34 On this method of execution, see note 29 above.

power, a statement proven by the fact that one of the seven wonders of the ancient world was located on this island. The second title of the fourteenth book of the *Digest* is entitled 'The Rhodian law of jettison' (*De lege Rodia de iactu*). As mentioned in an earlier section, the *Digest* of Justinian consists of fragments of the writings of classical Roman jurists. These jurists discuss provisions of the so-called 'Rhodian law of jettison' and comment on the rules governing what is nowadays known as general average. General average concerns cases in which the captain of the ship is forced to throw cargo overboard in order to save the ship in bad weather. In such cases, the loss of the person whose cargo has been sacrificed for the common good is spread evenly among all those concerned. We do not know whether these provisions on general average were actually included as such in an ancient text deriving from Rhodes.

A Greek version of these Latin *Digest* fragments is found in the *Basilica*, the laws that were promulgated around 900. In a later chapter we will discuss the *Basilica* in detail. At this point it is suffices to mention that the *Basilica* contain the Greek summaries of all four parts of Justinian's legislation.[35] What is interesting is that the Byzantine collection known as the *Rhodian Sea Law* was also included as a whole in the eighth title of the fifty-third *Basilica* book. This raises some questions. For example, since the *Digest* fragments about jettison have already been transmitted in the *Basilica*, why did the compilers feel the need to also include in the *Basilica* the jettison provisions found in the *Rhodian Sea Law*? Moreover, there is some discussion on whether the *Rhodian Sea Law* was inserted into the text of the *Basilica* as a regular title or as a supplement. This is not the place to examine in detail all these questions. Based on the literature and on recent studies, it seems that the *Rhodian Sea Law*, as far as jettison and shipwreck is concerned, had a supplementary character to the *Digest* fragments, which may explain why the entirety of the *Rhodian Sea Law*—with the exception of its preface—was also included in the *Basilica*. For example, in the *Rhodian Sea Law* we find several rather detailed provisions which deal with the rewards for salvaging wrecked goods (see TEXT 20). In the *Basilica* part which transmits the *Digest* fragments about maritime issues, we do not find any such provisions addressing the rewards given to those who find of wrecked goods.

Moreover, in the *Rhodian Sea Law*, the rules on general average are extended to more cases than those just concerning strict average. All kinds of potential troubles and dangers to which a ship sailing the sea was exposed were examined in this Byzantine source; the *Rhodian Sea Law* thus distinguishes the various roles of the different parties involved in maritime activities, and the degree of negligence of each party was taken into consideration when estimating the legal consequences (see TEXT 19). In any case, the fact that the whole text of the *Rhodian Sea Law* is included in the *Basilica* demonstrates the importance of this maritime law collection. We quote in the following examples some fragments of the *Rhodian Sea Law*.

35 Little, however, is rendered of the *Institutes*. On the *Basilica*, see below, pp. 123–129.

TEXT 18 The *Rhodian Sea Law*, Part III, chapters 3 and 5[36]: about theft committed by a sailor and fights between sailors

3. ἐὰν ναύτης κελεύσει τοῦ ναυκλήρου κλοπὴν ποιήσῃ ἐμπόρου ἢ ἐπιβάτου καὶ καταληφθεὶς κατασχεθῇ, ὁ ναύκληρος διπλᾶ ἀποδιδότω τοῖς τὰ σύλα παθοῦσιν, ὁ δὲ ναύτης λαμβανέτω ξυλαγώγια ἑκατόν. ἐὰν δὲ ναύτης αὐτοβούλως συλήσῃ μέν κατασχεθῇ δὲ ἢ καὶ διὰ μαρτύρων ἐλεγχθῇ, σφοδρῶς βασανιζέσθω, ἐὰν καὶ μάλιστα τὰ σύλα χρυσίον ᾖ, καὶ τὴν ἀποκατάστασιν τῷ συληθέντι ποιείτω.	3. If a sailorman robbing a merchant or passenger at the captain's command is caught and arrested, then the captain must pay twice the value to the victim, and the sailor is given 100 strokes of the cane. But if the sailor steals on his own initiative and is caught in the act or if proven guilty by means of witnesses, then he will suffer severe torture, especially if it is a theft of gold, and repay to the victim.
5. ἐὰν ναῦται μάχην ποιήσωσι, λόγοις ποιείτωσαν καὶ μηδεὶς κρουέτω τὸν ἕτερον. ἐὰν δὲ καί τις κρούσῃ εἰς κεφαλὴν καὶ ἀνοίξῃ ἢ ἑτέρως πῶς κυλλώσῃ, παρεχέτω ὁ κρούσας τοὺς μισθοὺς τοῖς ἰατροῖς καὶ τὰ ἀναλώματα τῷ ἀδικηθέντι καὶ τὸν μισθὸν ὅλου τοῦ χρόνου τῆς ἀργίας καὶ ἐπιμελείας.	5. If sailors are fighting, they must do so by means of words instead of hitting each other. If somebody nevertheless hits someone else on the head and causes an open wound, or causes his invalidity in any other way, then the one who gave the blow must pay the doctors' wages and the expenses made by the victim and his wages of the whole period during which he is unable to work and is being nursed.

TEXT 19 The *Rhodian Sea Law*, Part III, chapters 10, 26, 28, 29[37]: about shipwreck, liability and contribution

10. ἐὰν ναύκληρος ἅμα τοῖς ναύταις ἀμελήσῃ καὶ συμβῇ ζημίαν ἢ ναυάγιον, ὁ ναύκληρος καὶ οἱ ναῦται ὑποκείσθωσαν τῷ ἐμπόρῳ εἰς τὴν ἀπόδοσιν τῆς ζημίας. εἰ δὲ ἀπὸ ἀμελείας τοῦ ἐμπόρου συμβῇ	10. If the captain, together with the crew, is negligent and some damage or shipwreck occurs, the captain and the crew are liable to make restitution to the merchant for the loss. However, if it is through the negligence

36 All cited Greek passages of *The Rhodian Sea Law* are from the critical edition of W. Ashburner, *The Rhodian Sea-Law* (Oxford: 1909; repr. Aalen: 1976).

37 The English translation of all the following fragments of *The Rhodian Sea law* is from M. Humphreys, *The Law of the Isaurian Era: The Ecloga and its Appendices* (Liverpool: 2017).

TEXT 19 (*cont.*)

ἀπώλειαν τοῦ πλοίου καὶ τοῦ γόμου γενέσθαι, ὑποκείσθω ὁ ἔμπορος ἐν τῇ ζημίᾳ τοῦ ναυαγίου καὶ τοῦ πλοίου, εἰ δὲ τοῦ ναυκλήρου μὴ ἐμποδίσαντος μηδὲ τῶν ναυτῶν μηδὲ τοῦ ἐμπόρου συμβῇ ζημίαν ἢ ναυάγιον, τὰ σωζόμενα μέρη τοῦ πλοίου καὶ τῶν φορτίων εἰς συμβολὴν ἐρχέσθωσαν.

of the merchant that the ship and cargo are lost, then the merchant is liable for the loss of the ship and the wreck. But if there is no negligence by the captain or the crew or the merchant and a wreck happens, then the salvage from the ship and the cargo shall come into the contribution.

26. ἐάν τινος τῶν ναυτῶν ἢ ναυκλήρων ἐκκοιτοῦντος ἐκ τοῦ πλοίου συμβῇ ἀπώλειαν γενέσθαι τοῦ πλοίου νυκτὸς ἢ ἡμέρας, πᾶσαν τὴν ζημίαν ἐφορᾶν τοὺς ἐξωκοιτοῦντας ναύτας ἢ ναυκλήρους· τοὺς δὲ εἰς τὸ πλοῖον μείναντας ἀζημίους μένειν· τοὺς δὲ ἀμελήσαντας προσφέρειν τῷ δεσπότῃ τοῦ πλοίου τὴν διὰ τῆς αὐτῶν ἀμελείας προσγενομένην ζημίαν.

26. If any of the sailors or the officers sleep off the ship and it happens that the ship is lost, at night or day, all the losses shall be borne by the sailors and officers who slept off the ship, while those who remained on board shall not be liable. Those who are negligent must make good to the owner of the ship the damage caused by their negligence.

28. ἐὰν πλοῖον ἐν τῇ ἐμβολῇ ἐμποδισθῇ ὑπὸ τοῦ ἐμπόρου ἢ κοινωνοῦ πληρωθείσης τῆς προθεσμίας, καὶ συμβῇ ἀπὸ πειρατείας ἢ πυρκαϊᾶς ἢ ναυαγίου ἀπώλειαν γενέσθαι τοῦ πλοίου, ὁ τὴν ἐμπόδιον ποιήσας ἐμφερέτω τὰς ζημίας.

28. If a ship is hindered while loading by the merchant or partner and the time fixed for loading passes, and it happens the ship is lost due to piracy, fire or shipwreck, the one who caused the delay shall bear the loss.

29. ἐὰν ὁ ἔμπορος ἐν τῷ τόπῳ ὅθεν συγγράψονται μὴ παράσχῃ τὰ φορτία πληρωθείσης τῆς προθεσμίας, καὶ συμβῇ ἀπὸ πειρατείας ἢ πυρκαϊᾶς ἢ ναυαγίου ἀπώλειαν γενέσθαι, ἐφορᾶν πᾶσαν τὴν ζημίαν τοῦ πλοίου τὸν ἔμπορον. ἐὰν δὲ μὴ πληρωθέντων τῶν ἡμερῶν τῆς προθεσμίας συμβῇ τι τῶν εἰρημένων, εἰς συμβολὴν ἐρχέσθωσαν.

29. If the merchant does not provide the cargo at the place agreed, and the agreed time passes, and it happens that the ship is lost to piracy, fire or shipwreck, then the merchant shall bear all the losses of the ship. If the days set have not passed and one of these said things happens, then they shall all come into contribution.

The rationale behind the provisions in the preceding (TEXT 19) is to establish a fair distribution of damages amongst all parties in the event of shipwreck or damage. Chapter ten sets out the general rule: if the captain and crew are negligent, they have to compensate the merchant for his loss; if, however, the merchant's negligence causes the shipwreck, then he alone is held liable. Chapters twenty-six, twenty-eight and twenty-nine describe particular cases of liability concerning the captain and crew on one hand, and the merchant on the other. In chapter twenty-six, a distinction is made between the sailors and masters who slept on shore, and are thus liable if the ship is wrecked, and the ones who remained on board and who presumably—because they were on board—did their best to save the ship and, as a result, are not liable. If the ship is lost because of the merchant's fault, then the merchant alone must pay for the damage done, as chapters twenty-eight and twenty-nine prescribe. There are many more rules related to claims regarding 'contribution'[38] and jettison in the *Rhodian Sea Law*. We quote in the following passage the last three chapters of this text, which refer to the rewards for people who save wrecked goods:

TEXT 20 The *Rhodian Sea Law*, Part III, chapters 45–47: about shipwreck, salvage and rewards

45. ἐὰν ἐν πελάγει πλοῖον στραφῇ ἢ διαφθαρῇ, ὁ ἀποσώζων τι ἐξ αὐτοῦ ἐπὶ τὴν γῆν λαμβανέτω ἀντὶ μισθοῦ οὗ ἀποσώζει τὸ πέμπτον μέρος.	45. If a ship in open sea is capsized or destroyed, then anyone who brings to safety anything from it to land shall receive as a reward a fifth portion of what they saved.
46. ἐὰν κάραβος ἀπὸ ἰδίου πλοίου τὰ σχοινία διαρρήξας ἀπόληται ἅμα καὶ τοῖς ἐμπλέουσιν ἐν αὐτῷ, ἐὰν οἱ πλέοντες ἀπόλωνται ἢ ἀποθάνωσι, τὸν μισθὸν τὸν ἐνιαυσιαῖον ἀποδιδότω ὁ ναύκληρος εἰς πλῆρες τοῦ ἐνιαυτοῦ τοῖς τούτων κληρονόμοις. ὁ δὲ τὸν κάραβον ἀποσώζων σὺν τῶν ἐφολκίων, καθὼς ἐν ἀληθείᾳ εὑρίσκει, πάντα ἀποδώσει, λαμβάνων οὗ ἀποσώζει τὸ πέμπτον μέρος.	46. If a boat breaks away from the ropes of its ship and is lost with all her crew, then if those on board are lost or die, the captain shall pay their annual wages for a whole year to their heirs. Anyone who brings the boat to safety along with its rudders shall return everything just as he found it, and he shall receive a fifth part of what he saves.

38 'Bring in contribution' or 'goods come into contribution' or 'the right to contribution' means here that the person whose property has been thrown overboard in order to save the ship, can ask that the loss will be proportionally shared by everyone onboard the ship.

TEXT 20 (*cont.*)

47. ἐὰν χρυσίον ἢ ἀργύριον ἢ ἕτερόν τι ἐκ βυθοῦ ἐπάρθῃ ἀπὸ ὀργυιῶν ὀκτώ, λαμβανέτω ὁ ἀποσώζων τὸ τρίτον μέρος. ἀπὸ δὲ ὀργυιῶν δεκαπέντε, λαμβανέτω ὁ ἀποσώζων τὸ ἥμισυ διὰ τὸν κίνδυνον τοῦ βυθοῦ. τῶν δὲ ἐκριπτομένων ἀπὸ θαλάσσης εἰς γῆν καὶ εὑρισκομένων ἢ ἐπιφερομένων ἐπὶ πῆχυν ἕνα, λαμβανέτω ὁ ἀποσώζων δέκατον μέρος τῶν ἀποσωζομένων.	47. If gold or silver or anything else is lifted up from a depth of eight fathoms, then the salvager shall receive a third share. If from fifteen fathoms, the salvager shall receive half due to the danger of the depth. When things are cast from the sea onto land and are found there or are carried as far as one cubit, then the salvager shall receive a tenth part of the salvage.

These three chapters set different criteria for the actual estimation of the rewards for those who find of wrecked goods. The reward is not always the same, but varies depending on different factors. The location of the wrecked good played a role in the actual estimation of the reward, such as whether the good was found in the sea or cast ashore. If the good was in the sea, the estimation of the reward further depended on the exact depth of the sea in the place where the good was found. The deeper it was found and saved, the higher the reward, since it was more difficult to bring it ashore. Finally, the *Rhodian Sea Law* also includes interesting provisions about maritime partnerships and maritime loans.

9 Select Bibliography

Primary Sources

Ashburner, W. 'The Byzantine Mutiny Act', *The Journal of Hellenic Studies*, 46 (1926), pp. 80–109.

Ashburner, W. 'The Farmer's Law', *The Journal of Hellenic Studies*, 30 (1910), pp. 85–108 and 32 (1912), pp. 68–95 (repr. in JGR, II, pp. 65–71, as *Farmer's Law: Leges Rusticae*).

Ashburner, W. *The Rhodian Sea-Law*. Oxford: 1909; repr. Aalen: 1976.

Burgmann, L. *Ecloga. Das Gesetzbuch Leons III. und Konstantinos' V*, Frankfurt am Main: 1983.

Burgmann, L. and Sp. Troianos. 'Appendix Eclogae', FM, 3 (1979), pp. 24–125.

Humphreys, M. *The Laws of the Isaurian Era: the Ecloga and its Appendices*. Liverpool: 2017.

Koder, J. *Nomos Georgikos. Das byzantinische Ladwirtschaftsgesetz. Überlegungen zur inhaltlichen und zeitlichen Einordnung. Deutsche Übersetzung*. Vienna: 2020.

Konidaris, J. 'Die Novellen des Kaisers Herakleios', FM, 5 (1982), pp. 33–106.

Medvedev, I. et al. *Vizantijskij zemledel' českij zakon* [= critical edition of *The Farmer's Law: The Nomos Georgikos*]. Leningrad: 1984.

Rodolakis, G.E. *Από το Νόμο Ροδίων στο 53° βιβλίο των Βασιλικών. Συμβολή στη μελέτη του βυζαντινού ναυτικού δικαίου* [in Greek = From the 'Law of the Rhodians' to the 53rd Book of the *Basilica*.

Contribution to the Study of Byzantine Maritime Law]. Athens: 2007 [this book contains the most recent critical edition of Book 53 of the *Basilica*].

Rodríguez Martín, J.-D. *El Tratado De Actionibus y sus Apéndices*. Santiago de Compostela: 2016.

Ščapov, J.N. and L. Burgmann, eds. *Die slavische Ecloga*. Frankfurt am Main: 2011.

Simon, D. and A. Siphoniu-Karapa. 'Eine Fragmentesammlung aus dem Baroccianus 173', FM, 3 (1979), pp. 1–23.

Simon, D. and Sp. Troianos. *Das Novellensyntagma des Athanasius von Emesa*. Frankfurt am Main: 1989.

Sitzia, Fr. *Le Rhopai*. Naples: 1984.

Sitzia, Fr. *De actionibus*. Milan: 1973.

Secondary Literature

Brubaker, L. and J. Haldon. *Byzantium in the Iconoclast Era, c. 680–850: A History*. Cambridge: 2011.

Burgmann, L. 'Die Nomoi Stratiotikos, Georgikos und Nautikos', *Zbornik Radova Vizantološkog Instituta*, 46 (2009), pp. 53–64.

Burgmann, L. 'Ἀθανάσιος δίγλωσσος. Latina in der Novellenbearbeitung des Athanasios von Emesa', SG, 4 (1990), pp. 57–82.

Claus, A. *Ὁ Σχολαστικός* (PhD Diss., University of Cologne). Cologne: 1965.

Humphreys, M., ed. *A Compantion to Byzantine Iconoclasm*, Leiden/Boston: 2021.

Lascaratos, J. and P. Dalla-Vorgia. 'The Penalty of Mutilation for Crimes in the Byzantine Era (324–1453 A.D.)', *International Journal of Risk and Safety in Medicine*, 10/1 (1997), pp. 51–56.

Letsios, D. *Νόμος Ῥοδίων Ναυτικός. Das Seegesetz der Rhodier. Untersuchungen zu Seerecht und Handelsschiffahrt in Byzanz*. Rhodes: 1996.

Loukaki, M. 'Σχολαστικός. Remarques sur le sens du terme à Byzance (IVe–XVe siècles)', *Byzantinische Zeitschrift*, 109/1 (2016), pp. 41–72.

Paradiso, A. 'Mutilations par voie de justice à Byzance. L'ablation du nez dans l'Eklogê de Léon III l'Isaurien', in J.-M. Bertrand, ed. *La violence dans les mondes grec et romain*. Paris: 2005, pp. 307–320.

Penna, D. 'Finders Keepers, Losers Weepers? Byzantine Shipwreck and Salvage in the Eleventh and Twelfth Centuries', in L. Sicking and A. Wijffels, eds. *Conflict Management in the Mediterranean and the Atlantic, 1000–1800: Actors, Institutions and Strategies of Dispute Settlement*. Leiden/Boston: 2020, pp. 43–66.

Scheltema, H.J. 'Subseciva. XVII. La Collectio Novellarum d'Athanase', RIDA, 13 (1966), pp. 349–352 (= *Opera minora*, pp. 155–157).

Schminck, A. 'Probleme des sog. "Νόμος Ῥοδίων ναυτικός"', in E. Chrysos, D. Letsios, H. Richter, and R. Stupperich, eds. *Griechenland und das Meer. Beiträge eines Symposions in Frankfurt im Dezember 1996*. Mannheim/Möhnesee: 1999, pp. 171–178.

Simon, D. 'Das Novellenexemplar des Athanasios', FM, 7 (1986), pp. 117–140.

Simon, D. 'Review of A. Claus, *Ὁ Σχολαστικός* (PhD Diss., Universität zu Köln: 1965)', *Byzantinische Zeitschrift*, 59/1 (1966), pp. 158–161.

Sinogowitz, B. *Studien zum Strafrecht der Ekloge*. Athens: 1956.

Sitzia F. 'Il Breviarium Novellarum di Theodoro di Ermopoli', SG 9 (2014), pp. 187–241.

Sitzia, Fr. 'Theodorus e l'insegnamento degli σχολαστικοί nella storia del diritto bizantino', in J.H.A. Lokin and B.H. Stolte, eds. *Introduzione al diritto bizantino. Da Giustiniano ai Basilici.* Pavia: 2011, pp. 189–237.

Troianos, Sp. 'Bemerkungen zum Strafrecht der Ecloga', in B. Kremmudas, Chr. Maltezou, and N. Panayiotakis, eds. *Festschrift Nikos Svoronos*, vol. 1 ('Αφιέρωμα στὸν Νίκο Σβορῶνο). Rethymno: 1986, pp. 97–112 (repr. in Sp. Troianos, *Historia et Ius*, vol. 1, *1969–1988*. Athens: 2004, pp. 455–472).

Troianos, Sp. 'Zum Aufbau des Titels περὶ διαφόρων ἀναγνωσμάτων im Novellensyntagma des Athanasios', in L. Burgmann, M.Th. Fögen, and A. Schminck, eds. *Cupido legum.* Frankfurt am Main: 1985, pp. 235–244 (repr. in Sp. Troianos, *Historia et Ius*, vol. 1, *1969–1988*. Athens: 2004, pp. 443–454).

Watson, A., ed. and trans., *The Digest of Justinian*, 4 vols., Philadelphia: 1985 (rev. edn, Philadelphia: 1998).

FIGURE 4 Detail from a Byzantine Gospel of the eleventh century, depicting workers in a vineyard (bottom) and receiving their payment (top).
PARIS, BNF, COD. GR. 74. (HTTPS://GALLICA.BNF.FR/ARK:/12148/BTV1B10722121J/F85.ITEM). HTTPS://UPLOAD.WIKIMEDIA.ORG/WIKIPEDIA/COMMONS/B/BD/BYZANTINE_AGRICULTURE.JPG. LAST ACCESSED MARCH 14, 2022

CHAPTER 4

Macedonian Renaissance

1 Introduction

The iconoclastic period ended in 843 and icon veneration was allowed again. The restoration of Orthodoxy and icon worshipping was part of a general cultural revival in many fields including art, literature and law. This period of cultural revival is known as 'the Macedonian Renaissance'. It takes its name from the Macedonian emperors, the Byzantine dynasty that reigned from 867 until 1056. The founder of this dynasty, Basil I, came from the *theme* of Macedonia: hence the name 'Macedonian dynasty'.[1] Basil I ruled from 867 up to 886. He was succeeded by his second son Leo VI the Wise or Philosopher, who reigned from 886 up to 912. There is another name that must be mentioned when it comes to Macedonian legislation: that is the scholar Photios (born *c.* 810, died after 893), one of the greatest intellectuals in Byzantium, who became patriarch of Constantinople twice (858–867 and 877–886) and played an influential role in the legislative work of the Macedonian emperors, as we will see. Photios was interested in the literature of antiquity. One of his most important works is the *Bibliotheca* or *Myriobiblon* (Μυριόβιβλον = 'ten thousand books'), which is something like an encyclopaedia and contains summaries, reviews and extracts from the writings of classical authors (Aristotle, Plato, Herodotus, etc.), many of which are now lost. Photios was not popular with everyone. As a patriarch, in particular, he was rather controversial. Although Photios had been a tutor of Leo VI the Wise, he was nevertheless deposed from his patriarchal see in Constantinople by Leo VI himself.

The Macedonian emperors proved very active in the legal field. As we mentioned in an earlier chapter, the majority of Justinian's legislation had been promulgated in Latin, and that posed a problem for the majority of his subjects who could neither read nor understand it. Greek was, after all, the dominant language in the Byzantine empire. That is why, shortly after Justinian's legislation was promulgated, jurists had started to make Greek summaries and Greek commentaries on this legislation. As a result, by the time of the Macedonian dynasty at the end of the ninth century, several Greek legal texts existed, based on translations, summaries and commentaries on the Justinianic legislation. For this reason, the Macedonian emperors carried out the so-called 'purge of the laws', the *anakatharsis tōn nomōn* (ἀνακάθαρσις τῶν νόμων), meaning the purification of laws. In other words, their intention was to clear out the legislation and impose some order on the legal chaos that existed. The results were new legal collections. We will examine the

1 A *theme* was a term for a military and administrative division in Byzantium, see ODB, vol. 3, pp. 2034–2035. See also ODB, vol. 2, pp. 1262: 'In Byz. terminology of the 10th–12th C. the name *Macedonia* was applied to Thrace …'.

 | DOI:10.1163/9789004520684_005

following legal works that were produced during this period: the *Prochiron*, the *Eisagoge*, the *Basilica*, the *Novels* of Leo VI the Wise and the *Prefect's Book*.

2 The *Prochiron* and the *Eisagoge*

The first two legal works of the Macedonian dynasty are the so-called *Prochiron* (Manual) and *Eisagoge* (Introduction). In earlier studies of Byzantine law, the *Eisagoge* was known by the name *Epanagoge*, but in the mid-1980s, the German scholar A. Schminck proved with sound arguments that the actual title of this work was the *Eisagoge* and not *Epanagoge*, as was believed up to then.[2] Both the *Prochiron* and the *Eisagoge* are practical legal compendia of the type of the *Ecloga*, since they both cover in principle the same ground. This raises questions about their status. It is understandable that the Macedonian emperors wanted to replace the *Ecloga* of the emperors whom they considered as heretics (i.e. the iconoclastic emperors) and who had ruled before them. But why, then, produce two similar legal books? There has been a lot of discussion on this matter, including questions about the actual dating and status of these two law texts. Some scholars believe that the *Prochiron* was issued first, between 870–879; others suggest that it was issued after the *Eisagoge*, sometime around 907.

Although both legal works seem similar, there are also important differences. First of all, the *Prochiron* is briefer than the *Eisagoge*. They are both divided into forty titles, but the *Prochiron* does not refer to matters of public or administrative law, whereas the *Eisagoge* does. The *Prochiron* simply starts with life and ends with death or, in legal terms, it starts with marriage and ends with law of succession. The *Eisagoge*, however, starts with a general treatment of the functions and responsibilities of the emperor and the patriarch (see below, TEXT 3). Here then lies the second main difference between the two works. The *Eisagoge* must have been influenced by Photios, and parts of it (or all of it?) were most likely written by him. This is evident from the treatment of some subjects in the *Eisagoge*—especially the title concerning the position of the patriarch—and from its preface, which is filled with philosophical arguments and theological matters, as we will see (TEXT 2).

Both texts, and in particular their prefaces, give us some information about the genesis of the *Basilica*. We will paraphrase in the following examples parts of the prefaces of both the *Prochiron* and the *Eisagoge*, and then compare the information each provides.[3]

2 A. Schminck, *Studien zu mittelbyzantinischen Rechtsbüchern* (Frankfurt am Main: 1986).

3 A. Schminck has edited and translated into German the prefaces of both the *Prochiron* and the *Eisagoge*, whose numeration of the lines of both prefaces we follow here (TEXTS 1 and 2), using the edition of A. Schminck, *Studien zu mittelbyzantinischen Rechtsbüchern* (Frankfurt am Main: 1986).

TEXT 1	Summarised preface to the *Prochiron* (Manual)
1–4	In the name of our lord Jesus Christ our God, the Emperors and Caesars Basil, Constantine and Leo, the fortunate, pious, famous, victorious, triumphant, ever venerable, faithful Augusti:
5–25	We do our best to serve God and the people He put under our care. The best way to serve God is justice, according to Solomon and Isaiah: justice is a necessary ingredient of society and God demands us to be just.
26–32	Justice is synonymous with law, viz. the law which God gave us to help us: see Isaiah.
33–36	That is why we take an interest in legislation.
37–41	It was a good thing that we occupied ourselves with it, for the legal literature had reached enormous dimensions.
42–47	Due to this vastness, people were afraid to study the texts. Scholars had attempted to facilitate its study, ⟨but with little success⟩. Seeing that instruction in the law is indispensable, we had to come up with something better.
47–51	So we selected from that enormous quantity the main issues, presenting them in this concise legal handbook (τῷδε τῷ προχείρῳ νόμῳ).
52–57	We have (1) summarised, (2) translated into Greek, (3) made changes and corrections, (4) supplemented. The result is (1) clearness, (2) reasonable scope, (3) correctness, (4) completeness.
57–62	We have arranged this selection into forty titles. Further details can be found in the unabridged complete corpus, which we have lately 'purged' (ἀνακεκαθαρμένῳ).
63–76	It is true that there already exists **a so-called handbook**, but that is full of horrible mistakes, hence not suitable for students. It did not find favour with our predecessors either, at least parts of it did not. Our own work, by contrast, is legally as well as didactically correct.
77–82	As for the '**purge**' mentioned above: everything which is no longer valid is recognisable as invalid by being assembled into **one book (ἓν τεῦχος)**. The rest of the old laws can be consulted in cases where the Prochiron is insufficient. We have left them in their original forms and arranged them into 60 **books.**
82–83	The *Prochiron* starts where our nature starts: ⟨betrothal, marriage, etc.…⟩

TEXT 2 Preface to the *Eisagoge* (Introduction)

1–4	Law of the emperors Basil, Leo and Alexander.
5–7	A law book like the present one is most important, for the law comes from God.
7–16	For: God created man from matter and spirit, and then gave a law (a good one) to keep these components together. In this way He intended to make it clear that (1) both components, although entirely different, have their origins in one single principle, (2) and that this Principle is good.
17–23	Ad 1: He created man from both substances, which indicates that He also made these components themselves. Ad 2: what keeps man together is a good law, hence the Creator is good too (and one): contra [dualistic] Manicheans.[4]
23–27	By creating (1) spirit, (2) matter and (3) the law which keeps them together, God intended to indicate that His monarchy consists of three substances. Thus He suggests to us His wish to be venerated as a Trinity.
28–31	As the emperors were in some mysterious way initiated in this truth, they have showed themselves dedicated supporters of this good law. It was in need of (1) restoration, (2) general dissemination.
31–40	So the work was done in two stages: (1) to **'purge'** (clear out) the vast amount of old laws and to arrange the remainder into **40 books**; (2) to throw out the rubbish of the Isaurians, which undermined the theological dogma explained above, and to replace it by an Introduction (*Eisagoge*, Εἰσαγωγή) into those forty books, consisting of forty titles.
41–46	This law, then, must have the highest authority for our subjects, because, as we all know, God has made the law emperor, so to speak, over the faithful, so the law comes from emperors—from orthodox emperors, of course.
47–53	We have pointed out that the law was given by God, which directly strengthens our [dual] nature. In this respect it is unique among all good things. Therefore the law should be given priority above everything else.
53–62	Hence the study of the law, too, differs from other useful studies, in that it directly supports our very nature. Other occupations may contribute to happiness, but justice is happiness and it is indispensable for our salvation. So the study of law also deserves priority.

4 Manichaeanism was a religious movement that was influenced by Gnosticism and Judeo-Christianity and elaborated a dualistic view of the world: the struggle between a good world of light and an evil world of darkness. It takes its name from the Persian religious leader Mani (born in Babylonia in AD 216). Christians considered it a heresy.

TEXT 2 *(cont.)*

63–65	Moreover, justice is God's most characteristic quality. His justice is shown by the justice and equality of His works, where everyone receives his due. For God created the world after a blueprint in which each part received the right ('just') proportions; in other words, the creation is characterised by order and 'law'.
74–83	In ourselves this God-given law regulates our emotions and desires, thus effectuating 'equality' and justice. In promoting justice, the law must eventually result in complete goodness.
84–86	In short: take this Introduction seriously, for it comes from God Himself.
87–113	**Arrangement of the Introduction:**
87–90	Title 1 about law and justice. Through the law, Christ reigns as supreme emperor.
90–94	The following titles (2–7) deal with the functions of the **emperor, patriarch** and magistrates. This picture of the hierarchical structure of the state reflects the hierarchy in heaven.
95–101	Since our empire is a Christian state, we go on with the titles (8–11) about its spiritual aspects, namely about ecclesiastical offices and initiations.
102–108	In order to be 'complete', man must lead an active life. For that reason we added titles (12–28) which regulate the social aspects of society: betrothal, marriage etc., the law of obligations, witnesses and documents.
109–110	Finally (titles 29–36): regulations about the end of life: the law of inheritance.
110–113	As an appendix (37–40): everything which would ideally be superfluous: slavery, delicts, criminal law.

The heading of both of *Prochiron* and the *Eisagoge* begins with the names of the emperors responsible for its promulgation. In Byzantium, as in Rome, there was a system of co-emperors, i.e. one main emperor who shared his authority with one or several others, mostly his sons. The reason behind this co-emperorship was to ensure that the sons would succeed the emperor after his death. Basil I, founder of the Macedonian dynasty, had three sons, but he always ruled with no more than two of them as co-emperors. At the time the *Prochiron* was issued, his co-emperors were his sons Constantine and the later emperor, Leo VI. After the death of Constantine in 879 AD, his brother Alexander succeeded him as Basil I's co-emperor.[5] Given the specific names of the emperor and

5 When Basil I died himself in 886, his son Leo VI the Wise succeeded him and continued the legal activity of his father.

co-emperors mentioned in the headings of both legal works, it makes sense to conclude that the *Prochiron* should indeed be dated earlier than the *Eisagoge*, since it still refers to Constantine, whereas the *Eisagoge* (see TEXT 2) mentions the succeeding co-emperor Alexander instead. Furthermore, in both prefaces emphasis is placed on the task of a good emperor to take care of legislation and justice, noting that he has been entrusted to fulfil this task by God, a pattern that we have seen in other prefaces of Byzantine legal writings. The legislative activities of the emperor are more or less dictated by God Himself.

In lines 52–62 of the *Prochiron*'s preface, we learn about the process underlying the compilation of the text. The words 'translated into Greek' must refer to the technical legal jargon, such as the Latin names of actions, etc.[6] Since the *Prochiron* is no more than a manual, arranged into forty titles, the reader is instructed to refer to the 'unabridged complete corpus' for further details. This complete corpus can be identified with what we call the *Basilica*, or one of their immediate predecessors. Lines 77–82 of the *Prochiron*'s preface shed some light on the making of the *Basilica*: there we find a reference to 'the one book' and another arrangement into sixty books. This 'one book' or 'one volume', which has not been preserved, consisted of invalid laws, and the emperors subsequently arranged the remaining laws into sixty books. The *Basilica* as we know them consist indeed of sixty books. We see that the *Eisagoge* preface, by contrast, says that the emperors have arranged the material into forty books. This discrepancy can be used as an argument in favour of the hypothesis that the *Prochiron*, being more in-line with the *Basilica* as we now have them, postdates the *Eisagoge*. Another piece of information that plays a role in the discussion about the relation between the *Prochiron* and the *Eisagoge* is found in lines 63–76 of the *Prochiron*'s preface, where we read about the rejection of an earlier, existing manual. The name of this manual is not mentioned, an omission which has led to two contrasting hypotheses. Either, this nameless text must be the *Ecloga* of the 'heretic' iconoclastic emperors if you follow the hypothesis that the *Prochiron* antedates the *Eisagoge*, or it may be the *Eisagoge* itself, if you were to accept the hypothesis that the latter work was written before the *Prochiron*.

In lines 31–40 of the *Eisagoge*'s preface we also read about the famous purge of old laws and the arrangement of the remaining laws into a new volume—this time, into forty books instead of sixty, even though the *Basilica* as we now know it consisted of sixty books. It is also stated that the new legislation will replace the 'rubbish' of earlier emperors, presumably meaning the Isaurian emperors. This last piece of information has been advanced as an argument in favour of the hypothesis that the *Eisagoge* was promulgated first, before the *Prochiron*.

Lines 87–101 refer to the first titles of the *Eisagoge* itself. The *Eisagoge* preface is a much more ambitious and pretentious text than that of the *Prochiron*, a feature that is generally attributed to the direct influence of Photios. In the *Eisagoge* preface we see a real, theo-

6 See the following section of the present chapter for further discussion about the *Basilica*.

logical refutation of the iconoclastic movement of the Isaurian dynasty and we find an argument explaining that there is a direct connection with the law (see TEXT 2). Moreover, the second and third titles of the *Eisagoge* (see TEXT 3, further on) describe the functions of the emperor and the patriarch and, accordingly, the relationship between the state and the church:

TEXT 3 Extracts from the *Eisagoge*, titles 2 and 3: about the emperor and the patriarch[7]

ΤΙΤΛΟΣ ΔΕΥΤΕΡΟΣ Περὶ βασιλέως Κεφ. α'. Βασιλεύς ἐστιν ἔννομος ἐπιστασία, κοινὸν ἀγαθὸν πᾶσι τοῖς ὑπηκόοις, μήτε κατὰ ἀντιπάθειαν τιμωρῶν, μήτε κατὰ προσπάθειαν ἀγαθοποιῶν, ἀλλ' ἀνάλογός τις ἀγωνοθέτης τὰ βραβεῖα παρεχόμενος. [...]	SECOND TITLE About the Emperor (1) The emperor is the legal authority, common good for all subjects: he is not led by personal dislike in punishing, nor by sympathy in allowing advantages, but administers judgments as an unbiased arbitrator. [...]
δ'. Ὑπόκειται ἐκδικεῖν καὶ διατηρεῖν ὁ βασιλεὺς πρῶτον μὲν πάντα τὰ ἐν τῇ θείᾳ γραφῇ γεγραμμένα, ἔπειτα δὲ καὶ τὰ παρὰ τῶν ἑπτὰ ἁγίων συνόδων δογματισθέντα, ἔτι δὲ καὶ τοὺς ἐγκεκριμένους ῥωμαϊκοὺς νόμους. [...]	(4) It is the emperor's task to maintain and observe, first, everything written in the holy scripture, then also the canons of the seven councils, and furthermore the accepted Roman laws [...]
ΤΙΤΛΟΣ ΤΡΙΤΟΣ Περὶ πατριάρχου Κεφ. α'. Πατριάρχης ἐστὶν εἰκὼν ζῶσα χριστοῦ καὶ ἔμψυχος, δι' ἔργων καὶ λόγων χαρακτηρίζουσα τὴν ἀλήθειαν. [...]	THIRD TITLE About the patriarch 1. The patriarch is the living and animate image of Christ, representing the truth by his words and actions. [...]
δ'. Ἴδια πατριάρχου τὸ εἶναι διδακτικόν, τὸ πρὸς πάντας ὑψηλούς τε καὶ ταπεινοὺς ἀστενοχωρήτως ἐξισοῦσθαι, καὶ πρᾷον μὲν εἶναι ἐν δικαιοσύνῃ, ἐλεγκτικὸν δὲ πρὸς τοὺς ἀπειθοῦντας, ὑπὲρ δὲ τῆς ἀληθείας καὶ τῆς ἐκδικήσεως τῶν δογμάτων λαλεῖν ἐνώπιον βασιλέως καὶ μὴ αἰσχύνεσθαι. [...]	4. The patriarch is characterised by being a good teacher, by behaving equally unrestrained towards highly and lowly placed persons, mild in justice, but severe towards the disobedient, and by addressing the emperor without reservations on behalf of the truth and of maintaining the doctrines. [...]

7 The Greek text of the *Eisagoge* is cited from JGR, vol. II.

TEXT 3 (*cont.*)

η'. Τῆς πολιτείας ἐκ μερῶν καὶ μορίων ἀναλόγως τῷ ἀνθρώπῳ συνισταμένης, τὰ μέγιστα καὶ ἀναγκαιότατα μέρη βασιλεύς ἐστι καὶ πατριάρχης. [...]	8. The state consists of limbs and parts, just as man. The biggest and most essential limbs are the emperor and patriarch. [...]
θ'. Ὁ κωνσταντινουπόλεως θρόνος βασιλείᾳ ἐπικοσμηθεὶς ταῖς συνοδικαῖς ψήφοις πρῶτος ἀνεῤῥήθη, αἷς οἱ θεῖοι κατακολουθοῦντες νόμοι καὶ τὰς ὑπὸ τοὺς ἑτέρους θρόνους γινομένας ἀμφισβητήσεις ὑπὸ τὴν ἐκείνου προστάττουσιν ἀναφέρεσθαι διάγνωσιν καὶ κρίσιν. [...]	9. The patriarchal see of Constantinople, as it is adorned with the emperorship, has come first in the synodical decisions.[8] Following their example, the holy statutes lay down that disputes which find place among the other sees are also to be referred to his decision and judgment [= of the patriarch of Constantinople.] [...]

It is clear that the author of these titles is not at all modest when describing the position and functions of the patriarch. This lack of modesty is an added argument in favour of the patriarch Photios's influence on the *Eisagoge*, an influence possibly even extending to direct authorship. He claims a position of considerable authority and power; it is therefore not difficult to understand that Photios was not universally liked, nor that the next emperor, Leo VI, apparently did not like him at all, forcing him to resign as patriarch. In fact, the title of the *Eisagoge* which refers to the authority of the patriarch is one of the most compelling reasons to date the *Prochiron* later than the *Eisagoge*, contrary to what the lists of co-emperors indicate: it would then have had the function of doing away with a legal text that contained a few controversial titles which undermined the position of the emperor, and which had been made under the influence of someone who had since fallen into disgrace.[9] We should also point out that the *Eisagoge* is the only legal compilation in which the functions of the emperor and the patriarch are described, and in that respect, it is a unique piece of Byzantine legal literature.

3 The *Basilica* Puzzle

We have mentioned the *Basilica* more than once by now. In this section we will finally focus on and explain the *Basilica*. Hopefully, this will make earlier references to this work clear as well.

8 Decisions of synods are technically called canons see below, pp. 191–197.

9 As already mentioned, Photios was a controversial figure in Byzantium; for a few titles from the vast literature on this subject, see the bibliography provided at the end of this chapter.

Put briefly, the *Basilica* (τὰ Βασιλικὰ νόμιμα) or the 'Imperial laws' amount to the Greek rendering of Justinianic legislation. They epitomise the 'purge' of laws that the Macedonian emperors wanted to achieve. The idea behind the making of the *Basilica* was to create one law that would consist of the different parts of Justinian's legislation, but produced in the Greek language. By the time of the Macedonian dynasty, as mentioned earlier, there were many Greek legal works related to or deriving from Justinian's legislation, such as Greek *summae* and *indices* of the *Digest*, the *Code*, etc. The *Basilica* compilers thought that instead of consulting all these Greek summaries, versions and commentaries on Justinian's legislation, it would be better and more convenient to have one law in Greek that would consist of all four parts of Justinian's legislation: the *Code*, the *Digest*, the *Institutes* and the *Novels*, though the majority of the latter had been issued in Greek anyways. The result was the *Basilica*, a massive compilation of laws consisting of sixty books that rendered in Greek the different parts of Justinian's legislation.[10]

The *Basilica* were published in about 900 under Leo VI the Wise (886–912), after the death of his father Basil I, but preparation for the work had begun earlier, as noted in the prefaces of both the *Prochiron* and the *Eisagoge*. In fact, the information contained in these two prefaces can be confusing because they mention the *Basilica* as if they were already completed, whether in forty or sixty books. What is actually meant by this is that the real work of 'purging' the laws had been completed, but the physical books themselves had not yet been written. The *Basilica* compilers had made a list of all the abolished and outdated laws: that was the 'one volume' or the 'one book' mentioned in the *Prochiron*. Consequently, everything that was not listed in this one volume remained valid. In other words, at that stage, if you were confronted with a law text you could simply check your 'one volume of abolished laws', and if a particular rule or provision could not be found there, then it was valid. In addition, all the remaining (i.e. non-purged) laws were rearranged. Instead of having fifty books of the *Digest*, twelve of the *Code* and one hundred sixty-eight of the *Novels*, there were now sixty *Basilica* books. Each *Basilica* book was subdivided into titles, and each title contained the relevant parts of the *Digest*, the *Code* and the *Novels* as well as parts of the *Institutes* in a few cases. This was indeed a lot of work, especially if, according to some sources, the compilers suddenly decided to reduce this material into forty books, rather than sixty, even if they then they changed their minds and produced sixty books after all.

The theory, therefore, is that in the time of Basil I there were only lists, like a kind of table of contents, which would have looked like this: '*Basilica* book A title 1 deals with subject B and it consists of *Digest* C, *Code* D and *Novels* E'. Next, if you wanted to know what these laws actually said, you had to consult your own Greek copy of the *Digest* and *Code*. If you had to consult the *Digest*, you could, for example, look in the works of Stephanos or Dorotheos; and if you wanted to consult the *Code*, you would look in the work of Thalelaios, Anatolios or Isidoros, depending on what volumes were at your disposal. Thus, the

10 Little has been included from the *Institutes* in the *Basilica*.

first stage of compiling the *Basilica* was to draw up these table of contents. The next logical step was to fill in these contents with Greek texts. At this stage, the *Basilica* compilers apparently selected a sixth-century version for the official *Basilica* text. For the *Digest*, they chose the *Digest summa* of 'the Anonymos Senior'; for the *Code* they chose the Code *index* of Thalelaios, except for book eight, where they used the *Code summa* by Anatolios instead because they did not possess Thalelaios's version for book eight at that time. For the *Novels*, there was no one standard version: often, the compilers took the original, since it was in Greek anyway, but in some cases, they used the works of Athanasios and Theodoros. This 'filling in', as we call it, was done under Leo VI the Wise and the result was the *Basilica*. In a way, the compilers of the *Basilica* had to assemble a puzzle. They had the tables of contents in their hands, and their task was to try and find equivalent Greek versions to fill in and complete this puzzle.

Hence, the *Basilica* basically consist of sixth-century texts. As mentioned in an earlier section,[11] the sixth-century jurists, the *antecessores*, had not translated technical legal terms into Greek, but instead preferred to use the original Latin legal terminology, sometimes transliterated in Greek letters.[12] In some cases, the *Basilica* compilers used a Greek equivalent word for a Latin technical term. In other words, they sometimes attempted to 'exhellenizein' (ἐξελληνίζειν), i.e. to use Greek words for the Latin legal terms. These Greek adaptations, the *exhellenismoi*, were not all made at the same time. We know this because of the fact that the *exhellenismoi* are not always the same in the surviving manuscripts. In many of his writings, N. van der Wal has examined the problems related to these Greek adaptations and, more generally, to linguistic issues concerning the *Basilica* text and scholia.[13] The *Basilica* were issued around 900, as mentioned above. In a later stage, scholia were added to the *Basilica* text and these scholia are divided, as we will see, into the 'old' ones, which date from the sixth century, and the 'new' scholia, which date from the eleventh and twelfth centuries.[14]

The latest critical edition of the *Basilica* was made in Groningen by H. J. Scheltema, N. van der Wal and D. Holwerda. This monumental edition, which took many years to complete (1953–1988), comprises eight volumes containing the *Basilica* text (series A), and nine volumes containing the *Basilica* scholia (series B). Thus, text and scholia have been edited separately. The Groningen *Basilica* edition is now available online, published by Brill (see: https://referenceworks.brillonline.com/browse/basilica-online (date of access: 08/11/2021)). This digital Groningen edition of the *Basilica* is accompanied by two texts which are extremely useful for any scholar of Byzantine law, and in particular for those who want to use the Groningen *Basilica* edition and study any subject related to the *Basilica*. The first text, written by B.H. Stolte, is called the new *praefa-*

11 See above, pp. 40–42.

12 See above, pp. 41–42.

13 See the bibliography at the end of this chapter.

14 See below, pp. 137–143 and 152–164.

tio, i.e. a new introduction to the online Groningen *Basilica* edition.[15] It is intended to remedy the lack of a comprehensive introduction to the completed print edition (Prolegomena), which otherwise has to be gathered together from the Latin prefaces of the various volumes and from a number of separate papers. Stolte provides not only a background to the *Basilica* text and scholia, but also discusses the manuscript tradition of the *Basilica* and the previous editions that had been made of the *Basilica*; he further elaborates information on the Groningen edition itself, including information on how to actually use this edition. To take a simple but important example: Stolte explains all the signs and abbreviations that appear throughout the critical apparatus. The second text that accompanies the Groningen *Basilica* online edition is an extended bibliography by Th.E. van Bochove. This bibliography is very useful because he has selected and categorised on a subject-by-subject basis all bibliography that is related to the *Basilica*. Moreover, van Bochove not only provides the relevant bibliography per *Basilica* subject, but he often provides a short explanatory introduction to every *Basilica* subject that precedes each bibliographical subject. In short, both texts—that of Stolte and that of van Bochove—not only help scholars who are familiar with the *Basilica*, but they are also invaluable to 'beginners' of Byzantine law who would like to study *Basilica* subjects and use the Groningen edition. It is therefore very beneficial indeed that both texts by Stolte and van Bochove can be consulted online and free of charge on the relevant site by Brill.[16]

For the following examples, we use two pages from the Groningen edition of the *Basilica*, to illustrate the description just provided (TEXT 4).[17] The example concerns *Basilica* book twenty-four, second title, which deals with reclaiming payments made for an immoral or illegal purpose. The actual legal subject is not of interest at this point, and for this reason we do not provide the translation; we use these two pages of the Groningen edition (pages BT 1152–1153) only to illustrate the composition of the *Basilica*. As we can see in the underlined red box, the *Basilica* text B. 24,2,1 corresponds to the *Digest* fragment D. 12,5,1. The Greek text used to render the Latin *Digest* fragment is taken from the *summa* of 'the Anonymos Senior', as described above. At the end of page 1152, we see that the editors helpfully point out the existence of *Basilica* scholia on this *Basilica* fragment. The relevant preserved scholia are listed under the word **Scholia** in bold letters. For example, we can see that there are two scholia preserved in manuscript Pa, scholia no. 1 and no. 2 that refer to line 3 of this page, which is the rubric, i.e. the title of this *Basilica* book. To consult these scholia one has to look in the B series of the Groningen edition. If scholia to any given title survive in more than a single manuscript, then the scholia of each manuscript have been edited separately. On the same page (BT 1152), after mention-

15 This text has also been published: B.H. Stolte, 'Praefatio to the Basilica On-Line', FM, 13 (2021), pp. 239–264.
16 Mentioned above.
17 BT 1152–1153. With kind permission of Brill.

ing whether any *Basilica* scholia have been preserved for this part, references are given to these *Basilica* fragments insofar as they also are found in other Byzantine legal sources. These references are cited after the word **Testimonia** in bold letters. In the Testimonia, legal sources are abbreviated; for example, the abbreviation Tip. stands for *Tipoukeitos*, a work that we will explain in the next chapter.[18] Finally, at the end of the page we see the relevant critical apparatus for this page. In the critical apparatus the authors point out differences with other manuscripts.

On the next page of the Groningen edition that we provide here (BT 1153), we have underlined in a red box the *Basilica* fragment B. 24,2,10, which corresponds to the *Code*, part C. 4,7,1. The Greek version of the *Code* for this *Basilica* part is taken from the *Code index* by Thalelaios, as explained above. Again, at the end of the page, we see whether any relevant *Basilica* scholia have been preserved for this *Basilica* part, and one can consult these scholia in the series B of the Groningen edition. Existing scholia are cited after the word **Scholia** in bold letters. Under the word **Testimonia** in bold letters we find references to these *Basilica* fragments in other Byzantine legal sources. Finally, at the end of the page the relevant critical apparatus is given for this page.

A last point regarding the *Basilica* concerns the question of whether or not they can be considered a codification. Most scholars believe that the *Basilica* were not considered a codification at the time that they were issued. We have seen that Justinian had paid particular attention to the exclusivity of his codification. He had made clear that what was not included in his codification would not henceforth be valid. The exclusivity clause is a basic element for meeting the criteria of codification. When the *Basilica* were issued, no exclusivity clause was included. It was only later on, during the time of Manuel I Komnenos (1120–1180), that the emperor ordered that the *Basilica* were to replace the Justinianic legislation and that they were to be exclusive. The emperor ordered this because of a legal question that arose concerning the appointment of a bishop, a case that we will discuss in detail in the chapter about canon law.[19]

---

18 See below, pp. 164–167.
19 See below, pp. 199–200.

TEXT 4 From the *Basilica* (BT 1152–1153)

1152 LIB. XXIV — TIT. II

LIBRI XXIV TITULUS II

Τίτλος β΄.

Περὶ ἀπαιτήσεως πράγματος ἐπὶ αἰσχρῷ ἢ ἀδίκῳ διδομένου

B XXIV, 2, 1 = D XII, 5, 1. Πᾶν διδόμενον ἢ διὰ πρᾶγμα δίδοται
ἢ διὰ αἰτίαν, τὸ δὲ διὰ αἰτίαν ἢ σεμνὴν ἢ αἰσχράν· καὶ ἡ αἰσχρότης ἢ τοῦ
1 διδόντος ἐστὶ μόνου ἢ τοῦ λαμβάνοντος ἢ ἑκατέρου. Τὸ μὲν οὖν ἐπὶ σεμνῷ
2 πράγματι δοθὲν τότε ἀναλαμβάνεται, ὅτε μὴ γένηται. Εἰ δὲ αἰσχρότης ἐστὶ
τοῦ λαβόντος, κἂν ἐποίησε τὸ πρᾶγμα ἐφ᾽ ᾧ ἔλαβεν, ἀποδίδωσιν,

Digest *summa* of 'the Anonymos Senior'

B XXIV, 2, 2 = D XII, 5, 2. ὡς ἔνθα τις λάβῃ ἐπὶ τῷ μὴ φονεῦσαι
1 2 ἢ μὴ ἱεροσυλῆσαι ἢ μὴ κλέψαι, ἢ ἐπὶ τῷ δοῦναι παραθήκην ἢ δικαίωμα. Εἰ
δὲ καλὴν δίκην ἔχων παράσχω τῷ δικαστῇ ἐπὶ τῷ ὑπὲρ ἐμοῦ ψηφίσασθαι,
εἰ καὶ ἀναλαμβάνω, ὅμως ἔγκλημα πλημμελῶ τὸν δικαστὴν ὑποφθείρων καὶ
ἐκπίπτω τῆς δίκης.

B XXIV, 2, 3 = D XII, 5, 3. Εἰ δὲ αἰσχρότης ἐστὶ τοῦ διδοῦντος καὶ
τοῦ λαμβάνοντος, ἀργεῖ ἡ ἀνάληψις, ὡς ἔνθα δικαστὴς λάβῃ ἐπὶ τῷ κακῶς
ψηφίσασθαι.

B XXIV, 2, 4 = D XII, 5, 4. ἢ ἐπὶ πορνείᾳ, ἢ ὁ συσχεθεὶς μοιχὸς
1 2 ἢ κλέπτης. Εἰ δὲ μόνου τοῦ λαμβάνοντός ἐστιν αἰσχρότης, ἁρμόζει ἀνάληψις,
3 ἔνθα τυχὸν δέδωκά σοι διὰ τὸ μὴ ὑβρίσαι με. Τὸ διδόμενον πόρνῃ οὐκ ἀναδίδο-
ται· ἐπειδὴ γάρ ἐστι πόρνη, οὐκ ἔστιν αἰσχρὸν τὸ λαβεῖν αὐτήν, εἰ καὶ αἰσχρὸν
4 ἐστι τὸ εἶναι αὐτὴν πόρνην. Οὔτε τὸ διδόμενόν τινι ἐπὶ τῷ καταμηνῦσαι τὸν
κλέπτην ἢ τὸν φυγάδα, εἰ μὴ αὐτὸς ὁ κλέπτης ἢ ὁ κοινωνήσας αὐτῷ ἢ τῷ
φυγάδι ἔλαβε τὸ μήνυτρον. Εἰ δὲ ἀπὸ τοῦ φυγάδος μου λάβῃς, ἵνα μὴ καταμη-
νύσῃς αὐτόν, ἐνέχῃ μοι ὡς κλέπτης.

Scholia:
Rubr. 3 περὶ: Pa 1, 2
B XXIV, 2, 1 7 πράγματι: Pa 1 | 8 ἔλαβεν: Pa 2
B XXIV, 2, 2 10 παραθήκην: Pa 1 | 11 καλὴν: Pa 2, 3
B XXIV, 2, 3 14 ἐστὶ: Pa 1
B XXIV, 2, 4 17 συσχεθεὶς: Pa 1 | 19 διδόμενον: Pa 2 | 21 οὔτε: Pa 3, 4

References to *Basilica* scholia edited in series B

Testimonia:
Rubr. A | A^{i} | Tip. | ICb || **B XXIV, 2, 4** A | Syn. Δ, XXX, 9

References of these *Basilica* fragments in other sources

---

3 διδομένου: A A^{i} Tip. ICb, διδομένων Pa

Critical apparatus

TEXT 4 *(cont.)*

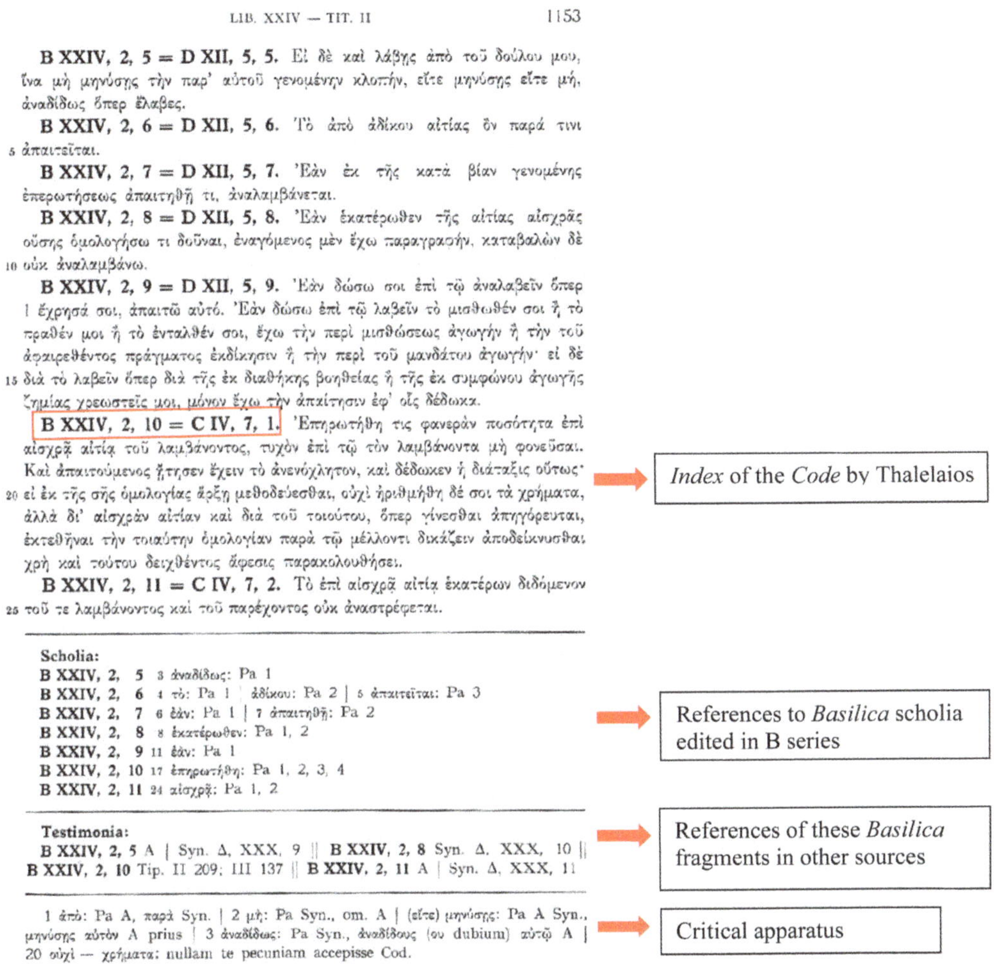

LIB. XXIV — TIT. II 1153

B XXIV, 2, 5 = D XII, 5, 5. Εἰ δὲ καὶ λάβῃς ἀπὸ τοῦ δούλου μου, ἵνα μὴ μηνύσῃς τὴν παρ' αὐτοῦ γενομένην κλοπήν, εἴτε μηνύσῃς εἴτε μή, ἀναδίδως ὅπερ ἔλαβες.

B XXIV, 2, 6 = D XII, 5, 6. Τὸ ἀπὸ ἀδίκου αἰτίας ὂν παρά τινι ἀπαιτεῖται.

B XXIV, 2, 7 = D XII, 5, 7. Ἐὰν ἐκ τῆς κατὰ βίαν γενομένης ἐπερωτήσεως ἀπαιτηθῇ τι, ἀναλαμβάνεται.

B XXIV, 2, 8 = D XII, 5, 8. Ἐὰν ἑκατέρωθεν τῆς αἰτίας αἰσχρᾶς οὔσης ὁμολογήσω τι δοῦναι, ἐναγόμενος μὲν ἔχω παραγραφήν, καταβαλὼν δὲ οὐκ ἀναλαμβάνω.

B XXIV, 2, 9 = D XII, 5, 9. Ἐὰν δώσω σοι ἐπὶ τῷ ἀναλαβεῖν ὅπερ ἔχρησά σοι, ἀπαιτῶ αὐτό. Ἐὰν δώσω ἐπὶ τῷ λαβεῖν τὸ μισθωθέν σοι ἢ τὸ πραθέν μοι ἢ τὸ ἐνταλθέν σοι, ἔχω τὴν περὶ μισθώσεως ἀγωγὴν ἢ τὴν τοῦ ἀφαιρεθέντος πράγματος ἐκδίκησιν ἢ τὴν περὶ τοῦ μανδάτου ἀγωγήν· εἰ δὲ διὰ τὸ λαβεῖν ὅπερ διὰ τῆς ἐκ διαθήκης βοηθείας ἢ τῆς ἐκ συμφώνου ἀγωγῆς ζημίας χρεωστεῖς μοι, μόνον ἔχω τὴν ἀπαίτησιν ἐφ' οἷς δέδωκα.

B XXIV, 2, 10 = C IV, 7, 1. Ἐπηρωτήθη τις φανερὰν ποσότητα ἐπὶ αἰσχρᾷ αἰτίᾳ τοῦ λαμβάνοντος, τυχὸν ἐπὶ τῷ τὸν λαμβάνοντα μὴ φονεῦσαι. Καὶ ἀπαιτούμενος ᾔτησεν ἔχειν τὸ ἀνενόχλητον, καὶ δέδωκεν ἡ διάταξις οὕτως· εἰ ἐκ τῆς σῆς ὁμολογίας ἄρξῃ μεθοδεύεσθαι, οὐχὶ ἠριθμήθη δέ σοι τὰ χρήματα, ἀλλὰ δι' αἰσχρὰν αἰτίαν καὶ διὰ τοῦ τοιούτου, ὅπερ γίνεσθαι ἀπηγόρευται, ἐκτεθῆναι τὴν τοιαύτην ὁμολογίαν παρὰ τῷ μέλλοντι δικάζειν ἀποδείκνυσθαι χρὴ καὶ τούτου δειχθέντος ἄφεσις παρακολουθήσει.

B XXIV, 2, 11 = C IV, 7, 2. Τὸ ἐπὶ αἰσχρᾷ αἰτίᾳ ἑκατέρων διδόμενον τοῦ τε λαμβάνοντος καὶ τοῦ παρέχοντος οὐκ ἀναστρέφεται.

Scholia:
B XXIV, 2, 5 3 ἀναδίδως: Pa 1
B XXIV, 2, 6 4 τό: Pa 1 | ἀδίκου: Pa 2 | 5 ἀπαιτεῖται: Pa 3
B XXIV, 2, 7 6 ἐάν: Pa 1 | 7 ἀπαιτηθῇ: Pa 2
B XXIV, 2, 8 8 ἑκατέρωθεν: Pa 1, 2
B XXIV, 2, 9 11 ἐάν: Pa 1
B XXIV, 2, 10 17 ἐπηρωτήθη: Pa 1, 2, 3, 4
B XXIV, 2, 11 24 αἰσχρᾷ: Pa 1, 2

Testimonia:
B XXIV, 2, 5 A | Syn. Δ, XXX, 9 || **B XXIV, 2, 8** Syn. Δ. XXX, 10 || **B XXIV, 2, 10** Tip. II 209; III 137 || **B XXIV, 2, 11** A | Syn. Δ, XXX, 11

1 ἀπό: Pa A, παρὰ Syn. | 2 μή: Pa Syn., om. A | (εἴτε) μηνύσῃς: Pa A Syn., μηνύσῃς αὐτὸν A prius | 3 ἀναδίδως: Pa Syn., ἀναδίδους (ου dubium) αὐτῷ A | 20 οὐχὶ — χρήματα: nullam te pecuniam accepisse Cod.

4 The *Novels* of Leo VI the Wise

Leo VI the Wise is the second most productive emperor who issued *Novels*, the first of course being Justinian. There are 113 *Novels* of Leo VI collected in one volume. It has been suggested that Leo VI wrote most of these *Novels*, or, if he did not write the whole text of the laws, he at least wrote the prefaces to them, which are usually rather long and rhetorical. A *Novel*, as we have explained in the section of Justinian's legislation,[20] is a new law, a

20 See above, p. 30

new imperial constitution issued by an emperor. In the case of Justinian, the *Novels* were the new laws that Justinian issued after 534, that is, after the promulgation of his second *Code*. Likewise, one would therefore expect that the *Novels* of Leo VI were issued after the *Basilica*; yet, the *Novels* of Leo VI have a different character, as M.Th. Fögen has discovered.[21] Fögen proved that the *Novels* of Leo were not issued after the completion of the *Basilica* (as were the Theodosian and the Justinianic *Novels*) but during the process of the completion of the *Basilica*, and the *Novels* thus served to settle disputes that arose during the making of the *Basilica*. In this respect, they resemble the Fifty Decisions of Justinian rather than his *Novels*.[22]

We will demonstrate the character of the *Novels* of Leo VI with an example, his *Novel* 65. We will first quote the relevant fragments from the *Code* (TEXT 5.1), then the *Code summa* by Anatolios (TEXT 5.2) and *Novel* 65 of Leo (TEXT 5.3), before commenting upon all texts and linking them to a fragment of the *Basilica* text (TEXT 5.4) and one *Basilica* scholion (TEXT 5.5).

TEXT 5.1 C. 9,18,4:[23] the constitution which will be revised by Leo VI in *Novel* 65

4. *Idem A. et C. [= Constantinus] ad Bassum pp.*	4. The Same Emperor and Caesar [= Constantine] to Bassus, Urban Prefect.
pr. *Eorum est scientia punienda et severissimis merito legibus vindicanda, qui magicis adcincti artibus aut contra salutem hominum moliti aut pudicos animos ad libidinem deflexisse detegentur.*	pr. The knowledge of those who are found by means of magic arts to plot against the health or lives of men, or turn chaste minds to licentiousness, should be punished, and repressed by the severest laws.
1. *Nullis vero criminationibus implicanda sunt remedia humanis quaesita corporibus aut in agrestibus locis innocenter adhibita suffragia, ne maturis vindemiis metuerentur imbres aut ruentis grandinis lapidatione quaterentur, quibus non cuiusque salus aut aestimatio laederetur, sed quorum proficerent actus, ne divina munera et labores hominum sternerentur.*	1. Those, however, who seek remedies for the ailments of humanity, or, while in the country, innocently exert themselves to preserve grapes from showers, or from the effects of rain or hail, ought not to be liable to criminal accusations, as their efforts are directed not to the injury of the health or reputation of mankind, but to prevent the gifts of God and the labours of humanity from being destroyed.

21 See M.-Th. Fögen, 'Legislation und Kodifikation des Kaisers Leon VI', SG, 3 (1989), pp. 23–35.

22 See above, p. 23.

23 The Latin text of this constitution is cited from P. Krüger (= C.).

TEXT 5.1 (*cont.*)

D.x k. Iun. Aquileiae Crispo et Constantino cc. conss.	Given at Aquileia, on the tenth of the Kalends of June, during the Consulate of Crispus and Constantinus [321 AD].

TEXT 5.2 **Anatolios' *summa* of C. 9,18,4 (preserved not in the *Basilica*, but in the *Excerpta Vaticana et Laurentiana* 76)[24]**

76. Ἡ γοητεία ἡ ἕλκουσα εἰς ἔρωτα λογισμοὺς ἀπαγορευέσθω. Ἡ μέντοι ἐπὶ θεραπείᾳ σωμάτων γινομένη ἢ διὰ τὸ ἐπισχεῖν βροχὴν ἢ χάλαζαν σωτηριώδης οὖσα φυλαττέσθω, μηδενὶ κίνδυνον φέρουσα.	76. The kind of magic which draws reasonable minds into lust must be forbidden. On the other hand, that which is practised for medical purposes or which is beneficial in that it stops rain or hail must be protected, because it will not harm anybody.

TEXT 5.3 ***Novel* 65 of Leo VI the Wise:[25] amendment to C. 9,18,4 (see TEXT 5.2)**

Ὁ μὲν εἰπὼν μέμφεσθαι τῷ οἴνῳ καὶ τὸ τούτου εὔθυμον ἀποστρέφεσθαι διὰ τὸ τῶν μεθύσων κακόθυμον ἔοικε διὰ φαύλην χρῆσιν τὸ μὴ καθ' ἑαυτὸ φαῦλον ὂν διασύρειν. Ἐγὼ δὲ νόμον ἐκτεθειμένον ὑπὸ τῶν πάλαι νομοθετῶν διασκεπτόμενος ὃς γοητείαν μὲν φαύλην ἡγούμενος τιμωρεῖται, πάλιν δ' αὐτὴν ἀποδέχεται, οὐκ ἐκ τῆς τῶν χρωμένων αὐτῇ προαιρέσεως φαύλην δεικνυμένην, ἀλλ' οἴκοθεν πηγάζουσαν τὴν κακίαν, ὥσπερ οἱ κοπρῶνες τὴν δυσωδίαν, μέμφεσθαι τοῖς νενομοθετηκόσιν οὐκ ἂν φαίην, ἵνα δὲ	Those who blame the wine and deny themselves its cheerfulness because of the bad temper of drunks, seem to depreciate because of its abuse something that is not inherently bad. That is not what I do when I am now going to evaluate a law which was issued by legislators of ancient times. On the one hand, this law condemns and punishes magic, but on the other hand it accepts it all the same, though magic is not just found [to be] evil depending on the user's intentions, but is fundamentally a source of evil, just as sewers are a source of stench. I would not

24 The Greek text and English translation are from J.H.A. Lokin and R. Meijering, *Anatolius and the Excerpta Vaticana et Laurentiana, Edition and Commentary* (Groningen: 1999).

25 The Greek text is cited from the edition of P. Noailles and A. Dain, *Les Novelles de Léon VI le Sage* (Paris: 1944).

TEXT 5.3 (*cont.*)

μὴ μέμφοιντο τὸ τὴν μέμψιν ἔχον νομοθέτημα ἐκκαθαίρειν δικαιῶ τοῦ τῶν νόμων ἐδάφους.

wish to criticize the law-givers, but in order to prevent this disputable law from being criticised by others, I find it best to remove it from the field of law.

Βούλεται μὲν γὰρ εὐθύνειν γοητείαν, ὅτι τὸ σῶφρον τοῦ νοῦ ἀφαιρουμένη ἀναβακχεύει τοὺς λογισμοὺς πρὸς οἴστρους καὶ μανίας ἐρωτικάς, ἀποδέχεται δὲ πάλιν αὐτὴν ὡς σπερμάτων καὶ καρπῶν θεραπείαν καὶ ἄλλων δέ τινων καλῶν, ὡς οἴεται, χορηγόν, καὶ ὅπερ ὡς ἐπίβουλον κολάζει, τοῦτο πάλιν ὡς εὐεργέτην τιμᾷ.

On the one hand it does want to make magic punishable, because it takes away the sanity of mind and rouses to sexual and erotic frenzy; on the other hand, however, it accepts it too as having a beneficial effect on seeds and fruits and leading to certain other salutary—or so it seems—results. So what it punishes as evil, that is honoured by the same law as something beneficial.

Ἡμεῖς δὲ τὴν τοιαύτην μαγγανείαν ὀλεθρίαν μὲν ὑπάρχειν πειθόμεθα, καλοῦ δέ τινος αἰτίαν οὐκ ἂν πεισθείημεν. Εἰ δὲ καὶ φαίνοιτό τι φέρειν τοιοῦτον, ὡς δοκεῖ τῷ ταύτην ἀποδεχομένῳ νόμῳ, οὐ χρηστόν—ἀλλὰ δέλεαρ καὶ πάγην πρὸς τὸ τῶν κακῶν ἔσχατον τὴν τοῦ ὄντος ἀγαθοῦ ἔκπτωσιν ἁλίσκουσαν—ἴσμεν τε καὶ ἔγνωμεν τοὺς πειθομένους δαιμονίοις σκαιοῖς ἀντὶ τοῦ Πλάστου καὶ Δεσπότου προσανέχειν παρασκευάζοντας βλάβας διὰ τῆς τῶν ἐκτὸς ἀλυπίας εἰς τὴν ψυχὴν δέχεσθαι τοὺς ταύτην ἀποδεχομένους· ὅπερ πολλάκις οἱ πρὸς τὰς πληγὰς δειλοὶ πάσχουσιν, οὐ βουλόμενοι ταύτας ἐπὶ τῶν χειρῶν δέξασθαι, κατὰ τῆς κεφαλῆς ἢ τῆς γαστρὸς ὑποδέχονται.

We, however, do believe that such sorcery is pernicious, and we cannot believe that it might cause anything good. And even if any such result might seem possible, as in the opinion of the law that accepted it (and rather than something positive it would be a lure, leading the victim into the worst possible trap: the loss of the true good), even then we know and are convinced that people who listen to false demons instead of following the Creator and Lord achieve that those who embrace this kind of magic, precisely by escaping from pain on the outside, suffer damage to their souls. This experience is very common also in people who duck away from blows: not wanting to be struck on their hands, they are knocked on their heads or hit in their stomachs.

Εἴ τις δὴ ὅλως τοιαῦτα φωραθείη μαγγανευόμενος, εἴτε προφάσει τῆς τοῦ σώματος θεραπείας, εἴτε ἀποτροπῆς τῆς τῶν καρπίμων βλάβης, τὴν ἐσχάτην

Hence, if anyone at all is caught practising magic, whether it is on the pretext of some physical therapy or of averting damage to the crops, he will suffer the severest possible

TEXT 5.3 (*cont.*)

εἰσπραττέσθω ποινήν, τὴν τῶν ἀποστατῶν κόλασιν ὑφιστάμενος.	punishment, being punished as an apostate.

According to C. 9,18,4, a constitution from the year AD 321, there are two kinds of magic (see TEXT 5.1): black magic, which is forbidden, and 'beneficial' magic which is allowed. In the following text (TEXT 5.2), the *antecessor* Anatolios faithfully summarises this constitution, saying that 'beneficial' magic is indeed allowed; the type of 'beneficial' magic he has in mind is, for instance, the magic used for medical purposes or magic that stops the rain, because this kind of magic does not harm anyone. Note, by the way, that this is an Anatolios fragment preserved outside the *Basilica*. Leo VI revises this constitution with his *Novel* 65 (see TEXT 5.3). As we can see, Leo does not believe in 'beneficial' magic, so he changes this law and forbids any kind of magic. If we look into the relevant *Basilica* text (TEXT 5.4) we can see that this revision of Leo VI has been taken into consideration, and that the law was changed accordingly.

TEXT 5.4 **BT 3009/9–11: the *Basilica* text, adapted to the *Novel* 65 of Leo VI**

B. 60, 39, 25 = C. 9,18,4 Ἡ διάταξις βούλεται τὸν ἐπιδειξάμενον γοητείαν ἕλκουσαν εἰς ἔρωτα τοὺς σώφρονας λογισμοὺς ἢ κατὰ τῆς σωτηρίας ἀνθρώπων μηχανησάμενον δημεύσει καὶ ἐξορίᾳ τιμωρεῖσθαι.	The constitution demands that a person who practices magic, which draws reasonable minds into lust, or plots against the salvation of men, is punished by confiscation and exile.

This adaptation has been noticed by the author of a *Basilica* scholion, as we can see in the following fragment:

TEXT 5.5 **BS 3759/9–13 (sch. 1Pe ad B. 60,39,25 = C. 9,18,4): *Basilica* scholion commenting about the 'purged' *Basilica* disagreeing with the 'Platos' [*index* of Thalelaios?]**

Πρόσκειται τῇ διατάξει ἐν τῷ Πλάτει· ὅσα δὲ πρὸς θεραπείαν ἀνθρώπων γίνονται ἢ πρὸς γεωργίαν ἢ πρὸς τὸ τοὺς	In the **'Extensive version' (*Platos*)** of this constitution there is the additional clause 'but what is done with the purpose of

TEXT 5.5 (*cont.*)

καρπούς μὴ ἀπὸ ὄμβρων ἢ ἀπὸ χαλάζης βλαβῆναι, ταῦτα παντὸς ἀπαλλάττεσθαι κινδύνου χρή. Ἀλλ', ὡς ὁρᾷς, οὐκ ἐδέχθη ἐν τῇ ἀνακαθάρσει.	healing people or for the benefit of agriculture or to prevent damage to crops by heavy rain or hail, that must be exempt from all risk'. **But, as you see, this has not been accepted in the purged version.**

The scholiast here notes that the exception about magic for beneficial purposes is present in the 'Extensive version (*Platos*)', but 'as you see', it 'has not been accepted in the purged *Basilica*'. The conclusion is that the committee which made the *Basilica* text adapted it to the *Novel* of Leo, so the *Novels* were chronologically earlier than the *Basilica*. The question that arises is what is meant by the 'Extensive version' (*Platos*) here? It is not the first time that we come across this word. 'Platos', which can be translated as 'extensive version' or 'breadth', is a tricky word in Byzantine law because it can refer to many things. For example, the word 'platos' might refer to the work of Stephanos or to the work of Thalelaios, but it may also be related to the preparatory work that was done for the *Basilica*, or even to the *Basilica* themselves. The author of this scholion, in using the term 'platos', could be referring to the work of Thalelaios, that is the original *Code index* by Thalelaios. Judging from this example, we might be inclined to conclude that Leo's *Novels* were duly taken into consideration by the *Basilica* compilers. However, the compilers did not do so in every case, as has been shown by M.Th. Fögen.

5 The *Prefect's Book*

The last item produced in this period is very different from the other contemporary sources. It was issued in AD 911/12 during the reign of Leo VI the Wise and is called the *Prefect's Book* (the Eparchikon biblion/Ἐπαρχικὸν βιβλίον) because it is a law book addressed to the prefect (eparch) of Constantinople. The prefect was responsible for the guilds (*suntechniai*, συντεχνίαι); these were corporations of specific tradesmen in the Byzantine capital. The *Prefect's Book* is divided into twenty-two chapters and refers to issues concerning the organisation and functioning of different guilds: notaries, silk-merchants, jewelers, candlemakers, soap-boilers, butchers, fishmongers, etc. We quote some fragments of the *Prefects's Book* in the following examples.

TEXT 6.1 The *Prefect's Book*, chapter 1: about notaries[26]

1. Περὶ ταβουλλαρίων [...] 1.2 Ὁ προχειρισθησόμενος ὀφείλει ἐπὶ στόματος ἔχειν τοὺς τεσσαράκοντα τίτλους τοῦ ἐγχειριδίου νόμου καὶ τῶν ἑξήκοντα βιβλίων τὴν γνῶσιν, παιδευθῆναι δὲ καὶ τὴν ἐγκύκλιον παίδευσιν, ὡς ἂν μὴ διαμαρτάνῃ ἐν ταῖς ἐκδόσεσιν, ὀλισθαίνῃ δὲ καὶ περὶ τὴν λέξιν· ἔχειν δὲ καὶ τὸν χρόνον πληρέστατον τοῦ διατρανοῦσθαι καὶ τῷ νοΐ καὶ τῷ σώματι. Χειρὸς δὲ γραφῇ ἐκτυπούτω ἐν τῷ συλλόγῳ τοῦ μή τι τῶν ἀδοκήτων διαπράττεσθαι. εἰ δὲ φωραθείη, ἐκπιπτέτω τοῦ βαθμοῦ.	1. About notaries [...] 1.2 The person who is to become (a notary) has to know by heart the forty titles of the legal manual[27] and to have knowledge of the sixty books,[28] he also has to have a general education, so that he does not make mistakes in his acts and slips into linguistic mistakes; he should also have reached full maturity so that he has been developed mentally and physically. He has to sign before the assembled guild that he will not do anything improper; if he is detected to do that he will fall out of his office.

TEXT 6.2 The *Prefect's Book*, chapter 12: about soap-boilers

12. Περὶ σαπωνοπρατῶν 12.1. Ὁ ἄνευ εἰδήσεως τοῦ ἐπάρχου καὶ τοῦ κατὰ τὴν ἡμέραν προστάτου ἕτερον πρόσωπον μὴ ὂν ἐκ τοῦ συστήματος ἐκδιδάσκων τὴν τοιαύτην τέχνην, ζημίᾳ εἰκοσιτεσσάρων νομισμάτων ὑποκείσθω.	12. About soap-boilers 12.1. If anyone, without the knowledge of the prefect and the acting chairman (of the guild), teaches the trade to an apprentice who is not a member of the guild, he pays a penalty of 24 coins (*solidi*).[29]
12.2. Ὁ τοῖς σαπωνοπράταις καταριθμεῖσθαι μέλλων ἐμφανιζέσθω τῷ ἐπάρχῳ, καὶ τηνικαῦτα παρὰ τοῦ συστήματος εἰσδεχέσθω, καὶ ἐργαστήριον ἀνοιγέτω, μαρτυρούμενος	12.2. If anyone wishes to be accepted among the soap-boilers, he must make it known to the prefect and will then be accepted by the guild and can open a

26 The Greek text of all cited fragments from the *Prefect's Book* comes from the edition by J. Koder, *Das Eparchenbuch Leons des Weisen* (Vienna: 1991).

27 This must refer to the *Prochiron*.

28 These must refer to the *Basilica*.

29 A *solidus* was a golden coin.

TEXT 6.2 (*cont.*)

δηλονότι καὶ ἀσφάλειαν ἀπαιτούμενος τοῦ μηδὲν παρὰ τὰ διατεταγμένα διαπράττεσθαι. παρεχέτω δὲ πρὸς μὲν τὸν δημόσιον νομίσματα ἓξ καὶ ἐν τῷ βασιλικῷ βεστιαρίῳ νομίσματα ἕξ. ὁ δὲ παρὰ ταῦτα κατατολμῶν ὑπεισελθεῖν ἐκδιωκέσθω τοῦ συστήματος.	workshop. Of course he must declare and guarantee in the presence of witnesses that he will not act against the rules of the guild. He must pay six coins to the state and six to the emperor's purse. If anyone tries to enter the guild without keeping to these rules, he must be excluded.
12.3. Ὁ καινὸν ἀνοῖξαι ἐργαστήριον σαπωνοπράτου μέλλων ἐκφευγέτω ἀπὸ τοῦ παλαιὸν χρηματίζοντος ἐργαστήριον πήχυς ἑπτὰ καὶ πόδας δώδεκα· ὁ δὲ ἐντὸς τῆς τοιαύτης διαστολῆς πειρώμενος ἀνοῖξαι ζημιούσθω εἰκοσιτέσσαρα νομίσματα καὶ ἐκδιωκέσθω.	12.3. If anyone wishes to set up a new soap-boiler's shop, he must keep a space of seven yards and twelve feet from the nearest existing workshop; if he tries to set up a shop within this distance, he pays a penalty of twenty-four coins and is thrown out of the guild.
12.4. Ὀφείλει ὁ σαπωνοπράτης μήτε γάλλικον πωλεῖν μήτε τοῖς μεταπράταις ἀπεμπολεῖν σαπώνιον τοῖς μὴ ὑπὸ τὴν αὐτὴν οὖσι τέχνην. ὁ δὲ μὴ οὕτω ποιῶν τῇ προειρημένῃ ὑποκείσθω εὐθύνῃ.	12.4. Soap-boilers are not allowed to sell Gallic soap, nor to sell soap to middlemen; if they do, they are punished as above.

The *Prefect's Book* is a valuable source shining a light on the economic activities that took place in tenth-century Constantinople; it also illuminates the practices of merchants and, more broadly, daily life in the Byzantine capital. It provides information not only about the various professional guilds and their organisation, but also about manufacture, commerce and state policy concerning all sorts of products. For example, the production of silk was considered an important craft, and the *Prefect's Book* provides detailed rules governing the protection of the secrets of this craft, including severe punishments for transgressors. We quote in the following two examples some relevant fragments concerning silk production and commerce from the *Prefect's Book*.

TEXT 6.3 ***The Prefect's Book*: provisions protecting silk production and commerce**

6. Περὶ τῶν μεταξοπρατῶν 6.16 Οἱ μεταξοπράται μὴ ἀπεμπολείτωσαν τὴν μέταξαν Ἑβραίοις ἢ ἐμπόροις πρὸς τὸ διαπιπράσκειν αὐτὴν ἔξω τῆς πόλεως.	6. About silk-merchants 6.16 The silk-merchants should not sell the silk to Jews or merchants who would want to resell it outside the city. Whoever does

TEXT 6.3 (*cont.*)

οἱ δὲ τοῦτο ποιοῦντες τυπτέσθωσαν καὶ κουρευέσθωσαν. [...]	this will be beaten and their hair will be cut off. [...]
8. Περὶ σηρικαρίων 8.7 Ὁ οἰκέτην, ἢ μισθωτὸν ἢ ἐκλέκτην, ἐξωτικοῖς ἢ ἐθνικοῖς πιπράσκων χειροκοπείσθω.	8. About silk-manufacturers 8.7 He who sells a slave or a hired worker (skilled in silk) or a worker who sorts out the silk[30] to foreigners or provincials will have his hand cut off.

6 The 'Old' *Basilica* Scholia

The *Basilica* were promulgated around 900 during the reign of Leo VI the Wise. Leo died in 912 and was succeeded by his son Constantine VII the 'Porphyrogennetos', an epithet that means in Greek 'the purple-born'. This needs some explanation. Leo VI was married four times, and his only son Constantine VII was the offspring of his fourth marriage with Zoe Karbonopsina. There were questions about the legitimacy of the fourth wedding of Leo VI, an issue that is known in literature as the conflict over the tetragamy of Leo VI. The epithet 'purple-born', used after the name of Constantine VII, was meant to emphasise his legitimate imperial title, because the colour purple, the 'porphyra', was the imperial colour. It was a custom for the empress to give birth in the purple chamber of the imperial palace. All legitimate children of the reigning emperors were born in this chamber. The epithet 'Porphyrogennetos', 'purple-born', thus indicates that Constantine VII was born in this room and was therefore a legitimate child of the contemporary reigning emperor, Leo VI the Wise. Constantine had been crowned co-emperor—probably in 908—and when his father died, he officially succeeded him to the throne; in reality, however, he was too young to reign, and his actual, personal rule began from 945.

Constantine VII is better known as a scholar emperor. He promoted the compilation of encyclopaedic works, such as the *Geoponika* (Περὶ γεωργίας ἐκλογαί), which was an encyclopaedia on agriculture commissioned by the emperor and was based on excerpts from ancient writers. The author of this work begins with a long and flattering dedication to Emperor Constantine VII. The author praises the emperor for his achievements, for serv-

30 It is unclear how to translate the word 'ἐκλέκτην'. It has been suggested that this term could indicate the worker who sorted out the silk and selected the silk based on its quality. Koder translates the term in German as 'Sortierer (Titrierer?)'. See J. Koder, *Das Eparchenbuch Leons des Weisen* (Vienna: 1991), p. 105.

ing his subjects in the best way, and for showing an interest in and improving all aspects of the sciences and art. Moreover, under the name of Constantine VII, several works survive that talk about the administrative system of the empire and its foreign relations; one such example is the work *De administrando imperio* ('On the Governance of the Empire'), which can be characterised as a manual by the emperor for his son. In fact, the Greek title of this work is 'To [my] own son Romanos' (Πρὸς τὸν ἴδιον υἱὸν Ρωμανόν). This work gives us information about the relations between Byzantium and its neighbours, and about Byzantine diplomacy more broadly. It was probably on the initiative of Constantine VII that the so-called 'old' *Basilica* scholia were added to the *Basilica* from the middle of the tenth century onwards.

The 'old' *Basilica* scholia are extracts from mostly sixth-century (and a few early seventh-century) commentaries and versions of the *Digest*, the *Code* and the *Novels*. In other words, the 'old' *Basilica* scholia are fragments of writings mostly produced by the *antecessores*. It is important to recognise at this point that this is how the *antecessorian* writings have been preserved in their vast majority: they have been selected and re-used as *Basilica* scholia and have been preserved as such. The *Digest index* and *paragraphai* by Stephanos, for example, or the *Code index* by Thalelaios, have been preserved indirectly in the manuscripts either as the *Basilica* text or as scholia to this text. As mentioned above, the *Basilica* scholia have been edited separately in the Groningen edition. We will now first show one page from this edition with examples of 'old' scholia (see TEXT 7 on the next page).[31] The actual content of these scholia is not important at this point, so we will not translate them, and instead only indicate the names of the so-called scholiasts in a box in the margin of the page. Further below we will also give examples of 'old' scholia with translations (see TEXTS 8, 9, 10 and 11 on pp. 141–143).[32]

A question that arises is why the 'old' scholia, i.e. these sixth-century (and a few early seventh-century) fragments were added to the *Basilica* text from the tenth century onwards. Again, one has to take into account the actual nature and composition of the *Basilica*. Put simply, the *Basilica* text, as we explained in an earlier section, consists of sixth-century writings. The *Basilica* were promulgated in Greek around 900, but they do reflect Justinianic legislation. In this respect, it makes sense to read and use fragments from the sixth century that explain Justinianic legislation, because such fragments can help people better understand the *Basilica* text itself. In other words, the sixth-century (and a few early seventh-century) fragments that were added in the *Basilica* text and are now known as 'old' *Basilica* scholia clearly help in the interpretation of the *Basilica* text itself. Obviously, the people who added them thought it would be a pity not to include them because they were helpful for the reader. Thus, the 'old' *Basilica* scholia date from the sixth century and are in fact originally scholia not on the *Basilica*, but on

31 BS 1735. With kind permission of Brill.

32 In the next chapter we will discuss the so-called 'new' scholia, see below, pp. 152–164.

TEXT 7 The 'old' *Basilica* scholia: example of the lay-out in the Groningen edition

LIB. XXIV — TIT. II (Pa) 1735

SCHOLIA AD BASILICORVM LIB. XXIV TIT. II
E COD. MS. PAR. GR. 1348 *(Pa)*.

Ad rubricam.

1. Βιβ. β'. τῶν Διγ. τιτ. ε'. καὶ βιβ. ιβ'. τῶν Διγ. τιτ. [ε'.], τῶν DERÉBUS α'.

2. Βιβ. β'. τῶν Διγ. τιτ. ε'.· βιβ. ιβ'. τῶν Διγ. τιτ. ε'., α'. τῶν δερ[έβους].

B XXIV, 2, 1 = D XII, 5, 1.

1. Κυρίλλου. Τὸ διὰ σεμνὴν αἰτίαν δοθέν, ἐὰν μὴ γένηται ἡ αἰτία, ῥεπετι- Hb III 15 τεύεται. Τὸ δὲ δι' αἰσχρὰν αἰτίαν τοῦ λαβόντος δοθέν, κἂν γένηται ἡ αἰτία, ῥεπετιτεύεται· οἷον δέδωκά σοι, ἵνα μὴ φονεύσῃς ἢ ἀποδῷς μοι ὃ παρεθέμην σοι δικαίωμά μου, ἢ δικαστῇ, ἵνα ὑπὲρ ἐμοῦ ψηφίσηται εἰς καλὸν πρᾶγμα, εἰ καὶ τοῦτο ποιῶν ἐκπίπτω τῆς δίκης καὶ ὑπόκειμαι καὶ τῷ δεφάλσις. Εἰ δὲ κακὸν πρᾶγμα εἶχον, οὔτε ῥεπετιτεύω· ἑκατέρου γὰρ αἰσχρά ἐστιν αἰτία. Ταὐτόν ἐστι κἂν ὡς στροῦπτον ἢ κλοπὴν ποιήσας δῶ, ἵνα μὴ προδοθῇ. Ὅτε μόνου τοῦ λαβόντος αἰσχρά ἐστιν αἰτία, οἷον ἐὰν δῶ σοι, ἵνα μὴ ὑβρίσῃς με, χώρα τῇ ῥεπετιτίονι.

→ scholion taken from the *Digest summa* of Cyrillus

2. Στεφάνου. Ὅτι ἔνθα αἰσχρὰ αἰτία μόνου τοῦ λαβόντος ὑπόκειται, κἂν γένηται ἡ αἰτία, ἐφ' ᾗ ἐδόθη, τὰ διδόμενα ῥεπετιτεύεται.

→ scholion taken from the *paragraphai* of Stephanos

B XXIV, 2, 2 = D XII, 5, 2.

1. Τὸ αὐτὸ καὶ ἐπὶ τῆς κομοδάτης καὶ ἐπὶ τῆς ἐξτεσταμέντο καὶ τῆς ἐξστιπουλάτου. Δύναται δὲ καὶ αὐτὴ ἡ δεποσίτι βοναφίδε οὖσα κινεῖσθαι εἰς ἀπαίτησιν τῶν δοθέντων διὰ τὸ ἀναδοθῆναι τὸ παρατεθέν, ὡς μανθάνεις ἐν τῷ τελευταίῳ διγέστῳ τῆς δεποσίτι τοῦ παρόντος συντάγματος.

2. Σημείωσαι, ὅτι κἂν καλήν τις ἔχῃ ὑπόθεσιν, χρήματα δὲ παράσχῃ τῷ δικαστῇ, ἵνα φυλάξῃ αὐτῷ τὸ δίκαιον, τὰ μὲν δοθέντα ῥεπετιτεύει διὰ τοῦ OBTURBEMCAŨSA κονδικτικίου, ἐγκλήματι δὲ ὑποπίπτει.

3. Στεφάνου. Ὁ τὸν δικαστὴν ὑποφθείρων τῷ Κορνελίῳ δεφάλσις κατέχεται, ὡς ὁ Μαρκιανὸς ἐν τῷ μη'. τῶν Διγ. βιβ. τιτ. ι'. διγ. α'. φησίν. Ἐκπίπτει δὲ καὶ τῆς δίκης ὁ τὸν δικαστὴν ὑποφθείρων, ὡς ὁ Οὐλπιανὸς ἐν τῷ γ'. τῶν Πρώτων βιβ. τιτ. DECALUMNIATÓRIS διγ. α'. φησίν. Ἀλλ' εἰ καὶ τῷ Κορνελίῳ Hb III 16 δεφάλσις ὑπόκειται ὁ τὸν δικαστὴν ὑποφθείρας, ὅμως οὐ τὴν ἐκ τοῦ Κορνελίου

→ scholion taken from the *paragraphai* of Stephanos

4 sch. 1 rubro scriptum est | 12 πρᾶγμα εἶχον: bis Pa | 13 στροῦπτον: i. e. stuprum

→ critical apparatus

SCHELTEMA, *Basilica*, VIII. 2

Justinian's legislation. That is why they are also useful for a better understanding not only of Justinian's legislation, but of Roman law more broadly as well, since Justinian had codified Roman law in his legislation. Let us also not forget that some of the *antecessores* had actually taken part in the committees responsible for drafting Justinian's legislation, notably Dorotheos and Theophilos. They knew very well what they were talking about when they explained or commented on parts of Justinian's legislation. Further, in some cases they could point out the problems that had arisen during the process of transmitting Roman law into Justinian's texts. In short, the 'old' *Basilica* scholia are valuable in many ways.

We will now present four short fragments of 'old' *Basilica* scholia. The fact that they are 'old' scholia is evident from the names mentioned in the headings of the scholia: Cyrillos and Stephanos lived in the sixth century and 'the Anonymos Junior' lived in the beginning of the seventh century. All four scholia deal with questions of partnership. Partnership (*societas*) was an agreement between two or more persons to cooperate and join forces for a common purpose. Before we quote the first actual scholion by Cyrillos, we will give a short explanation on how to cite a *Basilica* scholion.

***How to cite a *Basilica* scholion**

What is the best way of citing a *Basilica* scholion? We will use as an example the scholion by Cyrillos (see TEXT 8), which is cited as follows:

- BS 452/25–28 (scholion Ca 2 ad B. 12,1,4 = D. 17,2,4).

  This is the most complete and best way to cite a *Basilica* scholion because it provides the following data: the pages and lines of the *Basilica* Groningen edition, the manuscript information, the *Basilica* part that this scholion comments on, and the part of Justinian's legislation from which this *Basilica* part derives. Let us decipher the data given in this citation:
  - The BS refers to the Groningen *Basilica* edition, Series B, scholia (see Abbreviations).
  - The number 452 is the page of this edition, and numbers 25–28 indicate the lines of this page.
  - The data in the brackets give information on the actual scholion: its number in the Groningen edition, which manuscript it has been preserved in, which *Basilica* book it comments on, and the *Digest* fragment that this *Basilica* book derives from. In this case, it is scholion no. 2 of manuscript Ca (= Codex Graecus Coislianus 152)[33] commenting on B. 12,1,4, which derives from D. 17,2,4.

We will now quote the actual scholion by Cyrillos, or, to put it more precisely, the *summa* of Cyrillos that has become a *Basilica* scholion about partnership in which he describes how partnership is formed and how it is dissolved:

33 For the repertory of *Basilica* manuscripts containing descriptions of each, please consult the *Repertorium der Handschriften des byzantinischen Rechts* by L. Burgmann et al. (for details see section 8. Select Bibliography at the end of this chapter) and the *New Praefatio* (3. The manuscript tradition of the *Basilica*) by B.H. Stolte on the *Basilica* online edition, at the following link: https://referenceworks.brillonline.com/browse/basilica-online#part6 (date of access: 13/02/2022) and in FM, 13 (2021), pp. 239–264.

TEXT 8 **'Old' *Basilica* scholia: example of Cyrillos**
BS 452/25–28 (scholion Ca 2 ad B. 12,1,4 = D. 17,2,4)

Κυρίλλου. Κοινωνία συνίσταται πράγματι, ῥήματι καὶ δι' ἀγγέλου. Λύεται θανάτῳ, **κάπιτις δεμινουτίονε**, ἐκστάσει ἢ ἐνδείᾳ. Κοινωνία συνίσταται καὶ **τουτόρουμ βονόρουμ** καὶ ἑνὸς πράγματος, καὶ μεταξὺ καὶ ἀπόρου καὶ εὐπορωτέρου. Δωρεᾶς δὲ χάριν οὐ συνίσταται.	Of Cyrillos. A partnership is formed by act, words and by messenger. It is dissolved by death, reduction of civil status, renunciation or poverty. Partnership is formed either by (the contribution of) the whole property[34] or of one good, and between a person who is poor as well as someone who is richer. It is not formed, however, by way of a donation.

Note that Cyrillos does not translate into Greek some legal terms, but prefers to use the Latin terminology transliterated in Greek letters (what we have marked with bold letters in the Greek text): **κάπιτις δεμινουτίονε** = *capitis deminutione*, meaning literally 'of diminished capacity', i.e. of his legal capacity, deterioration of his status, and **τουτόρουμ βονόρουμ** = *totorum bonorum* which means 'of the whole property'.

Partnership in Roman law (and thus also in Byzantine law) was based on the mutual trust of the partners. The *actio pro socio* was the action that any partner could bring against his other partners because of breach of trust. If a partner was condemned by the *actio pro socio*, he also became infamous.[35] Stephanos speaks about this action in the following scholion:

TEXT 9 **'Old' *Basilica* scholia: example of Stephanos**
BS 468/11–15 (scholion Ca 6 ad B. 12,1,35 = D. 17,2,35)

Στεφάνου. Ἐν ᾧ μὴ μετὰ πίστεως ἀγαθῆς ἀνεστράφη περὶ τὰ ἐπίκοινα πράγματα. Τίς οὖν ἡ διαφορά; Ὅτι ὁ μὲν κοινωνὸς ἐναχθεὶς ἀτιμοῦται, ὁ δὲ κληρονόμος αὐτοῦ τῇ πρὸ σόκιο καταδικασθεὶς οὐκ	Of Stephanos. If he has not behaved with good faith with respect to the common goods. Now what is the difference? That the partner on one hand becomes infamous when he is sued, whereas his heir on the other hand does not become

34 That is, when all the goods of the contracting parties are included in the partnership.

35 Infamy (*infamia*) in Roman law was a penalty for wrongful and disgraceful conduct and brought about a restriction of certain rights.

TEXT 9 (*cont.*)

ἀτιμοῦται, καθὸ μὴ **σοῦο νόμινε**, ἀλλὰ **νερεδιταρίῳ** ὁ τοῦ κοινωνοῦ κληρονόμος ἐνάγεται, ὡς ὁ Οὐλπιανὸς ἐν τῷ γ΄. βιβ. τῶν *πρώτων* τιτ. ϛ΄. διγ. β΄. φησίν (D. 3, 2, 6).[36]	infamous when he is condemned because of the ***actio pro socio***, because the heir of the partner is sued not **in his own name** but in his **capacity of heir**, as Ulpian mentions in the third book of the ***Prota***, sixth title, second fragment [where this subject is dealt with.]

Stephanos explains that if the *actio pro socio* is brought and the malicious partner has been condemned but, in the meantime, he has died, then his heir does not become infamous because the heir had not acted in his own name. Stephanos also prefers to use the Latin legal terms transliterated in Greek letters (these are the words that we have marked with bold letters in the fragment). Further, he refers to the *Prota*, as expected. As we have already mentioned in an earlier chapter, the word *Prota* was used to refer to the first four books of the *Digest* that had to be studied (together with the *Institutes*) in the first year of legal studies, according to Justinian's programme.[37] In the following fragment, 'the Anonymos Junior' clarifies that the *actio pro socio* cannot be brought in cases where a time limitation was fixed for the partnership and this period has passed without fault (*culpa*):

TEXT 10 'Old' *Basilica* scholia: example of 'the Anonymos Junior'
BS 512/18–20 (scholion Ca 11 ad B. 12,1,63 = D. 17,2,65)

Τοῦ Ἀνωνύμου. Εἰ δὲ καὶ χρόνος ὡρίσθη τῇ ⟨κοινωνίᾳ⟩ καὶ παρῆλθεν ἄνευ κούλπας, ἀργεῖ ἡ προσοκίο, ὡς διγ. νβ΄. θεμ. ια΄.· ἀνάγνωθι καὶ τὸ πρῶτον τοῦ αὐτοῦ διγέστου ⟨θεμ.⟩.	Of the Anonymos. If there is a time limitation determined for ⟨the partnership⟩ and the period has passed without *culpa*, the action of partnership is not possible, as is said in fragment 52 section 11; read also the first section of the same fragment.

36 The Greek fragment mentions 'third book, sixth title, second fragment', that is D. 3,6,2, but the correct reference is D. 3,2,6.

37 See above, pp. 35–36.

'The Anonymos Junior', who is here commenting on D. 17,2,65, refers to multiple sources. First, he refers to 52 § 11 ⟨of the same title D. 17,2⟩, that is: D. 17,2,52 § 11; and, secondly, to ⟨D. 17,2⟩ 52 § 1. By looking up these two references of Anonymos, we can make the following remark: the first reference indeed makes excellent sense, but for the second reference (D. 17,2, 52 § 1), it seems that the Anonymos must have meant § 2 instead of § 1, or in any case what we now count as § 2.

Finally, in the fourth and last 'old' scholion that we cite here, Stephanos explains another action that is often relevant in partnerships: the *actio communi dividundo*, which was the action for dividing the common property.

TEXT 11 'Old' *Basilica* scholia: example of Stephanos
BS 516/23–25 (scholion Ca 32 ad B. 12,1,63 = D. 17,2,65)

Στεφάνου. Σημείωσαι, ὅτι τὰ μετὰ τὸ διαλυθῆναι τὴν κοινωνίαν εἰς τὰ ἐπίκοινα πράγματα παρ' ἑνὸς τῶν κοινωνῶν γενόμενα δαπανήματα οὐ διὰ τῆς **πρὸ σόκιο**, ἀλλὰ διὰ τοῦ **κομονιοβιδούμδο** ἀπαιτοῦνται.	Of Stephanos. Note that the costs that have been made on the common things by one of the partners after the dissolution of the partnership cannot be reclaimed with the action on partnership (***actio pro socio***) but with the action for dividing common property (***actio communi dividundo***).

These four fragments that we have cited are examples of 'old' *Basilica* scholia. The word 'old' suggests that there are also other kind of *Basilica* scholia that are 'new'. The 'new' *Basilica* scholia date from the eleventh and twelfth centuries and will be examined in the following chapter.[38] In that chapter, we will also explain how to distinguish 'old' *Basilica* scholia from 'new' ones, and the problems that arise from this classification. Before we finish with the tenth century, however, there are another two works that we would like to examine: the *Synopsis maior Basilicorum*, which also dates from this century, and the legal lexica.

7 The *Synopsis Maior Basilicorum* and the Legal Lexica

During the tenth century, all sorts of composite works appeared that combined elements of the *Prochiron*, the *Eisagoge* and even the old *Ecloga* of the iconoclastic emperors. We also see works related to the *Basilica* appearing. The most important of these latter is the

38 See below, pp. 152–161.

Synopsis maior Basilicorum, which dates from around the middle of the tenth century. It consists of selected *Basilica* fragments or their summaries arranged into alphabetical order based on a keyword of the fragment or of the summary. It is divided into twenty-four basic divisions, following the twenty-four letters of the Greek alphabet. Under each letter are the relevant title rubrics of the *Basilica*; for instance, in an English equivalent, the subject of 'sale' would be found under the letter 'S'. We quote a fragment from the table of contents from the Greek letter 'B' and, in example after this, a fragment from the main text of B 2 (about acorns, *balanos*) and B 3 (about the emperor, *basileus*, and the empress *basilissés*).

TEXT 12.1 ***Synopsis maior Basilicorum*: fragment from the table of contents:[39] Letter 'B'**

Περὶ βαθμῶν συγγενείας **Περὶ βαλάνου** **Περὶ βασιλέως καὶ βασιλίσσης ἤτοι αὐγούστης** Περὶ βασιλικῶν ἀντιγραφῶν καὶ διατάξεων καὶ κελεύσεων καὶ τύπων Περὶ βεβαιώσεως τῶν προκομιζομένων ἐγγράφων δικαιωμάτων Περὶ βίας	B 1: about degrees of kinship **B 2: about acorns** **B 3: about the emperor and the empress** B 4: about imperial rescripts and enactments and mandates and edicts B 5: about verifying written documents put forward as proofs B 6: about violence

TEXT 12.2 ***Synopsis maior Basilicorum*: from the main text: B 2 and B 3[40]**

B 2 **Περὶ βαλάνου** 1. Ἀνάγν. **βι. νη' τιτ. κδ' κεφ. κγ'**, ἐν ᾧ φησιν· Ἐὰν βάλανος ἐκ τοῦ ἀγροῦ μου εἰς τὸν σὸν πέσῃ, λέγει ὁ πραίτωρ ἐξεῖναί μοι ἐπὶ τρεῖς ἡμέρας ἐκλέγειν καὶ ἀφαιρεῖσθαι αὐτήν. τὸ αὐτὸ δεῖ νοεῖν καὶ ἐπὶ παντὸς καρποῦ.	B 2 About acorns 1. Read **book 58,24,23**, which says: 'If acorns from my field fall on your field, then the praetor says that I am entitled to collect and appropriate them within three days. You must accept the same rule as valid for all fruits.'

39 From the edition of JGR, vol. V, p. 16.
40 From the edition of JGR, vol. V, pp. 124–125.

TEXT 12.2 (*cont.*)

B 3 **Περὶ βασιλέως καὶ βασιλίσσης ἤτοι αὐγούστης**	B 3 **About the emperor and the empress**
1. Ἀνάγν. βι. β' τιτ. ϛ', οὗτινος ἐν τῷ α' κεφ. φησιν· Ὁ βασιλεὺς τοῖς νόμοις οὐχ ὑπόκειται. ἡ αὐγούστα δὲ ὑπόκειται. δίδωσι δὲ αὐτῇ ὁ βασιλεὺς τὰ ἑαυτοῦ προνόμια.	1. Read book 2 title 6, whose first chapter runs: 'The emperor is not submitted to the laws. The empress is, but the emperor gives her the same privileges that he has'.
2. Ἐν δὲ τῷ β' κεφ.· Ὅπερ ἀρέσει τῷ βασιλεῖ, νόμος ἐστίν, εἴτε δι' ἐπιστολῆς ἐνυπογράφου ὁρίσει ἢ διαγινώσκων ψηφίσεται ἢ ἐξ ἐπιπέδου ὁρίσει ἢ διὰ δόγματος προαγορεύει. καὶ λέγεται ταῦτα διατάξεις. τινὰ δὲ τούτων προσωπικά ἐστι καὶ οὐχ ἕλκονται πρὸς ὑπόδειγμα, εἴτε πρὸς φιλοτιμίαν εἴτε πρὸς ποινήν τινος ἐτέθησαν.	2. And in the second chapter: 'Whatever the emperor decides is the law, whether he declares it in a signed letter, or reads a verdict, or decrees from the ground (that is: not from his throne), or prescribes through a decree. They are called constitutions. Some of them are 'personal' and cannot be used as precedents, whether they were issued in order to honour a specific person or to punish him'.
3. Ἐν δὲ τῷ ιζ' κεφ.Ἡ μεταξὺ δύο τινῶν βασιλέως ἀπόφασις καὶ ἐπὶ τῶν παραπλησίων κρατείτω.	3. In chapter 17: 'The imperial verdict between two persons must also be valid in similar cases'.

There are also many Latin-Greek lexica. We cannot be quite so sure on the dating of these lexica. They presumably date from an earlier period, in the early Macedonian renaissance (i.e. the ninth century), but we thought that it would be appropriate to give some examples of such lexica in this section because we have already mentioned the alphabetical arrangement of the *Synopsis maior Basilicorum*. Most of these lexica have been published in the series of the *Fontes Minores*.[41] The quality of these lexica varies. The entries are basically Latin words, but written in Greek characters. The Latin words printed in capitals in the editions have been added for the benefit of the modern reader: it is not always easy to recognize the word, because it is often quite corrupt. For instance, the example in TEXT 13 is called 'Lexicon αὐσηθ' because the word 'αὐσηθ' (ausith) is the first entry. The Greek 'αὐσηθ' is a corrupted form of the Latin *absit*, 'let it be absent', which is the third-person singular, present subjunctive of the verb '*abesse*' (= be absent). Further, if we say

41 See FM in Abbreviations.

the entries are given in alphabetical order, it is according to the Greek alphabet, which implies that the Greek letter 'β' stands either for the Latin letter 'V' or 'B'.

TEXT 13 Lexicon αὔσηθ (= absit) B 9–20[42]

Latin entries/reconstruction	Greek translation(s)	English translation(s) of the Greek translation(s)
B 9 βίτιον/VITION	ἐλάττωμα, ψόγων αἰτία	fault, defect, shortcoming
10 βία/VIA	στράτα, ἔνθα πεζὸς καὶ μετὰ ὀχήματος πορεύεται	road, where a pedestrian also drives with a cart
11 βετρανός/VET(E)RANOS	πεπαλαιωμένος	veteran
12 βινδικτίοναι/VENDITIONE	πρᾶσις	sale
13 βινδικατίονε/VINDICATIONE	διεκδίκησις	vindication
14 βέρσον/VERSON	ἀναστροφή	refund
15 βουλγαρία/VULGARIA	πληθυντική	plural (??)
16 βονόρουμποσσέσορε / BONORUM POSSESSORE	ὑπάρχων νομεὺς πραγμάτων	being in possession of goods
17 βίτιον/VITION	ἐλάττωμα, αἴτιον ψόγων	flaw
18 βακαντία/VACANTIA	σχολαῖα	vacant
19 βικιναλία/VICINALIA	ὁδὸς ἡ εἰς κώμην ἄγουσα	road leading to a village
20 βίκους/VICUS	κώμη	village

Finally, some lexica are vocabularies applicable only to one specific text. For instance, there is a famous lexicon on the *Paraphrasis Institutionum* by Theophilos, the Lexicon 'Adet', which is a corruption of the Latin *habet*, 'he has', from the Latin verb *habere* (= to have).

8 Select Bibliography

When it comes to the bibliography of the *Basilica*, the following online bibliography, curated by Th.E. van Bochove for the *Basilica* Online Brill, remains indispensable: Basilica Online—Brill (https://referenceworks.brillonline.com/browse/basilica-online). This bibliography is divided into seven sections, as follows:

I. Preliminary works, story, and completion of the Groningen *Basilica* edition
II. Consulting, reading, and quoting the *Basilica cum scholiis*

42 From the edition of the *Lexicon αὔσηθ* by L. Burgmann in FM, 8 (1990), p. 300.

III. Evaluation and significance of the *Basilica cum scholiis*
IV. Critical editions of texts relating to the *Basilica* and recently discovered *Basilica* testimonies
V. Manuscript tradition of the *Basilica cum scholiis*
VI. Studies pertaining to the *Basilica cum scholiis*
VII. Legal education and *antecessores*

Other Literature related to This Chapter

Primary Sources

Burgmann, L. 'Das Lexikon αὐσηθ', FM, 8 (1990), pp. 249–337.
Fögen, M.-Th. 'Das Lexikon zur Hexabiblos aucta', FM, 8 (1990), pp. 153–214.
Koder, J. *Das Eparchenbuch Leons des Weisen*. Vienna: 1991.
Kollias, T. and M. Chroni. *Τὸ Ἐπαρχικὸν βιβλίον Λέοντος ϛ' τοῦ Σοφοῦ* [= The Book of the Eparch of Leo VI the Wise]. Athens: 2010.
Meijering, R. 'Ῥωμαϊκαὶ ἀγωγαί. Two Byzantine Treatises on Legal Actions', FM, 8 (1990), pp. 1–152.
Noailles, P. and A. Dain. *Les Novelles de Léon VI le Sage*. Paris: 1944.
Signes Codoñer, J. and F.J. Andrés Santos. *La Introducción al derecho (Eisagoge) del Patriarca Focio*. Madrid: 2007.
Stolte, B.H., R. Meijering, et al. 'The Prooimion of the Eisagoge: Translation and Commentary including the Appendices', SG, 7 (2001), pp. 92–145.
Stolte, B.H. 'The Lexicon Μαγκίπιουν', FM, 8 (1990), pp. 339–380.
Troianos, Sp. *Οι Νεαρές Λέοντος ϛ' του Σοφού* [= The *Novels* of Leo VI the Wise, Introduction, Text, Translation in Modern Greek, Indices and Appendix]. Athens: 2007.

Secondary Literature

Brandsma, F. 'The Usefulness of the Byzantine Tradition to the Interpretation of the Corpus Iuris Civilis', in J.H.A. Lokin and B.H. Stolte, eds. *Introduzione al diritto bizantino. Da Giustiniano ai Basilici*. Pavia: 2011, pp. 681–692.
Burgmann, L. 'Λέξεις ῥωμαικαί. Lateinische Wörter in byzantinischen Rechtstexten', in W. Hörandner and E. Trapp, eds. *Lexicographica byzantina. Beiträge zum Symposion zur byzantinischen Lexikographie*. Vienna: 1991, pp. 61–79.
Burgmann, L., M.-Th. Fögen, A. Schminck, and D. Simon. *Repertorium der Handschriften des byzantinischen Rechts. Teil I: Die Handschriften des weltlichen Rechts* (Nr. 1–327). Frankfurt am Main: 1995.
Chitwood, Z. *Byzantine Legal Culture and the Roman Legal Tradition*, 867–1056. Cambridge: 2017.
De Jong, H. 'Using the Basilica', SZ, 133 (2016), pp. 286–321.
Fögen, M.-Th. 'Reanimation of Roman Law in the Ninth Century: Remarks on Reasons and Results', in L. Brubaker, ed. *Byzantium in the Ninth Century: Dead or Alive? Papers from the Thirtieth Spring Symposium of Byzantine Studies, Birmingham, March 1996*. Aldershot: 1998, pp. 11–22.
Fögen, M.-Th. 'Byzantinische Kommentare zu römischen Aktionen', FM, 8 (1990), pp. 215–248.
Fögen, M.-Th. 'Legislation und Kodifikation des Kaisers Leon VI', SG, 3 (1989), pp. 23–35.
Lokin J.H.A. 'The *Novels* of Leo and the Decisions of Justinian', in Sp. Troianos, ed. *Analecta*

Atheniensia ad ius Byzantinum spectantia. Athens/Komotini: 1997, pp. 131–140 (= J.H.A. Lokin. *Analecta Groningana ad ius graeco-romanum pertinentia*, ed. Th.E. van Bochove. Groningen: 2010, pp. 175–182).

Lokin, J.H.A. 'The Significance of Law and Legislation in the Law Books of the Ninth to Eleventh Centuries', in A.E. Laiou, and D. Simon, eds. *Law and Society in Byzantium: Ninth—Twelfth Centuries*. Washington: 1994, pp. 71–91 (= J.H.A. Lokin. *Analecta Groningana ad ius graeco-romanum pertinentia*, ed. Th.E. van Bochove. Groningen: 2010, pp. 183–199).

Lokin, J.H.A. 'Habent sua fata Basilica. On the Occasion of the Completion of the Groningen Basilica Edition', SG, 3 (1989), pp. 1–10 (= J.H.A. Lokin. *Analecta Groningana ad ius graeco-romanum pertinentia*, ed. Th.E. van Bochove. Groningen: 2010, pp. 201–209).

Lokin, J.H.A. and Th.E. van Bochove. 'Compilazione—educazione—purificazione. Dalla legislazione di Giustiniano ai Basilica cum scholiis', in J.H.A. Lokin and B.H. Stolte, eds. *Introduzione al diritto bizantino. Da Giustiniano ai Basilici*. Pavia: 2011, pp. 99–146.

Lokin, J.H.A. and B.H. Stolte, eds. *Introduzione al diritto bizantino. Da Giustiniano ai Basilici*. Pavia: 2011.

Pieler, P.E. 'Ἀνακάθαρσις τῶν παλαιῶν νόμων und makedonische Renaissance', SG, 3 (1989), pp. 61–77.

Scharf, J. 'Photios und die Epanagoge', *Byzantinische Zeitschrift*, 49 (1956), pp. 385–400.

Scheltema, H.J. 'Über die Natur der Basiliken', *Tijdschrift voor Rechtsgeschiedenis*, 23 (1955), pp. 287–310 (= *Opera Minora*, B 11, pp. 290–306).

Scheltema, H.J. 'Probleme der Basiliken', *Tijdschrift voor Rechtsgeschiedenis*, 16 (1939), pp. 320–346 (= *Opera Minora*, B 2, pp. 170–188).

Schminck, A. 'Leges ou νόμοι? Le choix des princes slaves à l'époque de Photius et les débuts de l'ἀνακάθαρσις τῶν παλαιῶν νόμων', in Sp. Flogaitis and A. Pantélis, eds. *The Eastern Roman Empire and the Birth of the Idea of State in Europe*. London: 2005, pp. 309–316.

Schminck, A. 'Zur Einzelgesetzgebung der "makedonischen" Kaiser', FM, 11 (2005), pp. 269–323.

Schminck, A. *Studien zu mittelbyzantinischen Rechtsbüchern*. Frankfurt am Main: 1986.

Signes Codoñer, J. 'Las Novelas de León VI el Sabio', in J.H.A. Lokin and B.H. Stolte, eds. *Introduzione al diritto bizantino. Da Giustiniano ai Basilici*. Pavia: 2011, pp. 267–321.

Signes Codoñer, J. 'The Corpus of Leo's *Novels*: Some Suggestions Concerning their Date and Promulgation', SG, 8 (2009), pp. 1–33.

Stolte, B.H. 'Praefatio to the Basilica On-Line', FM, 13 (2021), pp. 239–264

Stolte, B.H. *Basilica Online—New Praefatio*, at https://referenceworks.brillonline.com/browse/basilica-online, New Praefatio (date of access: 02/12/2021).

Stolte, B.H. 'Thirty Years Later: Past, Present and Future of Editing the Basilica', SG, 10 (2019), pp. 163–186.

Stolte, B.H. 'The Value of the Byzantine Tradition for Textual Criticism of the Corpus Iuris Civilis. "Graeca leguntur"', in J.H.A. Lokin and B.H. Stolte, eds. *Introduzione al diritto bizantino. Da Giustiniano ai Basilici*. Pavia: 2011, pp. 667–680.

Svoronos N.G., *La Synopsis major des Basiliques et ses appendices*, Paris: 1964

Van Bochove Th.E., 'Tenth Century Constantinople: Centre of Legal Learning? Second thoughts concerning the addition of the older scholia to the Basilica text', FM, 12 (2014), pp. 69–96

Van Bochove Th.E., 'The Basilica between Quellenforschung and Textual Criticism', in J. Signes

Codoñer, and I. Pérez Martín (eds.), *Textual Transmission in Byzantium: between Textual Criticism and Quellenforschung*. Turnhout: 2014, pp. 539–575

Van Bochove, Th.E. *To Date and Not To Date: On the Date and Status of Byzantine Law Books*. Groningen: 1996 (translated into Greek by A.H. Nikolopoulos, *Χρονολογώντας και Εξακριβώνοντας*. Athens/Thessaloniki: 2007).

Van der Wal, N. 'Les termes techniques grecs dans la langue des juristes byzantins', SG, 6 (1999), pp. 127–141.

Van der Wal, N. 'Problèmes linguistiques rencontrés par les juristes byzantins', in M. Gosman and J. van Os, eds. *Non Nova, Sed Nove. Mélanges de civilisation médiévale dédiés à Willem Noomen*. Groningen: 1984, pp. 279–283.

Van der Wal, N. 'Die Schreibweise der dem Lateinischen entlehnten Fachworte in der frühbyzantinischen Juristensprache', *Scriptorium*, 37 (1983), pp. 29–53.

Van der Wal, N. 'Der Basilikentext und die griechischen Kommentare des sechsten Jahrhunderts', in A. Guarino and L. Labruna, eds. *Synteleia Vincenzo Arangio-Ruiz*. Naples: 1964, pp. 1158–1165.

FIGURE 5 From *The Madrid Skylitzes*, an illuminated manuscript of the *Synopsis of Histories* of John Skylitzes, a Byzantine historian of the late eleventh century. The future Leo VI the Wise offers a sword to his father, Emperor Basil I founder of the Macedonian dynasty.
WITH KIND PERMISSION OF THE BIBLIOTECA NACIONAL DE ESPAÑA, HTTPS://COMMONS.WIKIMEDIA.ORG/W/INDEX.PHP?CURID=32401733. LAST ACCESSED MARCH 14, 2022

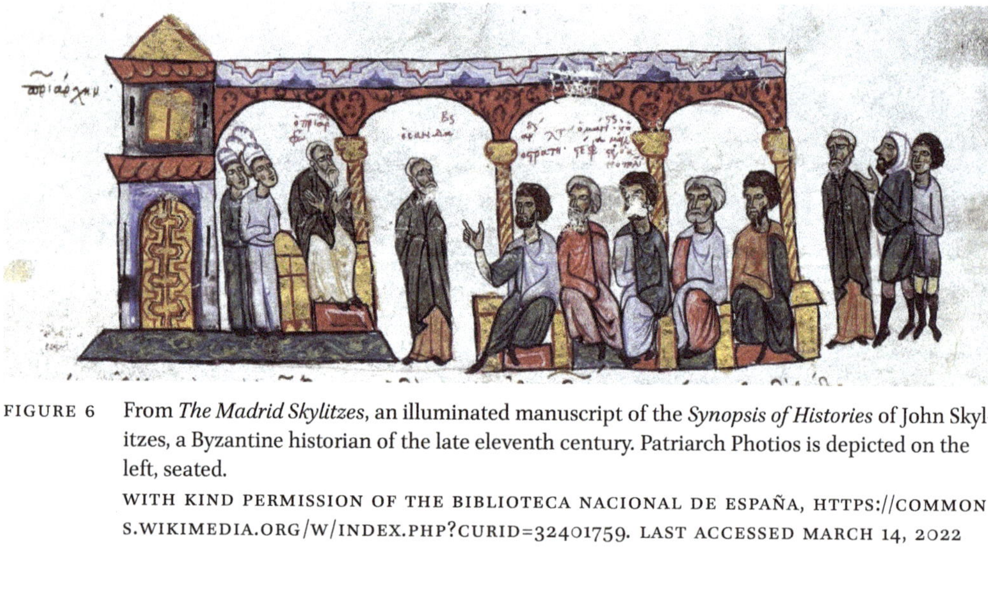

FIGURE 6 From *The Madrid Skylitzes*, an illuminated manuscript of the *Synopsis of Histories* of John Skylitzes, a Byzantine historian of the late eleventh century. Patriarch Photios is depicted on the left, seated.
WITH KIND PERMISSION OF THE BIBLIOTECA NACIONAL DE ESPAÑA, HTTPS://COMMONS.WIKIMEDIA.ORG/W/INDEX.PHP?CURID=32401759. LAST ACCESSED MARCH 14, 2022

FIGURE 7 From the Imperial Gate mosaic in the basilica of Hagia Sophia (Istanbul, Turkey). Emperor Leo VI the Wise bows down before Christ. In medallions: on the left of Christ, the Archangel Gabriel; on his right, Mary.
PHOTO: MYRABELLA, HTTPS://COMMONS.WIKIMEDIA.ORG/W/INDEX.PHP?CURID=24027371. LAST ACCESSED MARCH 14, 2022

CHAPTER 5

From the Eleventh Century up to 1453

1 The 'New' *Basilica* Scholia

In the middle of the eleventh century there was a revival of legal activity in Byzantium. This revival was connected to a law school that was founded in Constantinople around AD 1045 by Emperor Constantine IX Monomachos. The law school created by Constantine IX was not like the Justinianic law schools. It can be considered more as an imperial favour granted to one person, Ioannes Xiphilinos, who in 1064 became the patriarch of Constantinople and served as patriarch until his death in 1075. A *Novel* of Constantine IX has survived in which he appoints Xiphilinos head of the newly established law school. As this *Novel* phrases it, Xiphilinos is appointed as the 'nomophylax', a word that derives from the Greek noun 'νόμος', which means 'law', and the verb 'φυλάττω', which means 'to guard' or 'to observe'; a 'nomophylax' thus literally means 'the guardian of the laws'.

A lot has been written about the nature, the status and the dating of this *Novel*. It is generally accepted that behind the writing of this *Novel* is the scholar Ioannes Mauropous, who was a teacher in Constantinople and had as pupils a circle of young men of potential, including Ioannes Xiphilinos and Michael Psellos, the latter being one of the greatest intellectuals in the history of Byzantium. In fact, at the same time that Xiphilinos was the director of the law school in Constantinople, Psellos was appointed by the same Emperor Constantine IX Monomachos as the director of another school in the capital where philosophy was taught. The *Novel* sketches the role of the *nomophylax* and gives some information on the law school. We quote a relevant fragment from this *Novel*:

TEXT 1 From the *Novel* of Constantine IX Monomachos establishing a law school in Constantinople in *c.* 1045, from chapter 10a[1]

[...] καὶ τὸ ἀπὸ τοῦδε διδασκαλεῖον μὲν νόμων τὸ εὐαγέστατον οἴκημα κληθήσεται τοῦτο, νομοφύλαξ δὲ ὁ διδάσκαλος, οὐ μὲν οὖν ἁπλῶς οὐδ' ἀλόγως, ἀλλ' ὅτι νόμους διδάσκων καὶ φυλάττειν ἔλαχε νόμους –τοῦτο μὲν οἷς ἐνάξει τοὺς μαθητευομένους αὐτῷ πρὸς φυλακὴν καὶ	[...] and this brightest building (= the church of St George in Maggana) will be henceforth named the school of laws, the teacher (will be named) 'nomophylax', not just without sense or a good reason but because as a teacher of laws it is also his responsibility to guard the laws, on the one hand because he will lead his

1 The Greek text is cited from A. Salač, *Novella constitutio saec. XI medii: quae est de schola iuris Constantinopoli constituenda et legum custode creando* (Prague: 1954), p. 25.

 | DOI:10.1163/9789004520684_006

TEXT 1 (*cont.*)

συντήρησιν τῆς τῶν νόμων βουλήσεως, σαφηνίζων πάντα καλῶς καὶ παραδιδοὺς ὡς οἷον τε τὴν νομομάθειαν ἄπταιστον, τοῦτο δ', ὅτι φυλάξει καὶ τὰς βίβλους τῶν νόμων, ἃς ἐκ τῆς ἐκεῖσε βιβλιοθήκης παρὰ τοῦ εὐλαβεστάτου βιβλιοφύλακος εἰς ἐλευθέραν λήψεται χρῆσιν καὶ πρὸς τὸ δοκοῦν αὐτῷ μεταχειριεῖται, δηλαδὴ τὰς χρειωδεστέρας καὶ πρὸς τὴν διδασκαλίαν τῶν νόμων χρησιμοτέρας.	students to the observation and maintenance of the will (= *ratio*) of the laws clarifying everything always in a right way and delivering the most unfailing legal knowledge, and on the other hand, because he will guard the books of the laws, which he is allowed to use freely from that library by the most respected librarian and to use (them) in the way they should (be used), namely using them for the most necessary and useful teaching of the laws.

Based on this testimony, we can conclude that there was a library in Constantinople that housed important legal works, that the *nomophylax* had a duty to protect these works, and that he received a kind of privilege to use them, as he wanted. In the following chapters of the *Novel* the emperor addresses the *nomophylax* himself, giving him instructions and advice, and further on, the emperor addresses the students as well. The *Novel* also mentions, for example, that candidate notaries and advocates should henceforth learn diligently about the laws from the learned *nomophylax*, and that they should not be admitted into a guild before the *nomophylax* confirms that they have learned the laws and the other necessary skills of speech and writing. The author of this *Novel* imitates in many ways Justinian's laws, but contrary to the Justinianic introductory laws,[2] nothing is mentioned in Constantine IX's *Novel* about the actual teaching material or the law curriculum. The author of the *Novel* of Constantine IX Monomachos uses a highly rhetorical style.

The *nomophylax* of Monomachos' law school, Ioannes Xiphilinos and other jurists of the eleventh (and later of the twelfth) century, wrote comments, scholia, on the *Basilica* text. These scholia are known as the 'new' *Basilica* scholia. Hence the 'new' *Basilica* scholia date from the eleventh and twelfth centuries and are scholia on the *Basilica* themselves (and occasionally even on the 'old' *Basilica* scholia), whereas the 'old' *Basilica* scholia date from the sixth century and are actually scholia on the Justinianic legislation. The 'new' *Basilica* scholia can give us information about legal practice in the eleventh and twelfth centuries. The distinction between 'old' and 'new' *Basilica* scholia can be somewhat misleading, however, and one has to keep in mind that the study of scholia in general remains tricky. This is because scholia sometimes contain more than one layer, and it can be difficult to distinguish these layers, i.e. who wrote what and when. This is related to the whole

2 See above, pp. 34–40. on the *Constitutio Omnem*.

problem of the transmission of texts in manuscripts. To give a simple example: imagine that in the margin of the *Basilica* text a jurist of the eleventh century copies an 'old' scholion, a scholion deriving from *antecessorian* writings, because he rightly believes that it can help in understanding the *Basilica* text. He copies it and then adds his own comment under it. The resulting scholion then survives under his name, i.e. the scholion has as its heading the name of an eleventh-century Byzantine jurist. Can this scholion be considered an 'old' or a 'new' *Basilica* scholion? Later scholia can thus incorporate older scholia, and it is sometimes very difficult to distinguish these different layers. Another tricky point when studying scholia in general also concerns the name in the heading of the scholion. For example, if the heading of a *Basilica* scholion contains the name of Stephanos, we assume that it was he who wrote the text (*index* or *paragraphè*) from which it derives. But is that necessarily the case? Did Stephanos actually write it himself, or could it have been a student in the class of Stephanos who wrote down what the teacher said? In other words, who wrote that particular scholion, and how faithful is what has survived to the words that Stephanos actually said?

In any case, in the study of the *Basilica* scholia, we do make the distinction between 'old' and 'new', and we do speak of the scholia as being attributed to Stephanos, to Dorotheos, to Thalelaios, to Hagiotheodorites, to Nicaeus, etc., but it is worth keeping in mind the above observations whenever one studies them. The fact remains, however, that the scholia that do survive under the name Stephanos, for example, share some common characteristics. The same holds true for the scholia that survive under the name of a young scholiast, Hagiotheodorites, and further examples could be produced.

The following authors belong to the younger generation of the *Basilica* scholia: Xiphilinos, Kalokyros, Nicaeus, Doxapatres and Hagiotheodorites.[3] We will give some examples of 'new' *Basilica* scholia: of Ioannes Xiphilinos, of Nicaeus and of Hagiotheodorites. In these examples we will first quote the *Basilica* fragment that the scholiasts comment upon (where this is necessary to understand those comments), and then the actual scholion.

There are thirty-six scholia preserved with the term *nomophylax*, contained either in their headings, such as 'of the *nomophylax*', or in their main text, such as in the phrase 'according to the *nomophylax* ...'. There are several scholia preserved with the heading 'of Ioannes', but it is not certain whether all these scholia can be attributed to Ioannes Xiphilinos. Ioannes was a common name in Byzantium. Moreover some of the scholia that have the heading 'of Ioannes' can with certainty be attributed to an *antecessor* named Ioannes Kobidas.

The majority of Xiphilinos' scholia are brief. What is interesting is that he takes into account older legal material when he is interpreting the law. We will give one example of his scholia, first citing the *Basilica* fragment about which Xiphilinos writes his comments:

3 In a recent article, Simon suggests that *Basilica* scholia with the name Rhomaios are abstracts from the *Peira*: see D. Simon, 'Die Peira', FM, 13 (2021), pp. 323–343. More about Rhomaios can be found below, pp. 168–172.

TEXT 2.1 B. 13,1,18,3 (BT 717/19–20): this is the *Basilica* fragment on which Xiphilinos comments

Ὁ ἐν εἰδήσει χρήσας ὑπαίτια σκεύη τοῦ ἐν αὐτοῖς βληθέντος ἐκχυθέντος ἐνέχεται.	The person who knowingly lends defective vessels is liable when something is poured in and leaks out again.

This *Basilica* fragment refers to a loan for use only (*commodatum*). According to the *Basilica*, the lender is liable if he has deliberately given a defective vessel and, as a result of this defect, the liquid that was poured in leaks out. In other words, the good was not suitable to be lent because it was defective. Xiphilinos explains in the following scholion that the case mentioned in the *Basilica* is not the only possible example of defect. What is more: he points out that both the *rheton* and Stephanos mention the possibility that the vessel was not so much leaky *per se*, but defective in a way that affected the quality of its contents. So, he criticizes the *Basilica* text: the rule should be extended to all cases in which some kind of damage takes place.

TEXT 2.2 'New' *Basilica* scholia: example of Ioannes Xiphilinos about *commodatum* BS 622/10–13 (scholion Ca 15 ad B. 13,1,18 = D. 13,6,18)

Τοῦ **Νομοφύλακος**. Ἢ ἄλλως βλαβέντος δηλονότι· τὸ γὰρ παρὸν ῥητὸν κορόπτουμ ἔχει, ὃ δηλοῖ τὴν φθοράν. Τούτῳ τῷ ῥητῷ συνᾴδει ὁ Στέφανος ἐν ταῖς παραγραφαῖς. Φησὶν γάρ, ὅτι οὐκ ἐξεχύθη μὲν ὁ οἶνος ἢ τὸ ἔλαιον, μετεποιήθη δέ.	Of the ***nomophylax***. Or damaged in another way; for the present *rheton* has the word '*corruptum*', which indicates the damage. And Stephanos agrees with this *rheton* in his *paragraphai* because he says that the wine or the olive oil did not leak out, rather it changed.

Xiphilinos makes reference to the *rheton*, a term that is used—as we have seen in an earlier chapter—by the *antecessores* when referring to the original Latin text of Justinian's legislation.[4] This raises the question of whether Xiphilinos has actually consulted the original Latin text here. What is certain from this scholion is that Xiphilinos has consulted the relevant *paragraphai* of Stephanos, which confirm what is mentioned in the *rheton*, as Xiphilinos points out.

4 See above, p. 41.

As far as Nicaeus is concerned, there are eighty-five *Basilica* scholia which either have the name Nicaeus in their heading or in their text. Different suggestions have been advanced as to the identification of this jurist. In most of the headings of his scholia we simply read 'of Nicaeus' (τοῦ Νικαέως), without a first name. In a very few scholia, the first name Constantine is added. Within this period, and in particular at the end of the eleventh century, there are also sources which refer to a high-court judge named Georgios Nicaeus. It has further been suggested that the name Nicaeus may refer to the place of origin of this Byzantine jurist, i.e. a jurist who came from Nicaea. Nicaeus, whoever he was, commented on different books of the *Basilica*, but the majority of his scholia deal with the law of procedure. In most cases they are brief. We present in the following one example of Nicaeus' scholia. Once again, we will begin with the *Basilica* fragment on which Nicaeus comments:

TEXT 3.1 B. 21,2,6,6 (BT 1034/20–24): this is the *Basilica* fragment on which Nicaeus comments

Ἐπὶ δὲ τῆς ἐπιτροπῆς καὶ τῆς κοινωνίας οὐ καταδικάζεται κληρονόμος οἰκείῳ ὀνόματι, ἐπειδὴ μήτε διαβαίνει ταῦτα εἰς κληρονόμους, ἀλλ' ὑπὲρ τοῦ χρέους τοῦ τελευτήσαντος ἐνάγεται.	In cases of mandate (*mandatum*) and partnership (*societas*), the heir is not condemned in his own name, because these do not pass to the heirs, but he is liable (only) for the debt of the deceased.

According to this *Basilica* fragment, in the case of a mandate and of a partnership, the heir is not condemned in his own name, but he is liable only for the debt of the deceased. Nicaeus comments on this *Basilica* fragment explaining in detail the case of partnership.

TEXT 3.2 'New' *Basilica* scholia: example of Nicaeus about partnership BS 1298/5–12 (scholion 27 Pa ad B. 21,2,6 = D. 3,2,6).

Τοῦ **Νικαέως**. [...] Εἰ δὲ ὡς κοινωνοί τι πράξουσιν οἱ τῶν κοινωνῶν κληρονόμοι, ὡς ἀπὸ νέας συναινέσεως χώρα τῇ περὶ κοινωνίας ἀγωγῇ. Ἀνάγνωθι καὶ τὴν ἐν τῷ λζ'. κεφ. παραγραφὴν λέγουσαν· **ἐν ᾧ μὴ μετὰ πίστεως ἀγαθῆς ἀνεστράφη περὶ τὰ ἐπίκοινα πράγματα. Τίς οὖν ἡ διαφορά; Ὅτι ὁ μὲν κοινωνὸς ἐναχθεὶς ἀτιμοῦται, ὁ δὲ κληρονόμος τῇ προσοκίο καταδικασθεὶς οὐκ ἀτιμοῦται, καθὸ μὴ**	Of **Nicaeus**. [...] If, however, the heirs of the partners will act as partners, the action of partnership is available based on a new consent. Read also the *paragraphè* in the thirty-seventh chapter, which mentions: **if he has not behaved with good faith with respect to the common goods. Now what is the difference? That the partner on one hand becomes infamous when he is sued, whereas the heir on the other hand does not become**

TEXT 3.2 (*cont.*)

σουνόμινε ἀλλὰ γερμιταριονόμινε ὁ τοῦ κοινωνοῦ κληρονόμος ἐνάγεται, ὡς ἐν τῷ γ'. βιβ. τῶν Πρώτων τιτ. β'. διγ. ς'. φησὶν ὁ Οὐλπιανός, οὗπέρ ἐστι τὸ προκείμενον θέμα.	**infamous when he is condemned because of the *actio pro socio*, because the heir of the partner is sued not in his own name (*suo nomine*) but in his capacity of heir (*hereditario nomine*), as Ulpian mentions in the third book of the *Prota*, sixth title, second fragment**, where this subject is dealt with.

Partnership was an agreement between two or more persons to cooperate for a common purpose. Partnership in Roman law (and, consequently, Byzantine law) was based on the mutual trust of the partners. The *actio pro socio* was the action that any one partner could bring against another partner who acted maliciously. A partner who was condemned in the *actio pro socio* was also punished by *infamia*, i.e. loss of honour or reputation, because he was deemed to have betrayed the trust he was given. Nicaeus explains that the partner's heir is not punished by *infamia*, since he is not sued in his own name. Nicaeus, just as Xiphilinos, refers to older material. In this case, Nicaeus advises his audience to consult a relevant *paragraphè*. The *paragraphè* to which Nicaeus refers has been preserved and derives from the *antecessor* Stephanos.[5] If we compare Stephanos's *paragraphè* to the lines that we have marked with bold letters in the scholion of Nicaeus (TEXT 3.2), it is clear that the latter quotes Stephanos on this point. It is Stephanus who refers to the *Digest* and uses the term *Prota*,[6] as expected, and Nicaeus quotes Stephanos' words.

Regarding the *Basilica* scholia by Hagiotheodorites nearly two-hundred scholia have been preserved which contain the name Hagiotheodorites either in their heading or in their text. They never mention the first name of this jurist, which has stimulated discussion about the identity of this *Basilica* scholiast. The problem is that the Hagiotheodorites family had produced several functionaries in the secular and ecclesiastical field in the twelfth century. In the past it has been suggested that the Hagiotheodorites who wrote the *Basilica* scholia was either Michael Hagiotheodorites, who served as a high

5 BS 468/11–15 (sch. CA 6 ad B. 12,1,35 = D. 17,2,35): 'Στεφάνου. Ἐν ᾧ μὴ μετὰ πίστεως ἀγαθῆς ἀνεστράφη περὶ τὰ ἐπίκοινα πράγματα. Τίς οὖν ἡ διαφορά; Ὅτι ὁ μὲν κοινωνὸς ἐναχθεὶς ἀτιμοῦται, ὁ δὲ κληρονόμος αὐτοῦ τῇ πρὸ σόκιο καταδικασθεὶς οὐκ ἀτιμοῦται, καθὸ μὴ σοῦο νόμινε, ἀλλὰ νερεδιταρίῳ ὁ τοῦ κοινωνοῦ κληρονόμος ἐνάγεται, ὡς ὁ Οὐλπιανὸς ἐν τῷ γ'. βιβ. τῶν πρώτων τιτ. ς'. διγ. β'. φησίν (3, 2, 6)'. D. 3,2,6 is the correct reference, added by the editors, but in fact the text says D. 3,6,2.

6 *Prota* were the first four *Digest* books that were taught during the first year of Justinian's curriculum of legal studies, see above, p. 36.

imperial functionary (*logothetes tou dromou*) probably from 1054, or, alternatively, the jurist was Nicholas Hagiotheodorites, who served as the metropolitan of Athens in the 1160s and 1170s and died in 1175. Recent studies tend to confirm the opinion of other scholars who had proposed Constantine Hagiotheodorites as the author of these *Basilica* scholia, a well-known jurist according to contemporary accounts.

Most of the *Basilica* scholia written by Hagiotheodorites are lengthy. The scope of material of his scholia deals in particular with issues related to the wrongful damage to property, theft, penalties, delicts, liability, etc. Hagiotheodorites must have been a law teacher, and his scholia reflect the style of classroom teaching. Similar to Xiphilinos and Nicaeus, he sometimes also uses older material that derived from the works of the *antecessores*. Furthermore, Hagiotheodorites makes broad use of *antecessorian* elements in his teaching; for example, he often outlines a piece of theory in advance designed to help the student, and regularly employs fictitious cases and question-and-answer forms. His style is elaborate but at the same time, easy to follow. There is a clear structure to his scholia. Despite the complexity of some of his topics, Hagiotheodorites successfully manages to convey his material to pupils in a pleasant way by using vivid examples and *antecessorian* methods. A good example of his vivid figure of speech is the following scholion in which he asks the students to pay particular attention to the issue he is explaining, and in which he makes use of a rather funny metaphor:

TEXT 4.1 BS 3444/13–16 (scholion Pe 5 ad B. 60,12,91 = D. 47,2,91): Hagiotheodorites—example of vivid speech

Εἰ δ' ἀφεὶς ἐπιπόλαιον προσέχειν τοῖς λεγομένοις καὶ μὴ λούεσθαι, ἀλλ' ἀλείφεσθαι ἐθέλειν,[7] καὶ τὰ ἐν τῷ ζ. βιβ. παραγραφέντα θαυμάσεις καὶ τὸ παρὸν οὐ προσκρούσει πρὸς ἐκεῖνα τὰ τοῦ ιη'. τιτ. τοῦ ζ'. βιβ. θέματα, ἐφ' οἷς καὶ παρεγράφη σοι. [...]	But if you leave the surface and are willing to listen to what is said and not (just) to take a bath, but to anoint yourself, you will admire what has been explained in the margins of the seventh book; and the present text does not conflict with those cases in the eighteenth title of the seventh book, about which explanations have been given to you. [...]

The following scholion is another good example of Hagiotheodorites' style, reflecting classroom teaching methods:

7 The editors point out in the critical apparatus that 'ἐθέλειν' ('to be willing') seems to be a corruption of 'ἐθέλεις' ('you are willing').

TEXT 4.2 BS 3392/21–23 (scholion Pe 38 ad B. 60,12,48 = D. 47,2,48): Hagiotheodorites—example of classroom teaching

Πολλαχοῦ γὰρ τοῦτο ἔμαθες. Τὸ γὰρ **φούρτιβον**, κἂν εἰς μυρίους καλῇ πίστει νομεῖς περιέλθῃ, **φούρτιβον** μέν ἐστι καὶ ⟨οὐκ⟩ **οὐσουκαπιτεύεται** […]	You have learned this in many places. The stolen good (*furtivum*), even if it comes to countless good faith possessors, is nevertheless a stolen good (*furtivum*) and cannot be acquired by acquisitive prescription (*usucapio*) […]

Hagiotheodorites' scholion refers to the concept of acquisitive prescription (*usucapio*). According to Roman law (and Byzantine law), five requirements had to be met in order for the possessor to become owner of a thing by *usucapio*: i. the thing had to have the capacity to be owned, ii. the claimant must have the thing in possession, iii. the claimant had to be in good faith, at least at the beginning of his possession, iv. the claimant had to have gained possession by a valid cause (*iusta causa*) and v. the claimant had to have possessed the thing for a particular period of time. Stolen things were excluded from *usucapio*. Even if the claimant was in good faith, stolen things (or things taken by force) could never be acquired by *usucapio*. This was a basic restrictive requirement for acquiring ownership by *usucapio*, and Hagiotheodorites reminds his pupils of this rule in a characteristic way: 'the stolen good, even if it comes to countless good faith possessors, it is nevertheless a stolen good and cannot be acquired by *usucapio*'. By sentences like these, you can easily picture Hagiotheodorites standing before the class and delivering his lecture. Note also that he uses Latin legal terms transliterated in Greek letters and combined with Greek endings (see the terms in bold letters in TEXT 4.2): 'φούρτιβον' derives from the Latin *furtivum*, which means 'stolen', and here the scholiast has transliterated the term in Greek letters and added the Greek neutral ending -ον. Also, the verb 'οὐσουκαπιτεύεται' derives from the Latin noun *usucapio*, meaning 'acquisitive prescription', and is combined with the Greek ending for verbs in third-person singular form -τεύεται.

We will at this point give an example of a typical scholion of Hagiotheodorites. As with the scholia of the other 'new' *Basilica* scholiasts, we will begin with the *Basilica* fragment which Hagiotheodorites then explains in his comment:

TEXT 4.3 B. 60,12,83(82),2 (BT 2850/1–2): this is the *Basilica* fragment on which Hagiotheodorites comments

Ὁ διὰ ἡδονὴν δούλην μὴ οὖσαν πόρνην κλέψας ἐνέχεται τῇ περὶ κλοπῆς	He who has stolen out of lust a female slave who is not a prostitute is liable for the action for theft;

TEXT 4.3 (*cont.*)

ἀγωγῇ· εἰ δὲ κρύψει, καὶ τῇ τῶν ἀνδραποδιστῶν ἀγωγῇ.	if he conceals her (he is) also (liable) for the action for kidnapping.[8]

TEXT 4.4 **BS 3439/18–30 (sch. Pe 13 ad B. 60,12,83 = D. 47,2,83): 'new' *Basilica* scholia, example of Hagiotheodorites about the different actions available if a female slave is stolen**

Τοῦ αὐτοῦ.	Of the same person (**Hagiotheodorites**).[9]
Ἔμαθες, ὅτι ὁ κλέψας πρᾶγμα, κἂν μὴ ἐπὶ τῷ κερδᾶναι ὅλον, ἀλλὰ μόνην τὴν νομὴν ἢ χρῆσιν αὐτοῦ, ἐνέχεται τῇ φούρτι, ὡς κεφ. α'. θεμ. β'., καὶ ἐπὶ τοῦ ἄλλως χρησαμένου τῷ πράγματι, ὃ κατὰ κίχρησιν ἔλαβεν, ὡς κεφ. μ' [...] Κατὰ ταύτην οὖν τὴν διδασκαλίαν καὶ ἐνταῦθά φησιν, ὅτι ὁ κλέψας δούλην, εἰ μὲν διὰ τοῦτο μόνον ἔκλεψεν αὐτήν, ὥστε ἀπολαῦσαι τῆς ἐξ αὐτῆς ἡδονῆς καὶ μετὰ τὴν ἀπόλαυσιν ἀντιστρέψαι πάλιν αὐτὴν τῷ δεσπότῃ, ἐνέχεται μὲν τῇ φούρτι, πλὴν οὐκ εἰς πᾶσαν τὴν δούλην, ἀλλ' εἰς ὃ ἔκλεψε δίκαιον. Ἔκλεψε δὲ τὴν αὐτῆς νομὴν ἢ χρῆσιν, ὡς καὶ ὁ ἐν τῷ μ'. κεφ. Εἰ δὲ κρύψει ταύτην τελείως, τουτέστιν εἰ δὲ παρακρατήσει καὶ θελήσει κερδᾶναι τελείως τὴν δούλην, ἐνέχεται μὲν τῇ φούρτι καὶ εἰς ὁλόκληρον τὴν δούλην, ἐνέχεται δὲ πρὸς ταύτῃ καὶ	You have learned that he who has stolen a good, even if he did not do so with the intention of mere financial gain, but only to enjoy its possession or its use, is liable to the action for theft (*actio furti*), as in the first chapter, the second paragraph, and, about someone who has used the good that he has received for use in a different manner, as in the fortieth chapter [...] According, therefore, to this teaching he says here too, that he who stole a female-slave, if he has stolen her only for this purpose, to enjoy the pleasure that comes from her and after the enjoyment to return her to the owner, he is liable indeed to the action of theft (*actio furti*), yet not for the entire value of the female-slave, but only for the right he has stolen. And what he stole was the possession or use of her, as is also in the fortieth chapter. If, however, he conceals her completely, namely, if he holds her and wants to profit from the female-slave completely, he is liable on one hand to the action for theft (*actio furti*) and for the whole female-slave, and, on the other hand, he is also

8 This action arises on the basis of the *lex Fabia*.

9 In this case, of Hagiotheodorites, because the previous scholion was written by him; see BS 3439/10 (sch. Pe 12 ad B. 60,12,83 = D. 47,2,83).

TEXT 4.4 *(cont.)*

τῇ κατὰ τῶν ἀνδραποδιστῶν ἀγωγῇ τῇ τε ἐγκληματικῇ, περὶ ἧς φησὶν ὁ μη'. τιτ., καὶ τῇ χρηματικῇ ἤτοι τῇ σέρβι κορούπτι, περὶ ἧς φησι τιτ. ϛ'. κεφ. α'. θεμ. δ'. καὶ κεφ. δ'. καὶ κα' [...]	liable for her with the action against kidnappers, by a criminal action, which the forty-eighth chapter speaks of, and by a civil action, namely the *servi corrupti*,[10] which the sixth title, first chapter, fourth paragraph and fourth and twenty-first chapters speak of [...]

In this scholion, Hagiotheodorites explains the different kinds of actions that are available when someone steals a female slave, differentiating them based on the reason of theft, i.e. stealing the female slave for your own use and returning her to the owner afterwards, or stealing the female slave to keep her and profit from her.

2 Recognising 'Old' and 'New' *Basilica* Scholia

How do we recognise whether a *Basilica* scholion is 'old' or 'new'? The problem is that in manuscripts, 'old' and 'new' scholia have been inserted randomly without a system, i.e. it is not that in the manuscript first we have the 'old' scholia and then follow the 'new' ones. This means that 'old' and 'new' scholia are found in a random order even within those manuscripts in which two columns of scholia surround the *Basilica* text. For example, in one manuscript, a scholion by Hagiotheodorites is followed by a scholion of Dorotheos (see the photo of the manuscript codex Parisinus graecus 1350 on the next page).[11]

So, the name in the heading definitely provides a good start, but it nevertheless remains somewhat tricky, as we explained above.[12] Moreover, sometimes mistakes in the heading can be made by a copyist. Regardless, in order to find some kind of system in the *Basilica* scholia the general rule is that when you see a name in the heading of a *Basilica* scholion, you can probably attribute the scholion to this author, and you know by the name of the attributed author whether it is an 'old' or 'new' scholion. Sometimes a scholion with a name in the heading (for example, of Hagiotheodorites) is immediately followed

10 This is the *actio servi corrupti* (*de servo corrupto*), the action that a slave's owner has against someone who corrupts his slave.

11 The manuscript is kept in the National Library of France (Bibliothèque nationale de France—BnF) and is available online: https://gallica.bnf.fr/ark:/12148/btv1b10722500s/f51.item (date of access 17/02/2022).

12 See, under section 1. The 'new' *Basilica* scholia, the remarks about the authorship of scholia in general, concerning the question of whether it was Stephanos himself who wrote the scholion, or a student who had taken his class.

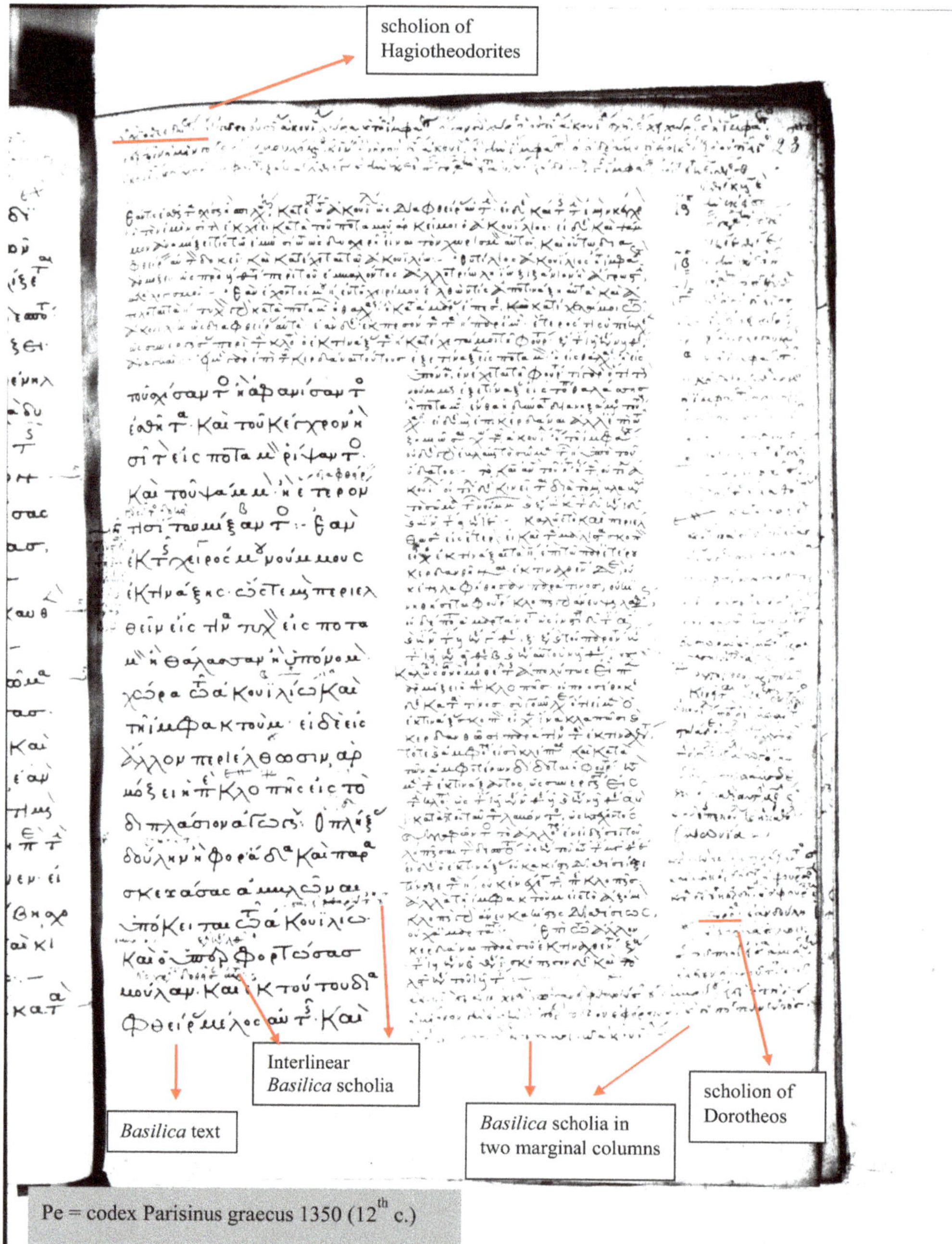

FIGURE 8 Codex Parisinus graecus 1350
NATIONAL LIBRARY OF FRANCE (BIBLIOTHÈQUE NATIONALE DE FRANCE—BNF), AVAILABLE ONLINE: HTTPS://GALLICA.BNF.FR/ARK:/12148/BTV1B10722500S/F51.ITEM (DATE OF ACCESS 30/08/2022)

by another one with the words 'of the same (author)' (τοῦ αὐτοῦ), which is an argument in favour of attributing it to the author of the previous scholion, in this case Hagiotheodorites.

Many scholia survive without a name in the heading. How then can you determine whether they are 'old' or 'new'? There are some words and references that can help you in such cases. For example, if you see in the scholion that there are references to the *Basilica* books, you can presume that this one is 'new', since it has been written after the *Basilica* were made. However, sometimes even Justinianic references have been converted into *Basilica* references. One must always be cautious when dealing with the *Basilica* scholia in general, as explained in the introduction of this chapter. Furthermore, if a later work is mentioned, for example a *Novel* of Leo VI the Wise or later canons,[13] you can safely assume that the scholion is again a 'new' one. If there are references to the *Corpus Iuris*, e.g. to the *Digest*, you can infer that it is an 'old' scholion; however, as explained above,[14] younger scholiasts sometimes incorporated older material and copied old references as well. If you see words that are directly related to the Justinianic curriculum of law studies, like, for instance, the words *partes* or *de iudiciis*, you would also expect that the scholion is an 'old' one and, in particular, derived from an *antecessorian* text; but once more, keep in mind the problems described above.[15] Again, if you see words related to the *antecessorian* teaching method, for example, the word *rheton*, you would expect this to be an 'old' scholion, but there are also 'new' scholia attributed to Xiphilinos with the word *rheton* (see TEXT 2.2 cited above). The question in such a case is how does Xiphilinos use this word: does he copy it from an older scholion or does it belong to his own terminology? This is certainly not the place to examine these questions.

Sometimes you can attribute a scholion to a particular scholiast on the basis of the content of the scholion and the personal style, wording and interests of the scholiast. For example, scholia of Stephanos are usually long and rather elaborate, and he shows a predilection for specific words. You also know that Stephanos' scholia derive from his teaching, so they can only refer—as far as the *Digest* is concerned—to the books of the *Digest* that were dealt with in class according to the Justinianic curriculum of legal studies.[16] Hagiotheodorites often uses examples with the names Peter and Paul. All these hints can help you trace the origin of a *Basilica* scholion. But ultimately, you can never be sure about the attribution of any particular scholion, and one must be extremely cautious when dealing with *Basilica* scholia.

As far as the transition of the scholia is concerned, it has been suggested that 'old' and 'new' scholia were added to the text of the *Basilica* during the eleventh century under the

13 On canon law, see below, pp. 191–213.
14 See section 1. The 'new' *Basilica* scholia.
15 See section 1. The 'new' *Basilica* scholia.
16 See above, pp. 39–40.

direction of Xiphilinos, thus forming a continuous commentary on the *Basilica*, which scholars describe as the so-called *glossa ordinaria* or *catena*. However, there are serious arguments against this theory since we have, for example, at least one copy of the *Basilica* with older scholia which antedates the foundation of the law school in the middle of the eleventh century.

3 The *Ponema Nomikon*, *Tipoukeitos* and the *Synopsis Legum*

The *Ponema Nomikon* is an anthology of the *Basilica* text. It was composed around AD 1073/74 by the high-court judge Michael Attaleiates, on the order of the Byzantine emperor, Michael VII Doukas. The aim of this work was to create a practical legal manual that would summarise the *Basilica*. In the following example (TEXT 5), we provide a summarised version of the preface to show what people knew of legal history at that time, and also to show the difference between the preface of an imperial law book and one made by a private person. In the *Ponema Nomikon* there is no more talk of God having made the emperor responsible for issuing law, no philosophy about the nature of justice and law, no Biblical quotations, etc.

TEXT 5 *Ponema Nomikon* by Michael Attaleiates: summary of the preface[17]

(pr.) The Emperor (Michael VII Ducas: 1071–1078) told me to make a concise and clear survey from the vast legal literature. As an introduction, I [= Attaleiates] will sketch in this preface the **history of law**.

(1) Long ago, when Rome was not yet governed by emperors but by two yearly elected magistrates, not all laws were written in books: most law was customary law.

(2) Later, ten men, among whom was Appius Claudius, made the so-called law of the **Twelve Tables**. These tables contained all the laws of Rome and also pieces from the Athenian laws of Solon and Dracon. This situation lasted for a very long time.

(3) Then came the ***iurisconsults***, Gaius etc., who created new legislation and refined the system of legal actions.

(4) Then these were supplemented by the imperial **constitutions**.

17 Based on the edition of L. Sgoutas, reprinted in JGR, vol. VII; see the select bibliography at the end of this chapter.

(5) Later we had the famous emperor **Justinian**, who commissioned learned men to assemble the chaotic legal texts into fifty books, which he called *Digest* or *Pandect*. In the same way he gave instructions for the three *Codices*, sc. the *Gregorianus*, the *Hermogenianus* and the *Theodosianus*, as well as the subsequently issued constitutions, to be collected and put into order by the *antecessores* **Thalelaios, Anatolios** and **Isidoros**, in a separate work: the twelve books of *Codices*. Further he issued the *Institutes*, a concise introduction to the law for beginners. Finally, he had **Tribonian** assemble the *Novels* in a separate book. Tribonian was very learned but also a real money-grubber. For this reason, lots of litigants bribed him while he was writing it, either to induce him to adapt the law to suit their own purposes, or also to formulate the text in a dubious and ambiguous way.

(6) Then, finally, the great emperor **Leo** [VI] got the ambitious idea to order a committee of jurists to assemble everything that was strewn throughout the *Digest*, *Code*, *Institutes* and Justinianic *Novels* and to remake it all into one corpus, consisting of **sixty books** and six volumes.

(7) We shall now first deal with the law of persons and the law of things, in thirty-five titles. We shall use short and everyday language, in order that non-specialists will also be able to understand the law.

Another work of this period is the *Tipoukeitos* by Michael Patzès, who was a judge. The title of this work is rather odd, and means 'the what text is found where' (Τί ποῦ κεῖται): it is a sort of an index of the *Basilica*. It summarises the *Basilica* chapters in their own original order, but its main importance for us lies in its references. The summary of each chapter is followed by references to related chapters. Generally speaking, the references to related *Basilica* chapters is not itself unusual, but in the *Tipukeitos*, the references also include the opening words of those chapters. Thus, a typical reference in the *Tipoukeitos* looks like this: 'look also in *Basilica* book A title B chapter C, the beginning of which runs: "…"'. That information is especially helpful because the *Basilica* laws have not completely been preserved in the manuscripts: because we lack completed *Basilica* books, the *Tipukeitos* and other works like it have been instrumental in allowing editors to partially reconstruct the missing *Basilica* books. The *Tipukeitos* is thus a very helpful tool in the reconstruction of lost *Basilica* books since it gives us the actual wording of the beginning of a chapter.

Below, we will give an example demonstrating the utility of *Tipoukeitos* when it comes to reconstructing the *Basilica* text in the Groningen edition. First, we will provide a fragment from *Tipoukeitos* (TEXT 6.1 on p. 166) and then a part of the *Basilica* Groningen edition (TEXT 6.2 on p. 167).[18] The words that are marked with bold letters in *Tipoukeitos*

18 BT 929. With kind permission of Brill.

are used in the edition of the *Basilica* for reconstructing a *Basilica* part that is lost, i.e. a part for which no manuscripts have been preserved. The word 'restitutus' in the edition indicates that it is a reconstructed part of the *Basilica*; conversely, the dots that you see on the page of the edition indicate that these *Basilica* parts are lost, and the editors have been unable to reconstruct them. Finally, at the end of the page of this *Basilica* edition (TEXT 6.2 on p. 167), you can see that the editors refer to the 'Testimonia', the sources that they have used for the reconstruction of the text in question.

TEXT 6.1 Michael Patzes, *Tipoukeitos* 9,4

Τίτλος δ′ Περὶ ὁμολογησάντων	Fourth title About persons who have made stipulations
Περὶ τοίνυν ὁμολογησάντων, καὶ ποῖαι τῶν ὁμολογιῶν ἔρρωνται καὶ ποῖαι οὐκ ἔρρωνται, ζήτει βι. μζ′ τι. α′ καὶ βι. ζ′ τι. ϛ′ καὶ τι. ιϛ′ καὶ τὰς ἐν αὐτῷ παραπομπάς, καὶ τοῦ κδ′ βι. τι. δ′ καὶ τι. η′ καὶ τοῦ ιθ′ βι. τι. γ′ κε. β′ οὗ ἡ ἀρχή· **Τὸ εἰπεῖν ἐὰν εἴσω τῆσδε τῆς προθεσμίας** [...][19]	About those who have made stipulations and which stipulations are valid and which are not see forty-seventh book, first title and seventh book, sixth and sixteenth title and the references there and twenty-fourth book, fourth and eighth titles and the nineteenth book, third title, second chapter, which begins as follows: **if someone has said 'if within this deadline'**. [...]

Another work of this period is the *Synopsis legum* (Σύνοψις τῶν νόμων) by Michael Psellos (1018–1078). Psellos is a well-known figure in Byzantine culture, and has been characterised as a polymath because of his profound knowledge of different disciplines. He wrote about history as well as philosophy and rhetoric. He was the head of the philosophy school at the same time that Xiphilinos was the head of the law school, and it is said that they taught each other. The *Synopsis legum* is, as its title implies, a synopsis of the laws, but it has a different form compared to other legal collections. It is a long didactical poem, which consists of 1410 lines of poetry about law, all written for the benefit of the future Emperor Michael VII. On the next page (TEXT 7) we provide a fragment from the introduction of the *Synopsis legum*.

19 The Greek text cited from C. Ferrini and J. Mercati (eds.), *M. Κριτοῦ τοῦ Πατζῆ Τιπούκειτος. Librorum LX Basilicorum summarium. Libros I–XII* (Rome: 1914).

TEXT 6.2 B. 19,3 (BT 929): example of the use of *Tipoukeitos* for reconstruction of lost *Basilica* text in the Groningen *Basilica* edition

LIB. XIX — TIT. III (RESTITUTUS) 929

LIBRI XIX TITULUS III

RESTITUTUS

> Τίτλος γʹ.

> Περὶ νόμου καταπιστευτέου, ὅστις κινεῖται μεταξὺ πράτου καὶ ἀγορα- > στοῦ, ἡνίκα πρᾶγμα ἐπὶ συμφώνῳ πραθῇ τοῦ ἐντὸς τῆς προθεσμίας > τῆς ὡρισμένης καταβληθῆναι τὸ τίμημα

. . . .

B XIX, 3, 2 = D XVIII, 3, 2. > Τὸ εἰπεῖν 'ἐὰν εἴσω τῆσδε τῆς προ- > θεσμίας μὴ καταβάλῃς τὸ τίμημα, ἀναγόραστός ἐστιν ὁ ἀγρός' ὑπὲρ τοῦ > πράτου ἐστί· καὶ δύναται αὐτῷ μὴ χρήσασθαι μήτε τὴν πρᾶσιν ἀναλύειν.

From *Tipoukeitos*
See the bold letters in Text 6.1

B XIX, 3, 3 = D XVIII, 3, 3. > Οὐ γὰρ ἄκων κέχρηται τῷ προτεθέντι > ὅρῳ. Ἐν δὲ τῷ μεταξὺ τῷ ἀγοραστῇ κινδυνεύεται τὸ πραθέν.

B XIX, 3, 4 = D XVIII, 3, 4. . . . .

The dots indicate that the *Basilica* text here is lost and the editors have not been able to reconstruct it.

. . . .

> 4 Καὶ χωρὶς ὀχλήσεως ὀφείλει καταβαλεῖν ἐμπροθέσμως ὁ ἀγοραστής . . .

B XIX, 3, 5 = D XVIII, 3, 5. > Ἐν τῷ μεταξὺ μὲν οἱ καρποὶ τοῦ > ἀγοραστοῦ γίνονται· διὰ δὲ τῆς ἀπαιτήσεως τοῦ τιμήματος δίδωσι τῷ πράτῃ > αὐτούς. Οὐδὲν γὰρ ἐκ τοῦ πράγματος μένει παρ' αὐτῷ.

B XIX, 3, 6 = D XVIII, 3, 6. > Τὰ δὲ δοθέντα λόγῳ ἀρραβῶνος ἢ > 1 ἑτέρας αἰτίας παρακρατεῖ ὁ πράτης, καὶ οὐ δίδωσι τὴν συμφωνηθεῖσαν > 2 προσθήκην. Μετὰ τὴν προθεσμίαν δεχόμενος ὁ πράτης τὸ λοιπὸν τοῦ τιμή- > ματος . . .

. . . .

Testimonia:
Rubr. Tip. | ICb || **B XIX, 3, 2** Syn. A, V, 1 | Tip. I 108 || **B XIX, 3, 3** Syn. A, V, 1 || **B XIX, 3, 4** Tip. I 154; s. l. || **B XIX, 3, 5** Pira XLIV, 5 || **B XIX, 3, 6 pr. § 1** Pira XLIV, 5 | Tip. I 166 | **§ 2** Tip. II 97

Tip. = *Tipoukeitos*

TEXT 7 Michael Psellos, *Synopsis legum*, 1–22[20]

Τοῦ σοφωτάτου Μιχαὴλ τοῦ Ψελλοῦ καὶ ὑπερτίμου Σύνοψις τῶν νόμων διὰ στίχων ἰάμβων καὶ πολιτικῶν πρὸς τὸν βασιλέα κῦριν Μιχαὴλ τὸν Δοῦκαν ἐκ προστάξεως τοῦ πατρὸς αὐτοῦ καὶ βασιλέως.

Of the very learned and highly honoured Michael Psellos, a survey of the law in iambic and political[21] verse, addressed to the emperor Michael Ducas as ordered by his imperial father.

Πολὺ καὶ δυσθεώρητον τὸ μάθημα τοῦ νόμου, ἐν πλάτει δυσπερίληπτον, ἀσάφες ἐν συνόψει,

The study of law is vast and difficult: hard to grasp in its entirety, unclear in

20 The Greek text is cited from L.G. Westerink, *Michael Psellus: Ponemata* (Stuttgart/Leipzig: 1992).

21 Political verse is a form of metre used in secular Byzantine Greek poetry.

TEXT 7 (*cont.*)

ἐν λόγῳ δυσερμήνευτον, ἀλλ' ὅμως ἀναγκαῖον· καὶ δεῖ τὸν αὐτοκράτορα τούτου μᾶλλον φροντίζειν, δικαίως γὰρ τὸ δίκαιον ἐν δίκαις φυλακτέον. ὅθεν ἐγώ σοι τὰ πολλὰ τοῦ λόγου συνοψίσας εὐθήρατόν τι σύνταγμα πεποίηκα τῶν νόμων.	summary form, linguistically hard to interpret: yet, it is indispensable, and the emperor especially has to study it, for he must justly maintain justice in the law-court. Therefore I have summarized for you the great quantity of texts, thus making a manageable manual of law.
Πρῶτον δ' ἑρμηνευτέον σοι πόσα τοῦ νόμου μέρη, τὸ μὲν γὰρ τούτου **Κώδικες** οὕτως ὠνομασμένον, πτυχίον δωδεκάβιβλον, ὅ φασι Διατάξεις· ἔχει δὲ τοῦτο, δέσποτα, δόγματα βασιλέων, ἀντιγραφάς τε νομικὰς καὶ δικῶν ἀποφάσεις.	First of all I must explain to you how many parts of the law there are. One part is called Codices; it consists of twelve books and contains what they call constitutions. Those are, Your Majesty, decrees of emperors, rescripts and judgements pronounced in court.
Τὸ δὲ καλοῦσι **Δίγεστα**, Ῥωμαϊκὴ δ' ἡ κλῆσις, ὑπάρχει δὲ τὰ Δίγεστα Ἑλληνικῶς **Πανδέκτης**, ὅτι καὶ νόμων πέφυκε παντοδαπῶν δοχεῖον καὶ πλεῖστοι συνεγράψαντο τοὺς νόμους τοῦ Πανδέκτου.	Another part is what they call *Digest*, a Latin word, in Greek the 'πανδέκτης' [that which contains everything], because it is a container of all sorts of laws. These laws of the *pandektes* were written by many different authors.
τῶν δὲ Διγέστων, δέσποτα, παντοδαπὰ τὰ μέρη· τὰ μὲν γὰρ **πρῶτα** λέγουσι, περὶ συναλλαγμάτων, τετράβιβλος δ' ἡ σύνταξις, κλῆσις πρῶτα τῶν πρώτων.	The *Digest*, Your Majesty, in its turn consists of various parts, for there is one part which they call *Prota*, about contracts. The four first books are called *Prota* [First].
Τὸ μετὰ ταῦτα πέφυκεν ἑπτάβιβλον πτυχίον, Ῥωμαϊκῶς λεγόμενον οὕτω, **διουδικίης**, ἤτοι τῶν περὶ κρίσεων, εἴ τις ἐξελληνίζει [...]	Then there follow seven which have the Latin name *de iudiciis*, i.e. translated into Greek, the law of procedure. [...]

4 The *Peira*

The so-called *Peira* (Πεῖρα), which means 'sample' or 'experience', dates from around the middle of the eleventh century. It is a legal collection containing the advice and verdicts of the judge Eustathios Rhomaios, who served at the imperial court in Constantinople in this period. We have already come across the name of Eustathios Rhomaios when we referred to the 'new' *Basilica* scholia; there are some *Basilica* scholia preserved under his name, and other scholiasts sometimes refer to him. Eustathios' verdicts and other statements were selected and published in the *Peira* by one of his pupils or admirers. From the text of the *Peira*, it is not always clear how the author obtained his information, nor what his relationship to Eustathios was. It is however evident from several passages of the work that the author knew Eustathios in person and had discussed cases with him (see TEXT 8.1). The work consists of seventy-five chapters (named titles), further divided into paragraphs. Some chapters are very brief and others very lengthy. The main part of the *Peira* derives from the collection of *hypomnèmata* (ὑπομνήματα), a work by Eustathios Rhomaios himself. An *hypomnèma* was a lengthy text written by one of the court's judges and which expressed his legal opinion on the case, explaining the arguments he used to reach a decision in detail. This text formed the basis for the court's decision, the *semeioma* (σημείωμα), which was more concise. The *Peira* is one of the few sources that reflect real legal practice. We quote the following fragment from the *Peira*.

TEXT 8.1 Eustathios Rhomaios, *Peira*, 6,16[22]

Ὅτι ἐὰν γράψω οὕτως· 'ὑποτίθημί σοι γενικῶς πᾶσαν τὴν οὐσίαν μου', ὑπεξαιρεῖται τότε 'ὅσα πιθανόν ἐστιν ἰδικῶς μὴ ὑποτίθεσθαι τὸν χρεώστην, οἷον ἡ οἰκοσκευὴ καὶ ἡ ἐσθὴς καὶ τὰ πρὸς χρῆσιν ἀναγκαῖα ἀνδράποδα', οἷον ὁ μάγειρος καὶ ἕτερός τις πρὸς χρείαν ἀναγκαίαν πάνυ ἐπιτήδειος, 'καὶ τὰ πρὸς διάθεσιν φερόμενα', οἷον νοτάριος, φροντιστὴς μειζότερος, 'καὶ τὰ πρὸς καθημερινὴν χρῆσιν, καὶ ἡ παλλακὴ καὶ οἱ φυσικοὶ παῖδες καὶ οἱ θρεπτοί.' ἀνάγνωθι βι. κε' τ. β' κεφ. ς'.	If I write: 'I give you a general hypothec on my whole property', then an exception is made for 'what it is probable that the debtor would not have mortgaged separately, such as his household goods and clothes and the slaves whom he daily needs', e.g. his cook and others who are essential to his daily life, 'and those whom he personally likes', e.g. his secretary and his bookkeeper, 'and what he needs every day and his favourite female slave and his natural children and his domestic slaves'. Read book twenty-five, second title, chapter six.
Οὕτω τοῦ νόμου φράζοντος ἠρώτησα· 'καὶ πῶς, ὅτε καταδικάζεταί τις ἀπὸ χρέους, οὐχ ὑπεξαιροῦνται ἃ ὁ νόμος διέξεισι;' καὶ ὁ μάγιστρος· ὅτι 'μὴ θεματίσῃς τὸν χρεώστην ἄπορον, ἢ τοσαύτην	**This being the letter of the law, I asked:** 'But how can it be, then, that if someone who is condemned to pay a debt (bankrupt), no exception is made for what the law mentions here?' And the *magistros*[23] replied: 'That is

22 The Greek text is cited from JGR, vol. IV.

23 Rhomaios had received the high rank title of *magistros*. On this title, see ODB, vol. 2, p. 1297.

TEXT 8.1 (*cont.*)

κεκτημένον περιουσίαν, ὅσον ἐστὶ τὸ χρέος, ἀλλ' εὔπορον τοῦτον θές, τὸν δὲ δανειστὴν λέγοντα· ἐπεὶ ὑποτεθειμένην ἔχω πᾶσαν τὴν οὐσίαν σου, καὶ χρυσίον οὐ παρέχεις μοι, δίδωσι δέ μοι νόμος ἐπιλογὴν λαμβάνειν ἃ βούλομαι τῶν πραγμάτων σου, θέλω λαβεῖν τὴν οἰκοσκευὴν καὶ τὸν μάγειρον ἢ τὸν νοτάριον. διὰ τοῦτο οὖν διαστέλλων ὁ νόμος λέγει ὅτι, ὅτε ὑποτίθησιν ἄνθρωπος γενικῶς πᾶσαν τὴν οὐσίαν αὐτοῦ, εὔπορος ὢν καὶ μικρὰ δανειζόμενος, οὐ δοκεῖ ἐνθυμεῖσθαι, ἵνα δῷ εἰς ὑποθήκην τὰ ἀναγκαῖα καὶ πρὸς χρῆσιν αὐτῷ ἐπιτήδεια, ἀλλ' ἃ ῥητῶς συμφωνεῖ καὶ τίθησιν εἰς ὑποθήκην. καὶ οὐ δύναται ὁ δανειστής, ἔχων λαβεῖν ἑτέρωθεν τὸ ἱκανὸν τοῦ χρέους, ἀναγκάζειν τὸν χρεώστην δοῦναι πρὸς αὐτὸν ἃ εἰς διάθεσιν ἔχει ἢ εἰς ὑπουργίαν ἀναγκαιοτάτην.'	because you should not hypothesise that the debtor (pledger) is insolvent, or that his property suffices precisely to pay the debt. Instead you must imagine the situation as follows: he has quite a substantial property and the creditor says: "As I have a general mortgage on your property and as you do not give me money, and as the law allows me to choose from your property what I want, I want your household goods and your cook and your secretary". That is why the law declares that if someone gives a general mortgage on his whole property, supposing that he is a wealthy person and that it is a small debt, he is not assumed to intend a mortgage on what is indispensable and essential for him, but only what he explicitly agrees with. So, if there is another possibility for the creditor to have his debt settled, he cannot force the debtor to give him what he (the debtor) personally likes or what he cannot dispense with'.
καὶ οὕτως **ἔλυσε τὸ ζήτημα ὁ πάνσοφος μάγιστρος**, ἀποδοξάμενος καὶ ἐμὲ τῆς ἐρωτήσεως, παραγγείλας προσέχειν καί, ὅτε διάφοροι νόμοι περὶ τοῦ αὐτοῦ λέγουσι πράγματος καὶ τυποῦσι πῶς ὀφείλει κρίνεσθαι, μή, εἴπερ ἕτερόν τι ἓν νόμιμον εὑρεθῇ ἴσως ἐναντιόφανον, αὐτῷ μόνῳ προσέχειν, ἀλλὰ κατὰ τὴν τῶν πολλῶν νόμων ἔννοιαν ἑρμηνεύειν καὶ τὴν τοῦ ἑνός.	In this way **the very learned *magistros* solved the problem** and made me ashamed for my stupid question, warning me to keep in mind that, if various laws deal with the same subject and prescribe how we must judge it, and if then there may be found one little rule which seems to contradict them, we must not pay attention solely to this one, but interpret the exception in accordance with the meaning of the majority of the laws.

It is clear from the above fragment that the author of the *Peira* is an admirer of Eustathios. It seems that in this case, the author had face-to-face discussions with Eustathios, and this impression is evident from other fragments of the *Peira* as well. In some cases, the author mentions that he had assisted the judge. When it comes to the application and interpretation of the law, it has been remarked that in order to justify his decision or opinion, Eustathios sometimes refers not only to laws but also, for example, to literary authors, such as Homer or Aristotle. In some cases, he exhibits leniency, and prefers to apply a lesser penalty; and sometimes he bases his decision on his common sense. The moderation of penalties is related to a Byzantine concept called 'oikonomia' (deliberate modification), which also appears in Byzantine ecclesiastical literature (and other genres too). When choosing between two penalties, a Byzantine judge would sometimes apply 'oikonomia': he would then choose the less harsh penalty because he believed that this was the most sensible thing to do. Showing mildness (φιλανθρωπία, philanthropy) was after all a virtue that a good jurist should have, according to Byzantine authors.

All the above observations on the interpretation of law by Eustathios should not be taken to mean that Rhomaios was a judge who did not take into account the laws when formulating his decisions and opinions. In various studies, scholars have shown that Eustathios knew the laws and was able to understand and apply concepts of Roman law. Moreover, the fact that he referred to literary authors could also be considered as an expression of his broad knowledge. In other words, it is true that these literary references could help his argumentation and that is why he added them, but, on the other hand, the use of these references could also be viewed as a simple display of knowledge by Eustathios, or by the author who actually wrote the *Peira*, a person who deeply admired Eustathios and wanted to show that this judge was indeed a very learned man. We quote at this point a brief passage from the *Peira* that refers to the application of foreign laws.

TEXT 8.2 Eustathios Rhomaios, *Peira*, 14,16[24]

[...] καὶ ἐσημειώσατο ὁ μάγιστρος οὕτως ὅτι ὁ διαθέμενος, εἰ καὶ βαρβαρικοῦ γένους ἦν, ἀλλὰ τῇ ῥωμαϊκῇ βασιλείᾳ προσεληλυθὼς καὶ ἀξιώματι μεγάλῳ τιμηθεὶς καὶ πολλῶν δωρεῶν ἀξιωθείς, ἀνάγκην εἶχε τοῖς ῥωμαίων ἕπεσθαι νόμοις καὶ μὴ ἐθνικῶς διατίθεσθαι [...]	[...] and the master noted down the following: that the person who made the will, although he was a foreigner because he had immigrated to the Roman Empire and had been honoured with an important office and many grants, he was nevertheless to follow the Roman laws and could not make a will in the foreign ways [...]

What is interesting from this passage is that Eustathios discusses here the possibility of applying foreign law to a case regarding succession law. If a foreigner is involved in a case, should the Byzantine judge, in this case Eustathios, take into consideration foreign laws? According to this fragment, Eustathios argued that the testament was not valid for the

24 The Greek text is cited from JGR, vol. IV.

following reasons: this particular foreigner had lived within the Byzantine empire and had immigrated to the Roman Empire, he had held an important imperial office, and had been given considerable grants. This meant that the foreigner needed to follow Roman, i.e. Byzantine law, and thus his estate was not to be distributed according to foreign rules. Even if this man was not entirely aware of this law, Eustathios added, he should have asked and been informed about it. The decision made by Eustathios reflects the Roman legal principle of *ignorantia legis non excusat*, which means that 'the ignorance of the law is no excuse'. Hence, if the deceased man had not immigrated to the Roman Empire, had not held an important imperial office and had not accepted grants, his testament (the provisions of which were governed by foreign law) would have been valid. This is concluded from an *a contrario* interpretation of Eustathios' judgment. There are also other cases included in the *Peira* addressing situations in which foreign law could be applied by the judge. Here we are given an interesting view of what we would call Byzantine 'international private law'.

5 The *Ecloga Basilicorum*[25]

The so-called *Ecloga Basilicorum*, which means 'selection of the *Basilica*', is indeed a selection of the first ten *Basilica* books accompanied by a commentary. It is dated to the middle of the twelfth century and was likely composed around 1142 AD. The first ten *Basilica* books mainly cover issues related to justice, such as the organization of the courts, jurisdictional matters and the competency of courts, advocates, appeals, etc. The commentator offers lengthy comments on these books of the *Basilica*. The *Ecloga Basilicorum* is therefore valuable because it is one of the few works that can give us some information about actual Byzantine legal practice in the twelfth century. It is also a precious source of commentary on the first ten *Basilica* books; this is especially useful because not many scholia have been preserved on this first part of the *Basilica*. We now quote two fragments from the *Ecloga Basilicorum*.

TEXT 9.1 ***Ecloga Basilicorum*, comment on B. 2,2,225,2**[26]

B. 2,2,225,2 = D. 50,16,234,2	**B. 2,2,225,2 = D. 50,16,234,2**
Τῷ ῥήματι τοῦ ζῆν καὶ τροφὴ καὶ ἐσθὴς καὶ στρώματα περιέχεται.	The word 'living' includes food, clothing and blankets.

25 Please note that part of this section on the *Ecloga Basilicorum* is based on an article published in the *SG*: see the bibliography at the end of this chapter.

26 The Greek texts of the *Ecloga Basilocorum* are cited from the edition of L. Burgmann, see the select bibliography at the end of this chapter.

TEXT 9.1 (*cont.*)

The comment in the *Ecloga Basilicorum*: Ἐὰν εἴπῃ τις οὕτως· ‘βούλομαι τὸν κληρονόμον μου τῷ δεῖνι διδόναι κατ’ ἔτος τὰ πρὸς τὸ ζῆν ἐπιτήδεια, ἀνθ’ ὧν εἰς ἐμὲ ἐκεῖνος εἰργάσατο ἀγαθῶν’, οὐ μόνον τροφὴν αὐτῷ ὁ κληρονόμος ὀφείλει διδόναι, ἀλλὰ καὶ πάντα τὰ πρὸς τὸ ζῆν συμβαλλόμενα χορηγεῖν ὀφείλει αὐτῷ, τουτέστιν ἐσθῆτα καὶ στρώματα καὶ τὰ ὅμοια· χωρὶς γὰρ τούτων ἄνθρωπος οὐ δύναται ζῆν.	**The comment in the *Ecloga Basilicorum*:** If someone says: ‘I wish for my heir to give to so-and-so every year the necessities of life, because of the favours he has conferred upon me’, the heir must give him not only food, but provide him with everything that allows him to live, i.e. clothing, blankets and the like; for without those, a man cannot live.

TEXT 9.2 ***Ecloga Basilicorum*, comment on B. 2,2,226,1**

B. 2,2,226,1 = D. 50,16,235,1 Τέκτονας ξύλων λέγομεν οὐ μόνον τοὺς τὰ ξύλα πελεκῶντας, ἀλλὰ πάντας τοὺς οἰκοδόμους.	**B. 2,2,226,1 = D. 50,16,235,1** By ‘carpenters’ we indicate not only woodworkers, but all construction workers.
The comment in the *Ecloga Basilicorum*: Ὥστε, ἐάν τις συμφωνήσῃ μετά τινος ποιῆσαι τὸν δοῦλον αὐτοῦ [τεχνίτην] τέκτονα ξύλων, οὐ μόνον ὀφείλει αὐτὸν καταστῆσαι πρὸς τὸ τὰ ξύλα πελεκᾶν, ἀλλὰ καὶ πρὸς πᾶσαν ἄλλην οἰκοδομὴν ἐπιτήδειον.	**The comment in the *Ecloga Basilicorum*:** So, if someone agrees with somebody else to make his slave a skilled carpenter, he must not only train him in woodwork, but in all construction work necessary to build a house.

In both passages the language of the commentator is clear and uncomplicated, and his examples are easy to understand. The intention of the author of the *Ecloga Basilicorum* is to explain the law in a simple and easy way, and this is evidently reflected in his style of writing. He begins his comments several times by providing an explanation in advance on the subject he is about to comment upon; moreover, he uses fictitious cases, and very often he poses a question and then gives the answer in a form of a definition or an example. It has been suggested that the style of the author of the *Ecloga Basilicorum* indicates that this work was connected with contemporary legal teaching and legal practice. As far as his material is concerned, it has been suggested that the commentator of the *Ecloga Basilicorum* must have had at his disposal texts related to the teaching of the *antecessores*. We will try to illustrate this with the following fragment from the *Ecloga Basilicorum*.

TEXT 9.3 ***Ecloga Basilicorum*****, comment on B. 2,3,168 = D. 50,17,168 (BT 63/13–14)**

B. 2,3,168 = D. 50,17,168
Ἐν τοῖς ἀσαφέσι τὸ φιλάγαθον ἑρμηνεύομεν.

B. 2,3,168 = D. 50,17,168
In unclear cases we interpret [the law] in a mild way.

The comment in the *Ecloga Basilicorum*:
Οἷον ὡς ἐπὶ θέματος· τελευτῶν τις ἔγραψεν ἐν τῇ ἰδίᾳ διαθήκῃ· 'ἡ δούλη μου Μαρία ἔστω ἐλευθέρα, ἐὰν ἄρρεν πρῶτον τέκῃ'· μετὰ τελευτὴν τοῦ διαθεμένου τέτοκεν ἡ Μαρία ἐν μιᾷ γαστρὶ καὶ ἄρρεν καὶ θῆλυ, καὶ δῆλον οὐκ ἦν, ποῖον πρῶτον ἐτέχθη, καὶ ἦν ἀμφιβολία, ἆρα γενήσεται ἐλευθέρα ἡ Μαρία καὶ ἔσονται καὶ τὰ τεχθέντα ἐλεύθερα ὡς ἀπὸ ἐλευθέρας γεννηθέντα ἢ μή τί γε διὰ τὸ εἶναι ἄδηλον καὶ ἀσαφὲς τὸ ποῖον πρῶτον ἐτέχθη, καὶ ἡ Μαρία ἐναπομενεῖ τῷ ζυγῷ τῆς δουλείας τρυχομένη καὶ τὰ τεχθέντα ἔσονται δοῦλα. Λέγομεν οὖν, ὅτι καὶ ἡ Μαρία ἐλευθερωθήσεται καὶ τὰ τεχθέντα εὐγενῆ ἔσονται ὡς ἀπὸ ἐλευθέρας τεχθέντα· ἐν γὰρ τοῖς ἀσαφέσι καὶ μὴ καθαρῶς καταλαμβανομένοις τὸ φιλάγαθον ἑρμηνεύομεν, φιλάγαθον δέ ἐστι τὸ εἰπεῖν πρῶτον γεννηθῆναι τὸ ἄρρεν καὶ διὰ τοῦτο γενέσθαι καὶ πάντας ἐλευθέρους.

The comment in the *Ecloga Basilicorum*:

To take an example; someone at his death wrote in his own will: 'Let my slave Maria be free if she gives birth first to a boy'. After the death of the testator, Maria gave birth at the same delivery to a boy and a girl, and it was not clear which (child) was born first; and there was doubt whether Maria will become free and the born (children) will also become free, as having been born from a free woman, or, because it is unclear and doubtful which was born first, Maria continues to be worn out by the burden of slavery, and the children will also be slaves. Well, we say that both Maria will become free and the children will be freeborn, because they have been born from a free woman; for in obscure and not clear cases, we interpret in a mild way; and it is mild to say that the boy was first born and that because of this, all will become free.

Καὶ ἄλλους δὲ πολλοὺς προσφόρους εὑρήσει τις θεματισμοὺς τῷ παρόντι κανόνι, οἷον ὡς ἐπὶ θέματος· Πέτρος τις ἐτελεύτησε καταλιπὼν ἄνηβον παῖδα ὑπὸ ἐπίτροπον· ἀνεφύη τούτῳ Παῦλός τις καὶ ἔλεγε δανεῖσαι τούτῳ νομίσματα καὶ δέξασθαι καὶ ἐγγυητάς· ὁ ἄνηβος ὤμοσε μὴ χρεωστεῖν. Καὶ ζήτησις ἦν, ἆρα συνηλευθερώθησαν τῆς ἐνοχῆς καὶ οἱ ἐγγυηταὶ ἢ μή τί γε ὁ μὲν ἄνηβος ἐσεῖται ἐλεύθερος, οἱ δὲ ἐγγυηταὶ ἀπαιτηθήσονται·

And one will find many other fictitious cases relevant for this rule; to provide an example: someone named Peter died leaving behind a son in the age of puberty under a guardian; a certain Paulus came forward against him and said that he [Paulus] had lent money to him [the boy] and had also received sureties. The son under puberty swore that he did not owe [this]. And the question was, whether the sureties were also freed from the obligation, or the boy under puberty will be free

TEXT 9.3 (*cont.*)

ἐποίει δὲ τὴν ζήτησιν ἡ τοῦ ὅρκου ἀσάφεια· οὐδὲ γὰρ ἐδήλωσεν ἐν τῷ ὅρκῳ ὁ ἄνηβος, ὅτι 'οὐ χρεωστῶ, διότι οὐδ' ὅλως ἐδανεισάμην', ἢ ὅτι 'οὐ χρεωστῶ διὰ τὸ μὴ παρεῖναι τὸν ἐπίτροπόν μου κατὰ τὸν καιρὸν τοῦ δανείου'. Τοιαύτης οὔσης τῆς ἀμφιβολίας διὰ τὴν ἀσάφειαν τοῦ ὅρκου λέγομεν καὶ τοὺς ἐγγυητὰς συνελευθεροῦσθαι διὰ τὸ τὰ ἀσαφῆ πρὸς τὸ φιλάγαθον ἑρμηνεύεσθαι· φιλάγαθον δέ ἐστι τὸ λέγειν ἐλευθεροῦσθαι καὶ τοὺς ἐγγυητὰς σὺν τῷ ἀνήβῳ.	(from the obligation), but there will be a claim against the sureties. It was the uncertainty of the oath that caused the question because the boy in puberty did not specify in the oath 'I do not owe because I have not borrowed at all', or 'I do not owe because my guardian was not present at the time of the loan'. Since this doubt was due to the uncertainty of the oath, we say that the sureties are also freed, because unclear cases are interpreted in a mild way; and it is mild to say that the sureties are also freed together with the boy in puberty.
Τὸ δὲ ἑρμηνευθὲν νόμιμόν ἐστι κεφ. ρξη' τοῦ γ' τιτ. τοῦ β' βιβ.	The legal rule that has been interpreted here is the hundred-sixtieth-eight section of the third title of the second book.

The last title of the final book of Justinian's *Digest* (title seventeen) addresses the various rules of law. This title includes many of the basic maxims of Roman law. The D. 50,17,168, from which B. 2,3,168 derives, sets out a general rule for interpretion in doubtful and otherwise unclear cases. The *Digest* fragment has been transmitted in the second book of the *Basilica*. In fact, the two final titles of the *Digest*, namely titles sixteen and seventeen, which deal with the meaning of words, expressions and various rules and maxims, are found at the beginning of the *Basilica*, in the second book. The author's comment in the *Ecloga Basilicorum* for the *Basilica* fragment B. 2,3,168 is very lengthy (see TEXT 9.3). There is only one *Basilica* scholion preserved for this part, and in that scholion, its author advises the reader to check some other references in other *Basilica* books and their commentaries.[27] The comment in the *Ecloga Basilicorum* corresponding to the *Basilica* passage B. 2,3,168 (TEXT 9.3) is thus a typical example of the style of the commentator of the *Ecloga Basilicorum*. Rather than referring to the law in theory, he prefers to use examples to illustrate what the law means in practice. The first example that he uses, about the female slave and the twins, refers to legacies and confirms the rule of the law: if there are doubts, the milder, the more philanthropic solution should be followed. What is interest-

27 BS 20/11–12 (sch. P 1 ad B. 2,3,168 = D. 50,17,268).

ing in this comment is that the first example that he uses—i.e. about the female slave and twins—is found in another part of the *Basilica*, not as a scholion, but as part of the text of the *Basilica* itself.[28] If one compares the original *Digest* fragment from which the *Basilica* text derives with the comment in the *Ecloga Basilicorum*, one sees striking similarities between the *Digest* fragment and the example used by the commentator of the *Ecloga Basilicorum* about the female slave and the twins. The most plausible scenario to explain this would be that the commentator had another text at his disposal, something presumably related to the writings of the *antecessores* and it was in these *antecessorian* writings that he saw relevant examples and used them in his commentary. There are additional examples that confirm the theory that the commentator of the *Ecloga Basilicorum* must have had *Basilica* manuscripts with *antecessorian* commentaries at his disposal. The question to arise at this point thus concerns the extent to which he used this earlier material, something that has been much examined by scholars, but we will not discuss this question here.[29]

In some parts of the *Ecloga Basilicorum*, the commentator informs us about what the legal practice was in his own time, using such expressions as, 'today (σήμερον) this and this occurs', or similar wording, and he further supplies contemporary information about the law of procedure. He also provides the names of contemporary judges and makes reference to officials who lived in his own day; and he sometimes also mentions contemporary political situations. According to some scholars, the *Ecloga Basilicorum* allows us to reconstruct the framework of twelfth-century courts and the rules governing their jurisdictions. What seems most plausible is that the commentator of the *Ecloga Basilicorum* must have been someone at home in the courtroom and someone who was well acquainted with the legal practice of the day; most probably, he was a judge himself because in one of his comments he does, in fact, refer to a judgment in which he had taken part.

6 The *Novel* of Manuel I Komnenos on Procedural Law

We learn a lot about courts and procedural law from a long *Novel* issued by Emperor Manuel I Komnenos (1118–1180) in 1166 and which still survives. This law offers valuable information on Byzantine legal procedure of the twelfth century, since it is the only law actually referring to court procedure in a systematic way. The emperor's aim was to speed up court procedure, for he was concerned about how effectively the court system operated at this time. The emperor begins his law by describing the problem: trials took far too long. Time was wasted, and because of these delays, litigants could not find any legal remedy for their complaints. This is, by the way, a common way to begin a *Novel*; in most of the prefaces to various *Novels*, the emperor refers to the problem that has led him to

28 B. 44,18,10 = D. 34,5,10 (BT 2043/12–15).
29 See the bibliography at the end of this chapter.

the decision of issuing the law. Manuel I's description of lengthy trials is vivid. He mentions that people who are wounded by injustice are knocking on the proverbial doors of the courts, but they find no legal remedy there; instead, their wounds worsen and grow painful. Therefore, the emperor decided to take measures to redress this problem. The *Novel* deals with issues concerning court sessions and the categories of judges, the duties of the defendants and of the advocates, lawsuits and the timeframes in which they must be terminated, disputes that are settled by oaths, appeals, etc. We provide a fragment from this *Novel* which deals with the duties of the advocates and the length of time within which trials should be terminated:

TEXT 10 From the *Novel* of Manuel I Komnenos on law procedure, twelfth century[30]

Ἐπεὶ δὲ καὶ τῇ τῶν συνηγορούντων ἀπεραντολογίᾳ καὶ τῇ πολλῇ τούτων ἐνστάσει προσωχθίκει ἡ βασιλεία μου -σπούδασμα γὰρ αὐτοῖς κατεφώρασε πολλάκις ὥρας ὑποσυλᾶν καὶ σεσοφισμένως φυγοδικεῖν, οἷς τὰς αυτὰς πολλάκις δικαιολογίας ἀνακυκλοῦσι, καὶ τῶν προτέρων δυσαποσπάστως ἐξεχόμενοι προκόπτειν οὐκ ἐῶσι τὸ δικαστήριον—διορίζεται μετὰ συστολῆς ἱσταμένους τοὺς συνηγόρους ὡς τὸ πρὶν δικάζεσθαι καὶ μὴ συγκαθῆσθαι τοῖς δικασταῖς ἐν τῷ δικάζεσθαι, καὶ μὴ κατὰ ταὐτὸν τοῖς λόγοις χωρεῖν, ἀφ' ὧν συγχεῖται μὲν ἡ ἀκρόασις, ἐκκρούεται δὲ καὶ τῶν δικαστῶν ἡ ἀκριβὴς καὶ συντετηρημένη διάγνωσις, ἀλλὰ θατέρου μέρους ἐφησυχάζοντος μετ' εὐταξίας καὶ καταστάσεως τὰ οἰκεῖα δίκαια προτείνειν τὸν προλογίζοντα, εἶτα τὸν μὲν ἠρεμεῖν, ἀντιδικαιολογεῖσθαι δὲ μετὰ τῆς ἴσης ἀδείας τὸν ἕτερον· καὶ οὕτω λέγειν τοὺς δικαστὰς ἃ διαγινώσκουσι. [...]	Since My Majesty is weary of the endless speeches of those who plead in court and their great obstruction—for It detected in them many times an attempt to while away time and cunningly shirk trial, in which they often repeat the same arguments and, clinging to their previous pleas with great tenacity, they prevent the case from making progress—It determines that the advocates should conduct the case as formerly, with economy, standing up, and should not sit with the judges during the litigation, and should not proceed to speak at the same time—in consequence of which on the one hand, hearing is confused, on the other, the precise and strictly observed examination of the judges is frustrated. Instead while one party remains silent the first speaker should put forward his own proofs with good order and discipline, then, keeping still, the other should plead the opposing case with equal license. And then the judges say what they decide. [...]

30 The Greek text and English translation are cited from R. Macrides, 'Justice under Manuel I Komnenos', FM, 6 (1984), pp. 127–129 and 136–137 (lines 54–65, 83–90, 96–101, 200–205).

TEXT 10 (*cont.*)

Ἵνα οὖν μὴ τοῦ λοιποῦ ἀπέραντα εἴη τὰ δικαστήρια, τὸν ἐν διαφόροις βιβλίοις τῶν βασιλικῶν ἐγκατεστρωμένον ἀναζωπυροῦμεν νόμον, καὶ νενεκρωμένον οἷον εἰπεῖν καὶ ἀργίαν παντελῆ κατεψηφισμένον ἀνιστῶμεν, διοριζόμενοι κατ' ἐκεῖνον, τὰ μὲν ἐγκληματικὰ τῶν δικαστηρίων ἐντὸς διετίας περατοῦσθαι, τοῖς δὲ χρηματικοῖς τὸν τῆς τριετίας χρόνον ἐξαπλοῦμεν· αὔταρκες γὰρ αὐτοῖς τὸ τοσοῦτον διάστημα τοῦ καιροῦ, κἂν εἰ καὶ ἴσως τινὲς ὑποθέσεις πολὺ τὸ γρῖφον ἔχουσαι καὶ τὸ δυσχερὲς εὑρίσκοιντο καὶ τὴν λύσιν οὐκ εὐμαρῶς παραδεχόμεναι. […]	So that, then, hereafter lawsuits are not endless, we resurrect and restore to life the law which is registered in various books of the *Basilica* and which is, so to speak, dead and has been condemned to complete disuse, ordaining in accordance with that law that criminal suits be terminated within two years, while with regard to the civil suits we extend the time to three years; for this length of time is sufficient for these, even if perhaps some cases, being very obscure, should meet with difficulty and not easily admit a solution. […]
εἰ δὲ τῶν μερῶν σχολαζόντων αἴτιοι τῆς ἀπράκτου παραδρομῆς τοῦ καιροῦ οἱ δικάζοντες γένοιντο, τῶν προσόντων αὐτοῖς δικαστικῶν ὀφφικίων μετακινηθήσονται· ποῦ γὰρ ἂν εἴη δίκαιον, τοὺς ἐπὶ σωτηρίᾳ τῶν κακῶς πασχόντων τὸ δικάζειν λαχόντας, εἶτα πρὸς συντριβὴν αὐτῶν κεχρημένους τῷ λειτουργήματι, καὶ ἔτι δικαστικῶν ὀφφικίων προΐστασθαι, ἢ συνδικάζειν τοῖς τούτων προϊσταμένοις; […]	If the parties are conscientious but the judges are responsible for the unprofitable passing of time, they will be removed from the judicial offices which belong to them. For how can there be justice when those chosen to sit in judgment for the salvation of those who fare ill then use the function to oppress these peoples, yet still head judicial offices or sit in judgment along with their heads? […]
Ἐπεὶ δὲ καὶ τὰ πρόστιμα τὰ τοῖς ἐγγράφοις ἐντιθέμενα ἐξ ὁμολογίας τῶν συναλλαττόντων δι' ἀσφάλειαν καὶ παραφυλακὴν τῶν συμπεφωνημένων ἐγγράφονται, ὥστε τὸν ἀθετοῦντα τούτοις ὑποπέσειν, νῦν δὲ καὶ τοῦτο εἰς παντελῆ ἀχρηστίαν ἦλθεν, ἅτε τῶν δικαστῶν ἐφ' οἷς οὐ χρὴ φιλανθρωπευομένων, καὶ ἐν ἀλλοτρίαις συμφοραῖς μαλθακιζομένων καὶ χαυνουμένων, ἐπὶ τῷ τοῦ καλοῦ ζήλῳ καὶ τῇ τῶν ἀδικουμένων ἐκδικήσει διοριζόμεθα (…)	And since the fines inserted into the documents are written in by agreement of those who have entered into contract, for the security and safeguarding of the things agreed, so that he who has broken faith falls subject to them, but now this too has fallen into complete disuse, because judges show kindness where it does not befit, and are softened and weakened by others' misfortunes, in the desire for honour, and in vindication of those who are wronged, We prescribe (…)

When discussing the length of time that lawsuits should take to be concluded, the emperor refers to the *Basilica*. He mentions that criminal suits should be terminated within two years, whereas civil suits may require up to three years. He explicitly mentions that these provisions of the *Basilica* had fallen into disuse, and he makes clear that they are to be revived again and applied in practice. Interestingly, this was the same emperor who ordered that the *Basilica* were to replace the Justinianic legislation, and that they were to become the exclusive source of law, a decision made after a legal question had arisen concerning the appointment of a bishop.[31] Another issue that is settled in the aforementioned fragment refers to the interpretation of the judges. It is mentioned that although fines are provided in contracts in order to secure what is agreed, these fines are nevertheless not applied in practice, because judges show too much kindness. In the Greek text, the word that is used for kindness derives from the word 'φιλανθρωπία' (philanthropia = mildness, kindness). The emperor states that these fines should be applied in accordance with legal decrees. In an earlier section of this chapter, we referred to the concept of 'oikonomia' and the mildness (φιλανθρωπία) that the Byzantine judges showed in some cases when interpreting the law.[32] As we said there, Byzantine authors considered philanthropy, the display of kindness, to be a virtue of a good judge. The emperor, however, is not pleased with the excessive kindness that judges display in certain situations: he orders them to stick to the law and ensure the payment of any fines that are included in contracts.

7 The Decisions and Statements of Chomatenos

In the beginning of the thirteenth century, Byzantium was faced with dramatic changes. In 1204, Constantinople was sacked by the participants of the Fourth Crusade, and the city of Constantinople—as well as most of the Byzantine empire—was divided among rulers from Western Europe, the so-called Latin rulers. This period from 1204 until 1261 is also known as the Latin Empire. But the Latins were not in control everywhere. Three Byzantine successor states were formed within this period. The first was the Empire of Nicaea extending over a large area of Asia Minor. The second was the Despotate of Epirus covering mainly a large part of nowadays north-western part of Greece and Albania. The third was was the Empire of Trebizond at the southern coast of the Black Sea. Eventually it was Nicaea that prevailed. The Nicaean emperors issued *Novels* that came to be accepted as Byzantine law after 1261. Constantinople was recaptured by the Empire of Nicaea in 1261, and the Byzantine Empire was then restored under the Palaiologos dynasty. In 1453 the Byzantine capital was sacked by the Ottomans, thus marking the end of the Byzantine Empire. Nevertheless, even after 1453, one can see Byzantine influence in many fields, not least of which was law.

---

31 See below, pp. 199–200.

32 See above, p. 171.

In the late Byzantine period, ecclesiastical courts flourished, especially in the Despotate of Epirus and in Constantinople. It was not unusual for bishops to judge and settle cases. Already from the time of Constantine the Great (272–337), emperors had allowed the bishops to exercise jurisdiction over secular disputes (*audientia episcopalis*). Sometimes, ecclesiastical courts were the only competent courts in which to hear particular cases, such as lawsuits where the parties were clerics (*privilegium fori*). Moreover, in the Despotate of Epirus, the personality and knowledge of particular bishops also attracted legal cases to their courts. In the Despotate of Epirus, Archbishop Chomatenos also settled matters of secular law. We know this because he published his replies. Demetrios Chomatenos or Chomatianos was born in the middle of the twelfth century and died around 1236. He served as the archbishop of Ohrid (today in North Macedonia) from 1216 to 1236. His decisions and statements covered many fields of law, including issues about marriage law, succession and criminal law. The decisions, statements and letters of Chomatenos are important because they give us information on the applicable law and the sources used in this period, and they give us a good impression of what kinds of cases were brought before a bishop's court. The same can be said for the acts of another churchman of this period, Ioannes Apokaukos (born *c.* 1155, died 1233), who served as a bishop in Naupactus, a city in present-day western Greece. As far as Chomatenos is concerned, scholars believe that he must have had a remarkable collection of books because he often cites fragments of the sources he uses. In the following example, we provide a fragment from one of Chomatenos' statements which concerns family law.

TEXT 11 Chomatenos, Statements (Ponemata diaphora), n. 5[33]

Ὅτι οὐκ ἔστι τοῖς νόμοις δεκτὴ ἡ ἐκ θέσεως ἀδελφότης καὶ διὰ τοῦτο οὐδὲ γαμικὰ συναλλάγματα ἐμποδοστατεῖ.	That the brotherhood-by-adoption is not recognised by laws and therefore it does not become an obstacle to marriage contracts either.
1. Ὁ ἀνδρικώτατος στρατιώτης Ἀλέξανδρος ὁ Νεοκαστρίτης τοιάνδέ τινα ἐρώτησιν ἔθετο πρὸς ἡμᾶς εἰπών, ὡς μέσον αὐτοῦ τε καὶ τοῦ ἀποιχομένου στρατιώτου Χύδρου συνέστη διὰ θέσεως ἀδελφότης· θέλει γοῦν αὐτὸς λαβεῖν εἰς γυναῖκα τὴν θυγατέρα τοῦ στρατιώτου	1. The most courageous soldier Alexander from Neokastra came to us with the following question. He said that he was related to the deceased soldier Chydros by means of brotherhood-by-adoption. Now he would like to marry the daughter of the soldier Basos, who is a full brother of this Chydros. He asks

33 The Greek text is cited from G. Prinzing, *Demetrii Chomateni Ponemata diaphora* (Berlin: 2002), p. 41.

TEXT 11 *(cont.)*

Βάσου, αὐταδέλφου ὄντος τοῦ εἰρημένου Χύδρου καὶ ἐζήτει μαθεῖν, εἰ κωλύεται τὸ τοιοῦτον συνάλλαγμα, ἀπὸ τοῦ γενέσθαι θετὸν ἀδελφὸν τοῦ Χύδρου τὸν αὐτὸν ἀδελφόν.	us to tell him whether such a marriage relationship would be forbidden, because of the fact that Chydros' brother would be his own adoptive brother.
2.Ἤκουσε δὲ παρ' ἡμῶν, ὡς οὐκ ἔστιν ἀθέμιτον τὸ τοιοῦτον συνάλλαγμα διὰ τὸ τὴν θέσιν τῆς ἀδελφότητος μὴ εἶναι τοῖς νόμοις δεκτήν· φησὶ γὰρ τὸ ιε' κεφάλαιον τοῦ ιγ' τίτλ. τοῦ λε' βιβλίου ῥητῶς οὑτωσί· *Μὴ δὲ παρὰ ξένοις τοῖς ἔξω Ῥώμης οἰκοῦσι διὰ θέσεως ἀδελφότης συνιστάσθω, κἂν τις ὡς ἀδελφὸς προληφθεὶς κληρονόμος γραφῇ, ἐκπιπτέτω τῆς κληρονομίας.*	2. He was told by us that such a marriage is not forbidden, because brotherhood-by-adoption does not exist according to the law. For book 35 title 13 fragment 15 [of the *Basilica*[34]] says in so many words: 'Foreigners who live outside Rome are not allowed to adopt each other as brothers, and if anyone is [nevertheless] appointed as heir on the grounds of being an "adopted brother", he must lose that inheritance'.
Ἐπεὶ γοῦν ἀπόβλητος παντάπασιν ἡ ἀδελφοθεσία τοῖς φιλευσεβέσι νόμοις ἐστίν, ἄρα γε οὐδὲν ἐμποδοσ<τα>τήσει τὰ ἐν αὐτῇ γινόμενα γαμικὰ συναλλάγματα, ἀλλ' ἐάσει ταῦτα προβαίνειν ὡς συγκεχωρημένα καὶ καλῶς συνιστάμενα καὶ μόνην τὴν ἐξ ἀγχιστείας ἴσως ἢ συγγενικοῦ αἵματος νόμιμον ἐγγύτητα ὑφορώμενα. Συγγένειαν γὰρ ἐκ θέσεως μόνην τὴν ἐκ τῆς ἀναδοχῆς τῆς ἀπὸ τοῦ ἁγίου βαπτίσματος καὶ τὴν ἐξ υἱοθεσίας ἀπὸ τῶν ἱερῶν κανόνων καὶ τῶν φιλευσεβῶν νόμων τηρεῖν παρελάβομεν, τὰς δ' ἄλλας ὡς ἀποβλήτους καὶ ἀσυστάτους ἀποκρουόμεθα· ἡ θέσις, γάρ φασι, μιμεῖται τὴν φύσιν. Ἡ φύσις δὲ υἱὸν μὲν ἐπιγινώσκει διὰ γεννήσεως, ἀδελφὸν δὲ	So, seeing that brotherhood-by-adoption is completely dismissed by the laws, it evidently does not in the least prevent marriage contracts. So let them go ahead, for they are allowed and entirely legal. The only legal impediment [for marriage] is kinship or blood relationship. The only form of relationship by adoption which we acknowledge is that by way of the holy baptism and the adoption of sons, according to the holy canons and the pious laws: all other forms of adoption are rejected as unacceptable and theoretically impossible. For adoption, they say, imitates nature, and nature does acknowledge the generation of sons, but not of brothers. So if nature does not recognise (the generation of) a brother,

34 The correct *Basilica* fragment is B. 35,13,17 = C. 6,24,4 (BT 1620/7–9). This *Basilica* part has been reconstructed by the editors of the Groningen *Basilica* edition.

TEXT 11 (*cont.*)

οὐδαμῶς. Εἰ δὲ ἀδελφὸν ἡ φύσις ἀγνοεῖ, ἄρα καὶ ἡ θέσις. Πῶς γάρ τι γεννήσει ἑαυτῷ ἀδελφόν; Εἰ δὲ τοῦτο ἀδύνατον, ἄρα οὐ θετὸν ἀδελφὸν εἶναι χρεών·	the same must be said of adoption. For how could anyone possibly generate himself a brother? And if that is impossible, it must also be impossible to create one by adoption.
ἀκώλυτον οὖν καὶ τὸ παρόν ἐστι συνάλλαγμα καὶ γενόμενον ἔσται ἄμεμπτον καὶ ἀκατηγόρητον. Ταῦτα πρὸς τὰ ἀφηγηθέντα.	So the marriage contract under discussion is not forbidden, and if it takes place it will be perfectly correct and inviolable. So far our reply.

The issue in question is whether brotherhood-by-adoption forms an impediment to marriage. Brotherhood-by-adoption or ritual brotherhood was a brother-making ceremony in Byzantium. Two men could become 'related' through this ceremony and were considered 'brothers', not by blood, i.e. biological brothers, but 'adoptive' brothers. In our case, Alexander was 'related' as an adopted brother to Chydros who had a biological brother named Basos. Alexander intended to marry a daughter of Basos and the question raised was whether this would be allowed, and whether Basos could also be considered an 'adoptive' brother to Alexander. According to Chomatianos, brotherhood-by-adoption does not have any legal basis in the first place. This is illustrated by a text in the *Basilica* where an adopted brother is not accepted as a brother in an inheritance case. Accordingly, it cannot form a legal impediment for entering a marriage either, and Alexander is allowed to marry the daughter of Basos. Most interesting in Chomatianos' argumentation is his reference to the *Basilica*.

Finally, an important source concerning ecclesiastical jurisprudence is the register of the Patriarchate of Constantinople, produced over the fourteenth and into the early fifteenth century and, which survives in two manuscripts, the Codices Vindobonenses historici graeci 47 and 48, now kept at the Austrian National Library. It contains, among other things, a considerable number of judicial decisions made by the patriarchal court of Constantinople, which was the highest ecclesiastical court. The documents date from 1315 to 1402.

8 The *Hexabiblos* by Harmenopoulos

The *Hexabiblos*, also called the *Prochiron Nomon* (Manual of laws), is a legal collection composed by the judge Constantine Harmenopoulos in Thessalonica around 1345. Harmenopoulos based this work on many legal texts. His main source was the *Prochiron*, but he used other works as well, such as the *Synopsis maior Basilicorum*, the *Synopsis minor*, the *Peira*, the *Rhopai*, the treatise of Julian of Ascalon, the *Ecloga*, et al. His aim was to create a practical law manual that would be easy to use in legal practice. The *Hexabiblos* ended up having a tremendous influence. With the fall of Constantinople in 1453, when the city was conquered by the Ottomans, the Byzantine empire collapsed. During the following centuries of Ottoman rule, the Greek population was allowed to continue to use their own law for some internal affairs. Because of its simplicity, the *Hexabiblos* became an influential text in the eastern part of Europe. It was rendered many times into Modern Greek, it was reprinted several times in Greece and it was used in legal practice up to the promulgation of the first Greek civil code in 1946. It has also been translated into Slavic languages and spread throughout the Balkan region. The *Hexabiblos* also received considerable attention in Western Europe, as is proven by the numerous critical editions and translations of this work. It was translated into Latin and German, and the sixth book of the *Hexabiblos*, which deals with criminal law, has also been translated into English.

An interesting element of the *Hexabiblos* is the actual structure of the material. Harmenopoulos did not follow the traditional threefold division of Roman law into persons, things and actions. Instead, he divided his material into six books, which is what the word *Hexabiblos* means: i.e. the six books. Civil law consists of the following five books: i. a general part, ii. property law, iii. law of obligations, iv. family law and v. succession law. The last book is on criminal law. Harmenopoulos' choice for having a general part in the beginning and then moving into the particular parts of civil law resembles the structure of modern codes.

We cite in the following example a fragment from the *Hexabiblos*, which is about 'bare' or simple agreements (*pacta nuda*). As a preliminary remark, we note that in Roman law there was a limited number of actions and, in consequence, a limited number of contracts. This meant that there was only a specific number of contracts that were actually binding, i.e. for which you had a right of action in the event of a breach of contract. A simple agreement (*pactum nudum*) was not binding in Roman law. Only those agreements or contracts that were recognised by the magistrates were legally binding. There was even a maxim that reflected this situation in Roman law: *pacta nuda non valent*, which means simple or bare agreements (literally 'naked agreements') are not valid and thus are not binding. Leo VI the Wise (866–912) had ordered in his *Novel* 72 that bare agreements which bore the sign of the cross or contained a reference to the Holy Trinity were nevertheless binding. Harmenopoulos refers to this *Novel* in the following fragment.

TEXT 12.1 **The *Hexabiblos*, 1,9,7: about pacts**[35]

7. Τὸ ψιλὸν σύμφωνον ἀγωγὴν οὐ τίκτει, ἀλλὰ παραγραφήν. Ψιλὸν δὲ σύμφωνόν ἐστι, ἡνίκα μὴ προηγήσηται δόσις, ἀλλὰ μόνον συστῇ ἐπὶ δόσει· ἐν ἀρχῇ δὲ γινόμενον τυποῖ τὴν ἀγωγήν, ὡς ἐπὶ τῶν καλῇ πίστει δικαστηρίων· εἰ δὲ μετὰ χρόνον συμφωνηθῇ τι, τῷ μὲν ἐνάγοντι οὐ συμβάλλεται, τῷ δὲ ἐναγομένῳ τίκτει παραγραφήν. Ἡ δὲ τριακοστὴ ὀγδόη νεαρὰ τοῦ καίσαρος Λέοντος οὕτω φησί· θεσπίζομεν οὖν ἐν παντὶ συμφώνῳ, ἐν ᾧ ἂν τὸ ἐκ τῶν θείων συναντιλήψεων ἐχέγγυον πρὸς τὴν ἀξιοπιστίαν προσῇ, τὴν ἰσχὺν παρεῖναι κραταιάν τε καὶ ἄλυτον, κἂν μηδεὶς λόγος προστιμήσεως συνεγέγραπτο.	7. The bare agreement does not raise an action but an exception. An agreement is bare when there is no preceding payment, but it is created only by payment. If it is made straightaway, it does produce the action, as in the proceedings of the good faith; if, however, something has been agreed afterwards, this does not benefit the plaintiff, but it does raise an exception for the defendant. The thirty-eighth *Novel* of the emperor Leo[36] says the following: 'We order therefore that in every agreement in which the guarantee for the credibility is present in one of these divine ways, the validity is strong and indissoluble, even if the text does not have a hint of a penalty clause'.

Several scholia are also preserved that comment on fragments of the *Hexabiblos*, some of them apparently written by Harmenopoulos himself. For the above cited *Hexabiblos* fragment, the following scholion has survived, which better explains the content of Leo's *Novel* 72 and its relevance:

TEXT 12.2 **The scholion for *Hexabiblos* 1,9,7**[37]

Ἡ νεαρὰ αὕτη οὐχὶ τὰ παράνομα κυροῖ σύμφωνα, εἴπερ ἐν ὀνόματι τοῦ θεοῦ γένοιτο (ἐκεῖνα γὰρ καὶ οὕτως οὐκ ἔρρωται), ἀλλὰ τὰ ἔννομα μέν, ψιλὰ δέ, ἅπερ εἰσὶ τὰ χωρὶς ἐπερωτήσεως καὶ προστί-	This *Novel* does not ratify the illegal contracts if they have been made in the name of God (because those are not valid even in this way), but those that are legal even if (they are) bare; these are the agreements that

35 From the 'practical' edition of C.G. Pitsakis, *Κωνσταντίνου Ἀρμενοπούλου, Πρόχειρον Νόμων ἢ Ἑξάβιβλος* (Athens: 1971), p. 61. This is not a new critical edition of the *Hexabiblos*, as the author notes in his introduction. Pitsakis uses the edition of Heimbach (Leipzig: 1851; repr. Aalen: 1969), but adds a long introduction and several notes.

36 This is *Novel* 72 by Leo VI the Wise.

37 From M.-Th. Fögen, 'Die Scholien zur Hexabiblos im Codex vetustissimus Vaticanus Ottobonianus gr. 440', FM, 4 (1981), pp. 256–345, at p. 304, which is the most recent critical edition of this scholion.

TEXT 12.2 *(cont.)*

μου γενόμενα. διὸ καί φησι· *κἂν μηδεὶς λόγος προστιμήσεως συνεγέγραπτο*. τοῦ γὰρ νόμου τὰ ψιλὰ σύμφωνα μὴ στέργειν κελεύοντος, ἡ νεαρὰ αὕτη καὶ ταῦτα στέργειν παρακελεύεται, εἴγε μόνον ἐπ' ὀνόματι τοῦ ζῶντος θεοῦ γένοιτο. τοιαῦτα δέ εἰσιν οἷα τὰ παρ' ἡμῖν ταβελλιωνικά, ἃ τὴν ἀρχὴν ἐκ τοῦ ὀνόματος τοῦ πατρὸς καὶ τοῦ υἱοῦ καὶ τοῦ ἁγίου πνεύματος ἔχουσιν.	have been made without a stipulation and a penalty clause. That is why it says: 'Even if the text does not have a hint of a penalty clause'. For although the law orders (us) not to approve of bare agreements, this *Novel* orders to approve of them too, provided that they have been made in the name of the living God. Such are what we know as 'tabellionika' (notary ones), which have as a beginning 'in the name of the Father, the Son and the Holy Spirit'.

9 Select Bibliography

For this chapter, we recommend that the reader consults the online bibliography that Th.E. van Bochove has made for the *Basilica* and every subject related to them, and available at the following link: https://referenceworks.brillonline.com/browse/basilica-online.

Primary Sources

Burgmann, L. *Ecloga Basilicorum*. Frankfurt am Main: 1988.

Ferrini C. and J. Mercati, eds. *M. Κριτοῦ τοῦ Πατζῆ Τιπούκειτος. Librorum LX Basilicorum summarium. Libros I–XII*. Rome: 1914.

Heimbach, G.E. *Const. Harmenopuli Manuale legum sive Hexabiblos cum appendicibus et legibus agrariis*. Lipsiae: 1851; repr. Aalen: 1969.

Macrides, R. 'Justice under Manuel I Komnenos', FM, 6 (1984), pp. 99–204.

Pitsakis, C.G. *Κωνσταντίνου Ἀρμενοπούλου, Πρόχειρον Νόμων ἢ Ἑξάβιβλος* [= Constantine Harmenopoulos' Procheiron Nomon or Hexabiblos]. Athens: 1971.

Prinzing, G. *Demetrios Chomatenos, Ponemata diaphora. Das Aktenkorpus des Ohrider Erzbischofs Demetrios Chomatenos. Einleitung, kritische Edition und Indizes*. Berlin/New York: 2002.

Salač, A. *Novella constitutio saec. XI medii: quae est de schola iuris Constantinopoli constituenda et legum custode creando*. Prague: 1954.

Sgoutas, L. 'Μιχαὴλ Ἀνθυπάτου καὶ Κριτοῦ τοῦ Ἀτταλειώτου. Ποίημα νομικὸν ἤτοι Πραγματεῖα ποιηθεῖσα κατὰ κέλευσιν τοῦ Βασιλέως Μιχαὴλ τοῦ Δούκα [= *Ponema Nomikon by Attalleiates*]', *Θέμις*, 8 (1861), pp. 47–155 (repr. in JGR, vol. VII, pp. 409–497).

Simon, D. and R. Reinsch, *Ἡ Πεῖρα—Die Peira. Text, Übersetzung, Kommentar*. Berlin: 2022 (forthcoming).

Westerink, L.G. *Michaelis Pselli Poemata*. Stuttgart/Leipzig: 1992.

Secondary Literature

Bénou, L. *Pour une nouvelle histoire du droit byzantin. Théorie et pratiques juridiques au XIVe siècle.* Paris: 2011.

Burgmann, L. 'Peira 51. Übersetzung und Kommentar', in Sp. Troianos, ed. *Κατευόδιον. In memoriam Nikos Oikonomides.* Athens: 2008, pp. 5–26.

Burgmann, L. 'Kalokyros "Sextos". Anmerkungen zu einem Basiliken-scholiasten', SG, 3 (1989), pp. 11–21.

Burgmann, L. and M.-Th. Fögen. 'Florilegium Lesbiacum', FM, 5 (1982), pp. 107–178 (repr. in L. Burgmann. *Ausgewählte Aufsätze zur byzantinischen Rechtsgeschichte.* Frankfurt am Main: 2015, pp. 7–83).

Chitwood, Z. *Byzantine Legal Culture and the Roman Legal Tradition*, 867–1056. Cambridge: 2017.

Fögen, M.-Th. 'Hexabiblos aucta. Eine Kompilation der spätbyzantinischen Rechtswissenschaft', FM, 7 (1986), pp. 259–333.

Fögen, M.-Th. 'Humanistische Adnotationes zur edition princeps der Hexabiblos', *Ius Commune*, 13 (1985), pp. 213–242.

Fögen, M.-Th. 'Zum Rechtsunterricht des Michael Psellos', JÖB, 32/2 (1981), pp. 291–302.

Fögen, M.-Th. 'Die Scholien zur Hexabiblos im Codex vetustissimus Vaticanus Ottobonianus gr. 440', FM, 4 (1981), pp. 256–345.

Gastgeber Ch., E. Mitsiou, J. Preiser-Kapeller and V. Zervan, eds., *A Companion to the Patriarchate of Constantinople.* Leiden: 2021.

Gastgeber Ch., E. Mitsiou and J. Preiser-Kapeller, eds., *The Register of the Patriarachate of Constantinople. An Essential Source for the History and Church of Late Byzantium.* Vienna: 2013.

Howard-Johnston, J.D. 'The Peira and Legal Practices in Eleventh-century Byzantium', in M.D. Lauxtermann and M. Whittow, eds. *Byzantium in the Eleventh Century: Being in Between: Papers from the 45th Spring Symposium of Byzantine Studies, Exeter College, Oxford, 24–26 March 2012.* Oxford: 2017, pp. 63–76.

Lefort, J. 'Rhétorique et Politique. Trois discours de J. Mauropous en 1047', *Travaux et Mémoires*, 6 (1976), pp. 265–303.

Lokin, J.H.A. 'The Significance of Law and Legislation in the Law Books of the Ninth to Eleventh Centuries', in A.E. Laiou and D. Simon, eds. *Law and Society in Byzantium: Ninth—Twelfth Centuries. Proceedings of the Symposium on Law and Society in Byzantium, 9th–12th Centuries, Dumbarton Oaks, May 1–3, 1992.* Washington: 1994, pp. 71–91.

Oikonomides, N. 'The "Peira" of Eustathios Rhomaios. An Abortive Attempt to Innovate in Byzantine Law', FM, 7 (1986), pp. 169–192.

Papagianni, E. 'Οι αυτοκρατορικές Νεαρές στο Σύνταγμα κατά στοιχείον του Ματθαίου Βλάσταρη και στην Εξάβιβλο του Κωνσταντίνου Αρμενοπούλου' [= The imperial *Novels* in the *Syntagma kata stoicheion* of Matthaios Blastares and in the *Hexabiblos* of Constantine Harmenopoulos], in Εταιρεία Μακεδονικών Σπουδών. Γ'Επιστημονικό Συμπόσιο "Βυζαντινή Μακεδονία" (14–15 Μαΐου 2016 Θεσσαλονίκη). Thessaloniki: 2019, pp. 377–388.

Papagianni, E. 'Un témoin de la réalité juridique byzantine: la jurisprudence patriarcale au XIVe siècle', FM, 11 (2005), pp. 213–227.

Papagianni, E. *Η νομολογία των εκκλησιαστικών δικαστηρίων της βυζαντινής και μεταβυζαντινής περιόδου σε θέματα περιουσιακού δικαιόυ* [= The Case Law of the Ecclesiastical Courts of Byzantine and post-Byzantine Period in Matters of Property Law, 3 vols.]. Athens: 1992, 1997 and 2010.

Paparriga-Artémiadi L., 'Les scoliastes byzantins face aux ambiguïtés des lois' in *Revue des Études Byzantines*, 77 (2019), pp. 225–256.

Penna, D. 'The Eleventh-Century Byzantine Jurist Nicaeus. His Scholia on the Basilica Laws and his Connection to the *Meditatio de nudis pactis*', FM, 13 (2021), pp. 111–131.

Penna, D. 'A witness of Byzantine Legal Practice in the Twelfth Century: Some Remarks on the Construction of the *Ecloga Basilicorum*', SG, 10 (2019), pp. 139–162.

Penna, D. 'Hagiotheodorites: the Last Antecessor? Some Remarks on One of the 'New' *Basilica* Scholiasts', SG, 9 (2014), pp. 399–427.

Pitsakis, C.G. 'Un demi-siècle d'études sur Constantin Harménopoulos: un bilan', in Ch. Papastathis, ed. *Byzantine Law. Proceedings of the International Symposium of Jurists Thessaloniki, 10–13 December 1998*. Thessaloniki: 2001, pp. 135–164.

Prinzing, G. 'A Quasi Patriarch in the State of Epirus: The Autocephalous Archbishop of "Boulgaria" (Ohrid) Demetrios Chomatenos', *Zbornik radova Vizantoloskog Instituta*, 41 (2004), pp. 165–182.

Reinsch, D.R. 'Eustathios Rhomaios' Opusculum über das Hypobolon', FM, 7 (1986), pp. 239–252.

Schminck, A. *Studien zu mittelbyzantinischen Rechtsbüchern*. Frankfurt am Main: 1986.

Simon, D. and S. Neye. 'Harmenopoulos liest die Peira', FM, 13 (2021), pp. 179–237.

Simon, D. 'Die Peira', FM, 13 (2021), pp. 323–343.

Simon, D. 'Eustathios Rhomaios, kaiserlicher Rechter im Konstantinopel des XI. Jahrhunderts', *Travaux et Mémoires*, 22/1 (2018), pp. 481–496.

Simon, D. *Rechtsfindung am byzantinischen Reichsgericht*. Frankfurt am Main: 1973.

Sirks, B. 'Peira 45.11, a Presumed Succession Pact, and the Peira as Legal Source', in Ch. Gastgeber, ed. *Quellen zur byzantinischen Rechtspraxis. Aspekte der Textüberlieferung, Paläographie und Diplomatik. Akten des internationalen Symposiums Wien, 5.–7. 11. 2007*. Vienna: 2010, pp. 189–199.

Sirks, B. *How Legal Is the Peira? Cases and Problems*. Oxford: 2012, available online at https://ora.ox.ac.uk/objects/uuid:5a059028-3045-4956-95f3-0b598f06337a (date of access: 17/02/2022).

Sirks, B. 'The Peira: Roman Law in Greek Setting', in *Studi in onore di Remo Martini*, vol. III. Milan: 2009, pp. 583–591.

Speck, P. 'Konstantinopel—ein Modell für Bologna? Zur Gründung einer Rechtsschule durch Irnerius', in *Varia* III, Freie Universität Berlin. Byzantinisch-neugriechisches Seminar. Ποικίλα βυζαντινά, 11. Bonn: 1991, pp. 307–348.

Troianos, Sp. 'Η Νεαρά Κωνσταντίνου του Μονομάχου ἐπὶ τῇ ἀναδείξει καὶ προβολῇ τοῦ διδασκάλου', *Byzantina Symmeikta*, 22 (2012), pp. 243–263.

Troianos, Sp. 'Von der Hexabiblos zu den Basiliken', SG, 3 (1989), pp. 127–141.

Van Bochove, Th.E. 'Tenth Century Constantinople: Centre of Legal Learning? Second Thoughts Concerning the Addition of the Older Scholia to the Basilica Text', FM, 12 (2014), pp. 69–96.

Van der Wal, N. 'Probleme bei der Restitution verlorengegangener Basiliken-bücher', SG, 3 (1989), pp. 143–154.

Weiß, G. 'Die Synopsis legum des Michael Psellos', FM, 2 (1977), pp. 147–214.

Weiß, G. 'Hohe Richter in Konstantinopel. Eustathios Rhomaios und seine Kollegen', JÖB, 22 (1973), pp. 117–143.

Wolska-Conus, W. 'L'école de droit et l'enseignement du droit à Byzance au XIe siècle: Xiphilin et Psellos', *Travaux et Mémoires*, 7 (1979), pp. 1–107.

Wolska-Conus, W. 'Les écoles de Psellos et de Xiphilin sous Constantin IX Monomaque', *Travaux et Mémoires*, 6 (1976), pp. 223–243.

FIGURE 9 From a mosaic in Hagia Sophia Church depicting Emperor Constantine IX Monomachos on the left and on the right his wife Zoe.
PHOTO: MARIËTTE VERHOEVEN. WITH KIND PERMISSION.

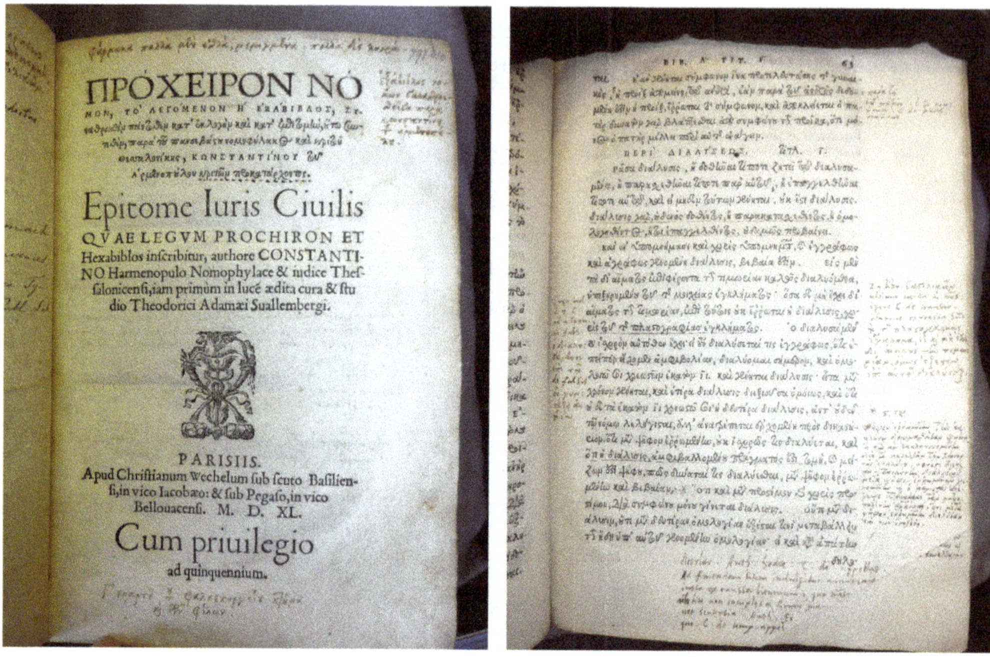

FIGURE 10 Two images of a copy of the first critical edition of Harmenopoulos' *Hexabiblos*, an edition that was made by Th.A. Suallemberg in Paris in 1540. This copy belonged to the humanist Gerard Falkenburg (c. 1538–1578), who made rich annotations to the text. This book is presently kept at the University Library of Leiden (shelf-number 759 C 50).
PHOTO: DAPHNE PENNA. WITH KIND PERMISSION OF THE UNIVERSITY LIBRARY OF LEIDEN.

CHAPTER 6

Canon Law

1 A Brief Outline of Byzantine Canon Law and Some Basic Terms

First, we must point out that in Byzantium, there was not a very strict separation between the state and the Church. For the Byzantines it was God who had placed the emperor as the head of the state. The emperor's authority derived from God and the emperor was naturally Orthodox. This explains, as we will see further on, why it was the emperor who summoned important ecclesiastical synods and why he was so interested in dealing with ecclesiastical matters. Religion was part of the state's affairs, and imperial legislation thus also dealt inevitably with religious issues. In other words, orthodoxy was state interest. Without a doubt, the subject of canon law in Byzantium could cover a whole book and, as already explained in the preface of this book, our aim is mainly to illustrate Byzantine law (and in this chapter, Byzantine canon law) through a selection of fragments of relevant sources.[1] Before presenting these sources, however, we will give an outline of the Eastern canonical sources and explain some basic terms of Byzantine canon law.

The Greek word 'canon' (κανών) literally means 'rule', 'measure'. Canon law deals with the rules and norms that regulate the Church. As is well known, the Christian church was first tolerated in the time of Constantine the Great. In AD 313, Emperor Constantine issued the Edict of Milan, the so-called 'tolerance edict', by which he allowed Christians to openly practise their religion. As a result of this edict, the persecution of Christians ceased and Christianity henceforth was made into a licit religion. Later, in AD 380/381 under Theodosius I, Christianity officially became the state religion. When Christianity was accepted and persecutions stopped, it could for the first time be organised properly. It was organised along lines analogous to the state: the church hierarchy followed the state hierarchy. That was when the first canons (rules, norms) were laid down. Canons of the church were established in meetings where all the bishops came together. Such a meeting was called a synod, from the Greek word 'synodos' (σύνοδος), or council, from the Latin *concilium*. As soon as Christianity emerged from secrecy and out 'into the open', dogmatic disputes and theological differences of opinion immediately surfaced as well. Church leaders did not tolerate this, nor did emperors put up with such sources of

1 There are two extensive general studies on Byzantine canon law in English: see Sp. Troianos, 'Byzantine Canon Law to 1100', and 'Byzantine Canon Law from the Twelfth to the Fifteenth Centuries', both published in W. Hartmann and K. Pennington (eds.), *The History of Byzantine and Eastern Canon Law to 1500* (Washington: 2012), pp. 115–169 and 170–214 respectively. These two studies are essentially English translations of the canon law sections in Troianos, *Pèges* = *Quellen*.

 | DOI:10.1163/9789004520684_007

turmoil. Hence, the bishops came together to settle all disputes. Their ambition was to reach doctrinal consensus. Those who chose to stick to minority views were labelled heretics as a consequence. This was the case, for example, with Arius (born *c.* 256, d. 336), a bishop in Alexandria who was denounced by the church as a heretic (see TEXT 1). This happened because he had different theological views about the Holy Trinity and the substantial relationship between the father and the son than those held by the majority of other bishops.

TEXT 1 Zonaras (twelfth century): about the first ecumenical council, Nicaea AD 325

Ἡ ἁγία καὶ οἰκουμενικὴ πρώτη σύνοδος γέγονε βασιλεύοντος τοῦ μεγάλου Κωνσταντίνου, ἀθροισθέντων ἐν Νικαίᾳ τῆς Βιθυνίας τριακοσίων δέκα καὶ ὀκτὼ ἁγίων Πατέρων, κατὰ Ἀρείου, γεγονότος πρεσβυτέρου τῆς κατὰ Ἀλεξάνδρειαν ἐκκλησίας, ὃς ἐβλασφήμει κατὰ τοῦ Υἱοῦ τοῦ Θεοῦ, τοῦ Κυρίου ἡμῶν Ἰησοῦ Χριστοῦ, λέγων μὴ ὁμοούσιον εἶναι αὐτὸν τῷ Θεῷ καὶ Πατρί, κτίσμα δέ· καὶ ὅτι ἦν, ὅτε οὐκ ἦν· ὃν καὶ καθεῖλεν ἡ ἁγία σύνοδος αὕτη, καὶ ἀνεθεμάτισε μετὰ τῶν ὁμοφρόνων αὐτοῦ· ἐδογμάτισε δὲ ὁμοούσιον τῷ Πατρὶ τὸν Υἱόν, καὶ Θεὸν ἀληθινόν, καὶ Δεσπότην, καὶ Κύριον, καὶ κτίστην τῶν κτιστῶν ἁπάντων· ἀλλ' οὐ κτίσμα, οὐδὲ μέντοι γε ποίημα. Πρώτη δὲ σύνοδος ἡ ἐν Νικαίᾳ αὕτη λέγεται πρὸς τὰς οἰκουμενικὰς ἀριθμουμένη· ἐπείτοι γε πρὸ αὐτῆς διάφοροι γεγόνασι σύνοδοι τοπικαί. Ἀλλὰ τῶν οἰκουμενικῶν αὕτη οὖσα πρώτη, προτέτακται τῶν λοιπῶν, τῶν πρὸ αὐτῆς γενομένων· τῆς ἐν Ἀντιοχείᾳ δηλαδή, κατὰ Παύλου τοῦ Σαμοσατέως, συγκροτηθείσης ἐπὶ Αὐρηλιανοῦ βασιλέως, τῆς τε ἐν Ἀγκύρᾳ, ἐν ᾗ ζήτησις γέγονε περὶ τῶν ἐν καιροῖς διωγμῶν τὴν πίστιν ἀρνησαμένων, καὶ μεταμελομένων, ὅπως δεῖ τούτους προσδέχεσθαι· καὶ τῆς ἐν Νεοκαισαρείᾳ, ἐν ᾗ

The first holy ecumenical council took place during the reign of Constantine the Great; 328 holy fathers gathered in Nicaea, Bithynia, against Arius, priest in the church of Alexandria, who told blasphemies about the Son of God, our Lord Jesus Christ, saying that He was not consubstantial with God the Father, but a creature, and that there was a time when He did not exist. He was condemned by the holy council under discussion and cursed, together with his followers. The council formulated the doctrine that the Son is consubstantial with the Father, and that He is the true God and Master and Lord, and the Creator of all things created; not a creature, and certainly not a produced being.

This council of Nicaea is called the first if one counts the ecumenical councils. It was preceded, however, by several local councils. But as this is the first of the ecumenical councils, it is dealt with before those that preceded it: those of Antioch, against Paulus of Samosata, which gathered during the reign of Emperor Aurelianus; of Ancyra, in which it was debated how the Church was to behave when confronted with some who had denied their faith during the persecutions but regretted it; and

TEXT 1 (*cont.*)

περὶ ἐκκλησιαστικῆς καταστάσεως κανόνες ἐξεφωνήθησαν.[2]	that of Neocaesarea, where canons were formulated about the ecclesiastical state.

As far as the bishops' councils are concerned, there is a difference between local and so-called universal or ecumenical councils. The word 'ecumenical' derives from the Greek word 'oikouméne' (οἰκουμένη), which means 'the inhabited world'. An ecumenical synod or council therefore is a general meeting of all the bishops. Already in the year after the Edict of Milan, for instance, there was a synod in Ancyra, but not all the bishops attended, so it did not count as ecumenical and was not recognised as valid—or at least, it was not valid at the beginning, although it would later on receive official authorisation and recognition. The first ecumenical synod was held in Nicaea (today's modern Turkish city of İznik, close to Istanbul) in 325 and was convened by Emperor Constantine the Great. TEXT 1 is a fragment from the commentary on this council by the twelfth-century canonist Zonaras,[3] where Nicaea is referred to as the first ecumenical council.

When bishops came together to settle their theological disputes, they also took the opportunity to settle legal matters. They were faced with questions such as: who is authorised to appoint a bishop; or, can someone who has denied his faith under the pressure of persecution still be admitted into church? So, canons, strictly speaking, are rules laid down by an ecumenical council. But they can also be other rules, such as those laid down in a local council or by a Church Father[4] if they have been officially accepted and authorised, that is, 'canonised'.

This is not the place to explain the relations between the Eastern Orthodox church and the Roman catholic. It suffices to mention that in the beginning of Christianity there was only one church, which means that both the Eastern Orthodox and the Roman Catholic church share a common early history. However, after many tensions between both churches, in AD 1054, the so-called East–West Schism or the Great Schism took place, which represented the final break between the Catholic Church and Eastern Orthodox Church. There are seven ecumenical councils. Or rather, to be more precise, there are seven councils recognized as ecumenical, as universal, by the Eastern Orthodox Church. The Roman Catholic Church recognises a few more, which were summoned by the pope. The seven ecumenical councils recognised by the Orthodox Church were all summoned by emperors and usually also presided by him or one of his representatives, as shown in the following table:

2 The Greek text is cited from the edition of RhP, vol. II, p. 113.

3 On Zonaras, see below, p. 199.

4 The Church Fathers were influential, authoritative Christian writers.

First	in 325 in Nicaea, summoned by Constantine the Great
Second	in 381 in Constantinople, summoned by Theodosius I
Third	in 431 in Ephesus, summoned by Theodosius II
Fourth	in 451 in Chalcedon, summoned by Marcianus
Fifth	in 553 in Constantinople, summoned by Justinian
Sixth	in 680–681 in Constantinople, summoned by Constantine IV
Fifth-Sixth Quinisextum Πενθέκτη (Penthekte)	in 691 in Constantinople, convened by Justinian II. This council is known as 'the council in Trullo' because it was held in the palace in a domed hall (*trullus*). This council systematised and confirmed the work of the Fifth and Sixth ecumenical councils and that is why it is called The Fifth-Sixth. It is not numbered as a separate ecumenical council because it is considered part of the Fifth and Sixth councils. The second canon of this ecumenical council confirmed or 'canonized' the so-called 'Apostle canons', i.e., those of the local councils and the writings of certain Church fathers.
Seventh	in 787 in Nicaea, convened by Constantine VI and his mother Eirene of Athens.

These ecumenical councils laid the theological foundations of the universal Christian faith through a process of eliminating dissident views about the nature of Christ, of the Holy Ghost, of Mary, etc. This universally accepted faith was formulated in the 'creed' or 'credo',[5] which is a statement and a symbol of Christian belief (in Greek: Τὸ Σύμβολον τῆς Πίστεως = the symbol of faith). The ecumenical councils took place in the East, that is, in the Greek-speaking part of the Roman Empire, but they were valid everywhere and were thus immediately translated into Latin. In the ninth century two more synods took place, which are not generally considered to be ecumenical: in 861, the so-called 'Primosecunda council', and in 879, the so-called 'Hagia Sophia council'. Both of these councils took place in Constantinople.

The canons issued by these councils were collected. The components of these collections are the following:

- Canons of the ecumenical councils; chronological.
- Canons of certain local, regional councils, which were automatically 'canonised' because they were included in the collection: Ancyra, Laodicea, Gangra.
- Pastoral letters of Church Fathers, like Basil of Caesarea (*c.* 329–*c.* 379) and Ioannes Chrysostom (*c.* 347–*c.* 407).
- The so-called 'Apostle Canons': rules ascribed to the Apostles themselves, although such an attribution was disputed.

5 The Latin verb *credo* means 'I believe'.

These were the canonical components of church law.

What complicates the situation even further is the fact that the Byzantine emperors also issued laws that, to a certain extent, covered the same ground as the church canons. Of course the emperor was not the head of the church, but he had considerable power and his constitutions about church matters were generally considered as legally valid.[6] However, they are not 'canons' in the strict sense of the word, but rather laws or 'nomoi'. These imperial constitutions issued by Justinian and others are mainly found in the first titles of the *Code* and in the *Novels*. For example, the first thirteen titles of the first book of Justinian's *Code* (from the second edition of the *Code*, the one that has survived) deal with church issues, such as the following: dogmatic principles that were settled in the ecumenical councils that had taken place by that time, issues regarding ecclesiastical property, clergy, monks, the administration of justice by bishops, heresies, sacraments, etc. There are also many Justinianic *Novels* that deal with, for example, ecclesiastical organisation and monastic life. These constitutions or 'nomoi' regarding ecclesiastical issues were at first listed in an appendix to the collections of canons, but later they were integrated within the collections themselves. The result is a combination of *canones*, i.e. canons of ecclesiastical origin and of 'nomoi', i.e. secular laws. Such a combination is technically called a 'nomocanon' (νομοκάνων). We will now briefly discuss the development of two of them.

The canons themselves were collected in their chronological order, called *Syntagma* (collection). This soon became unpractical: you simply could not find what you wanted if you did not happen to know which council had made a pronouncement about your chosen subject. Therefore, in addition to the chronological collection, systematic repertories were made to make the canons more accessible, based on the model of the *Codex Justinianus*. Two of these were of particular importance. First, in AD 550, Ioannes Scholastikos, who was a professional lawyer but later became the patriarch of Constantinople, arranged the canons into fifty titles. This Collection [of 'canones'] in Fifty Titles has an appendix with some *Novels* and a few Greek constitutions taken from the *Code*. After his death, the collection of canons and the appendix of nomoi were integrated into what we now know as the *Nomocanon of the Fifty Titles*.

A second attempt to make the canons more accessible was made in about AD 580, and is known as the *Syntagma canonum*. This collection of canons contained the full text of the canons and other sources that were recognised as canons and arranged them, as we said, not according to their subject-matter, but following the chronological order of the councils or other authorities that had issued them. This collection was then made accessible by a kind of register, which is referred to as the *Repertorium of Fourteen Titles*. This repertory is arranged according to the subject matter, and this time not into fifty

6 See the observations at the beginning of this chapter about the relation between the Byzantine Emperor and the Orthodox Church.

but fourteen titles, subdivided into chapters, with references to the relevant canons. The fourth title, for instance, is about baptism, and the separate chapters of this title deal with baptizing sick people or pregnant women, about baptizing people twice, about people baptized by heretics, etc. If, for example, you wanted information about baptizing a pregnant woman, you could consult the repertory and it would tell you to read canon 12 of Neocaesarea, canon 47 of Laodicea, etc. In this way you easily found what you wanted.

Then, to be sure that you did not miss anything essential, you could also consult a supplement to the *Syntagma canonum*, an appendix which contained summaries of texts of secular law regarding the church. These were texts taken from the *Corpus Iuris Civilis*; in other words, they were not canons but laws, *nomoi*. The first part of the appendix represents the first book of the *Codex Justinianus*, the second is taken from the *Digest* and the *Institutes*, and the third part from the *Novels* of Justinian. This arrangement into three different parts explains the name of the appendix: the *Collectio Tripartita* (also known as *Collectio constitutionum ecclesiasticarum*).

The next step in the evolution of this *Syntagma canonum* was a logical one that took place in the beginning of the seventh century (see the scheme of canon law further on, under 2 on p. 198): references to the *nomoi* in the *Collectio Tripartita* were inserted into the *Repertorium of Fourtıeen Titles*. After this combination of canons and *nomoi* it was no longer called the *Repertorium of Fourteen Titles*, but now the *Nomocanon of Fourteen Titles*. Actually, you not only find references to the relevant nomoi, but summaries of them as well. It is the jurist whom we already met in chapter 3,[7] 'the Anonymos Junior' or Enantiophanes who lived in the beginning of the seventh century, who was responsible for combining the references to the canons and the summaries of related nomoi, and he also added short commentaries if he felt they were needed. He did so in *c*. AD 612–619. In principle, his new systematisation made the *Collectio Tripartita* superfluous as a separate appendix, but it was usually nevertheless still included in the manuscripts, after the text of the canons themselves.

Just as in secular law, the time of Justinian and the generations after him are important for canon law as well. After the iconoclastic period, for which there were no major developments in canon law, we see a revival in the time of the Macedonian Renaissance, after the restoration of Orthodoxy in 843. Patriarch Photios, who as we have seen had played an influential role in the legislation of Basil I and especially in the *Eisagoge*, presumably also influenced canon law in this period. The *Syntagma canonum* was updated during the time of Photios' second patriarchate in AD 883.[8] This work of updating a text is exactly what one would expect at this stage: the text of the canons of the councils after AD 451

7 See above, pp. 91–96.

8 Photios was appointed patriarch of Constantinople twice. Between the periods of his appointments, he was banished and condemned.

(Chalcedon) were added and references to those canons were inserted into the *Nomocanon*. For centuries it was thought that the *Nomocanon of the Fourteen Titles* was written by Photios, and for this reason, the literature sometimes also calls this text the 'Nomocanon of Pseudo-Photios', even if we now know that the *Nomocanon in the Fourteen Titles* was originally compiled at the beginning of the seventh century and was revised during the time of Photios at the end of the ninth century. It is this revised text that has survived in the manuscript tradition.

In the ninth and tenth centuries, there was not much new ecclesiastical law, but there is one new source to pay attention to: the decrees of the patriarchs of Constantinople. Originally, the patriarch of Constantinople was just one of five patriarchs, nor was he even the main patriarch, but as time went on he gained in authority, at least in Byzantium. One of the reasons for this was because Alexandria, Jerusalem and Antioch were occupied by Arabs, and Rome was isolated politically. There also was a large concentration of bishops in Constantinople. While bishops for the occupied areas continued to be ordained, they were unable to travel to their posts, so they remained in the capital. There they came together in assemblies and ratified the decisions of the patriarch. This was not the official situation, and the decrees were not inserted in the *Syntagma*, but, in practice they were considered as valid church law. Moreover, no new secular law was included in the *Nomocanon*. Finally, there was another revision of the *Syntagma*, including the *Nomocanon*, in 1089 by Theodoros Bestes. Then we come to the twelfth century, which is important in canon law because of the work of the three so-called canonists.[9]

9 See below, pp. 199–204.

2 A Scheme of the Sources of Byzantine Canon Law until the Twelfth Century

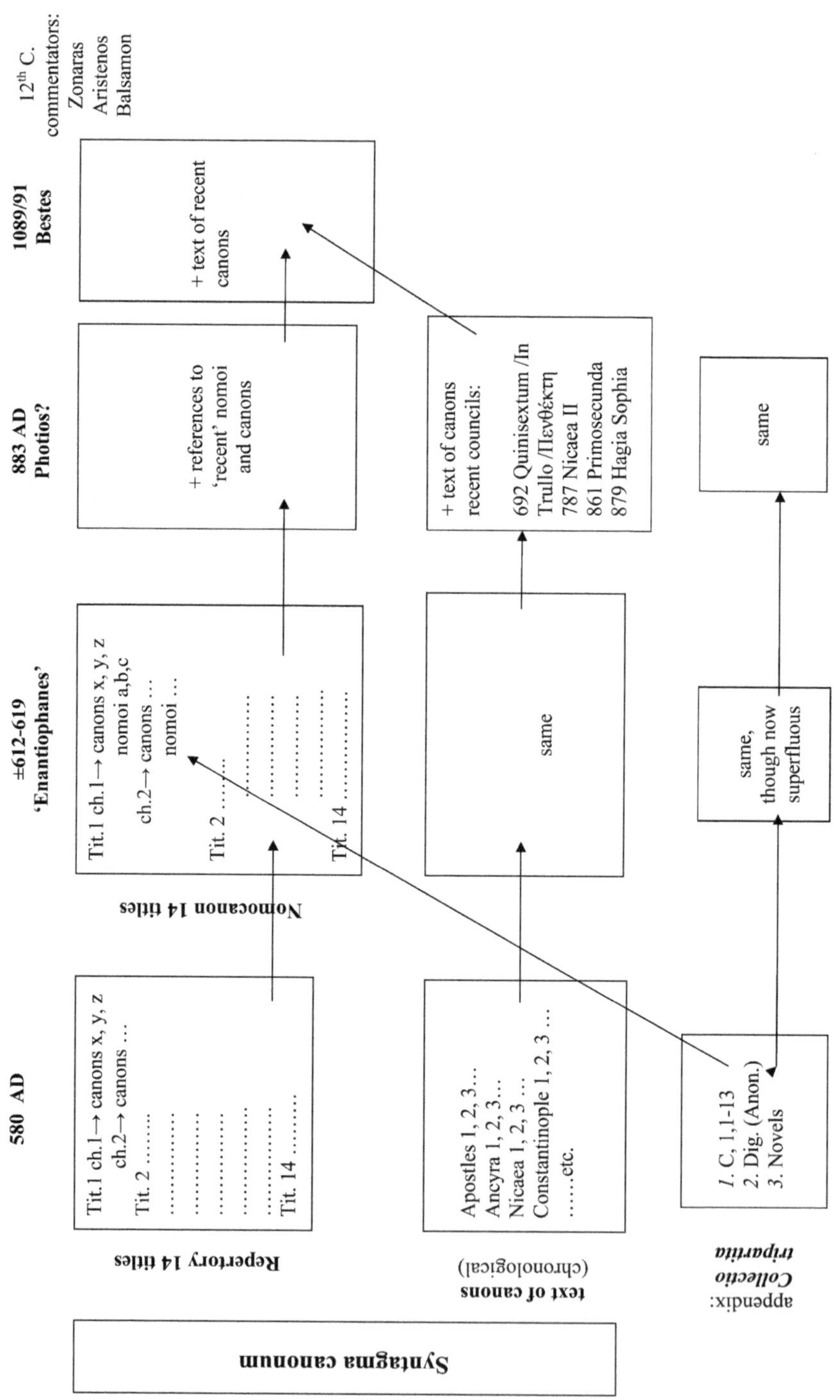

3 The Canonists of the Twelfth Century

As far as canon law in the twelfth century is concerned, the most important work is found in the writings of the three great canonists: Ioannes Zonaras, Alexios Aristenos and Theodoros Balsamon. They all wrote commentaries on the canons.

Zonaras was probably born towards the end of the eleventh century, and died sometime after 1159. He had held important secular offices and had served as a president at a high court. In later age, he became a monk at the monastery of St Glykeria at the Prince's islands, close to Constantinople. Zonaras not only wrote commentaries on the canons, but he also wrote theological works and a chronicle in which he describes the history from the creation of the world up to 1118. When it comes to canon law, Zonaras wrote an extensive commentary on the canons, i.e. the canons of the Apostles, of the councils (both ecumenical and local) and of the Church Fathers. Compared to the other two canonists, his work is more analytical than Aristenos' commentary but briefer than that of Balsamon. Another difference between Zonaras' commentary and that of Balsamon is that the former uses fewer sources of secular law in comparison to the latter.

Despite the fact that Zonaras was older than Aristenos, it was this latter who was the first to write a commentary on the canons, which means that Aristenos' commentary is the earliest of the three Byzantine canonists of the twelfth century. Aristenos was born presumably before 1100, and his death must have occurred after the year 1166, the year of a synod in Constantinople that we know he attended. He held important ecclesiastical and secular offices. In 1130, after an order of Emperor Ioannes II Komnenos (r. 1118–1143), Aristenos made a commentary on the canons based on a revision of the earlier *Synopsis canonum*, which was a summary of the canons, as its title implies. Aristenos wrote scholia on the canons of the Apostles, the ecumenical and the local synods, and on eighty-five canons of St Basil the Great or Basil of Caesarea, who was bishop of Caesarea (in Cappadocia, Asia Minor, nowadays Turkey) and one of the Church Fathers.

Theodoros Balsamon is the most well-known of the three canonists. He was born in Constantinople between *c.* 1130 and 1140 and died after 1195. He had occupied important ecclesiastical offices and became patriarch of Antioch (a city of ancient Syria and now in southern-central Turkey), although he remained in the Byzantine capital and never actually visited Antioch, which was under Latin occupation at that time. Balsamon's work is very extensive. His major hermeneutical work is his commentary on the *Nomocanon of the Fourteen Titles*. The background of this work is related to the status of the *Basilica*. As we have already mentioned, the *Basilica* were promulgated around AD 900. At the end of the twelfth century, there was a conflict between the patriarch of Constantinople and the metropolitan of Amaseia, a city on the Black Sea in present-day Turkey. The metropolitan had failed to appoint a bishop to the empty see of the city of Amisos, even after he had been requested to do so on three occasions. Since Amisos had been without bishop for over a year, the patriarch of Constantinople lost his patience. He then personally chose and ordained a bishop, and he claimed his right to do so on the basis of a Justinianic *Novel*. However, the metropolitan of Amaseia challenged that right, arguing that that particular *Novel* was not included in the *Basilica* and, therefore, that it was no longer valid. The question was then brought before Emperor Manuel I Komnenos, who, after consulting his advisers, decided that the metropolitan was right. In other words, he decided that those *Novels* that were not included in the *Basilica* had lost their force of law, implying that it was the *Basilica* that made up the codification, not the original, basically Justinianic corpus.

This decision, of course, had far-reaching consequences: the *Nomocanon of the Fourteen Titles* had been made before the *Basilica* and still contained laws that now suddenly ceased to be valid. Therefore, the emperor and the patriarch asked Balsamon, who was serving at that time as *chartophylax*, an ecclesiastical official with archival and notarial duties, to sort things out. For each law in the *Nomocanon* Balsamon had to check whether or not it was found in the *Basilica*. Then, apparently, he decided to set about writing a complete commentary. As far the *Basilica* are concerned, the following reply of Balsamon also sheds some light on the application of the *Basilica*.

According to this testimony, the *Basilica* laws were apparently rather hard to find, especially outside the Byzantine capital. Balsamon reassures the patriarch of Alexandria that he will be excused for not applying the *Basilica* because of the difficulty of acquiring them in his region. Nevertheless, he and others in his position should do their best in trying to find out the law of the *Basilica*. If they have done their best and have found nothing, then they are indeed excused.

TEXT 2 **'Canonical Questions' of His holiest patriarch of Alexandria, Marcus, and the replies given by His holiest patriarch of Antiochia, Theodoros Balsamon (Ἐρωτήσεις κανονικαὶ τοῦ ἁγιωτάτου πατριάρχου Ἀλεξανδρείας κυρίου Μάρκου, καὶ ἀποκρίσεις ἐπ' αὐταῖς τοῦ ἁγιωτάτου πατριάρχου Ἀντιοχείας, κυρίου Θεοδώρου τοῦ Βαλσαμών)**[10]

Ἐρώτησις δ' Τὰ ἑξήκοντα βιβλία τῶν νόμων, τὰ λεγόμενα βασιλικά, οὐ διεδόθησαν εἰς τὰς χώρας ἡμῶν· διὰ τοῦτο νυκτοβατοῦμεν ὅσον τὸ εἰς αὐτά. Ζητοῦμεν οὖν μαθεῖν, εἰ ἐντεῦθεν κατακρινόμεθα.	Question 4. Those sixty books of laws, those so-called *Basilica*, never reached our area. Hence we grope entirely in the dark for their contents. We would like to hear whether this can be a reason for us to be condemned.
Ἀπόκρισις Ὅσα ὁ νόμος λαλεῖ, τοῖς ἐν τῷ νόμῳ λέγει, κατὰ τὸν μέγαν Ἀπόστολον. Οἱ γοῦν αὐχοῦντες βίον ὀρθόδοξον, κἂν ἐξ	Reply: What the law says is said to those who are governed by that law, according to the great Apostle [Rom. 3:19]. Those who profess to

10 The Greek text is cited from the edition of RhP, vol. IV, p. 451.

TEXT 2 (*cont.*)

Ἀνατολῶν ὦσι, κἂν ἐξ Ἀλεξανδρέων, κἂν ἑτέρωθεν, Ῥωμαῖοι λέγονται, καὶ κατὰ νόμους ἀναγκάζονται πολιτεύεσθαι· τῷ νόμῳ δὲ τῷ φάσκοντι, "Οὐ δεῖ Ῥωμαῖον ἄνδρα νόμον ἀγνοεῖν", οὐ συσφίγγονται. Μόνοι γὰρ οἱ κατοικοῦντες τὴν Ῥώμην, τὴν βασιλίδα δηλονότι τῶν πόλεων, τὴν κατησφαλισμένην ὁμοίοις πυργώμασι, καὶ πολλοὺς πλουτοῦσαν νομομαθεῖς, ταῖς ἐκ τούτων σιδηροπέδαις κατέχονται. Διὸ οὗτοι μὲν ἀγνοῆσαι νόμον διενιστάμενοι οὐ συγγινώσκονται, κἂν χειρονάκται, κἂν ἀγύρται τινὲς ὦσι καὶ γραμμάτων ἀνήκοοι, ὡς δυνάμενοι τὰ τῶν νόμων μαθεῖν ἀπὸ τῶν συγκατοίκων αὐτῶν. Οἱ δὲ ἔξω τῆς Ῥώμης διάγοντες, ἀγρόται δηλονότι, καὶ λοιποί, πολλῷ δὲ πλέον Ἀλεξανδρεῖς, νόμον πολιτικὸν ἀγνοήσαντες συγγινώσκονται. Καλὸν γοῦν ἐστι καὶ τούτους ἐρωτᾶν, καὶ μανθάνειν τὰ νομικὰ παραγγέλματα. Εἰ δὲ δυσχερές ἐστι, συγγνώμης ἀξιωθήσονται.	lead an orthodox life, whether it is in Anatolia or in Alexandria or in any other place, are called Romans and are, therefore, necessarily governed by Roman law. Nevertheless they are not harmed by the decree that says: 'A Roman citizen is not allowed not to know the law.' Only the inhabitants of Rome—I mean, of course, the imperial city, the city fortified by bastions and rich in jurists—only they are chained by its [= that decree's] iron fetters. If these inhabitants of the capital do not know the law, then they are not forgiven, even if they are merely artisans or tramps or illiterate, because it is possible for them to ask their fellow-townsmen about the law. But those who live outside Rome, peasants, of course, and certainly people in Alexandria, they are forgiven for being ill-informed. Even so, it is obviously advisable for them to make enquiries, and to try to get acquainted with the legal regulations. Yet if they do not succeed, they will be excused.

Balsamon also wrote a commentary on the canons, i.e. the canons of the Apostles, the ecumenical and local synods and of the Church fathers. He is very analytical in his commentary providing the canon, then the explanation ('ermeneia') of this canon, the relevant 'nomos', then his commentary, before also adding the most recent laws and canons. Contrary to the other two canonists, Balsamon uses many sources of secular law. In fact, several *Novels* from after Justinian as well as numerous patriarchal documents have only been preserved in the work of Balsamon, in places where the canonist, for example, cites fragments of these documents or sometimes even adduces the whole text. Balsamon, after all, had easy access to the archives since he occupied the high ecclesiastical office of a *chartophylax*, who had archival and chancery-related duties.

In order to illustrate the differences between the three canonists and to compare their styles, we will now cite three fragments of their commentary on the same canon. The chosen canon is the first canon from the first ecumenical council of Nicaea in AD 325, and it is about whether amputated persons—and in particular castrated persons—can be members of the clergy. We will first cite the text of the canon itself (TEXT 3.1), and then fragments from the relevant comments on this canon by the three great canonists of the twelfth century in the following order: Aristenos (TEXT 3.2) because his commentary is the oldest, then Zonaras (TEXT 3.3), and, finally, Balsamon (TEXT 3.4).

TEXT 3.1 Nicaea, canon 1[11]

Εἴ τις ἐν νόσῳ ὑπὸ ἰατρῶν ἐχειρουργήθη ἢ ὑπὸ βαρβάρων ἐξετμήθη, οὗτος μενέτω ἐν τῷ κλήρῳ· εἰ δέ τις ὑγιαίνων ἑαυτὸν ἐξέτεμε, τοῦτον καὶ ἐν τῷ κλήρῳ ἐξεταζόμενον πεπαῦσθαι προσήκει, καὶ ἐκ τοῦ δεῦρο μηδένα τῶν τοιούτων χρῆναι προάγεσθαι. Ὥσπερ δὲ τοῦτο πρόδηλον, ὅτι περὶ τῶν ἐπιτηδευόντων τὸ πρᾶγμα καὶ τολμώντων ἑαυτοὺς ἐκτέμνειν εἴρηται, οὕτως εἴ τινες ὑπὸ βαρβάρων ἢ ὑπὸ δεσποτῶν εὐνουχίσθησαν, εὑρίσκοιντο δὲ ἄξιοι, τοὺς τοιούτους εἰς κλῆρον προσίεται ὁ κανών.	If a person was amputated by a doctor during illness, or gelded by barbarians, he is allowed to remain in the clergy. But if he castrated himself without being ill, he deserves after thorough examination to be excluded from the clergy. And in the future such people must not be admitted into the clergy at all. Just as it is clear that the preceding only speaks about those who have intentionally done so, who had the nerve to emasculate themselves, thus the canon does admit to the clergy those who were castrated by barbarians or by their masters but show themselves worthy.

TEXT 3.2 Commentary by Aristenos on Nicaea, canon 1[12]

Οἱ εὐνοῦχοι εἰς κλῆρον δεχέσθωσαν, οἱ δὲ ἐκτέμνοντες ἑαυτοὺς μὴ δεχέσθωσαν.[13]	Eunuchs must be admitted in the clergy, but those who mutilated themselves must not be accepted.
Εἴρηται καὶ ἐν τοῖς ἀποστολικοῖς κανόσιν, ἤγουν τῷ κβʹ, κγʹ καὶ κδʹ, τὸν ἄξιον ἱερωσύνης μὴ κωλύεσθαι εἰς κλῆρον προβιβάζεσθαι, εἴπερ ἀκουσίως ἐξευνουχίσθη· τὸν δὲ ἑκουσίως ἑαυτὸν ἀκρωτηριάσαντα ὡς αὐτοφονευτὴν	It is also said in the Apostle canons, more specifically in 22, 23 and 24, that someone who is worthy to become a priest should not be hindered from entering the clergy if he has been castrated against his will; if, however, he has amputated himself of his own free will as

11 The Greek text is cited from the edition of P.-P. Joannou, *Fonti Discipline Generale Antique* (*IIe–IXe* s.) *1.1: Les canons des conciles œcuméniques* (Rome/Grottaferrata: 1962), pp. 23–24.

12 The Greek text is cited from the edition of E. Papagianni, Sp. Troianos, L. Burgmann, and K. Maksimovič, *Alexios Aristenos: Kommentar zur Synopsis canonum* (Berlin/Boston: 2019).

13 This is a summary of the *Synopsis* that Aristenos used.

TEXT 3.2 (*cont.*)

ἑαυτοῦ εἰς κλῆρον ὅλως μὴ παραδέχεσθαι, ἀλλὰ καὶ κληρικὸν ὄντα καθαιρεῖσθαι. Τῆς αὐτῆς οὖν καὶ ὁ παρὼν κανὼν ἐννοίας ἐστίν.	a suicide, he should not be admitted into the clergy at all and even if he already belongs to the clergy he should be deposed. The present canon also has the same intent.

TEXT 3.3 **Commentary by Zonaras on Nicaea, canon 1**[14]

Διάφοροι κανόνες τῶν ἁγίων Ἀποστόλων τὰ αὐτὰ τῷ παρόντι κανόνι διατάττονται· καὶ οἱ τῆς πολιτείας δὲ νόμοι. Ἔοικε δὲ καταφρονηθῆναι τὸ πρᾶγμα καὶ μετὰ τοὺς κανόνας, καὶ αὖθίς τινας ἑαυτοὺς ἀκρωτηριάζοντας, προάγεσθαι εἰς κλῆρον· καὶ τοὺς ὑφ' ἑτέρων ἐκτμηθέντας κατ' ἐπήρειαν, μὴ προάγεσθαι. Διὰ τοῦτο οὖν καὶ οἱ τῆς συνόδου ταύτης τὸν παρόντα κανόνα ἐξέθεντο, διαταττόμενοι τὰ αὐτὰ τοῖς ἀποστολικοῖς κανόσι καὶ τοῖς νόμοις· ὥστε μήτε … κτλ.	There are various canons of the Apostles which decree the same as this one, and also secular laws. Yet it appears that the matter was disregarded even after these canons, so that it still happened that people who emasculated themselves were accepted into the clergy, while those who were gelded by others, as an insult, were not accepted. That is the reason why the fathers of this council again issued the canon under discussion, proclaiming the same rules as the Apostle canons and the secular laws, namely that (… etc.).

TEXT 3.4 **Commentary by Balsamon on Nicaea, canon 1**[15]

Οἱ ἀποστολικοὶ θεῖοι κανόνες ὁ κα.' ὁ κβ.' ὁ κγ.' καὶ ὁ κδ.' ἱκανῶς ἡμᾶς ἐδίδαξαν, τί ὀφείλει γίνεσθαι εἰς τοὺς ἀκρωτηριαζομένους τοὺς διδύμους. Ἀκολούθως οὖν τούτοις καὶ ὁ παρὼν κανὼν διατάττεται (…). Ἐπεὶ δὲ τοὺς ἀποστολικοὺς κανόνας ἑρμηνεύοντες, ἐγράψαμεν κολάζεσθαι τὸν μετὰ τὴν χειροτονίαν διὰ πάθος ἑαυ-	The Apostle canons 21, 22, 23, and 24 taught us clearly enough what to do with persons who mutilate their testicles. In accordance with those, the present canon also lays down that (…). In our commentary on the Apostle canons we wrote that someone who mutilates himself for medical reasons after being ordained as a priest is punished. The present canon, how- by

14 The Greek text is cited from the edition of RhP, vol. II, pp. 114–115.

15 The Greek text is cited from the edition of RhP, vol. II, pp. 115–116.

TEXT 3.4 (*cont.*)

τὸν ἀκρωτηριάσαντα· ἀπὸ δὲ τοῦ παρόντος κανόνος λέγοντος, Εἴ τις ἐν νόσῳ ὑπὸ ἰατρῶν ἐχειρουργήθη, οὗτος μενέτω ἐν τῷ κλήρῳ· καὶ αὖθις, Εἰ δέ τις ὑγιαίνων ἑαυτὸν ἐξέτεμε, τοῦτον, καὶ ἐν τῷ κλήρῳ ἐξεταζόμενον, πεπαῦσθαι προσήκει· εἶπόν τινες μὴ κολάζεσθαι τὸν μετὰ τὴν κλήρωσιν διὰ πάθος ἀκρωτηριασθέντα· φαμὲν ὡς ὁ τοιοῦτος κανὼν οὐ διαλέγεται περὶ τῶν ἀκρωτηριασθέντων μετὰ τὴν ἱερωσύνην, ἀλλὰ πρὸ τῆς ἱερωσύνης, μετὰ δὲ ταύτην, εἰς ἀμφιβολίαν ἐμπεσόντων. Εἰ δὲ καὶ πλέον ἀνθίσταταί τις, […], ἀκουσάτω ὡς ἡ ρμβ.' Ἰουστινιάνειος νεαρά, ἡ κειμένη ἐν βιβλίῳ ξ' τίτλῳ να.' κεφαλαίῳ τελευταίῳ, ἥτις καὶ κατεστρώθη ἐν κεφαλαίῳ ιδ.' τοῦ πρώτου τίτλου τοῦ παρόντος συντάγματος, ἐπιστομίζει αὐτόν. […]	ever, says, 'If someone was amputated a doctor during illness, or gelded by barbarians, he is allowed to remain in the clergy', and again: 'But if he castrated himself without being ill, he deserves after thorough examination to be excluded from the clergy.' This has led some to the inference that someone who mutilates himself for medical reasons after being appointed a priest is not punished. But in our opinion that canon does not speak of amputating after, but before priesthood and, after they become priests, they fall under suspicion. And if somebody should still contest this view, […], let him be told that the 142th *Novel* of Justinian, which is found in book 60 title 51, last chapter, which also found its way to chapter 14 of the first title of the present Syntagma [the Nomocanon of the Fourteen Titles], silences him. […]

Even from these short fragments from the work of the three canonists commenting on the same canon, it is clear that Balsamon's commentary is by far the most extensive, especially with its inclusion of specific references to secular law. For example, in the last sentences of his commentary on the first canon of the Council of Nicaea, he also points out that the Justinianic *Novel* has found its way both to the *Basilica* and to the *Nomocanon in the Fourteen Titles*.

Finally, from the late Byzantine period we will only mention the name of Matthaios Blastares who was a canonist of the fourteenth century. He was born in *c*. 1280 and died in *c*. 1350, after having spent most of his life at a monastery in Thessaloniki. His major work is the *Syntagma kata stoicheion* (Σύνταγμα κατὰ Στοιχεῖον), or *Alphabetical Syntagma* (= Collection in alphabetical order), which, as its title implies, is an alphabetical work mainly addressing ecclesiastical law, but also addressing some other fields of law, especially those that deal with the administration of justice. By the time Blastares was writing, the clergy was far more involved in the administration of justice than it had been before, and it has been suggested that Blastares' work aimed to help the clergy in the discharge of their judicial duties. The *Syntagma kata stoicheion* or *Alphabetical Syntagma* is divided into twenty-four parts, corresponding to the twenty-four letters of the Greek alphabet.

4 Byzantine Canon and Civil Law concerning Interest on Debts

In this final section, we will quote some fragments from both Byzantine canon and secular law. The subject of interest is ideal for illustrating the variety of Byzantine civil and canon law sources and the relation between them. The church was in principle against charging interest because it meant making profit at the expense of someone else. Clergymen were therefore not allowed to charge interest. We have added explanatory notes in bold letters in the right-hand column of the tables where this seemed helpful.

TEXT 4.1 ***The Nomocanon of the Fourteen Titles*, 9,27 (ninth century)**[16]

Ἀποστόλων κανὼν κε'. μβ'. μγ'. μδ'. Συνόδου Νικαίας κανὼν ιζ'. Τῆς ἐν Λαοδικείᾳ κανὼν δ'. νδ'. Τῆς ἐν Καρθαγένῃ κανὼν ε'. ις'. Συνόδου ς'. κανὼν ι'. κγ'. κδ'. ν'. να'. Συνόδου Νικαίας τὸ δεύτερον κανὼν δ'. Βασιλείου κανὼν ιδ'. ιζ'. κθ'.	Of the **Apostles canons** 25, 42, 43, **44**. Of the Council at **Nicaea canon** 17. Of the one in **Laodicea** 4, 54. Of that in **Carthage** 5, 16. Of the **Sixth council canons** 10, 23, 24, 50, 51. Of the second council of Nicaea canon 4. Of **Basil canons** 14, 17, 29.

The canons in bold letters are also found in the alphabetical work by Blastares under the Greek letter 'T' because the Greek word for 'interest', 'Τόκος' (Tokos), begins with the Greek letter 'T':

TEXT 4.2.1 **Blastares, *Alphabetical Syntagma*, Table of contents (fourteenth century)**[17]

Ἀρχὴ τοῦ **Τ** στοιχείου [...] κεφ. Ζ'. Ὅτι τόκους λαμβάνειν ἀπείρηται παντὶ κληρικῷ, καὶ περὶ τόκων	Beginning of letter **T** [...] chapter 7: That it is forbidden for every clergyman to charge interest; about interest

16 The Greek text is cited from the edition of RhP, vol. I, p. 202.

17 The Greek text is cited from the edition of RhP, vol. VI, p. 473.

TEXT 4.2.2 Blastares, *Alphabetical Syntagma*, T(*okos*) 7 (fourteenth century)[18]
Blastares' references to canons and civil laws about interest

Ἀποστόλων μδ'. Ὁ μδ'. τῶν ἁγίων Ἀποστόλων κανὼν [...]	Of the **Apostles 44** Canon 44 of the holy apostles [...]	**As in 4.1 Nomocanon; some of the TEXTS in 4.7.1–3**
Συνόδου πρώτης ιζ'. Ὁ ιζ'. τῆς α' Συνόδου πάντα κληρικὸν [...]	**First** synod canon 17 The 17th canon of the First Synod dictates that each member of the clergy [...]	
Συνόδου ἕκτης ι'. Τὰ αὐτὰ γὰρ καὶ ὁ ι'. τῆς ἕκτης λέξας Συνόδου [...]	**Sixth** synod canon 10 The same is also said by the 10th canon of the Sixth Council, which dictates [...]	
Λαοδικείας δ' Τούτοις ἕπεται καὶ ὁ τῆς ἐν Λαοδικείᾳ δ' κανών.	**Laodicea** canon 4 These examples are followed also by canon 4 of the council of Laodicea	**local, regional council**
Καρθαγένης ε'. Ὁ δὲ τῆς ἐν Καρθαγένῃ ε'., τὴν ἀπληστίαν πάντων τῶν κακῶν εἶναι μητέρα οὐδείς, φησιν, ἀγνοεῖ· [...]	Of **Carthage** canon 5 Canon 5 of the Council of Carthage says that no one doubts that greed is the mother of all evil things [...]	**another local council**
Βασιλείου ιδ'. Ὁ δὲ μέγας Βασίλειος ἐν ιδ'. κανόνι, Ὁ τόκους λαμβάνων κληρικός, φησιν, ἐὰν [...]	**Basil** canon 14 Basil the Great says in his 14th canon: 'The clergyman who charges interest [...]'	**One of the canonized Church Fathers**
Νόμοι Εἰ καὶ πολλοῖς τῶν πρὸ ἡμῶν ἔδοξε δεκτέαν εἶναι τὴν τῶν τόκων ἔκτισιν, ἴσως διὰ τὴν τῶν δανειστῶν	**Civil laws** Although many of our predecessors were of the opinion that charging interest was acceptable,	**This is from the *Prochiron*:**

18 The Greet text is cited from the edition of RhP, vol. VI, pp. 473–476.

TEXT 4.2.2 (*cont.*)

δυσκληρίαν τε καὶ ὠμότητα, ἀλλ' οὖν ὡς ἀναξίαν τῆς ἡμῶν τῶν Χριστιανῶν πολιτείας, ἀπευκταίαν εἶναι κεκρίκαμεν, ἅτε παρὰ τῆς θείας νομοθεσίας κεκωλυμένην· διὸ κελεύει ἡ ἡμετέρα γαληνότης, μηδενὶ μηδαμῶς ἐξεῖναι, ἐν μηδεμιᾷ ὑποθέσει τόκον λαμβάνειν, ἵνα μὴ νόμον φυλάττειν οἰόμενοι, νόμον Θεοῦ παραβαίνωμεν· ἀλλ' κἂν εἴ τις ὁσονδήποτε λάβοι, εἰς τὸ χρέος δὴ λογισθήσεται. Ὁ δὲ παλαιὸς νόμος, ῥητὴν ὁρίζει τοῖς τόκοις ποσότητα, τῇ ποιότητι μέν τοι τῶν προσώπων διαλλάττουσαν. Τοὺς μὲν γὰρ δανείζοντας ἀπὸ ἰλλουστρίων καὶ ἀνωτέρω, ἄχρι τρίτης ἑκατοστῆς καὶ μόνον κελεύει λαμβάνειν· ἀργυροπράτας δὲ καὶ ἐμπόρους, ἄχρι διμοίρου ἑκατοστῆς· τοὺς δὲ λοιποὺς πάντας ἄχρι ἡμισέως ἑκατοστῆς· εἰ δὲ πρὸς οἶκον εὐαγῆ τὸ δάνειον εἴη, ἄχρι τετάρτου ἑκατοστῆς.	perhaps in view of the possible loss and hardship of the creditors, yet we have decided that, being unworthy of our Christian State, it is abominable, seeing that it is forbidden by divine law. For that reason our Serenity dictates that nobody is allowed in any way to charge interest in any case, to prevent the situation where we believe to observe the law while we offend against the law of God. If someone nevertheless accepts whatever sum, this will be reckoned as part of the debt. But the **old law** defines a specific interest rate, which varies with the person's class. It tells those creditors who belong to the *illustres* and higher to limit the interest rate to 4%, bankers and merchants to 8%, and all others to 6%. If, however, the loan is to a sacred building, just 3%.	**see also below *Basilica* scholion 4 (TEXT 4.6.4)** **See B. 23,3,74 (BT 1134/14ff.) / C. 4,32,26 (Justinian 528AD)**

Blastares also makes reference to civil law provisions on interests. We will now cite fragments from Byzantine secular law sources about interest on debt, and we will point out the links between them and Blastares' references. The first fragment is from the *Synopsis maior Basilicorum*, an alphabetical work on the *Basilica*.[19]

19 On the *Synopsis maior Basilicorum*, see above, pp. 143–145.

TEXT 4.3 ***Synopsis Maior Basilicorum, T(okos)*** **[= interest], chapter 11 (tenth century)**[20]

Περὶ τόκων ἀπαιτουμένων καὶ μὴ ἀπαιτουμένων, καὶ ἀργυροπρατικῶν, καὶ τῶν μετὰ ὑπέρθεσιν ἀπαιτουμένων	About interest charged and not charged, and bankers, and about interest charged in case of default.	
1. Ἀνάγν. βι. ζ′ τί. ς′ κεφ. α′, ἐν ᾧ φησι· … 2. Ἀνάγνωθι καὶ βι. θ′ τί. γ′ […] 3. Ἀνάγνωθι καὶ βι. ιη′ τί. ζ′ […] **4. Καὶ βι. κγ′ τί γ′, οὗτινος ἐν τῷ α′ κεφ. φησίν·** Ἐπὶ τῶν καλῇ πίστει ἀγωγῶν ὀφφικίῳ τοῦ δικάζοντος ὁ τόκος ὁρίζεται πρὸς τὸ ἔθος τοῦ κλίματος, ἐν ᾧ τὸ συνάλλαγμα γέγονεν, ὥστε μέντοι μὴ ὑπερβαίνειν τὸν νόμιμον.	1. Read Bas. 7, 6,1, in which he says: … 2. Read also Bas. 9, 3 […] 3. Read also Bas. 18, 7 […] 4. And **Bas. 23, 3, which says in the first chapter**: 'In actions of good faith, the rate of interest is fixed at the judge's authority according to the custom of the place where the contract was made, so long as it does not exceed the legal rate.'	**See below, the *Basilica*, TEXT 4.5**

TEXT 4.4 **D. 22,1,1 (AD 533)**

Papinianus libro secundo quaestionum. Cum iudicio bonae fidei disceptatur, arbitrio iudicis usurarum modus ex more regionis ubi contractum est constituitur, ita tamen, ut legi non offendat. […][21]	*Papinian, Questions book 2*: In an action of good faith, the rate of interest is fixed at the judge's decision according to the custom of the area of contracting, so long as statute is respected. […]

TEXT 4.5 ***Basilica*, 23,3,1 (BT 1117/5–7)**

B.23, 3, 1 ≈ D 22,1,1. Ἐπὶ τῶν καλῇ πίστει ἀγωγῶν ὀφφικίῳ τοῦ δικάζοντος ὁ τόκος	In actions of good faith, the rate of interest is fixed at the judge's *officium* (author-

20 The Greek text is cited from JGR, vol. V.

21 The Latin text is cited from the standard edition of Th. Mommsen (= D.).

TEXT 4.5 (*cont.*)

ὁρίζεται πρὸς τὸ ἔθος τοῦ κλίματος, ἐν ᾧ τὸ συνάλλαγμα γέγονεν, ὥστε μέντοι μὴ ὑπερβῆναι τὸν νόμιμον.	ity) according to the custom of the place where the contract was made, so long as it does not exceed the legal rate.

There are many preserved scholia for this *Basilica* fragment. We will cite five of them (TEXTS 4.6.1–4.6.5).

TEXT 4.6.1 ***Basilica*** **scholion 1, BS 1621/6–11 (sch. Pa 1 ad B. 23,3,1 = D. 22,1,1)**

Ἐπὶ τῶν βοναφίδε δικαστηρίων ἐπιτέτραπται τῷ δικαστῇ διαγινώσκειν περὶ τῶν τόκων καὶ τούτους ὁρίζειν πρὸς τοὺς ἐν τῷ κλίματι συχνάζοντας τόκους, ἐν ᾧ καὶ γέγονε τὸ συνάλλαγμα, μόνον εἰ μὴ νόμῳ ἐναντιοῦται· τουτέστι τότε χρὴ τὸν δικαστὴν προσέχειν τῷ ἔθει τοῦ κλίματος, ὅταν ὁ τόκος ὁ συχνάζων ἐν τῷ κλίματι μὴ παρατρέχει τὴν ἡμιεκατοστήν.	In actions of good faith, the judge is allowed to decide about the interest and to define it according to the prevailing interest rate in the area where the contract was made, so long as it does not conflict with the law: *in other words, the judge must pay attention to the custom of the area unless the interest rate that prevails in the area exceeds 6%.*	**What is in italics is new information**

TEXT 4.6.2 ***Basilica*** **scholion 2, BS 1621/12 (sch. Pa 2 ad B. 23,3,1 = D. 22,1,1)**

Ἀνωνύμου. Ὁμοίως βιβ. γ′ τιτ. ε′ διγ. ς′ καὶ βιβ. ις′ τιτ. γ′ διγ. κδ′.	Similarly, D. 3,5,6 and 16.3,24	**'the Anonymos Junior' refers to the *Digest***

TEXT 4.6.3 ***Basilica*** **scholion 3, BS 1621/13–14 (sch. Pa 3 ad B. 23,3,1 = D. 22,1,1)**

Τοῦ αὐτοῦ. Τὸ ποσὸν τοῦ νομίμου τόκου μανθάνεις βιβ. δ′ τοῦ Κωδ. τιτ. λβ′ διατ. κς′.	The same. You learn the legal interest rate from C. 4,32,26.	**'the Anonymos Junior' refers to the *Code***

TEXT 4.6.4 ***Basilica*** **Scholion 4, BS 1621/15–23 (sch. Pa 3 ad B. 23,3,1 = D. 22,1,1)**

Ζήτει τοῦ Προχείρου κεφ. τελευτ. τιτ. ις'· εἰ καὶ πολλοῖς τῶν πρὸ ἡμῶν ἔδοξε δεκτέαν εἶναι τὴν τῶν τόκων ἔκτισιν, ἴσως διὰ τὴν τῶν δανειστῶν δυσκληρίαν καὶ ὠμότητα, ἀλλ' οὖν ὡς ἀναξίαν τῇ τῶν Χριστιανῶν πολιτείᾳ ἀπευκταίαν εἶναι κεκρίκαμεν ἅτε παρὰ τῆς θείας νομοθεσίας κεκωλυμένην. Διὸ κελεύει ἡ ἡμετέρα γαληνότης μηδενὶ μηδαμῶς ἐξεῖναι ἐν μηδεμιᾷ ὑποθέσει τόκον εἰληφέναι, ἵνα μὴ νόμον θεοῦ παραβαίνωμεν. Ἀλλ' εἴ τις ὅσον δήποτε λάβῃ, εἰς τὸ χρέος δὴ λογισθήσεται.	See the last chapter of title 16 of the ***Prochiron***: 'Although many of our predecessors were of the opinion that charging interest was acceptable, perhaps in view of the possible loss and hardship of the creditors, yet we have decided that, being unworthy of our Christian State, it is abominable, seeing that it is forbidden by divine law. For that reason our Serenity dictates that nobody is allowed in any way to charge interest in any case, to prevent that we should offend against the law of God. If someone nevertheless accepts whatever sum, this will be reckoned as part of the debt.'	**This is a 'new' BS because it refers to the *Prochiron* (see also TEXT 4.2.2 where Blastares refers to this part of the *Prochiron*)**
Ζήτει καὶ τὸν ι' κανόνα τῆς ἐν τῷ Τρούλλῳ τοῦ παλατίου συνόδου, ὅς φησι· πρεσβύτερος ἢ ἐπίσκοπος ἢ διάκονος τόκους ἢ τὰς λεγομένας ἑκατοστὰς λαμβάνων ἢ παυσάσθω ἢ καθαιρείσθω.	**See also Canon 10 of the Council in Trullo** of the palace, which says, 'A priest, bishop or a deacon who charges interest or the so-called hundredths (percentage) must either cease doing so or be deposed from office.'	**Refers also to canon law; see TEXT 4.7.3.**

TEXT 4.6.5 ***Basilica*** **Scholion 5, BS 1622/25–33 (sch. Pa 11 ad B. 23,3,1 = D. 22,1,1)**

Ὡς γάρ φησιν τὸ νβ' κεφ. τοῦ α'. τιτ. τοῦ β'. βιβ., τῆς συνηθείας καὶ τῆς χρήσεως ἡ αὐθεντία οὐκ ἐπὶ τοσοῦτον ἰσχύει, ὡς καὶ τὸν λογισμὸν καὶ τὸ νόμιμον ὑπερνικᾶν. Τὸ αὐτό φησι καὶ τὸ ογ'. κεφ. τοῦ παρόντος τιτ. περὶ τὰ τέλη διάταξις τυγχάνον. Ἀνάγνωθι βιβ. ιδ'. κεφ. ι'. θεμ. δ'. λέγον κατὰ	Because, as ⟨Bas.⟩2,1,52 (51) says, 'The authority of custom or usage **should not prevail to the extent of overcoming either reason or law.'** The same is said at the end of chapter 73 (74) of the present title (= Bas. 23,3), which is a constitution. Read Bas. 14,⟨1⟩,10 § 4 which begins with the words 'Also from joint use', and	**Other Bas. text** **+ another (from the *Code*)** **+ another**

TEXT 4.6.5 *(cont.)*

τὴν ἀρχήν· καὶ ἀπὸ συγχρήσεως, καὶ τὰς ἐκεῖ παραγραφὰς τοῦ παλαιοῦ. Πλὴν γίνωσκε, ὅτι ἐπὶ τῶν καλῇ πίστει δικαστηρίων τότε ὁ ἐν τῷ κλίματι συχνάζων τόκος ἀπαιτεῖται, ὅτε μὴ ἡ φύσις τοῦ συναλλάγματος ὡρισμένον ἔχει τὸν τόκον. Καὶ ἀνάγνωθι βιβ. ιγʹ. τιτ. βʹ. κεφ. λϛʹ. καὶ τὴν παραγραφὴν πᾶσαν τοῦ Θαλελαίου.	the *paragraphai* of the old (commentator) at that passage. You must realise, however, that in actions of good faith, the rate of interest is charged according to the custom of the area only when the nature of the contract does not have fixed interest. Read ⟨Bas.⟩ 13,2,36 and the whole *paragraphè* of Thalelaios.	+ 'old' BS + another + Thalelaios: = 'old' BS

In the last part of this section, we will cite a few relevant canons concerning interest that were referred to in the fragments that we have already quoted.

TEXT 4.7.1 Basil of Caesarea = Saint Basil the Great (fourth century), canon 14[22]

Ὁ τόκους λαμβάνων, ἐὰν καταδέξηται τὸ ἄδικον κέρδος εἰς πτωχοὺς ἀναλῶσαι, καὶ τοῦ λοιποῦ τοῦ νοσήματος τῆς φιλοχρηματίας ἀπαλλαγῆναι, δεκτός ἐστιν εἰς ἱερωσύνην.	If somebody who charges interest is willing to accept that this unjust profit is given to the poor and that he will in the future be free of the sick love of money, he is acceptable in priesthood.	See TEXT 4.1 (Nomoc.), and TEXT 4.2.2 (Blastares) and TEXT 4.6.4 (BS 4)

TEXT 4.7.2 Canon 17 of the First Council of Nicaea (AD 325)[23]

Ἐπειδὴ πολλοὶ ἐν τῷ κανόνι ἐξεταζόμενοι τὴν πλεονεξίαν καὶ τὴν αἰσχροκερδίαν διώκοντες ἐπελάθοντο τοῦ θείου γράμματος τοῦ λέγοντος· "Τὸ ἀργύριον αὐτοῦ οὐκ	Because many who are enrolled among the clergy chase greed and dishonorable gain, forgetting the sacred text saying 'He has not put out his money at interest' and	See TEXT 4.1 (Nomoc.) and TEXT 4.2.2 (Blastares)

22 The Greek text is cited from the edition of RhP, vol. IV, p. 134.

23 The Greek text is cited from the edition of P.-P. Joannou, *Fonti Discipline Generale Antique* (*IIe–IXe* s.) *1.1: Les canons des conciles œcuméniques* (Rome/Grottaferrata: 1962), p. 38.

TEXT 4.7.2 (*cont.*)

ἔδωκεν ἐπὶ τόκῳ",[24] καὶ δανείζοντες ἑκατοστὰς ἀπαιτοῦσιν, ἐδικαίωσεν ἡ ἁγία καὶ μεγάλη σύνοδος, ὡς εἴ τις εὑρεθείη μετὰ τὸν ὅρον τοῦτον τόκους λαμβάνων ἐκ μεταχειρίσεως, ἢ ἄλλως μετερχόμενος τὸ πρᾶγμα, ἢ ἡμιολίας ἀπαιτῶν, ἢ ὅλως ἕτερόν τι ἐπινοῶν αἰσχροῦ κέρδους ἕνεκα, καθαιρεθήσεται τοῦ κλήρου καὶ ἀλλότριος τοῦ κανόνος ἔσται.	charge a percentage on loans, this Holy and great Council judged it right that if anyone is found after this decision to still charge interest on an obligation, or uses a different way to achieve this purpose, or claims, or in general devises anything else for the sake of dishonorable gain, he will be deposed from the clergy and his name struck from the roll.	**Psalm 15,5: Lord, who may dwell in your sacred tent? (…) The one who lends money to the poor without interest**

TEXT 4.7.3 Greek version of Council In Trullo (= Quinisextum, AD 692) canon 10[25]

Ἐπίσκοπος ἢ πρεσβύτερος ἢ διάκονος τόκους ἢ τὰς λεγομένας ἑκατοστὰς λαμβάνων, ἢ παυσάσθω ἢ καθαιρείσθω.	A bishop, priest or a deacon who charges interest or the so-called percentage must either cease doing so or be deposed from office.	**See TEXT 4.1 (Nomoc.) and TEXT 4.2.2 (Blastares) and TEXT 4.6.4 (BS 4)**

TEXT 4.8 Enantiophanes in *Nomocanon* 9,27: addition of references to civil law (early seventh century)[26]

Ἡ δὲ κώλυσις τοῦ λαμβάνειν κληρικὸν τόκους, ἐμοὶ φαίνεται πανταχοῦ περὶ τῶν ἀπὸ δανείου ἤγουν συμφώνου λελέχθαι, οὐ μὴν περὶ τῶν σιωπηρῶς ἁρμοζόντων ἐξ ὑπερθέσεως ἐπὶ τῶν βοναφίδε	It seems clear to me that the prohibition for clergymen to charge interest concerns interest from a loan or a contract, certainly not the interests that is tacitly applicable on the grounds of delay in	**'Me' = Enantiophanes**

24 Psalm 15.5.

25 The Greek text is cited from the edition of P.-P. Joannou, *Fonti Discipline Generale Antique* (*IIe–IXe* s.) *1.1: Les canons des conciles œcuméniques* (Rome/Grottaferrata: 1962), p. 137.

26 The Greek text is cited from the edition of RhP, vol. I, p. 204.

TEXT *(cont.)*

ἀγωγῶν. Ἀμέλει καὶ ἡ γ'. διάτ. τοῦ β'. τίτ. τῶν νεαρῶν ἐπὶ ληγάτων εὐσεβῶν ἐξ ὑπερθέσεως εἶπεν ἀπαιτεῖσθαι καὶ τόκους καὶ καρπούς. Περὶ δὲ [...]	actions of good faith. Anyway, **the third constitution of the second title of the *Novels*** also said that in case of pious legacies both interest and fruits are charged on the grounds of delay. And about [...]	**= *Collectio Tripartita* III 2,3,14** [See **below TEXT 4.9**]

TEXT 4.9 ***Collectio Tripartita*** **III, 2,3,14 [= Nov. 131,12,1]**

Τὰ εὐαγέσιν οἴκοις ἢ ἐκκλησίαις ἢ συστήμασι καταλειφθέντα ληγάτα εἴσω μηνῶν ς' τῆς ἐμφανείας τῆς διαθήκης καταβαλλέσθω. Εἰ δὲ μή γε, ὁ τούτοις βεβαρημένος καρποὺς καὶ τόκους αὐτῶν καὶ ἐπαυξήματα προσδώσει.	Legacies that have been bequeathed to sacred houses or churches or institutions must be paid within six months upon registration of the will. If, however, this is not done, the one who is burdened has to pay them their fruits and interests and increments.

TEXT 4.10 **Balsamon's commentary to *Nomocanon* 9,27 (twelfth century)**[27]

Ἡ γ'. διάτ. τοῦ β'. τίτ. τῶν νεαρῶν ἐστὶ νεαρὰ Ἰουστιάνειος ρλα'., κειμένη ἐν βιβλίῳ τῶν βασιλικῶν ε'. τίτ. γ'. κεφ. θ'., καταστρωθέντι εἰς σχόλιον τοῦ α'. κεφ. τοῦ β'. τίτ. τοῦ παρόντος συντάγματος περὶ τὰς ἀρχάς. [...]	The third constitution of the second title of the *Novels* is *Novel* 131 of Justinian, which is found in *Basilica* book 5 title 3 chapter 9 (13) and also referred to in the scholion to the first chapter of the second title of this collection, near the beginning [...]	**This *Novel* also in Bas., so still valid also elsewhere in the *Nomocanon***

27 The Greek text is cited from the edition of RhP, vol. 1, p. 205.

5 Select Bibliography

Sp. Troianos' *Pèges* provides extensive bibliography after every section dealing with canon law in his book. For a general bibliography on Byzantine canon law, see the collected bibliography in W. Hartmann, and K. Pennington, eds. *The History of Byzantine and Eastern Canon Law to 1500*, Washington, D.C.: 2012 (part of which is also based on Troianos' contributions in that book).

Primary Sources

Beneševič, V.N. *Drevne-slavjanskaja Kormčaja XIV titulov bez tolkovanij / Syntagma XIV titulorum sine scholiis secundum versionem palaeo-slovenicam, adjecto textu Graeco e vetustissimis codicibus manuscriptis exarato*. St Petersburg: 1906; repr. Leipzig: 1974.

Joannou, P.-P. *Discipline générale antique (IVe–IXe s.), Pontificia Commissione per la redazione del Codice di diritto canonico oriantal—Fonti, fascicolo IX*, 4 vols. Rome/Grottaferrata: 1962–1964.

Messis, Ch. *Le corpus nomocanonique oriental et ses scholiastes du XIIe siècle. Les commentaires sur le concile in Trullo (691–692)*. Paris: 2020.

Papagianni, E., Sp. Troianos, L. Burgmann, and K. Maksimovič, eds. *Alexios Aristenos: Kommentar zur "Synopsis canonum"*. Berlin/Boston: 2019.

Pitra, J.B. *Iuris Ecclesiastici Graecorum Historia et Monumenta*, 2 vols. Rome: 1864, 1868.

Rhalles, G. and M. Potles, eds. *Σύνταγμα τῶν θείων καὶ ἱερῶν κανόνων*, 6 vols. Athens: 1852–1859.

Stolte, B.H. and N. van der Wal, *Collectio Tripartita: Justinian on Religious and Ecclesiastical Affairs*. Groningen: 1994.

Secondary Literature

Beck, H. *Nomos, Kanon und Staatsraison in Byzanz*. Vienna: 1981.

Beck, H. *Kirche und theologische Literatur im Byzantinischen Reich*. 2nd edn, Munich: 1977.

Brandes, W., A. Hasse-Ungeheuer, and H. Leppin, eds. *Konzilien und kanonisches Recht in Spätantike und frühem Mittelalter: Aspekte konziliarer Entscheidungsfindung*. Berlin: 2020.

Christophilopoulos, A. *Ἑλληνικὸν Ἐκκλησιαστικὸν Δίκαιον* [= Greek Canon Law]. Athens: 1965.

Gallagher, C. *Church Law and Church Order in Rome and Byzantium: A Comparative Study*. Brookfield, VT: 2002.

Gaudemet, J. *Église et cité: histoire du droit canonique*. Paris: 1994.

Helmholz, R.H. 'Canon Law and Roman Law', in D. Johnston, ed. *The Cambridge Companion to Roman Law*. Cambridge: 2015, pp. 396–422.

Hunger, H. 'Kanonistenrhetorik im Bereich des Patriarchats am Beispiel des Theodoros Balsamon', in N. Oikonomides, ed. *Byzantium in the 12th Century: Canon Law, State and Society*. Athens: 1991, pp. 37–59.

Kaufhold, H. 'Sources of Canon Law in the Eastern Churches', in W. Hartmann and K. Pennington, eds. *The History of Byzantine and Eastern Canon Law to 1500*. Washington, D.C.: 2012, pp. 215–342.

Konidaris, I. *Εγχειρίδιο εκκλησιαστικού δικαίου* [= Textbook of Canon law]. Thessaloniki: 2000.

Konidaris, J.M. Ζητήματα βυζαντινού και εκκλησιαστικού δικαίου [= *Subjects of Byzantine and Ecclesiastical Law*], 2 vols. Athens: 1990 and 2008.

Macrides, R. 'Nomos and Kanon on Paper and in Court', in R. Morris, ed. *Church and People in Byzantium*. London: 1990, pp. 61–86.

Nedungatt, G. and M. Featherstone, eds. *The Council in Trullo Revisited*. Rome: 1995.

Papagianni, E. '4.2. Canon Law and its Status in the Byzantine Legal System', in J.N. Dillon, ed., and D.A. Smart, trans. *Brill's New Pauly Supplements II—Volume 10: History and Culture of Byzantium*, published online: 2018 (orig. as M. Landfester, J. Rupke and H. Schneider, eds. *Byzanz: Historisch-kulturwissenschaftliches Handbuch*. Der Neue Pauly—Supplemente, 2, ed. F. Daim. Stuttgart: 2016).

Perentidis, S. 'Un canon peut-il être périmé? Mentalités et autorité du texte canonique du XIIe siècle', in N. Oikonomides, ed. *Byzantium in the 12th Century: Canon Law, State and Society*. Athens: 1991, pp. 141–147.

Pieler, P.E. 'Johannes Zonaras als Kanonist', in N. Oikonomides, ed. *Byzantium in the 12th Century: Canon Law, State and Society*. Athens: 1991, pp. 601–620.

Pitsakis, C.G. 'Le droit canonique. Droit de l'Eglise et droit romain', in J.H.A. Lokin and B.H. Stolte, eds. *Introduzione al diritto bizantino. Da Giustiniano ai Basilici*. Pavia: 2011, pp. 325–350.

Pitsakis, C.G. 'La συναλληλία, principe fundamental des rapports entre l'Église et l'État: idéologie et pratiques byzantines et transformations contemporaines', *Kanon: Jahrbuch der Gesellschaft für das Recht der Ostkirche*, 10 (1991), pp. 17–35.

Potz, R. and E. Synek, *Orthodoxes Kirchenrecht: eine Einführung*. Freistadt: 2007.

Schminck, A. 'Das Prooimion der Bearbeitung des Nonokanons in 14 Titeln durch Michael und Theodoros', FM, 10 (1998), pp. 357–386.

Stevens, G.P. *De Theodoro Balsamone. Analysis operum ac mentis iuridicae*. Rome: 1969.

Stolte, B.H. 'In Search of the Origins of the Nomocanon of the Fourteen Titles', in Ch. Papastathis, ed. *Byzantine Law. Proceedings of the International Symposium of Jurists Thessaloniki, 10–13 December 1998*. Thessaloniki: 2001, pp. 183–194.

Stolte, B.H. 'A Note on the un-Photian Revision of the Nomocanon XIV Titulorum', in Sp. Troianos, ed. *Analecta Atheniensia ad ius Byzantinum spectantia*, vol. 1. Athens/Komotini: 1997, pp. 115–130.

Stolte, B.H. 'Balsamon and the Basilica', SG, 3 (1989), pp. 115–125.

Troianos, Sp. 'Byzantine Canon Law to 1100' and 'Byzantine Canon Law from the Twelfth to the Fifteenth Centuries', in W. Hartmann and K. Pennington (eds.), *The History of Byzantine and Eastern Canon Law to 1500*. Washington, D.C.: 2012, pp. 115–169 and pp. 170–214.

Troianos, Sp. and G. Poulis. *Εκκλησιαστικό Δίκαιο* [= Ecclesiastical Law]. Athens/Komotini: 2003.

Troianos, Sp. 'Nomos und Kanon in Byzanz', *Kanon: Jahrbuch der Gesellschaft für das Recht der Ostkirche*, 10 (1991), pp. 37–51.

Troianos, Sp. 'Kirche und Staat. Die Berührungspunkte der beiden Rechtsordnungen in Byzanz', *Ostkirchliche Studien*, 37 (1988), pp. 291–296 (repr. in Sp. Troianos, *Historia et ius*, vol. 1. Athens: 2004, no. 20, pp. 497–502).

Wagschal, D. *Law and Legality in the Greek East: The Byzantine Canonical Tradition, 381–883*. Oxford: 2015.

Wagschal, D., 'Orthodox Canon Law: The Byzantine Experience' in A. Casiday (ed.), *The Orthodox Christian World*, Abingdon: 2012, pp. 383–397.

Wagschal, D. *The Nature of Law and Legality in the Byzantine Canonical Collections, 381–883* (PhD Diss., Durham University). Durham: 2010.

Wessel, S. 'The Formation of Ecclesiastical Law in the Early Church', in W. Hartmann, and K. Pennington (eds.), *The History of Byzantine and Eastern Canon Law to 1500*. Washington, D.C.: 2012, pp. 1–23.

FIGURE 11 Icon from the Holy Monastery of the Great Meteoron in central Greece, representing the First Ecumenical Council of Nicaea AD 325, with the condemned Arius in the bottom of the icon.
PHOTO: JJENSEN, CC BY-SA 3.0, HTTPS://COMMONS.WIKIMEDIA.ORG/W/INDEX.PHP?CURID=4610911. LAST ACCESSED MARCH 14, 2022. WITH KIND PERMISSION OF THE EPHORATE OF ANTIQUITIES OF TRIKALA AND OF THE HOLY MONASTERY OF THE GREAT METEORON.

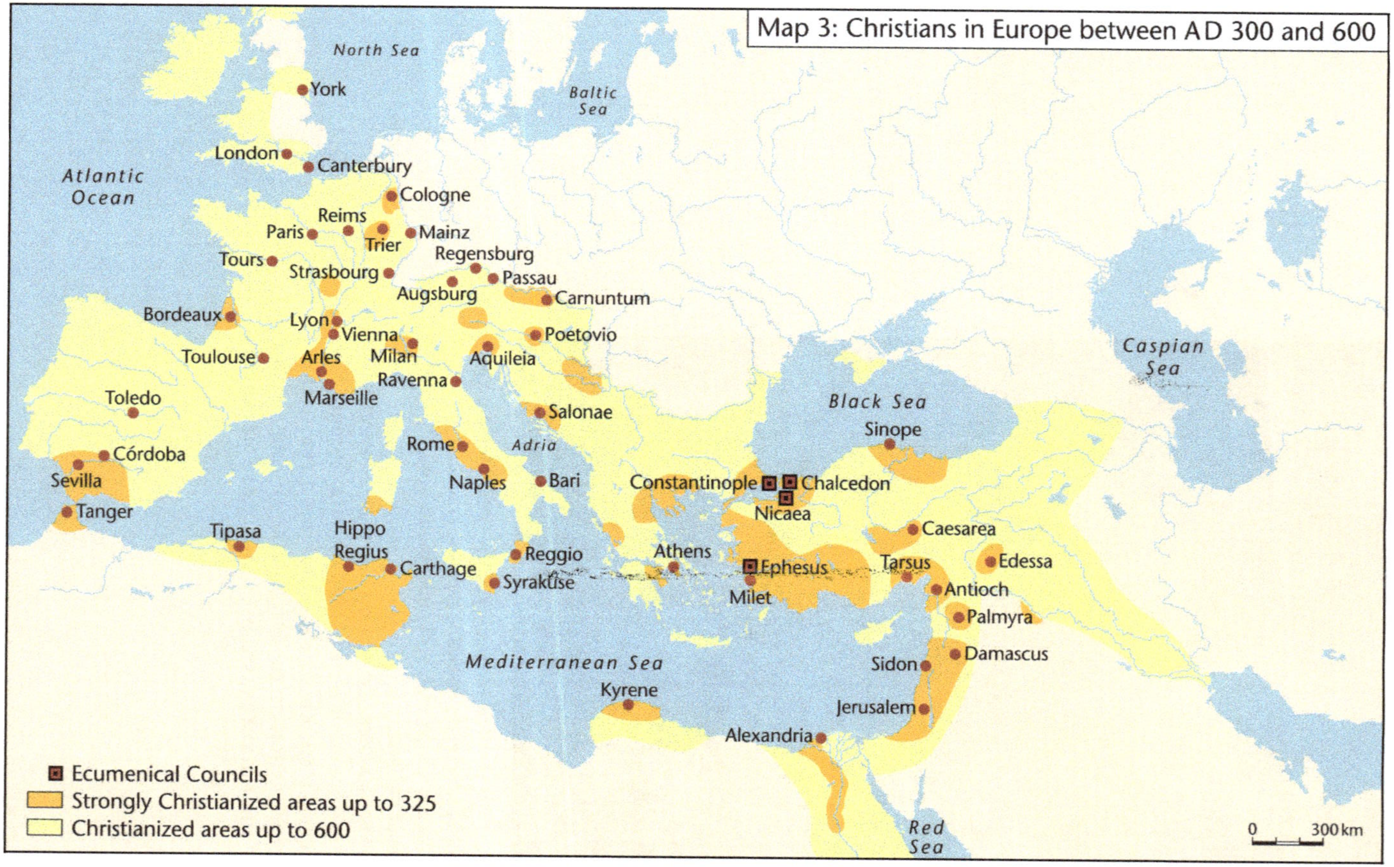

MAP 3 Christians in Europe between AD 300 and 600
DRAWING: PETER PALM

Appendix

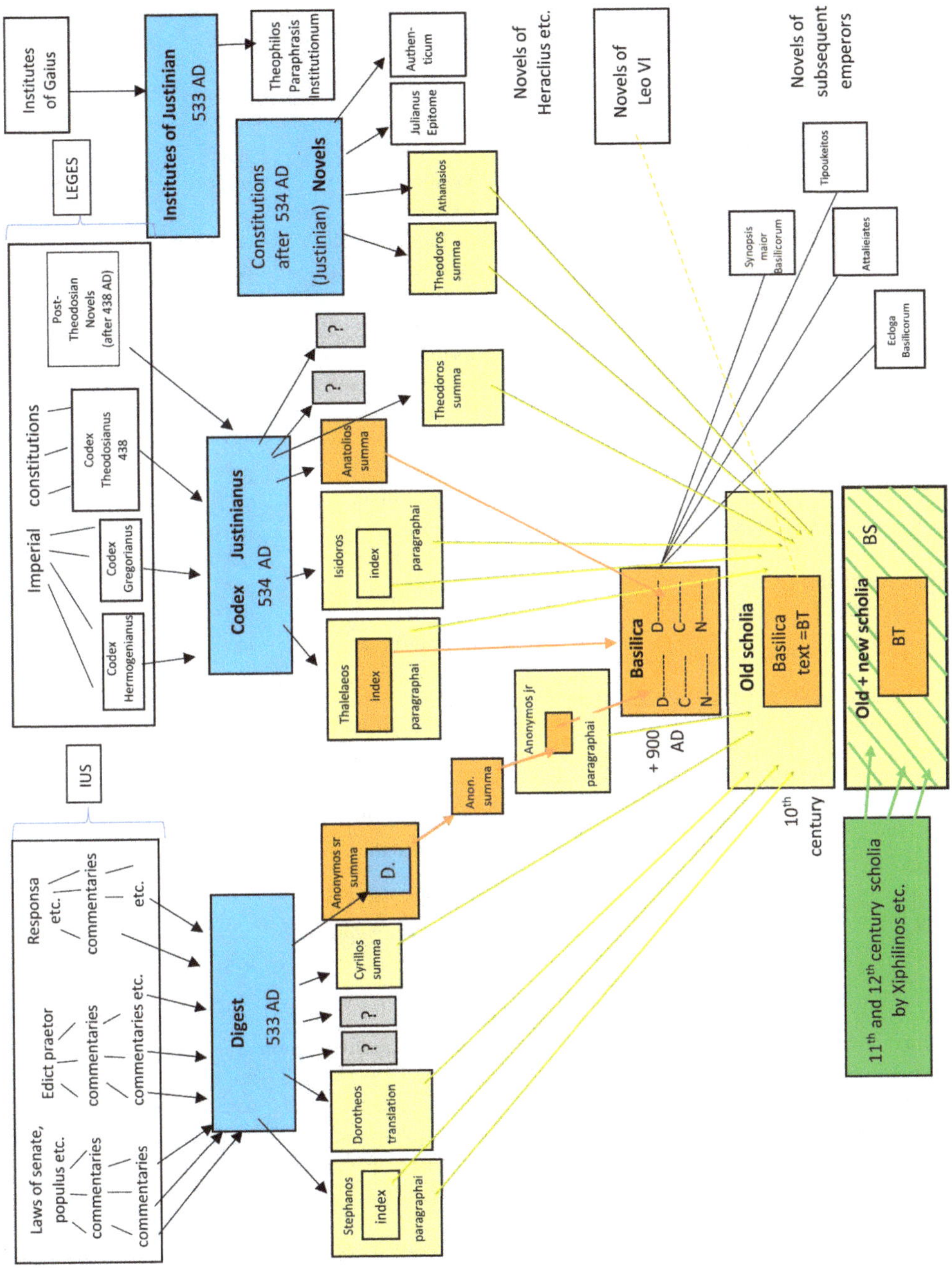

A Schematic Approach of Some Sources of Byzantine Law and Their Relations to Roman Law

 | DOI:10.1163/9789004520684_008

Index of Sources

Please note: for general references to the sources in this book please consult the Table of Contents. In the following index we include specific fragments of sources that are referred to in the book.

Index of Personal Names

Index of Place Names

www.ingramcontent.com/pod-product-compliance
Lightning Source LLC
Chambersburg PA
CBHW080936240926
51849CB00004BA/468
* 9 7 8 9 0 0 4 5 1 4 7 0 6 *